DISMANTLING DESEGREGATION

Dismantling Desegregation

The Quiet Reversal of

Brown v. Board of Education

Gary Orfield
and the Harvard Project

Susan E. Eaton
on School Desegregation

THE NEW PRESS — NEW YORK

LIBRARY OF CONGRESS CATALOGING-IN-PUBLICATION DATA

Orfield, Gary.
    Dismantling desegregation: the quiet reversal of Brown
v. Board of Education / Gary Orfield, Susan E. Eaton, and the
Harvard Project on School Desegregation.
        p. cm.
    Includes bibliographical references and index.
    ISBN 1-56584-401-7
    1. Segregation in education—United States—Case studies.
    2. School integregation—United States—History.
    3. Educational law and legislation—United States.
    I. Eaton, Susan E. II. Harvard Project on School
    Desegregation. III. Title.
LC212.62.072   1996
370.19'342'0973—dc2095-25315   CIP

PUBLISHED IN THE UNITED STATES BY THE NEW PRESS, NEW YORK
DISTRIBUTED BY W. W. NORTON & COMPANY, INC., NEW YORK

*Established in 1990 as a major alternative to the large, commercial publishing houses,
The New Press is the first full-scale nonprofit American book publisher outside
of the university presses. The Press is operated editorially in the public interest,
rather than for private gain; it is committed to publishing in innovative ways works
of educational, cultural, and community value that, despite their intellectual merits,
might not normally be commercially viable. The New Press's editorial offices
are located at the City University of New York.*

Book design *by* Hall Smyth *and* Gordon Whiteside *of* BAD
Production management by Kim Waymer

Printed in the United States of America

9 8 7 6 5 4 3 2

Contents

Foreword

It has been forty-two years since the Supreme Court decided *Brown v. Board of Education*, the landmark case that dealt a death blow to legal segregation. For half of those forty years, school desegregation proceeded at a snail's pace in southern school districts as civil rights lawyers waged trench warfare in federal courts. School boards and state officials engaged in dilatory and evasive maneuvers aimed at nullifying *Brown*'s command. Alabama's Governor Orville Faubus openly defied a federal court order to desegregate Little Rock schools until another Supreme Court ruling was enforced by Federal troops. Prince Edward's County, Virginia, closed its public schools and subsidized private school tuition for white students rather than desegregate; once again the Supreme Court had to step into the fray.

The Civil Rights Act of 1964 brought further impetus to school desegregation. It outlawed discrimination in federally funded programs and gave the U.S. Department of Justice authority to bring school desegregation suits. It was not until 1971, however, when the Supreme Court decided *Swann v. Charlotte-Mecklenburg Board of Education*, that widespread desegregation of southern school districts became a reality. *Swann* recognized the "inextricable connection" between schools and housing, and the mutually reinforcing segregative effect they had on each other. In *Swann* the Court sanctioned the use of transportation, if necessary as a remedial tool. "Busing," as it pejoratively came to be called, helped to desegregate school districts throughout the South, but it also unleashed a storm of controversy that followed its use in the northern desegregation cases of the seventies and eighties. Busing became the lightening rod for desegregation opponents who now argued that they were deprived of their right to send their children to neighborhood schools. The furor around busing has never subsided.

Yet, it was the availability of student transportation remedies that finally brought about school desegregation in many communities in which residential patterns, which in part reflect the effects of school segregation, were intensely segregated. Contrary to a popular misrepresentation, in many school districts throughout the nation school desegregation was successfully achieved. Sadly, much of what was accomplished is being undone. *Dismantling Desegregation: The Quiet Reversal of* Brown v. Board of Education is a superb analysis and account of how and why the promise of *Brown* is being eviscerated. Gary Orfield, the nation's leading desegregation expert, and Susan Eaton, of the Harvard Project on School Desegregation, have examined some of the most important desegregation efforts in recent years and chronicled the trend toward resegregation.

In my hometown of Norfolk, Virginia, the school board successfully implemented a desegregation plan after a long struggle that led to a declaration of "unitary status" two decades after *Brown*. A few years later the Norfolk school district sought and was allowed to return to neighborhood schools, which meant a return to segregated schools. The school board's promise and predictions of increased test scores, Parent-Teacher Association participation and resources for minority schools have gone unfulfilled as the predictable consequences of racially and economically segregated schools have crushed equal educational opportunity. Even more central to the promise of *Brown*, however, was the belief that racial segregation in public education harms minority students and "may affect their hearts and minds in a way unlikely ever to be undone." This is so not because all-black institutions are inherently inferior because they are all black but because of continuing structural inequities directly attributable to race. Thus in Kansas City, Missouri, from almost precisely the moment the school district became majority black, the majority white electorate consistently voted against bond issues and tax levies, precipitating a catastrophic decline in the capital and educational resources of the school district. Without the highly controversial court ordered remedy in *Jenkins v. Missouri*, the deterioration of the school district would not have been arrested.

Lawyers for the NAACP Legal Defense Fund litigated *Brown, Swann, Riddick v. School Boards of the City of Norfolk, Jenkins*, and hundreds of other desegregation cases. We know what has been accomplished, and we know what has been undone. Most Americans do not know. As a nation, we have come to a point where we now honor *Brown* more in theory than we do in fact. The consequences are not solely of legal significance. Millions of American children are relegated to racially segregated schools with high concentrations of economically disadvantaged students. They gain little solace from the knowledge that at one point in time a federal court was able to take a judicial snapshot of a desegregated district before it was allowed to resegregate or that the segregation they experience has been judicially determined to be de facto.

Race continues to be America's greatest dilemma and education remains the best escape from segregation's effects. *Brown* ultimately may be abandoned, but *Dismantling Desegregation* is a valuable contribution to the effort to ensure that the story is fully told. That gives great comfort to those who continue the struggle to make *Brown*'s promise a reality.

Elaine R. Jones
Director-Counsel
NAACP Legal Defense and Educational Fund

Preface

Much of the work in *Dismantling Desegregation* began in a year-long research seminar based at the Harvard Graduate School of Education. The goal of the seminar was to examine the assumptions underlying recent Supreme Court decisions that limited rights under school desegregation law. Since the seminar ended in 1992, the scope of our work has grown considerably, culminating in a book we hope will stimulate informed debate about issues either ignored or misunderstood for too long.

This book reflects the work of many people who began this project in the research seminar. Edward Kirby and Joseph Feldman researched the original working paper on the results of *Milliken II*'s monetary compensation remedies. They both volunteered hours of free labor and abundant patience as the draft went through several rewrites. Original working papers by Elizabeth Crutcher (Prince George's County) and Christina Meldrum (Norfolk, Virginia) provided important information and frameworks on which to build the final chapters about those communities. Elizabeth Crutcher also provided important background research and initial data collection for the chapter on Montgomery County, Maryland. David Thronson authored key early legal analyses.

A very special thanks goes to Alison Morantz whose interest in and dedication to this project continued long after her participation in the seminar ended. While a Rhodes Scholar at Oxford University, Alison carried two working papers (Kansas City, Missouri, and Charlotte, North Carolina) to their final stages as chapters in this book.

This book is not a compilation of those working papers, though the original work was very important. The editing, addition of substantial new material, additional research, the organization, structure, the analysis, conclusions, all work on six of the chapters, and the final writing of all chapters are the responsibility of the coauthors.

Earlier versions of some of the case studies in this book were released to the public and to the press through the Harvard Project on School Desegregation. The discussion and debate generated by those documents helped inform the writing and research on other chapters.

This project was made possible by the support of the Spencer and Mellon foundations. We also extend thanks to the Joyce Foundation for its generous support, with special appreciation to Warren Chapman and Deborah Leff.

The coauthors wish to thank Gordon Whiteside, Hall Smyth, Jim Levendos, and our editor, Ellen Reeves, at The New Press.

Jennifer Jellison was an invaluable graduate student assistant, offering excellent critiques of draft chapters, displaying a rare talent for citation hunting and fact checking, and lending much-needed organization and order to the Project. For hard work and assistance, thanks also go to Alisha Ellis, who worked with us as an intern in the Summer of 1995 before her senior year at Spelman College.

Susan E. Eaton thanks her husband, Mark W. Kramer, for his understanding, love, and friendship during this time-consuming project.

Gary Orfield thanks his family for their patience and support and Susan Eaton for her fine and extensive editing work that greatly improved all parts of the manuscript, not merely those that bear her name as the principal author. This book would have been impossible without her work in weaving together many disparate contributions.

Both authors express their appreciation for the opportunity to work with a remarkably dedicated group of students. The student researchers in the Harvard Project on School Desegregation were Elizabeth Crutcher, Vicki Krupp, Earl Phalen, Gail Bates, David Silver, Edward Kirby, Joseph Feldman, Alison Morantz, David Thronson, Christina Meldrum, Sylvia Ellison, Rhonda Lehman, Alberto Pimentel, Sara Schley, Sean Reardon, and Jennifer Jellison. All participants have agreed to donate royalties to minority scholarships at Harvard.

Introduction

Two generations ago a unanimous Supreme Court, in *Brown v. Board of Education*, declared intentionally segregated schools "inherently unequal." So began the movement to rid public schools of a shameful segregated past.

Where are we now?

We are in Hartford, Connecticut. Ninety-three percent of the schoolchildren in the public schools are either Latino or African American. More that two-thirds of the city's students live in poverty. Six minutes away on the highway are affluent, nearly all-white, suburban, high-achieving school districts that seem a world away.

In 1995, a state court judge in Hartford determines that Connecticut officials bear no responsibility for reducing the segregation between city and suburb. As the governor celebrates the court decision with champagne, protests over the ruling erupt in African American and Latino communities.

We are in Norfolk, Virginia. Having won a federal court's permission to dismantle its desegregation plan, the city school board here reinstitutes segregated elementary schools. Forty percent of Norfolk's students are white, but almost 100 percent of the students in Norfolk's ten resegregated schools are African American. And on average, 93 percent of those students come from low-income families.

Norfolk officials' promises to improve educational performance in the segregated schools are not fulfilled. Academic achievement gaps between the resegregated schools and other district schools continue to widen.

The nation is quick to celebrate *Brown v. Board of Education*'s anniversaries. Every five years, columnists and commentators collectively reaffirm *Brown* as a sacred turning point in history. Yet, few educators or policy experts today even blink at Hartford and Norfolk's numerical portraits of racial and economic isolation; more than forty years after *Brown*, racial separation both between and within school districts is an ordinary, unnoticed fixture in K-12 education. And there is a great deal of evidence to support *Brown's* basic premise that in American society, separate schools are inherently unequal.

How did we move from the seemingly glorious *Brown* decision to places like Hartford and Norfolk and find ourselves in the midst of a trend of pervasive and increasing school segregation? Part of the answer can be found in *Brown* itself and in subsequent legal and political history, a history of progress toward, then retreat from, the goal of racially integrated education.

With these understandings of why we are here, can we bring *Brown's* spirit back to life? Despite the disappointment and defeat, there are signs that the exhausting, decades-long struggle for integrated schools—the struggle *Brown* triggered—will continue.

This book guides readers along that legal and political path since *Brown*. Its chapters illustrate the consequences of resegregation and offer direction and justification for a different, more constructive route toward a just future.

In chapter 1, we trace desegregation's legal history, examining how politics and presidential ideology shaped events. With the exception of the years from 1964 to 1968, courts—not the legislative or executive branches—have been the dominant policy setters in desegregation, with the ultimate power to weaken or strengthen *Brown*.

Soon after the 1954 ruling, both *Brown's* great power and considerable limitations became apparent. The Supreme Court's eloquent outlawing of segregation provided the legal underpinning for African Americans seeking equality and integration in all sectors of public life. Yet the Supreme Court in *Brown*, and in the subsequent *Brown II*, failed to spell out, either in educational or numerical terms, what successful desegregation should look like. At the start, then, progress toward eliminating segregation was predictably slow, as recalcitrant school districts tinkered with remedies but clung to segregation.

Finally, between 1968 and 1973—nearly a generation after *Brown* —the Supreme Court articulated and extended desegregation rights and requirements. But by 1974, as protests over the potential expansion of the northern pattern of desegregation intensified, the Supreme Court limited *Brown's* reach. With few exceptions, this is where we are today, some twenty years later. *Brown* has been stripped of much of its power and reach by subsequent Supreme Court decisions, by political maneuvers, and by the cumulative effects of uninformed, but often intense, public debate. The Supreme Court decisions of the 1990s offer instruction not about how to further desegregation but about how to dismantle it. By allowing for the dismantling of special programming for segregated schools, the 1995 Supreme Court decision, *Missouri v. Jenkins*, suggests that the Supreme Court will not even support enforcement of the "separate but equal" doctrine that *Brown* overturned.

In chapter 2, we look closely at the logic and rhetoric that encouraged this dismantling and find that the operant ideas echo those that dominated politics and public perception after Reconstruction and triggered the first backlash; the nation's second effort to increase opportunity for African Americans—the civil rights movement— triggered the second.

The drift toward increasing school segregation and its grave consequences are explored in chapter 3. For the first time since *Brown*, African American students face rising school segregation. For Latino students, school segregation continues to rise, as it has for decades.

A segregated African American or Latino school, we show, usually enrolls a large percentage of economically disadvantaged students. This concentrated poverty devastates schools; students are literally cut off from routes that lead to job and college opportunities. These students often lack family connections, money, and networks that allow movement into the mainstream economy.

A recently modish dig at integrationists says: "Black kids don't need white kids to learn." But that phrase misses the effective property of desegregation. The policy works not when paternalistic whites "help" minorities but when it provides avenues toward opportunity. The currently stratified opportunity structure denies economically disadvantaged minorities access to middle-class schools, and to the world beyond them.

After "recasting" desegregation in this way, chapter 4 evaluates the most common promises attached to the "separate but equal" remedies that have replaced desegregated schools. We show that judges and others often simply accept school officials' pledges to create high-quality segregated schools. Consequently, judges make usually irreversible decisions to release school districts from desegregation requirements.

In doing so, justices fail to see contradictory documentation or consider crucial facts from the civil rights side. But the dominant assumptions that underlie efforts to dismantle desegregation are simply incorrect, even though they hold sway over our public discussion and jurisprudence.

This leads us to narrative accounts gathered from communities across the country that have struggled with desegregation. Cumulatively, our case studies bring to life many of the themes in current debates about the policy and about the "separate but equal" plans that replace integration. Only through the experience of actual people and places can we understand how these unfounded assumptions about desegregation and segregation play out in reality.

In chapter 5, we look at the experiment of Norfolk, Virginia, with court-approved segregation, which failed to deliver on the promises school leaders made for it. Average academic achievement levels in the segregated schools have stayed extremely low. School officials dissolved the committee that had been appointed to protect black students in segregated schools.

Chapter 6 examines the effects of a Supreme Court decision that, after blocking efforts to integrate white suburbs with heavily minority cities, called for extra funds for segregated districts. We explore the limitation of this remedy and conclude that genuine efforts toward racial integration should by no means be abandoned in favor of the monetary approach.

Chapter 7 is an examination of the efforts of Charlotte, North Carolina, to alter aspects of its busing plan, which illustrates typical political movements that encourage communities to move away from efforts to desegregate. We analyze Charlotte's shift away from integrated education, highlighting the forces that threaten the district's hard-earned desegregation plan. School officials' efforts in this diverse southern county have run into trouble as equally determined forces fight to hang onto interracial schooling. The sweeping integrationist election victory in 1995 shows the appeal of desegregation in a properous area with full city-suburban desegregation, even in a conservative era.

In chapter 8, we move slightly north to Montgomery County, Maryland, where school officials have never been under a court order to desegregate. Instead, they have long used the type of locally controlled desegregation policies that today's courts and policymakers embrace. And in this affluent, liberal school district, the lofty goals for integration were largely forgotten, resulting in policies that are ineffective and at times counterproductive.

We look at one of the country's most controversial and expansive desegregation orders in chapter 9. Kansas City, Missouri, the subject of the 1995 Supreme Court decision that further limited desegregation remedies, administers a $1.5 billion plan to improve education and integrate its schools. This elaborate remedy, however, was implemented only after the court rejected a metropolitan plan that would have joined the minority students in Kansas City schools with those in its surrounding white suburbs. The limited success of the Kansas City plan, we conclude, suggests that the rejected metropolitan remedy may have been the more effective and possibly less expensive course. We lament the Supreme Court decision that encourages abandonment, rather than improvement of this remedy.

In chapter 10, we turn to another Maryland county, Prince George, which was praised in the 1980s for successfully finding a way to improve education and desegregate. We find that the praise of the school district and its policies were not rooted in fact. There are two lessons here. First, policymakers and the public need to scrutinize carefully the claims of all school officials who purport to have found a cure for low achievement and segregation. Second, housing-related policies that might make a desegregation plan viable should be in place.

The legal and social analyses of courts' treatment of housing segregation in chapter 11 outlines two contradictory judicial conceptions. The first is that "accidental" or "natural" housing segregation creates school segregation; and, therefore, school officials should not be responsible for correcting the condition. The second, which we find more in accord with history and research, holds that housing segregation results from government action, which should spur desegregation remedies.

For many school districts, the only hope for eradicating segregation in schools lies in chipping away at segregated housing. Another option too often overlooked is to include a larger share of a metropolitan area's housing market in a school desegregation plan. For this reason, we close chapter 11 with specific recommendations for mutually supportive housing and school desegregation policies. Without such cooperation between school and housing officials, desegregation plans may be doomed to failure, as increasingly segregated neighborhoods are reflected in the nation's classrooms.

People on all sides of the desegregation debate might, at first glance, think our research reports only bad news. Those who favor integrated schools and an integrated society will surely be discouraged by the increasing trend of segregation along with news of loosening court standards. But advocates of "separate but equal" education will find the actual results of such policies sobering and sad.

We do also find hope. Large majorities of Americans, of all races, still prefer racially integrated schools and support more efforts to create them. Students and parents who have actually experienced desegregation report overwhelming satisfaction with the experience. In several states and cities, plaintiffs continue to craft new legal and political strategies for gaining access to opportunities currently closed.

The successes of school desegregation have never received as much publicity as its purported failures. But in fact, integration's achievements are considerable. Research strongly suggests that desegregated schooling helps break a cycle of segregation later in life, thereby leading to better-integrated work places and neighborhoods. Other findings show that African American students who attended desegregated schools have been more likely to be successful in their higher education and jobs than were their counterparts in segregated schools. We suggest that universities and policy analysts further investigate these benefits. The alternative is to allow courts and policymakers to continue acting on baseless assumptions about segregation's benefits and desegregation's drawbacks.

Many of the case studies in this book grew out of work conducted in an interdisciplinary research seminar including students from the Harvard Graduate School of Education, Harvard College, and Harvard Law School. Directed by Gary Orfield, the seminar, which later evolved into the Harvard Project on School Desegregation, put students to work analyzing the underlying assumptions of the *Board of Education v. Dowell* (1991) and *Freeman v. Pitts* (1992) decisions. Students also examined the potential of resegregation and other alternatives to mandatory desegregation.

After the seminar ended, sections of this book were released, as working papers and reports to the media, to scholars and citizens in relevant communities, generating debate in many communities and continuous requests for reprints and information.

There have been many changes in desegregation policy and law since the Harvard Project on School Desegregation began its work in the original seminar more than three years ago. *Brown*'s fortieth anniversary was celebrated with fanfare in 1994. But the following year, in 1995, the Supreme Court's 5-4 *Missouri v. Jenkins* decision further diluted *Brown*'s diminishing power.

As we conclude this book, much work is left undone. Desegregation itself is certainly not a cure-all for inequality in society. Racial and socioeconomic integration in schools and housing should be viewed as preconditions for equalizing routes of access and an unequal structure of opportunity. What happens inside these desegregated schools —their curricula, teacher training, and other policies and programs— will determine whether desegregation's potential is harnessed.

Economic success and political stability in our increasingly diverse nation depends upon a well-educated, fully included, tolerant citizenry. More segregation and more racial division divert us from this goal by building in distrust, inequality, and encouraging a politics based upon fear of African Americans, Latinos, or the poor.

Today, *Brown*'s vision is being abandoned, but conservatives and liberals alike still treat the 1954 ruling as a source of pride. Schoolchildren commemorate *Brown*'s birthdays in ritualized celebrations of its central lesson about right's triumph over wrong. *Brown*'s promise, the children are informed, was that government would protect minority students' rights to equal opportunity in education. Meanwhile, slowly, quietly, and without the nation's comprehension, political and legal forces have converged to dismantle one of our greatest constitutional victories.

Can the meaning and power of *Brown* be retrieved? We believe it is not too late. But we fear that the nation is poised to do damage that could threaten our multiracial society for generations.

Susan E. Eaton
Gary Orfield
Cambridge, Massachusetts
June 1995

Leading Decisions on Desegregation 1896-1995

Plessy v. Ferguson, 163 U.S. 537 (1896). This case involved a challenge from Homer Plessy, a black man, to a Louisiana state law requiring that blacks and whites use separate train car facilities. The Supreme Court concluded that racial segregation did not constitute discrimination under the Fourteenth Amendment, so long as the separate facilities were equal. The doctrine of "separate but equal," meant that the federal government sanctioned segregation. Subsequently, laws requiring racial segregation in education and other social and political domains were enacted throughout the South.

Brown v. Board of Education of Topeka, 347 U.S. 483 (1954) ("Brown I"). In this decision, the Supreme Court unanimously concluded that state-imposed segregated schools were "inherently unequal" and must be abolished. This decision, regarded by many as the landmark Supreme Court decision of this century, struck down the "separate but equal" doctrine.

Brown II, 349 U.S. 294 (1955). Coming a year after *Brown I*, this was the Supreme Court's first attempt to define how and when school desegregation would be achieved. In Brown II, the Court hedged on Brown I's powerful antisegregation stand, setting no standard or deadline for desegregation to occur. Desegregation, the court said, should occur with "all deliberate speed" in plans developed in federal district courts. Consequently, desegregation was delayed in many Southern districts.

Green v. County School Board of New Kent County, 391 U.S. 430 (1968). This case challenged "freedom of choice" plans that had been implemented by school districts throughout the South. Such plans gave the students the option of transfer from a black to a white school. Such plans placed the burden of integration on blacks, who were reluctant to transfer in the face of intimidation. In *Green*, the Supreme Court ruled that schools must dismantle segregated dual (or segregated) systems "root and branch" and that desegregation must be achieved with respect to facilities, staff, faculty, extracurricular activities, and transportation. Subsequently, courts used these "*Green* factors" as a guide in crafting desegregation plans. More recently, however, the factors have become a standard by which to determine whether school districts have achieved "unitary status," or fully integrated schools.

Alexander v. Holmes County [Mississippi] Board of Education, 396 U.S. 19 (1969). Weary of the South's evasion of its obligation under *Brown I*, the Supreme Court unanimously declared that desegregated school systems be achieved "at once" and "…operate now and hereafter only unitary schools."

Swann v. Charlotte-Mecklenberg Board of Education, 402 U.S. 1 (1971). This decision struck down "racially neutral" student assignment plans that produced segregation by relying on existing residential patterns in the South. The Court in *Swann* ruled that desegregation must be achieved in each of a district's schools to the greatest possible extent and approved busing as a means to do so.

Keyes v. Denver School District No. 1, 413 U.S. 189 (1973). This was the first ruling on school segregation in the North and West, where there were no explicit statutes requiring segregation. Under *Keyes*, school districts were responsible for policies that resulted in racial segregation in the school system, including constructing schools in racially isolated neighborhoods and gerrymandering attendance zones. Once intentional segregation was found on the part of the school board in a portion of a district, the whole district was presumed to be illegally segregated. This case also recognized Latinos' right to desegregation, as well as that of African American students.

Milliken v. Bradley, 418 U.S. 717 (1974). In this decision, the Supreme Court blocked efforts for interdistrict, city-suburban desegregation remedies as a means to integrate racially isolated city schools. The Court prohibited such remedies unless plaintiffs could demonstrate that the suburbs or the state took actions that contributed to segregation in the city. Because proving suburban and state liability is often difficult, *Milliken* effectively shut off the option of drawing from heavily white suburbs in order to integrate city districts with very large minority populations.

Milliken v. Bradley II, 433 U.S. 267 (1977). In this case, the Supreme Court faced the challenge of providing a remedy for the Detroit schools, where *Milliken I* made long-term integration impossible. The Supreme Court ruled that a court could order a state to pay for educational programs to repair the harm caused by segregation.

Riddick v. School Board of the City of Norfolk, Virginia, 784 F.2d 521 (4th Cir. 1986). This was the first federal court case that permitted a school district, once declared unitary, to dismantle its desegregation plan and return to local government control.

Board of Education of Oklahoma v. Dowell, 498 U.S. 237 (1991). The Oklahoma City school district had been ruled unitary by a federal court. The school board subsequently voted to return to segregated neighborhood schools. The Court held that "unitary status" released the districts from its obligation to maintain desegregation.

Freeman v. Pitts, 503 U.S. 467 (1992). The Court ruled that school districts could be partially released from their desegregation responsibilities even if integration had not been achieved in all the specific areas outlined in the *Green* decision.

Missouri v. Jenkins, 115 S. Ct. 2038 (1995). The Supreme Court ruled that *Milliken II* equalization remedies should be limited in time and extent and that school districts need not show any actual correction of the education harms of segregation. The Court defined rapid restoration of local control as the primary goal in desegregation cases.

CHAPTER ONE

Turning Back to Segregation
Gary Orfield

Four decades after the civil rights revolution began with the Supreme Court's unanimous 1954 school desegregation decision, *Brown v. Board of Education*, the Supreme Court reversed itself in the 1990s, authorizing school districts to return to segregated and unequal public schools. The cases were part of a general reversal of civil rights policy, which included decisions against affirmative action and voting rights. After decades of bitter political, legal, and community struggles over civil rights, there was surprisingly little attention to the new school resegregation policies spelled out in the Court's key 1990s decisions in *Board of Education of Oklahoma City v. Dowell*,[1] *Freeman v. Pitts*,[2] and *Missouri v. Jenkins*.[3] The decisions were often characterized as belated adjustments to an irrelevant, failed policy. But in fact, these historic High Court decisions were a triumph for the decades-long powerful, politicized attacks on school desegregation. The new policies reflected the victory of the conservative movement that altered the federal courts and turned the nation from the dream of *Brown* toward accepting a return to segregation.

Dowell, *Pitts*, and *Jenkins*, spelled out procedures for court approval of the dismantling of school desegregation plans—plans that, despite the well-publicized problems in some cities—have been one of the few legally enforced routes of access and opportunity for millions of African American and Latino schoolchildren in an increasingly polarized society. Though now showing clear signs of erosion, the school desegregation *Brown v. Board of Education* made possible had weathered political attacks better than many had predicted it would.

But *Dowell*, *Pitts*, and *Jenkins* established legal standards to determine when a local school district had repaid what the Court defined as a historic debt to its black students, a debt incurred during generations of intentional racial segregation and discrimination by state and local policies and practices. Under these decisions, districts that, in the eyes of a court, had obeyed their court orders for several years could send students back to neighborhood schools, even if those schools were segregated and inferior. With the 1995 *Jenkins* decision, the Court further narrowed educational remedies.

This is a troubling shift. *Brown* rested on the principle that intentional public action to support segregation was a violation of the U.S. Constitution. Under *Dowell* and *Pitts*, however, public decisions that re-create segregation, sometimes even more severe than before desegregation orders, are now deemed acceptable. These new resegregation decisions legitimate a deliberate return to segregation. As long as school districts temporarily maintain some aspects of desegregation for several years and do not express an intent to discriminate, the Court approves plans to send minority students back to segregation.

Dowell and *Pitts* embrace new conceptions of racial integration and school desegregation. These decisions view racial integration not as a goal that segregated districts should strive to attain, but as a merely temporary punishment for historic violations, an imposition to be lifted after a few years. After the sentence of desegregation has been served, the normal, "natural" pattern of segregated schools can be restored. In just two years in the early 1990s, *Dowell* and *Pitts* had reduced the long crusade for integrated education to a formalistic requirement that certain rough indicators of desegregation be present briefly.

These resegregation decisions received little national attention, in part because their most dramatic impact was on the South, the region that became the most integrated after *Brown*. The Supreme Court's 1974 *Milliken* decision had already rendered *Brown* almost meaningless for most of the metropolitan North by blocking desegregation plans that would integrate cities with their suburbs. Resegregation decisions made no difference to Washington and New York City since there were no desegregation plans in place.

In this chapter, we analyze the effects of the *Dowell, Pitts,* and *Jenkins* decisions and describe the social and political forces that shaped their underlying philosophy. These three cases largely displace the goal of rooting out the lingering damage of racial segregation and discrimination with the twin goals of minimizing judicial involvement in education and restoring power to local and state governments, whatever the consequences.

The Supreme Court handed down the first of the three resegregation decisions in 1991. *Board of Education of Oklahoma City v. Dowell* outlined circumstances under which courts have authority to release school districts from their obligation to maintain desegregated schools.[4] A previously illegally segregated district whose desegregation plan was being supervised by a court could be freed from oversight if the district had desegregated its students and faculty, and met for a few years the other requirements laid out in the Supreme Court's 1968 *Green v. School Board of New Kent County* decision.[5] *Green* ordered "root and branch" eradication of segregated schooling and specified several areas of a school system—such as students, teachers, transportation, and facilities—in which desegregation was mandatory. Under *Dowell*, a district briefly taking the steps outlined in *Green* can be termed "unitary" and is thus freed from its legal obligation to purge itself of segregation. Unitary might best be understood as the opposite of a "dual" system, in which a school district, in essence, operates two separate systems, one black and one white. A unitary district is assumed to be one that has repaired the damage caused by generations of segregation and overt discrimination.

Under *Brown*, proof of an intentionally segregated dual system triggers desegregation mandates. But once the formerly dual system becomes unitary, according to the decisions of the 1990s, minority students no longer have the special protection of the courts, and school districts no longer face any requirement to maintain desegregation or related education programs.

In 1992, a year after *Dowell*, the *Freeman v. Pitts*[6] decision went even further, holding that various requirements laid out in *Green* need not be present at the same time. This meant, for example, that a once-segregated system could dismantle its student desegregation plan without ever having desegregated its faculty or provided equal access to educational programs.

The Court's 5-4 decision in the 1995 case, *Missouri v. Jenkins*, found the Court's majority determined to narrow the reach of the "separate but equal" remedies provided in big cities after the Supreme Court blocked city-suburban desegregation in 1974. Its 1995 decision prohibited efforts to attract white suburban and private school students *voluntarily* into city schools through excellent programs. Kansas City spent more than a billion dollars upgrading a severely deteriorated school system. The goal here was to create desegregation by making inner city schools so attractive that private school and suburban students would choose to transfer to them. Because possible desegregation was limited within the city system by a lack of white students, the emphasis was put on upgrading the schools. When the district court said that it would examine test scores to help ensure that the remedy actually helped the black children who had been harmed by segregation, the Supreme Court said no, emphasizing the limited role of the courts and the need to restore state and local authority quickly, regardless of remaining inequalities. Ironically, the conservative movement that claimed it would be more productive to emphasize choice and "educational improvement" over desegregation, won a constitutional decision in *Jenkins* that pushed desegregation in big cities toward simple, short-term racial balancing within a city, even where the African American and Latino majority is so large that little contact with whites is possible.

Under *Dowell, Pitts* and *Jenkins,* school districts need not prove actual racial equality, nor a narrowing of academic gaps between the races. Desegregation remedies can even be removed when achievement gaps between the races have widened, or even if a district has never fully implemented an effective desegregation plan. Formalistic compliance for a time with some limited requirements was enough, even if the roots of racial inequality were untouched.

This profound shift of judicial philosophy is eerily compatible with philosophies espoused by the Nixon, Reagan, and Bush administrations. This should not be much of a surprise, since the Supreme Court appointees of these presidents generally shared conservative assumptions about race, inequality, and schooling with the presidents who appointed them. Furthermore, under the Reagan and Bush administrations, even the federal civil rights agencies actively undermined desegregation while embracing a "separate but equal" philosophy. Clarence Thomas, first named by President Reagan to begin dismantling enforcement activities in the civil rights office at the Education Department, was appointed by President Bush to the Supreme Court and became the deciding vote on the Supreme Court in the 1995 *Jenkins* decision.

Civil rights groups, represented by only a handful of lawyers, had little money to resist powerful dismantling efforts by local school districts and their legal teams. The fiscal and organizational crises that in the 1990s plagued the NAACP, the most visible and important civil rights organization, compounded the problem. Local school boards seeking to dismantle their desegregation plans were allied in court not only with powerful state officials but also, in the 1980s, with the U.S. Department of Justice.

After *Dowell* and *Pitts,* many educational leaders thought that, with courts out of the way, racial issues might be set aside and attention would shift from the divisiveness of imposed desegregation plans to educational improvement for all children. With this idea in mind, many school systems, including some of the nation's largest, have filed or are now considering filing motions for unitary status that will make it easier for them to return to neighborhood schools. Living under antidesegregation rhetoric and loosening desegregation standards, still other school districts have adopted policies based on "separate but equal" philosophies. Such policies pledge to do what *Brown* said could not be done—provide equality within segregated schools. Some have tried new and fashionable approaches that focused less and less on desegregation and incorrectly view segregation and its accompanying concentration of poverty as irrelevant to educational quality.

Development of Law Before the Resegregation Cases

The school desegregation battle was for a lasting reconstruction of American education, not for desegregation as a temporary punishment for the quickly absolved sin of racial segregation. The significance of the *Dowell, Pitts,* and *Jenkins* decisions, in fact, is best understood within the historical context of this long, difficult and yet unfinished post-*Brown* struggle toward desegregated schooling. The quiet, gradual movement from the holdings of *Brown* to those of *Dowell, Pitts,* and *Jenkins,* expressed allegiance to *Brown* while chipping away at its spirit and its power. In many communities, *Brown* is left intact today in theory only.

The path toward *Brown* and the movement away from it reflect the larger social and political contexts in which the Supreme Court makes its decisions. It handed down the *Brown* decision less than a decade after the end of a world war against a racist Nazi dictatorship. Both the Truman and Eisenhower administrations had explicitly urged the High Court to act against racial segregation in the South.

Harry Truman, in fact, was the first president since Reconstruction to propose a serious civil rights program. In 1947, the Truman-appointed Committee on Civil Rights issued "To Secure These Rights," which called for ending segregation in American life. The report offered forty suggestions for eliminating segregation, among them a proposal for the Justice Department to enter the legal battle against segregation and discrimination in housing. Later that year, Truman called on Congress to prohibit lynching, the poll tax, and segregation in all interstate transportation.[7]

Dwight D. Eisenhower desegregated the military. His Justice Department urged the Supreme Court to end school segregation in the South, and he appointed chief justice, Earl Warren, who wrote the *Brown* decision.[8] Although Eisenhower never publicly endorsed the *Brown* decision, the civil rights tradition of the party of Abraham Lincoln still had important echoes in his administration.

The Supreme Court justices who handed down the *Brown* decision were appointed by Presidents Franklin D. Roosevelt, Truman, and Eisenhower. The Court that later expanded and crystallized *Brown*'s mandate through the 1968 *Green* decision and the *Keyes* and *Swann* decisions of the early 1970s, which expanded desegregation requirements to the North and approved student transportation as a means for integration, had been changed by the appointments made by Presidents John F. Kennedy and Lyndon B. Johnson.

After 1968, however, no Democratic president would make a Supreme Court appointment for nearly twenty-five years; all appointees in the 1970s and 1980s were chosen by presidents whose campaigns had promised a more conservative judiciary and weaker civil rights policies. Perhaps the starkest symbol of reversal was the appointment of Clarence Thomas, a staunch critic of civil rights policy, to the chair of Justice Thurgood Marshall, who had argued *Brown* as an NAACP Legal Defense Fund lawyer.

Amid all the changes, the central constitutional provision of the Fourteenth Amendment—the guarantee of "equal protection of the laws"—remained unaltered. The broad policy changes generally reflected the political views of the presidents who appointed the justices.

Brown and Its Unanswered Questions

The *Brown* decision had tremendous impact upon the consciousness of the country and was an important catalyst and support for the civil rights movement. It challenged the legitimacy of all public institutions embracing segregation. The decision established a revolutionary principle in a society that had been overtly racist for most of its history. But the statement of principle was separated from the commitment to implementation, and the implementation procedures turned out not to work. For this reason, *Brown* and its implementation decision, *Brown II*, might most accurately be viewed as flawed compromises that combined a soaring repudiation of segregation with an unworkable remedy.

Brown announced, in no uncertain terms, that intentional segregation was unconstitutional; unanimity was obtained, however, by putting off the decision about how to enforce the new constitutional requirement.[9] In order to win a unanimous vote, the High Court diluted the subsequent 1955 *Brown II* decision on enforcement. The enforcement decision was so weak that it could not overcome resistance from the Southern political leaders who were prepared to close public education to resist desegregation. The 1955 decision on enforcement, *Brown II,* ordered desegregation with "all deliberate speed." The Court did not define what either "desegregation" or "all deliberate speed" meant. *Brown II*'s ambiguity left decisions about implementing *Brown* to the federal district courts in the South, which were without clear guidance from either the High Court or the federal government for more than a decade.[10]

Under fierce local political pressure, most Southern federal courts reacted to the vague mandates by delaying desegregation cases for long periods and then, in the end, ordering limited changes. Often these plans amounted to allowing a few black schoolchildren to attend a few grades in white schools, while maintaining a school district's essentially segregated character. Sometimes this meant that no whites were ever transferred to the previously all-black schools, faculties remained segregated, and black-and-white schools offered educational programs that differed in content and quality.[11]

The Southern segregated school system remained largely intact a full decade after *Brown*. By 1964, only one-fiftieth of Southern black children attended integrated schools. Northern segregation, mean-

7

while, was virtually untouched until the mid-1970s. Most Northern districts even refused to provide racial data that could be used to measure segregation. For nearly two decades following *Brown*, the Supreme Court denied hearings to school desegregation cases from the North.

After the rise of the civil rights movement, Congress passed the 1964 Civil Rights Act, the first major civil rights law in ninety years. It was only when serious executive enforcement was tied to the principles of *Brown* that the revolutionary potential of the constitutional change became apparent. The 1964 law, which barred discrimination in all schools and other institutions receiving federal dollars, forced rapid and dramatic changes on the South. Under President Johnson, the federal government vigorously enforced desegregation. Federal rules and sanctions took hold in 1965, backed by cutoffs of federal aid to school districts and extensive litigation by Justice Department civil rights lawyers.[12] This commitment lasted for only about three years, dying shortly after Richard Nixon was elected president in 1968.

Just a few years of intensive enforcement was enough to transform Southern schools and create much stricter and clearer desegregation standards. Following the enactment of the 1964 Civil Rights Act and the issuance of executive branch desegregation standards, the Supreme Court established a clear obligation for rapid and thorough desegregation of the South. The guiding principle here was that far-reaching desegregation must be accomplished by immediate change in an unequal opportunity structure. Finally, districts were told what they must do to eliminate segregation, how their progress toward a unitary, nonsegregated system would be measured, and what would be done to force change if they resisted.[13] By 1970, the schools in the South, which had been almost totally segregated in the early 1960s, were far more desegregated than those in any other region. The few years of active enforcement had had huge impacts.

Even when the mandates for action were clear, some key questions remained unanswered. No one really knew how long it would take to repair the corrosive damage caused by many generations of segregation or when the courts' responsibility for oversight would be fulfilled. By the late 1970s, lawyers, educators, and politicians were asking when a court order would cease and what obligations to desegregate would continue once judicial supervision ended. In what would become an increasingly important question well into the 1990s, they asked: Would courts view a return to neighborhood schools, a move with the foreseeable effect of recreating segregation, as a "neutral" act, or as another constitutional violation? Through the 1980s, the Supreme Court justices left these questions unanswered.

A Turn to the Right: Nixon and His Court

Civil rights politics turned sharply to the right following the triumph of Nixon's "Southern strategy" in the 1968 presidential election, a strategy that wooed the Southern vote by attacking early busing policies and other targets of Southern conservatives.[14]

Following Nixon's election, H. R. Haldeman, Nixon's chief of staff, recorded in his diary the President's directives to staff to do as little as possible to enforce desegregation. An excerpt from early 1970 is typical of comments found throughout Haldeman's diary:

> Feb. 4 ...he plans to take on the integration problem directly. Is really concerned about situation in Southern schools and feels we have to take some leadership to try to reverse Court decisions that have forced integration too far, too fast. Has told Mitchell [Attorney General] to file another case, and keep filing until we get a reversal.[15]

Early on in his first term, Nixon had fired Leon Panetta, then director of the Department of Health, Education, and Welfare's civil rights office, because Panetta had enforced school desegregation requirements. Nixon supported strong congressional action, even a constitutional amendment, to limit urban desegregation.[16]

Against the strong opposition of the Nixon administration, the Supreme Court's 1971 *Swann* decision ruled that busing was an appropriate means of achieving desegregation. That same year, President Nixon named the deeply conservative Justice Department lawyer, William Rehnquist, to the Supreme Court. During his tenure, Nixon appointed four Supreme Court justices. Rehnquist, elevated to chief justice by Ronald Reagan fifteen years later, became the member of the Supreme Court most hostile to desegregation issues. In Rehnquist's first twelve years on the Court, a law review analysis concluded, he had "never voted to uphold a school desegregation plan."[17] When the Rehnquist Court was firmly installed by the end of the 1980s, the stage would be set for dismantling desegregation.

Rehnquist had been a clerk at the Supreme Court during the *Brown* case, and he wrote a memo expressing approval for the "separate but equal" doctrine established by the 1896 *Plessy* v. *Ferguson* decision, which was the very doctrine that *Brown* v. *Board of Education* overturned. (Rehnquist later claimed that the memo did not express his views, but was actually an expression of Justice Jackson's early views on the *Brown* case.)[18]

The Rehnquist memo said:

> I realize that it is an unpopular and unhumanitarian position, for which I have been excoriated by "liberal" colleagues, but I think *Plessy* v. *Ferguson* was right and should be reaffirmed.[19]

Professor Sue Davis's analysis of Rehnquist's actual decisions on the Supreme Court in the 1970s and early 1980s showed that, although Rehnquist accepted *Brown* in theory, he gave it a narrow interpretation and disagreed with many of the later Supreme Court decisions that spelled out *Brown*'s mandate.[20] Rehnquist was the first clear dissenter on school desegregation in the eighteen years after *Brown*. In the 1973 *Keyes* decision, Rehnquist argued against extending desegregation law to the North, calling the decision a "drastic extension of *Brown*." In a 1975 dissent, he attacked a decision from Wilmington, Delaware, which provided a metropolitan-wide desegregation remedy, calling it "more Draconian than any ever approved by this Court" and accused his colleagues of "total substitution of judicial for popular control of local education."[21]

In a 1979 case in which the Court decided to continue to desegregate entire urban districts rather than just individual schools, Rehnquist accused the majority of favoring a policy of "integration *über alles*," suggesting a parallel with the Nazi anthem, *"Deutschland über alles."*[22] By the time of the resegregation decisions of the 1990s, Rehnquist's views, long expressed in lonely dissents, would become the majority view of the Supreme Court. Rehnquist himself wrote the 1995 *Jenkins* decision.

Accepting Segregation in the North: The Turning Point in Detroit

The impetus of *Brown* and the civil rights movement for desegregating American schools hit a stone wall with the 1974 *Milliken v. Bradley* decision. The metropolitan Detroit decision, known as *Milliken I*, represented the first major Supreme Court blow against school desegregation. With *Milliken*, the Supreme Court was forced to grapple with the basic barrier to achieving urban school desegregation. After the Second World War, the pattern of white suburbanization in

Northern cities intensified; many districts were left with too few white students to achieve full and lasting desegregation. In response to this demographic pattern, lower courts hearing the *Milliken* case approved a desegregation plan that would include not only Detroit's central city, but the predominantly white suburbs around it. But, in the face of intense opposition from the Nixon administration and many state governments, the High Court rejected the metropolitan remedy by a 5-4 vote.

This decision was particularly devastating to civil rights advocates, because only the year before, the Court in *Rodriguez* had ruled that children had no constitutional right to equal school expenditures.[23] Taken together, *Rodriguez* and *Milliken* meant that illegally segregated minority students in school districts with high numbers of minority students had a right to neither equalization nor desegregation.

Milliken viewed desegregation as unfairly punishing the suburbs. The Court ruled that unless it could be shown either that suburban communities or discriminatory state action created the pattern of all-white suburbs and heavily black city schools, Detroit would have to desegregate by mixing its dwindling white enrollment with its huge and rapidly growing black majority. Chief Justice Warren Burger cited the "deeply rooted tradition" of local control of public schools as the legal rationale for denying a metropolitan remedy and allowing segregated schools to persist. Since the minority population in the industrial North is much more concentrated in a few big cities than it is in the South, this decision guaranteed that segregation would be limited and temporary in much of the North.

In his dissent, Justice Byron White challenged Burger, noting that school districts and municipal governments are not sovereign. State governments and state law created and empowered these districts; thus states have the power to change or dissolve them, White said. The basic tradition of U.S. law is not the independence of local government and school systems, but their existence as subdivisions of state government. He argued that the Supreme Court had ample authority to order the state to craft an interdistrict remedy. Justice William O. Douglas argued in his dissent that "metropolitan treatment" of various problems, such as sewage or water, is "commonplace" and that regional approaches could be used to accomplish the basic constitutional mandate of desegregation.[24]

Justice Thurgood Marshall challenged his colleagues about what he thought was the Court's real reason for denying the suburban-city remedy: suburban political and racial resistance.

The Court did not even consider the ways in which suburban governments around Detroit had perpetuated and contributed to the segregation of housing that led to the segregated schools across Detroit's metropolitan area.

Three years later, in the second Detroit case, *Milliken II*, the Court approved a plan ordering the state to pay for compensatory programs to redress the harms of segregation. But as the judge who later presided over the monetary remedies in Detroit said in 1993, *Milliken II* has been a "limited form of reparations." In Detroit and other cities analyzed in this book, the *Milliken II* remedy has not been implemented successfully.[25]

Rejection of city-suburban desegregation brought an end to the period of rapidly increasing school desegregation for black students, which began in 1965.[26] No longer was the most severe segregation found among schools within the same community; the starkest racial separations occurred between urban and suburban school districts within a metropolitan area. But *Milliken* made this segregation almost untouchable. By 1991, African Americans in Michigan were more segregated than those in any other state.[27] When the Supreme Court, through *Milliken I*, slammed the door on the only possible desegregation strategy for cities with few whites, it shifted the attention of urban educators and civil rights lawyers away from desegregation and toward other approaches for helping minority children confined to segregated and inferior city schools.

The outcome in *Milliken v. Bradley* reflected Nixon's goal of weakening desegregation requirements. His four appointees made up four of the five votes to protect the suburbs. *Milliken* was consistent with Nixon's fervent attacks on busing and on efforts to open up suburban housing to black families. He had derided suburban housing initiatives as "forced integration of the suburbs" just before firing the leading advocate for the initiatives, Housing and Urban Development Secretary George Romney. John Ehrlichman, Nixon's top domestic policy advisor, said the strategy was based on politics and on Nixon's conviction that blacks were *genetically inferior* to whites.[28]

Writing to his chief of staff early in 1972, the year of his reelection campaign, Nixon called for emphasis on three domestic issues in the campaign: inflation, the drug problem, and his opposition to busing.[29]

Writing two months later to Ehrlichman, Nixon said it was time for the administration to abandon "the responsible position" on desegregation and "come to a Constitutional Amendment" in order to express a clear difference with the Democrats.[30] "We are not going to gain any brownie points whatsoever by being so responsible that we appear to be totally ineffective," he wrote.[31]

Nixon repeatedly declared that mandatory measures to achieve desegregation were unnecessary, and that Congress must stop courts from imposing "complicated plans drawn up by far-away officials in Washington, D.C." Fearing a constitutional crisis if Congress tried to override the authority of the Supreme Court to interpret the Constitution, the Senate narrowly blocked Nixon's attempt to limit judicial power by statute.[32] After he was reelected, the Watergate crisis diverted his attention from the desegregation issue.

By the mid-1970s, the United States had become an increasingly suburban country with a corresponding powerful suburban political perspective. Presidential elections were largely about the suburban vote, reapportionment was about expanding suburban representation, and older suburbs themselves were struggling with the problems of aging facilities and an antitax, antigovernment mood.

After the sudden changes of the civil rights era, the country denied the need to deal with race and income differences. White suburbanites were increasingly isolated from, and more fearful of, rapidly declining central cities. Between the mid-1960s and the early 1970s, Gallup Polls showed that racial inequality and race relations fell from the top concern of Americans to one of their lowest priorities.[33]

But although Nixon's triumph in the *Milliken* case did lock millions of minority schoolchildren into inferior, isolated schools, it did not resegregate the South. In a handful of cases outside the South — in Louisville, Wilmington and Indianapolis — federal courts found grounds to mandate city-suburban desegregation in spite of *Milliken*. Civil rights advocates crushed by the *Milliken* defeat could at least celebrate the fact that millions of African American and Latino schoolchildren were enrolled in Southern school districts where desegregation was feasible and an increasingly accepted part of community life. This enduring desegregation was the special target of the 1990s resegregation decisions.

The South's Comparative Success in Desegregation

The South was the target of the most aggressive and persistent desegregation enforcement. In the late 1960s, the Justice Department had
launched a full-scale attack on Southern segregation under *Green*'s
"root and branch" mandate. In the early 1970s, after the Supreme
Court's *Swann* decision rejected the Nixon administration's efforts to
ban busing, the Justice Department reluctantly enforced urban desegregation. In a compromise between Congress and the Nixon administration, a substantial federal aid program for desegregated schools—
the Emergency School Aid Act—was passed in 1972.[34] After the
Nixon White House halted administrative enforcement of urban
school desegregation, federal courts in Washington found the administration in violation of the 1964 Civil Rights Act, which mandated
cutoff of federal funds to school districts not complying with desegregation law, and ordered that enforcement resume. As a result, scores of
Southern school districts were required to end local desegregation.[35]

The *Green* and *Swann* decisions, which required full and immediate
desegregation, had more impact on the South than they did in the
North. First of all, there were already hundreds of school districts in
the South that had been required, by *Brown* and the 1964 Civil Rights
Act, to adopt some kind of desegregation plan. Even though many of
these strategies were inadequate—they often consisted of "freedom
of choice" transfer options that did not lead to desegregation—there
was at least some plan in existence. This was not the case in much of
the North. In the South, plans were already on the books and districts were under court jurisdiction or federal administrative supervision. Thus it was a simple matter to file motions or issue regulations
to have a plan updated to the newer standards required by *Green* and
Swann. After *Swann*, more than a hundred districts rapidly implemented new desegregation plans, imposing a move to districtwide
orders for immediate and total desegregation of students, faculties,
and transportation.

It had been easy to find school districts in the South guilty of segregation, but the question of guilt in the North was always more
ambiguous. The South had overt segregation laws requiring separate
schools; reading the state laws was enough to prove that government
had imposed segregation, which itself was linked to many government
actions. Northern segregation was compounded by many complex

school policies such as the drawing of attendance zones or the construction of schools serving residentially segregated areas. This meant that civil rights lawyers in the North often had a more arduous task and a less certain outcome in their school desegregation cases. It would take years to prove guilt before anyone even began to talk about a remedy. By the time a plan could be drawn up, shifting demographics often made full, lasting desegregation within the city school system impossible.

Where a northeastern or midwestern metropolitan area had dozens of separate school districts, many metropolitan areas in some Southern states were contained within a single school district. Therefore, the South was much better equipped to institute long-term desegregation within single districts. Florida was an excellent example of this, with countywide districts including cities and suburbs across the state. The Supreme Court's decision against crossing district lines was much more damaging to Northern desegregation.

Many areas of the booming Sunbelt were experiencing white immigration from the North. This trend was in stark contrast to the declining cities and some metropolitan areas of the North that were losing white residents rapidly.

After *Milliken I*, desegregation law remained relatively stable through the 1980s, and the South maintained the relatively high levels of school integration achieved under *Green, Swann,* and civil rights regulations through 1988. The struggle over the meaning of the law was ongoing. In two 1970s cases originating in the Ohio cities of Dayton and Columbus, Justice Rehnquist failed in his attempt to roll back the citywide desegregation requirements laid out in *Keyes,* which had ruled that once intentional segregation was found in one part of a school system, lower courts should presume that segregation found in other parts of that system was also unconstitutional. This presumption meant that desegregation plans would be drawn for entire districts rather than for just a few schools. Trying to reverse the *Keyes* requirement, Rehnquist, on his own initiative, blocked the desegregation of 43,000 Columbus students just before school opened in 1978. The next year, in the Ohio cases, however, the Supreme Court reaffirmed its citywide desegregation stand.[36]

President Jimmy Carter expressed reservations about busing policies both as governor of Georgia and during his presidential campaign. Griffin Bell, Carter's attorney general, also had a record of opposition.[37] Once Carter was in office, however, he appointed civil rights officials who favored school desegregation, and a few important cases were filed by the Justice Department. These included the Indianapolis case, resulting in a metropolitan-wide desegregation remedy despite the *Milliken* constraints. In fact, the first successful lawsuit to link school and housing desegregation in a single city (Yonkers, N.Y.), was filed under Carter's presidency.

During this time, though, Congress voted to limit mandatory desegregation by prohibiting the use of the federal fund cutoff sanction in the 1964 Civil Rights Act to enforce civil rights compliance if busing was needed. Without this enforcement power, there was no potential for a nationwide executive branch desegregation policy. By the end of its term, however, the Carter administration was trying to craft coordinated school and housing desegregation policies. But the belated effort was aborted by President Reagan's election. Carter did not have the opportunity to appoint a Supreme Court justice.

The Reagan Era and the Movement to Dismantle

Opposition to mandatory desegregation reached a new intensity during the Reagan Administration. Although desegregation orders were still sufficiently well-rooted to prevent a clear trend toward resegregation, the shift toward a "separate but equal" philosophy manifested itself at the end of the 1980s. Not even the South's favorable demographics and enforcement history could withstand the dismantling policies and court appointments of the Reagan administration.

In its first months, the administration won congressional action to rescind the Emergency School Aid Act of 1972, cutting off the only significant source of public money earmarked for the educational and human relations dimensions of desegregation plans. This was the largest federal education program deleted in the vast Omnibus Budget Reconciliation Act, which slashed hundreds of programs with a single vote.[38] Only the part that provided funds to specialized "magnet schools" was later restored. This restoration reflected the administration's desire to focus on choice. (Magnet schools relied upon parent's choosing to send their children to a particular school in an effort to achieve desegregation.) The Reagan administration also tried to eliminate Desegregation Assistance Centers, the only federally funded organizations that provide even limited assistance to desegregating school districts. Congress refused wholesale elimination, but funding cuts meant that the number of centers declined by three-fourths during this time.

During President Reagan's administration, the Justice Department, under the direction of Assistant Attorney General for Civil Rights William Bradford Reynolds, supported some of the school districts the Justice Department had once sued for intentional segregation, but failed to file any new desegregation lawsuits.[39] The administration proposed reliance on voluntary parental "choice" measures, like those the Supreme Court had rejected as inadequate in 1968 in *Green*. The administration also shut down research on ways to make desegregation more effective, took control of the formerly independent U.S. Civil Rights Commission, and used it to assail urban desegregation and other civil rights policies.

In 1981, Assistant Attorney General Reynolds told a congressional committee that "compulsory busing of students in order to achieve racial balance in the public schools is not an acceptable remedy." This position, Reynolds said, "has been endorsed by the President, the Vice President, the Secretary of Education, and me." At that time, however, Reynolds said that the administration would not try to apply the anti-desegregation principle to end desegregation plans already in force. He said: "Nothing we have learned in the 10 years since *Swann* leads to the conclusion that the public would be well-served by reopening wounds that have long since healed."[40] This resolve was quickly abandoned. Soon Reynolds and others intervened in older cases in an effort to dismantle settled desegregation plans.

As early as 1982, the administration called on the Supreme Court to restrict busing in metropolitan Nashville.[41] The Justice Department also supported an ultimately successful move in Norfolk, Virginia, to dismantle desegregation and become the first district to get court approval to return to segregated neighborhood schools. The department actively encouraged similar moves toward dismantling in other cities.

By the mid-1980s, educators and policymakers in a number of cities were actively discussing the option of dismantling their desegregation plans. This discussion picked up steam in 1986, soon after the Rehnquist Supreme Court refused to hear the Norfolk case, thus allowing a federal court to permit a return to racially segregated schools.

During this period, the Justice Department insisted that the plans were failures, unfair to whites and to local school systems. The plans should be seen as temporary punishments only, and districts should be allowed to return to segregated neighborhood schools. The department supported neighborhood schools, even in cities with no history of neighborhood schools, where the pre-desegregation policy had sent students to black or white schools, often well outside their neighborhoods.

For most of the 1980s, however, desegregation was surprisingly persistent. In contrast to the widespread belief that desegregation was a fragile, self-destructing policy, school desegregation endured year after year of attacks. Although the Reagan administration continually denounced desegregation as a failure, segregation levels for black students declined slightly during the Reagan years, showing the durability of many local plans, even in the face of opposition from Washington. Public opinion became more supportive of desegregation, even of busing. As the notion that widespread desertion of public schools was caused by integration won favor, the proportion of U.S. students attending public schools actually rose during the decade. Between 1984 and 1991, public school enrollment rose 7.1 percent, while enrollment in private schools dropped 8.9 percent.[42] The political leadership had succeeded in creating the false impression that desegregation policy had failed and families were deserting public education.

The Reagan administration's campaign against desegregation was successful after Reagan left because it was built upon appointments to the Supreme Court and the lower federal courts. Presidents Reagan and Bush appointed a new majority in the Supreme Court, and President Reagan elevated Justice William Rehnquist, the Court's leading opponent of school desegregation, to chief justice. With this new elevation, Rehnquist gained power to assign opinions, thereby gaining tremendous influence within the Court, and became the nation's leading legal figure. A full 60 percent of sitting federal judges in 1995 had been appointed by Presidents Reagan and Bush.[43] They had been screened for ideology to an unprecedented degree with elaborate investigations by the Justice Department and the White House.[44] This is significant because lower federal court judges have extensive power to decide whether a school district is unitary, whether it has complied "in good faith" with the desegregation order, and, finally, whether the district can return to segregated schooling.

The impact of the conservative agenda was finally clear when the Supreme Court handed down the 1991 *Dowell* decision that spelled out the process by which districts could resegregate schools. *Dowell*, and then *Pitts* in 1992, created the means by which even the South might return to segregated education. *Milliken* had blocked desegregation in the North and Midwest; now the South, where rigorous enforcement had led to better levels of desegregation, was vulnerable.

The 1990s' Definition of Unitary Status

The Court expressed its philosophical shift away from *Brown's* principles most clearly by redefining the legal term "unitary status." In doing so, the Court managed to invent a kind of judicial absolution for the sins of segregation. Under the new resegregation decisions, if a court declared a school district "unitary," that school district could knowingly re-create segregated schools with impunity.

This new use of unitary status represented an important change. Ironically, unitary status had been first used by the Court in its 1968 *Green* decision as a standard that segregated school districts should strive to attain. *Green* posited a unitary school system with equitable interracial schools as a long-term, permanent goal, viewing any school board action that worked against or ignored the goal of total desegregation, to be impermissible.

By 1990, unitary status in that sense—discrimination-free, racially integrated education—was no longer the objective; it became merely a method of getting out of racial integration. The Court rejected not only the ideal of lasting integration, but also the idea that elements of a desegregation plan were part of an inseparable package necessary to break down the dual school system and create desegregated education.

Thus unitary status decisions now have profound consequences for racial integration in U.S. schools. A court-supervised district that has never been declared unitary is obligated under the law to avoid actions that create segregated and unequal schools. But after a declaration of unitary status, the courts presume any government action creating racially segregated schools to be innocent, unless a plaintiff proves that the school officials intentionally decided to discriminate. This burden of proof is nearly impossible to meet, as contemporary school officials can easily formulate plausible alternative justifications. They certainly know better than to give overtly racist reasons for the policy change. With local authorities expressing innocence and the courts inclined to accept any professed educational justification regardless of consequences, minority plaintiffs face overwhelming legal obstacles when they try to prevent resegregation and other racial inequalities. Many of the very same actions that were illegal prior to a unitary status declaration become perfectly legal afterward.

The unitary status ruling assumes two things: that segregation does not have far-reaching effects and that a few years of desegregation, no matter how ineffective, could miraculously erase residual "vestiges" or effects of segregation. In this way, the courts implied that generations of discrimination and segregation could be quickly overcome through formal compliance with *Green* requirements for just one-tenth or one-twentieth as much time as the segregation and discrimination had been practiced.

Many courts do not even investigate whether or not vestiges of segregation are ever remedied. For example, under *Pitts, Dowell,* and *Jenkins,* school districts do not need to show that education gains or opportunities are equal between minority and white children. Nor do courts require solid evidence that discriminatory attitudes and assumptions growing out of a history of segregation have been purged from the local educational system.

In practice, the shift in the burden of proof that results from the unitary status declaration may be the key difference that allows a system to resegregate its schools. For example, after an Austin, Texas Independent School District was declared unitary in 1983, the federal district court relinquished jurisdiction completely in 1986; one year later, the school board redrew attendance zones to create segregated neighborhood schools. By 1993, nearly one-third of the elementary schools had minority enrollments of more than 80 percent nonwhite in a district that still had a white majority.[45] The judge allowed this segregation, though the student reassignments created the segregation in fourteen of the nineteen imbalanced schools.[46] Since the school district had been officially proclaimed unitary, actions that created segregation were assumed to be nondiscriminatory as long as the school leaders claimed an educational justification for the new plans. In contrast, an attendance plan in Dallas, then a nonunitary system, was rejected because it would have created too many one-race schools.[47] (Dallas has since been declared unitary.)

After the *Dowell* and *Pitts* decisions of 1991 and 1993, the road to resegregation seemed to be wide open. Teams of lawyers and experts were available, usually at steep fees, to help school districts fight for a return to segregated schools.

By the mid 1990s, several large systems had already moved to reinstitute segregated neighborhood schools, at least for the elementary school grades, by going into court to win unitary status. In some cases, civil rights lawyers, desperate to hang on to whatever remedies they could, simply settled these cases for fear that a trial would result in courts ending all desegregation immediately.

By 1995, courts had granted unitary status in a number of cases. Oklahoma City had been allowed to operate segregated neighborhood schools with only perfunctory consideration of the issues in the Supreme Court guidelines. Austin, Texas, had been allowed to reinstate segregated elementary schools. In Savannah-Chatham County, the district was declared unitary after implementing a purely voluntary plan that failed to meet the guidelines of a 1988 order. In that case, District Judge B. Avant Edenfield's language expressed the views of many judges now supervising desegregation cases. He praised the district's "momentous efforts," claiming that requiring more would be "imposing an exercise in futility." His ruling terminated all supervision of the system.[48] Older central city desegregation plans were closed with settlement agreements. Such agreements were adopted in such cities as Cincinnati and Cleveland.[49] In September 1995, the plan that produced the first Supreme Court decision in the North (Denver) was dissolved and the plan that had made metropolitan Wilmington the most integrated urban center on the east coast was dropped the month before.[50]

Today, a great many school districts remain under desegregation orders and have not filed motions to dissolve their plans. Some, including many in Florida, have plans that are increasingly ineffective because of the tremendous growth of white suburbs and the expansion of city ghettos without any adjustment of attendance areas set up in the old court order.

Many communities are on the brink of initiatives to dissolve plans that had provided an important, if imperfect, route of access for minority schoolchildren. Even in the regions that integrated most successfully and stably in the decades following the *Brown* decision, school systems were debating a return to segregation.

Themes about the "failure" or irrelevance of desegregation echo in public debates in city after city. Proposals for resegregation and attacks on desegregation often sail smoothly through school boards without objection, not because they will produce gains or because they represent the goals of the public, but because the civil rights side has been weakened, poorly funded, and struggling for survival in an increasingly conservative society with deepening racial and economic divisions.

The NAACP, by far the largest civil rights organization and the one with the most influential local chapters, has been in decline during the mid-1990s. It has experienced bitter internal struggles, the removal of its executive director and board chairman, division, and bankruptcy, all of which threaten its viability. With all of the major civil rights programs and many substantive programs crucial to the black community under political and legal attack, weakened civil rights groups have been overwhelmed.

Does It Matter?

All this might be of only academic interest if it really were true that school desegregation had "failed," or had already been dismantled, or if the country had learned how to make separate institutions truly equal in a racially divided and extremely unequal society.

The truth, however, is that although urban desegregation has never been popular with whites, it is viewed as a success by both white and minority parents whose children experienced it. In the 1990s, there remains a widely shared preference in the society for integrated schools, though there is deep division about how to get them. Meanwhile, there is simply no workable districtwide model that shows that separate schools have actually been made equal in terms of outcomes or opportunities. A return to "separate but equal" is a bet that some unknown solution will be discovered and successfully implemented, and that local politics will now be sufficiently responsive to the interests of African American and Latino students that they can safely forego the protection of the courts before ever actually experiencing equal education.

CHAPTER TWO

Plessy Parallels
Back to Traditional Assumptions
Gary Orfield

Brown v. Board of Education is the fountainhead of modern U.S. law on race and schooling. It is universally honored as one of the great moments of American justice. Educators and lawyers usually describe segregation as an unfortunate earlier stage of national development. The generations before *Brown* are described as a backward era, and the *Plessy* "separate but equal" decision condemned as a terrible error. The celebration of desegregation as the true American norm continues, despite the fact that most black children attended either no school or legally segregated schools nine-tenths of the time since the first slaves were brought to colonial Virginia. Ignoring the past, we have come to think of segregation as no more relevant to contemporary American educational policy than 1890s' debates about "free silver" or the 1930 Smoot-Hawley tariff are to contemporary economic policy. Our rhetoric about education reform reflects this misperception. Racial inequality has been rarely mentioned in the national debates on the "excellence" movement to raise education standards that began with the 1983 *A Nation at Risk* report, a movement whose proponents included Presidents Reagan, Bush, and Clinton. We don't think about the problems because we think that we solved them.

The common wisdom passed down by teachers through the generations is that *Brown v. Board of Education* corrected an ugly flaw in American education and American law. We celebrate *Brown* and Martin Luther King Jr. in our schools, even when these very schools are still almost totally segregated by race and poverty. Millions of African American and Latino students learn the lessons of *Brown* while they sit in segregated schools in collapsing cities, where almost no students successfully prepare for college. We celebrate *Brown* as cities and courts consider returning African American children to low-achieving schools that are segregated by race and poverty, without requiring proof that the effects of the history of discrimination have actually been corrected.

Rarely does anyone point out the contradiction of celebrating the Supreme Court's desegregation decision, even as the current Court encourages resegregation. So deep is our resistance to acknowledging what is taking place that when a school district abandons integrated education, the actual word "segregation" hardly ever comes up. Proposals for racially separate schools are usually promoted as new educational improvement programs or efforts to increase parental involvement.

An October 1994 announcement of the return to segregated neighborhood schools in Portsmouth, Virginia, for example, starts this way: "Elementary schools in Portsmouth will be different next year! Here's what you can expect: Elementary students will be assigned to schools in their communities."[1] In the new era of "separate but equal," segregation has somehow come to be viewed as a type of school reform, something progressive and new. But whatever new name segregation adopts, be it "neighborhood schools," "community schools," "targeted schools," or "priority schools," segregation is not new. The Minneapolis plan in 1995 was called "community schools," and the report proposing it was called "Eliminating the Gap: Assuring that All Students Learn."[2] Segregation is not a new idea, however, and neither is the idea of making separate schools equal. It is one of the oldest and most extensively tried ideas in U.S. educational history. In reality, *Brown*'s commitment to integration and equality are the true anomalies in this history.

The central and dominant value in our law and policy has been the "separate but equal" principle of *Plessy v. Ferguson*, the infamous 1896 Supreme Court decision in which the Supreme Court explicitly approved segregation by government. *Plessy* set the stage for sixty years of rigid segregationist policies in seventeen states, and a general acceptance of coerced racial separation in housing and many other aspects of American life in all parts of the country. Decades of legal struggle by civil rights lawyers and the NAACP were directed against this great bastion of racial subordination.

The central finding of the Supreme Court in the *Brown* decision was that "in the field of public education, the doctrine of 'separate but equal' has no place. Separate educational facilities are inherently unequal." Nothing in the previous sixty years of school segregation indicated any likelihood that black schools would be treated equally.

Brown established a legal goal of bringing down the walls of racial separation in school systems, but it never became the country's dominant educational policy. Even at the peak of the civil rights movement and liberal political power in the 1960s, much larger resources were being invested in upgrading segregated schools than in desegregating them. The government and the courts always funneled much more energy and resources into the pursuit of "separate but equal" reforms than into desegregating schools or trying to achieve equity by equal access to curriculum, or supporting programs to improve race relations within integrated schools.

The only major federal program supporting desegregation, the Emergency School Aid Act, was repealed in 1981 after only nine years of operation. It was "zeroed out" in the first Reagan budget in spite of substantial research evidence of benefits to schools and widespread popularity in districts (this money could not be used for busing, but only for educational and human relations programs related to successful desegregation). The far larger compensatory education program that funds extremely poor, often segregated, schools has operated for thirty years without evidence of significant educational gains.

During the mid–1960s, a real commitment to racial desegregation in government and a willingness to spend substantial political capital to enforce desegregation existed, though it was never an exclusive strategy of Great Society liberals. The urgent focus of public opinion on civil rights lasted only two years, from 1963 to 1965. Congressional leadership weakened after 1965 as public opinion changed and the GOP gained seats; relatively strong presidential leadership, however, continued through 1968. The school desegregation requirements enforced by the Supreme Court reached their strongest level in the late 1960s and early 1970s. In those decisions, the Court set clear goals and permitted no delays. Except for those years, however, little impetus came from the government for increased desegregation, and it is during that period that the vast bulk of the actual progress in desegregation occurred. By the time the fortieth anniversary of *Brown* was celebrated in 1994, more than twenty years had passed since there had been any significant expansion of desegregation efforts by any branch of government. In fact, the Supreme Court was leading the nation in the opposite direction.

The *Brown* decision, and the *Swann* and *Keyes* decisions of the early 1970s that clarified and extended school desegregation mandates, are the true exceptions in U.S. history. They were the products of a very unusual combination of a large social movement, a rare liberal majority in Congress, strong presidential leadership, and a Supreme Court emphasis on racial justice. This unique alignment of favorable forces dissolved rapidly.

Racial segregation and unequal education have been the norm, combined with rhetoric about equal opportunity for all Americans to develop their educational potential. The commitment to equal education is used, in turn, to justify the industrial world's most limited system of social welfare and the largest criminal justice system, since education is said to offer everyone a full and fair chance to make it in the free market, and this equal opportunity makes it just to expect equal performance with minimal public help.

If we are moving back toward a rigid form of the tradition of separate and unequal education, it is important to understand how a similar turning point in the past was understood and justified, the period in which the dream of abolitionists and the goals of the Civil War gave way to the reality of apartheid in the United States. It is vital to understand these parallels because our current debate is almost wholly lacking in historical perspective.

The arguments a century ago when *Plessy* made "separate but equal" the legal justification for segregation, and the assumptions of courts and political leaders at that time, bear a resemblance to those heard in the school desegregation debates today. Since we know the consequences of *Plessy*, such parallels should warn us of the possible recurrence of problems of rigid separation, and political and economic subordination justified by racist theories about black inferiority and about the natural aversion of whites to make contact with blacks.

The 1896 *Plessy v. Ferguson* decision formalized the abandonment of equality and integration by making "separate but equal" a fundamental principle of our constitutional law. Today, historians and legal scholars view *Plessy*'s affirmation of "separate but equal" as a historic catastrophe that led to mandated segregation, even as we repeat its mistakes by adopting its logic. Recent Supreme Court decisions and school board actions dismantling desegregation rest on many *Plessy*-like beliefs.

As it did a century ago, the Supreme Court now accepts the assumptions that racial segregation is natural and unsolvable, and that local governments will fairly protect equal rights without intervention from courts or higher authorities. Even post-Reconstruction theories about the genetic inferiority of blacks that surfaced in the "survival of the fittest" theories after Reconstruction in the South are emerging again, in books such as the 1994 *The Bell Curve* and Dinesh D'Souza's 1995 book *The End of Racism*, as a new wave of such theories captured national attention. Like their counterparts a century ago, our politicians, critics, scholars, and opinion makers are largely silent on the increasing problem of segregated schools.

The United States used its governmental power in major ways to correct racial inequalities only twice in its history. The first was the Reconstruction, and the second was the 1960s, in which the Civil Rights Act of 1964 and the Voting Rights Act were enacted. Supreme Court decisions in the 1960s and early 1970s greatly expanded the constitutional requirements for desegregation and racial equity. After each period of racial reform, an intense backlash developed, and a general drift back toward earlier racial patterns followed.

Reconstruction ended with political changes and court decisions culminating in *Plessy* that approved government-enforced segregation. At the time, the retreat from equality was justified by theories about the importance of state and local rights, about needed limits on the power of the courts, and about unchangeable racial attitudes that law could not alter.

With the resegregation decisions of the 1990s, the Supreme Court exhumed some of *Plessy*'s basic assumptions. The Supreme Court has, once again, authorized lower courts to send minority children to segregated schools without any assurance that the schools will be genuinely equal. In fact, the resegregated institutions we have studied are unequal largely because segregation concentrates poverty, bringing with it social burdens that other schools do not have to confront. The unequal poverty of nonwhites is, of course, a continuing effect of other forms of a history of discrimination, particularly in jobs and education, as is an intense residential segregation of a sort never experienced by any other American group.[3] The current turn away from civil rights coincides with increasing denial of public responsibility for racial inequality, past and present. In 1995, for example, only one white in sixteen thought that racial discrimination was a "very serious" problem and three-fifths of whites thought that blacks were as well off or better off than whites in terms of education.[4]

As was true at the time of *Plessy*, this more recent turn toward segregation seems reasonable to many. In the 1890s, the *Plessy* decision was not seen as an outrage; it was merely an expression views of that had become common among white leaders. In the 1990s, the growing attacks on school desegregation, affirmative action, voting rights, and other civil rights policies produced few positive initiatives by white political leaders. In both periods, a battered African American community was internally divided.

A century ago, only one dissenter, Justice John Marshall Harlan, warned of the effects of *Plessy*. He predicted that the "separate but equal" policy would have a long-term "pernicious" effect on a country where "the destinies of the two races...are indissolubly linked together..."[5] "The thin disguise of 'equal' accommodations...will not mislead anyone, nor atone for the wrong this day done."[6]

History tells us that the "equal" part of the *Plessy* equation was never enforced and that the *Plessy* principle gave constitutional legitimacy to policies creating racial divisions that the political system was powerless to change for two-thirds of a century. Once segregation was openly recognized as legal, it was implemented with astonishing thoroughness, and the issue of desegregation vanished from politics for generations. *Plessy* did not command segregation, but once the Court legitimized it, there was little organized resistance to its expansion and institutionalization.

The more recent drift back toward segregation may very well build into our society new racial barriers to opportunity that are nearly as intractable as those that followed *Plessy;* it will certainly reinforce existing ones. This time, of course, segregation would not exist primarily in one region of a society that was nine-tenths white, but in a society where only half of the children will be white in twenty-five years and where racial segregation is a serious issue in all regions.

There has been no clear official repudiation or overturning of *Brown*, just as *Plessy* never officially rejected or nullified the Fourteenth Amendment's guarantee of "equal protection of the laws." Under *Plessy*, courts merely read "equal protection of the laws" in a way that permitted and legitimized racial separation and subordination, justifying this with an assumption that local authorities would assure fairness. In the contemporary resegregation decisions, the courts continue to praise *Brown* while approving official decisions that transfer children back to segregated schools.

This chapter explores the parallels between the reversals of the 1890s and the trends of the 1990s. This time around, the nation deserves a more self-critical discussion of our decisions, their underlying assumptions, and their implications. That discussion should be illuminated by reflecting on our national experience the last time we dismantled our civil rights laws.

Trends in the Law

The *Brown* decision overturned several generations of legal precedent as well as the basic educational structure of seventeen states and the nation's capital. The 1954 decision was an unprecedented recognition that educational inequality could never be reversed unless walls of imposed racial separation were broken down. Equal opportunity, the *Brown* court said, would not be achieved unless racially separate school systems, which perpetuated and reinforced inequality, were eliminated. The fundamental change centered on *Brown*'s grim judgment that inferior treatment of minority institutions was virtually inevitable given the depth of discrimination, the inequalities of resources, and the politics of racial polarization that had dominated the South for generations. The U.S. political system had shown conclusively, the Court recognized, that its elected leaders would not even admit, much less resolve, such fundamental inequities through our normal governmental processes.

Chief Justice Earl Warren, author of the *Brown* decision, commented in his memoirs about the Court's sensitivity to the radical transformation required by *Brown*, which rejected a fundamental feature of American life. Warren, who was chief justice for sixteen years, wrote: "In my entire public career I have never seen a group of men more conscious of the seriousness of a situation, more intent upon resolving it with as little disruption as possible, or with a greater desire for unanimity."[7] Warren saw *Brown* as the beginning of a massive process of change from the dominant "separate but unequal" rule, which he saw as "the real meaning of *Plessy v. Ferguson*."[8] After Warren's resignation in 1969, the Court would begin its return toward the philosophy of *Plessy* within five years.

The first "giant step backward," as Justice Thurgood Marshall described it, came with the Supreme Court's 1974 decision, *Milliken v. Bradley*.[9] By denying a school desegregation remedy that would have combined the overwhelmingly black Detroit school district with the surrounding, predominantly white suburban ones, *Milliken* meant that poor minority children would be confined to segregated central city schools as the remaining whites and, later, many middle-class minority families fled to suburbs. Outside the South, minority children were highly concentrated in central cities and virtually all of the nation's large city school districts have shrinking white minorities.

Although the Supreme Court made the *Milliken* case sound like a quarrel over the best means to an end, *Milliken* meant that there would be no remedy for unconstitutional segregation in much of metropolitan America. Dissenters' predictions that Detroit and other cities like it would become even more segregated by both race and economic class once they tried to desegregate inside a black city came true with a vengeance.

Milliken established "separate" as the constitutional norm for the metropolitan North; the "but equal" part came with the second Detroit decision in 1977, *Milliken II.* Under *Milliken II,* the Supreme Court authorized courts to order additional, special educational programming that was supposed to remedy the negative educational effects of enforced segregation. Separate schools, the *Milliken II* theory said, would become equal through compensatory programs. In its 1995 *Jenkins* decision, however, the Supreme Court put strict limits on the scope of "separate but equal" remedies supposedly guaranteed by *Milliken II.*

Up until 1974, the Court had been building a powerful set of requirements for implementing *Brown* in the urban context, from the 1968 *Green* decision through the 1973 *Keyes* case. As the first busing decision, the 1971 *Swann* case imposed a metropolitan plan on Charlotte, North Carolina, which had a countywide school system, a plan that proved that city-suburban desegregation was feasible. In *Keyes,* the Supreme Court ruled against discriminatory practices in a Northern school district. This decision extended the reach of *Brown* to illegally segregated minority school districts outside the South. This effort, however, was quickly limited. Only one year after creating requirements for desegregation in Northern cities, the 5-4 *Milliken* case determined that there would be no feasible remedy for the millions of students there who were concentrated in city school districts with few white students and growing concentrations of poor minority children. The period of a unanimous Supreme Court spelling out specific ways to achieve genuine desegregation under *Brown* was now over. It was the beginning of a long period of retreat like that at the end of Reconstruction a century earlier.

Translating Politics into Law: The Long Buildup

The political and legal changes leading toward *Plessy* were two decades in the making; the journey from the urban prodesegregation cases of the early 1970s to the resegregation decisions of the 1990s was just as long. In both cases, changes in politics foreshadowed the shrinkage of civil rights.

The movement toward *Plessy* began as the national Republican party of the late 1800s faced severe political problems and retreated on efforts to achieve racial equality after it failed to win the support of Southern conservatives. In its campaign book for the 1888 presidential election, for example, the GOP focused almost entirely on economics and foreign policy and had virtually nothing to say about its heritage as the civil rights party of Lincoln. Lincoln was praised but his issue of racial justice was nowhere to be found.[10]

But the Republicans a century ago were never as ardent segregationists as the Democrats and could not outstrip their competition as racists. Democratic conservatives dominated the South well into the twentieth century, often putting down political challenges by stirring up racial fears.[11]

Rutherford B. Hayes, a Republican, won his presidency in 1876 in the electoral college, after a bitterly controversial count of the votes in several states. As part of a bargain with Southern congressional leaders to accept the decision of the special electoral commission, Hayes announced shortly before his election was affirmed by Congress that he would stop enforcing civil rights. He withdrew from the South federal troops that were protecting African Americans' exercise of their rights.[12] He and his successors rarely enforced civil rights laws against even white mob violence. Government increasingly ignored obvious racial crises, with presidents and other national leaders expressing the hope that these problems could be solved better at the state and local level.[13] In his 1905 tour of a South that had reimposed comprehensive segregation and enacted disenfranchisement laws, for example, President Theodore Roosevelt courted the Southern electorate: he "paid homage to Lee and the Confederacy and praised the

Southern people for loyalty to their traditions. He advised Negroes at Tuskegee to stay out of the professions and trust Southern whites as their best friends."[14]

Roosevelt's successor as president and future Supreme Court chief justice, William Howard Taft, continued the policy. According to a great historian of the South, C. Vann Woodward, Taft "reiterated the shibboleths of White Supremacy: 'the best friend that the Southern Negro can have is the Southern white man,' the history of Reconstruction was 'painful,' the fear of Federal enforcement of social equality was 'imaginary'..."[15]

The conservative shift of the Democratic party a century later, after the 1960s, was more gradual than that of President Hayes, but equally unsuccessful in blocking the progress of an opposition party willing to run as a virtually all-white institution and win by using racial fear to mobilize the white majority. Twentieth-century Republicans made a major breakthrough in the South in electing Nixon in the first presidential election after the civil rights reforms. Nixon's campaign promised civil rights retrenchment. The Democratic candidate, Hubert Humphrey, carried no Southern state except Texas.[16]

For three decades after the civil rights reforms, the only Democratic presidents were moderate Southern governors who deemphasized racial issues and supported turning additional power over to state and local governments.[17] Until the 1994 GOP takeover of the House of Representatives, however, strong liberal civil rights supporters retained power in some critical congressional committees.[18] The post-1960s backlash was resisted for a quarter century by a number of highly sophisticated, powerful African American and Latino leaders who gained power under the Voting Rights Act, and by the remains of the interracial coalitions formed through the civil rights movement, a movement that had captured an important part of the Democratic party. In the early years after the civil rights era, supporters of the reforms were much stronger than had been their counterparts a century earlier. The Republican presidents of the 1970s and 1980s induced legal change over time by changing the composition of the Supreme Court and lower federal courts, not by persuading Congress to repeal civil rights laws.

The Supreme Court became a central political target for conservatives after *Brown*, and when they finally reclaimed clear control under

Chief Justice William Rehnquist in the late 1980s, civil rights requirements rapidly eroded. As in the years before *Plessy*, there were a succession of Supreme Court decisions emphasizing the importance of state and local power and the need to limit federal power. The first signs of this trend in school desegregation law appeared in the 1974 *Milliken* case and the 1976 *Pasadena* case,[19] which limited the authority of federal courts to update desegregation plans as cities changed.

In the 1980s, the Supreme Court handed down decisions limiting voting rights, drastically cutting back affirmative action, and sharply constraining enforcement of the 1964 Civil Rights Act's key provision of cutting off federal aid from institutions engaging in discrimination. The Court also struck down minority contracting provisions in the 1989 *Croson* case, requiring local governments to prove that there had been a history of discrimination before setting aside a share of local contracts. Only because the Democratic coalition in Congress, with a shrinking group of Republican allies, responded by enacting amendments to laws giving civil rights agencies back most of the power the courts were trying to interpret away, was a major rollback of federal legal authority avoided. The Democratic party's ability to maintain control of the House of Representatives for four decades after the *Brown* decision and to hold the Senate (except from 1980 to 1986) were the political keys to this success.[20] From 1954 to 1996 there was never a time when the White House and both branches of Congress were all under the GOP control.

Even though Congress upheld basic civil rights laws, it could not assure their enforcement. During the Reagan and Bush years, the control of enforcement agencies was vested in officials who often used their authority (provided by the civil rights legislation) to weaken civil rights law and regulations. The wave of political reaction, igniting movements against immigrant rights and affirmative action, threatened civil rights policies and institutions. Civil rights advocates were almost continuously absorbed in endless defensive battles from the late 1960s to the mid-1990s.

Desegregation and Local Sovereignty

Milliken and the recent resegregation decisions of the 1990s echo some of *Plessy*'s basic themes and employ arguments paralleling some of those used to justify an end to Reconstruction-era civil rights law.

The Supreme Court in *Milliken* and the resegregation cases discussed in chapter 1, for example, held that the pursuit of equality and integration should cease at the point at which the struggle infringed seriously upon local government control. Autonomy of local school districts, these cases said, was a more important value than desegregation. Desegregation would either not occur at all, as in big city suburbs, or control would be turned back to local officials after a few years, as formerly de jure districts were declared free from the vestiges of segregation. In the 1995 *Jenkins* decision, the Court majority said that rapid restoration of state and local authority was much more important than efforts to assure that educational remedies produced actual gains for minority children.

The courts after Reconstruction also concluded that the authority of state and local governments was primary. The key decisions eroding or voiding laws from the Reconstruction period relied heavily on the power of state governments. In the 1873 *Slaughter House Cases,* the court ruled that states, not the federal government, had primary authority over civil rights. This decision rendered meaningless what had been considered key language about national rights included in the Fourteenth Amendment.[21] Both the 1896 *Plessy* decision and the 1990s' resegregation cases entrusted minority rights to local and state politics in the face of profound social and economic inequalities and racially polarized politics. After Reconstruction, courts affirmed state power even in the face of manifest plans to limit black opportunities. In the 1990s, power was turned back to local school districts in spite of the fact that almost every city and many states had strongly resisted desegregation and many were actively planning to resegregate. The anti–civil rights forces in Congress in the 1950s and 1960s often called themselves "States Righters," and that states were seen as principal barriers by the civil rights movement. In the 1980s and 1990s, state power was again seen as an important end in itself, and there was little concern about the probable racial consequences.

In the 1880s and 1890s, the self-styled "redeemers" in the South were restoring all-white rule under the Democratic party. In the present era, a virtually all-white Republican party with a strong anti–civil rights agenda controls many of the state governments and local school boards to which power to segregate is to be returned.

In both the post-Reconstruction period and during the conservative reaction following the civil rights era, the courts and many political leaders decided that the same state and local governments that had historically engaged in blatant discrimination would now be fair, and that race-related issues could safely be settled at the local level. This was simply assumed. Leaders clung to this ideology even when it rapidly became apparent that the result would be discrimination and inequality. There was a tendency to think positively about state and local control even when the experience raised red flags.

Just three years after *Plessy*, for example, the Supreme Court unanimously affirmed the Augusta, Georgia, school board's right to shut down its only black high school, saying it would overturn local action only if there was proof of "hostility to the colored population because of their race." It was not enough to show unambiguous racial inequality in treatment; plaintiffs had to prove the state of mind of the local officials, an almost impossible burden of proof. Ironically, this decision was written by Justice Harlan, the famous lone dissenter in *Plessy*, reflecting the speed with which unbridled local power to treat black children differently became the norm after the Court embraced "separate but equal". Not until after World War II did that Georgia county provide any high school education for blacks. In 1933, more than a third of a century after *Plessy*, white Southerners were three times as likely as blacks to go to high school.[22]

A century later, the Rehnquist Court, in the *Dowell, Pitts,* and *Jenkins* decisions, held that after just a few years under a court order, the rights of minority students deserved no federal judicial protection from local politics. Local districts with a proven history of intentional segregation for generations were restored an almost unlimited power to resegregate, unless the districts were caught explicitly deciding to intentionally hurt minority students. Such orders were reminiscent of a 1883 Supreme Court conclusion that the black man should recognize that

> there must be some stage . . . when he . . . ceases to be the special favorite of the laws, and when his rights as a citizen . . . are to be protected in the ordinary modes by which other men's rights are protected.[23]

In its 1995 *Jenkins* decision, both the Court's majority opinion and Justice Sandra Day O'Connor's and Justice Clarence Thomas's concurring opinions emphasized the need to restore local control. This, said Justice Rehnquist for the Court, was a fundamental "end purpose." Court efforts to assure educational gains for black students illegitimately "postpones the day when the KCMSD will be able to operate on its own."[24] In fact, however, the Kansas City school system did not want to be restored to local control—it lacked money to even continue operating the schools it had in place, and there was a consistent history of many generations of state leadership that never addressed the problems either of racial discrimination or of very severe urban educational decline, fully documented in the lower court decisions.

The courts assume today, as the *Plessy* Court did, that local agencies with a history of treating blacks unfairly could now be trusted to treat them fairly with no outside supervision. This prediction—that local officials would ensure equality—was dead wrong in *Plessy*, and the research presented in later chapters of this book indicates that the assumption is still wrong.

Increasing Inequality Under Local Control

After *Plessy* granted authority for segregation and it became clear that the "equal" part was meaningless, it did not take long for the architecture of segregation to become embedded in local law and governmental practice. The policies included key actions that built into U.S. metropolitan areas the extreme housing segregation[25] whose educational consequences the Supreme Court would try to partially remedy a century later with its busing decisions.

Segregated public schools became more dramatically unequal after *Plessy* made it clear that courts would not enforce substantive rights for black children. In the early 1870s, for example, North Carolina spent 63 percent of its average cost per white student on black students. But in 1910, well after *Plessy*, the rate of spending for blacks fell to 42 percent of that per white student. Over the same period of time in Alabama, the budget fell from 89 percent of the white level to 16 percent of the white level.[26] The equality part of the "separate but equal" doctrine, wrote historian Louis Harlan:

> was virtually ignored by the politicians and educational administrators who participated in the new era of Southern public school development which opened shortly after that decision.[27]

In 1900, the U.S. commissioner of education estimated that black children in the former slave states and the District of Columbia were receiving about half the level of funding given to whites for their education. But Harlan concluded that the reality was even worse, since statistics showed South Carolina spending only one-sixth as much, Georgia one-fourth as much, and Virginia one-third as much for the education of black children. In addition, the percent of young people enrolled in school was much lower among blacks than it was among whites, in part because not enough schools were built to accommodate black students. (Immediately after the Civil War, blacks had actually enrolled at higher rates than whites in some parts of the South.) The school year for black schools was also far shorter.[28]

Historian John Hope Franklin, an eminent black scholar who was educated in the apartheid schools of the South before *Brown,* described the racial consequences of the segregated system:

> White children were taught, if not directly then indirectly by their superior advantages, that they belonged to some kind of a master race....For the Negro children the task was an almost impossible one: to endure the badge of inferiority imposed on them by segregation, to learn enough in inferior Jim Crow schools to survive in a highly complex and hostile world, and, at the same time, keep faith in democracy.[29]

Less than two decades after *Plessy,* President Woodrow Wilson was implementing mandatory segregation in the federal executive agencies. Wilson blamed the race problem on Reconstruction and black political participation which, he said: had "left upon us the burden of a race problem well-nigh insoluble . . ."[30] The federal government did nothing to prevent state changes in voting laws that ended black political power in the South through a variety of strategies. In the 1990s, Supreme Court decisions were undermining the 1965 Voting Rights Act.[31]

Segregation as a Benefit

When a delegation of black leaders protested President Wilson's segregation policy, the president told the leaders that "segregation is not humiliating but a benefit, and ought to be so regarded by you gentlemen."[32] In the 1980s, President Reagan's Assistant Attorney General for Civil Rights, William Bradford Reynolds, delivered speeches that echoed some of Wilson's themes. The black students, Reynolds said, would be better off once neighborhood schools, which were often segregated, were restored.

Justice Clarence Thomas, appointed by President Bush after an epic battle with liberals and civil rights groups, became the first member of the Supreme Court since *Brown* to attack directly basic conclusions of the *Brown* decision and to suggest that segregated black schools might be better for their students. Attacking the idea that segregation harms children's "mental and educational development," Thomas claimed in his 1995 *Jenkins* opinion, that such a conclusion "rests on an assumption of black inferiority."[33] He added, "black schools can function as the center and symbol of black communities, and provide examples of independent black leadership, success, and achievement."[34]

A century earlier, the Supreme Court in *Plessy* had responded to the argument that segregated trains created a "badge of inferiority" by simply rejecting the idea that segregation was harmful: "If this be so," the Court said of the inferiority theory, "it is not by reason of anything found in the act, but solely because the colored race chooses to put that construction upon it."[35]

Plessy claimed that segregation was harmless. The reaction to the civil rights revolution sometimes went even further, to suggestions that it might have benefits.

The Legality of Local Actions That Increase Segregation

When the courts stand aside, there is still a question about what local authorities may legally do without triggering some new judicial intervention. Both at the time of *Plessy* and in the resegregation decisions of the 1990s, the basic answer of the Supreme Court has been that they can do anything for which they can produce a reasonable justification. The fact that the action produces segregation or inequality will not be enough to trigger judicial action. The *Plessy* court said that states could decide on any "reasonable regulation," and that legislatures should have "large discretion" in deciding what was reasonable. A legislature was "at liberty to act with reference to the established usages, customs and traditions of the people, and with a view to the promotion of their comfort, and the preservation of the public peace and good order."[36] This language was used for generations to legalize comprehensive mandatory segregation.

The modern resegregation decisions grant a similar broad discretion once a district has been declared unitary. While school districts may not take an action for the declared purpose of segregating children, they are free to take many kinds of actions that have that effect, so long as they can offer some educational reason.

When local control was restored and desegregation was dismantled, school systems then tended to dismantle institutions intended to protect the rights of black students. When courts reduced their pressure on school districts or released them from court control entirely, the school systems dismantled monitoring commissions that had been set up to protect the rights of minority schoolchildren. This dismantling occurred in such cities as Oklahoma City, Detroit, Norfolk, Virginia, and Austin, Texas. In school districts or states under no obligation to desegregate, the issue was rarely brought up, or was allowed to drift off the public agenda. Once the courts were out of the picture and local control was consolidated, issues of racial equity often disappeared. There was, in fact, some serious doubt that local school officials would even be permitted to take voluntary action consciously aimed at maintaining racial integration after being declared unitary. The Boston public schools, for example, were challenged in court by a white parent claiming that the city's voluntary affirmative policies to keep Boston Latin integrated amounted to discrimination against his daughter who might otherwise have been admitted.

Plessy *in the Cities*

The open acceptance of the legality of segregation after *Plessy* affected not only school policy, but laws and regulations that shaped neighborhood and community formation as twentieth-century cities grew. Segregation was immediately embraced by local officials and businessmen who had control over the form of rapid urban development in the Southern and border states.

In response to white pressures, Baltimore passed a law in 1910 that forbade residential movement of whites or blacks into areas zoned for the other race. Cities including Richmond, Norfolk, Portsmouth, Atlanta, Charleston, New Orleans, St. Louis, Oklahoma City, and Louisville adopted zoning by race.[37] Zoning officially defined where blacks were allowed to live, and defined other areas where only whites could legally reside.

The 1914 Louisville law, entitled "an ordinance to prevent conflict and ill-feeling between the white and colored races," was eventually challenged and struck down by the Supreme Court in 1917.[38] But some cities continued for decades to adopt and enforce such laws.[39]

State courts and the Supreme Court soon approved an almost equally effective segregative technique—court enforcement of racial covenants. Such covenants, written into mortgages, forbade the sale or rental of property to nonwhites.

Across the country, "neighborhood improvement associations" were organized to obtain agreements to covenants absolutely barring black residents. The borders of many black communities were completely closed in by such agreements.[40] Confinement of growing black communities to tiny parts of cities encouraged exploitation by landlords, and produced severe overcrowding, neighborhood deterioration, poor health conditions, and other problems that then perpetuated stereotypes of black inferiority and myths of declining property values after blacks entered a community. Those stereotypes and myths worked in a vicious circle to deepen housing segregation, particularly when false beliefs about property values were written into mortgage standards for the Federal Housing Administration's Home Loan Insurance Program, which set the ground rules for mortgage investments for decades.

Although restrictive covenants were invalidated by the Supreme Court in the late 1940s, the racial institutions and patterns of postwar suburbanization were set in place during a period of overt segregation, enforced by courts and imposed on developers seeking the federal mortgage insurance they needed for marketing their homes. Those patterns, which remain intact in most housing markets, helped create the severe metropolitan school segregation that led to the decades of struggle over busing. The complex interactions between school and housing segregation are discussed in chapter 11.

In very important ways, residential segregation was, at least in part, a product of *Plessy*'s affirmation of government-sanctioned segregation. It was ironic that limited judicial efforts to repair some of the educational damage from this racially exclusive form or urban development should, in a new century, trigger a movement reaffirming *Plessy*'s assumptions. *Plessy* led to government-enforced segregation of schools and neighborhoods; *Brown* eventually led to efforts to offset those patterns. Efforts to seriously enforce *Brown* in the cities gave rise to a political reaction that eventually transformed the courts and brought a new birth to the "separate but equal" principles.

The "Natural Forces" of Segregation: Parallel Justifications for Limiting Rights

During the time of *Plessy*, as now, socially accepted theories encouraged the view that segregation was a natural and inevitable force. In the last century, policymakers and courts were influenced by theories of genetic inferiority, social Darwinism, and the notion that racial attitudes were permanent and unchangeable. Once again, today, our courts and policymakers rely on theories about "natural preferences" to justify a return to segregated education.

In *Plessy*, the Supreme Court viewed civil rights as unattainable because "legislation is powerless to eradicate racial instincts...and the attempt to do so can only result in accentuating the difficulties of the present situation."[41]

Today the racial instinct argument pops up under less offensive terminology. More recently, courts cite as justification "incompatible residential preferences" documented in public opinion surveys.

In some cases, judges concluded that private attitudes would lead inevitably to the spread of housing and school segregation. In concluding that segregation was caused by "private" discrimination, the judges presumed that the courts, the schools, and other public agencies were powerless to change "inevitable" racial divisions. In the first Supreme Court resegregation decision, *Board of Education of Oklahoma City v. Dowell*, the Supreme Court quoted the trial judge's conclusion that "residential segregation was the result of private decision making and economics," ignoring what the three dissenting justices saw as extensive evidence of housing discrimination reinforced by school district actions.[42]

In the metropolitan Atlanta school case, the trial court concluded that it couldn't require school desegregation in spite of proof of many forms of official action to produce segregated housing. The judge said that the passage of time might have cured those problems, and he believed that current racial attitudes were major causes of housing segregation. In any case, he thought the issue was much more than courts could handle.[43]

The "preferences" for segregation were viewed neither as resulting from a history of discrimination, nor as beliefs that might be changed by different policies or experiences. As in the days of *Plessy*, racial preferences were seen as natural and immutable private racial attitudes.

The Supreme Court majority in *Pitts* reflected similar views. The Court found that it was "inevitable" that "the demographic makeup of school districts...may undergo rapid change" and cited evidence that "racially stable neighborhoods are not likely to emerge" because of preferences and "private choices." The Court said that it was "beyond the authority and beyond the practical ability of the federal courts to try to counteract these kinds of continuous and massive demographic shifts."[44]

If a similar analysis of "natural" preferences had been applied by the Court in *Brown*, desegregation of the South would never have been ordered. At the time, contemporary polls reported nearly unanimous Southern white opposition. After desegregation was actually imposed on the South, however, opposition to the policy of integration fell sharply. In 1954, 81 percent of white Southerners said they were opposed to school integration; by 1994 only 15 percent of white Southerners remained opposed to the policy.[45] When the Supreme Court in *Pitts* described resegregation as a product of private bias to which the courts must simply yield, it echoed *Plessy* and rejected *Brown*.

The natural forces argument was basic to the Supreme Court's *Jenkins* decision. The court held that white suburbanization was a natural fact that the courts must not try to change by creating city schools strong enough to lure suburban or private school white students. The Supreme Court held that the only permissible remedy in Kansas City was to implement central city desegregation, not to try to attract additional whites, and place all children in schools with large black majorities—the very conditions associated with the most rapid white decline.

The Court stated a preference, but not a requirement, for magnet schools, yet issued an order likely to cut drastically the funding for magnets and limit their duration.[46] In her concurring opinion, Justice O'Connor held that the "white exodus" was "caused by the District Court's remedial orders or by natural, if unfortunate, demographic forces..."[47] The courts were, however, ordering the least stable kind of desegregation orders—limited to central cities with big nonwhite majorities—because of the limitations imposed by the *Milliken* decision. Then they were defining the resulting white loss as a natural force.

During the *Plessy* era, the dominant social Darwinist research held that the nation's social hierarchy simply reflected the survival of the fittest. It was a law of nature, the Supreme Court held, that human law could not change. The theory had political currency; it reasoned that blacks' unequal status and success in society was due not to governmental discrimination, but to the natural inferiorities of their race.

"In essence," concludes historian Glen Altschuler, "the Court had adopted as law the dictum of social Darwinist [Yale Professor] William Graham Sumner, 'stateways cannot change folkways.'" Sumner concluded that "if we do not like the survival of the fittest, we have only one possible alternative, and that is the survival of the unfittest."[48] The Court accepted this theory.

In the following decades, the new science of standardized testing of intelligence would be interpreted as proving Northern European white superiority. Backed up by this "scientific" data, many agreed that white domination was natural. Overt claims of white supremacy came to dominate American society and was virtually unchallenged for generations.[49]

The same idea is taken seriously again by some in the 1990s. Claiming that education or changes in the opportunity structure will do little to remedy the inequities in our society and the IQ test gaps between minorities and whites, Charles Murray and Richard Herrnstein's *The Bell Curve*, argues:

> Putting it all together, success and failure in the American economy, and all that goes with it, are increasingly a matter of the genes that people inherit...Still further, we know that the correlation between intelligence and income is not much diminished by partialing out [controlling statistically for] the contributions of education . . ."[50]

Biologist and professor Stephen Jay Gould called the widely publicized book "anachronistic social Darwinism" reflecting "the depressing temper of our time."[51]

The important thing to remember when thinking about the social reasoning of contemporary courts is that the assumptions of *Plessy* seemed completely reasonable to white leadership and most white lawyers and intellectuals at the time. Scholars wrote monographs concluding that the entire enterprise of Reconstruction had been a futile attempt to change the unchangeable. The attitude was echoed a century later in much of the neoconservative writing about the futility of the civil rights reforms of the 1960s. Looking back, the great Southern historian C. Vann Woodward described the national response to *Plessy:*

> The country received the news of this momentous decision in relative silence and apparent indifference. Thirteen years earlier the *Civil Rights Cases* had precipitated pages of news reports, hundreds of editorials, indignant rallies, Congressional bills, a Senate report, and much general

debate. In striking contrast, the *Plessy* decision got only short, inconspic-
uous news reports and virtually no editorial comment outside the Negro
press. A great change had taken place...[52]

Looking back a century later, it is easy to see the tragic flaws in
the *Plessy* doctrine. University of Virginia Professor Robert J. Harris
described the *Plessy* decision as it looked after the *Brown* decision. In
1960, Harris described *Plessy* as:

> an opinion redolent with sociological speculation, permeated with theo-
> ries of social Darwinism, and carrying overtones of white racial
> supremacy as scientific truth...[53]

Today, policies that resegregated school systems have gone largely
unexamined by the nation's press and scholars. Supreme Court decisions that authorized segregation received little attention from legal
scholars and journalists. Rarely did journalists or scholars conduct
intensive investigations of the results.

Then, as now, there was a widespread belief that the well-meaning
efforts to enforce equality through law had failed. At the end of
Reconstruction, critics leveled a fierce, unyielding attack on social
policies to achieve racial equality. There was little critical discussion
or debate about the premises of "separate but equal" at the time.

We see some striking parallels a century later in a time when the
most popular president of the era, Ronald Reagan, attacked civil
rights policies and denied that discrimination was even a problem.
In his television debate with President Carter, Reagan said that when
he was growing up, he did not "know[the country] had a race problem."[54] In a 1981 speech to the NAACP, Reagan, in a typical statement, argued that government social programs had become "a new
kind of bondage" for blacks.[55] Before and after Reagan's election, he
consistently favored weaker civil rights requirements, more reliance
on the good will of local leaders and businessmen, and action against
individual incidents of clear discrimination rather than against systemic barriers to opportunity. The view of the Reagan administration
was that there were no systemic racial problems in the country. Those
had all been solved, the administration maintained, and the continuation of race-based remedies meant discrimination against whites.

The voluntary approach to solving racial inequalities resonated
with President Bush's "Thousand Points of Light" solution, which
honored volunteer philanthropy and service to the less fortunate.

Bush's "Thousand Points of Light" were routinely celebrated while assistance programs were cut back and civil rights policies reversed.

Though he celebrated voluntary solutions and denied serious racial problems, Bush won election in part by playing on stereotypes of black violence with the infamous "Willie Horton" ads. After Congress voted to strengthen civil rights laws after a series of 1989 Supreme Court decisions weakening policies against job discrimination, President Bush became the third president in U.S. history to veto a civil rights bill.[56] Later, Bush was to spend a great deal of political capital fighting to complete the redirection of the Supreme Court. He replaced Justice Thurgood Marshall with a black critic of court protection of civil rights, Justice Clarence Thomas, who was confirmed by the narrowest margin in U.S. history.[57] Thomas, who provided the fifth vote needed for strong conservative control of civil rights decisions, promptly began to make decisions reflecting the ideology of the Reagan and Bush administrations, becoming a solid supporter of the resegregation decisions.

Policies devised and implemented by the courts, and, indeed, the very composition of courts are the products of prolonged political battles over ideology. Realizing this, it is critical to ask whether the legal and factual assumptions of the new reaction against minority rights will turn out to be any more valid than those of the last century, and to study what actually happens after the policies change.

And so, just as *Plessy* set the norms of society for seven decades, another set of policies that institutionalize "separate but equal" might prove equally durable. When it was decided, *Plessy* reflected the commonsense understanding of the white community. The resegregation decisions of the 1990s reflect common white leadership views in what we consider to be a much more advanced society. In much the same way that Southern whites of the last century saw their apartheid system as a natural response, and saw civil rights laws as a futile and disruptive force, whites in contemporary metropolitan America tend to see residential segregation and all that derives from it as normal, and many view civil rights initiatives against school, housing, and job inequalities with skepticism. Studies in this book suggest that the assumptions and logic underlying current resegregation decisions may be as far off base as was the justification of *Plessy*.

After the Door Is Closed: Black Strategies

After Reconstruction, as at the end of the civil rights era, the exhausted and often defeated defenders of racial reform turned toward something that seemed more attainable. In the late nineteenth century, long before the *Plessy v. Ferguson* decision in May, 1896, the civil rights supporters lost their political initiative. Reformers tired of the effort, and many came to believe that their hopes had been in vain.

Historian Glen Altschuler describes the period in his study of American social thought from the Civil War through World War I: "During the 1870s and 1880s the Supreme Court adjudged that the federal government had done too much.... The Supreme Court's decisions reflected a consensus in which America, and former abolitionists, turned from government to voluntary philanthropy to aid blacks."[58]

White reformers could retire from the field in exhaustion. Black leaders were faced with devastating inequality, rigid color lines, and no possibility of a major public debate about segregation. In these circumstances, strategies for trying to make segregation work became popular, and the white community eagerly embraced leaders who openly accepted the basic racial order.

The racial structure of "separate but equal" policies today, as in the past, drastically curtails the options that minority leaders have. By rejecting efforts to use governmental power to overcome deeply rooted inequalities, the Court has foreclosed the strategy of integration for millions of children. With access denied, African American leaders often affirm, even against reasonable expectation, that minority pride and hard work within the minority communities can make segregation work. Racially polarized politics and the construction of segregated electoral districts under the Voting Rights Act only reinforce this tendency.

There is no real alternative for most black and Latino leaders. The press and white leaders tend to focus attention upon and reward those who promise contained progress within racially separate communities. Just as it was a century ago, this is what is considered the responsible position. Black leaders who continue to insist on racial change often are viewed as irrelevant or out of fashion. From this perspective, it should not be surprising that many African American and Latino administrators, forced to accept segregation as inevitable, are trying to turn it into an advantage.

Just as Booker T. Washington renounced the goals of Reconstruction and adopted "separate but equal" community-based development as an affirmative goal, we see some minority mayors and school superintendents in the 1990s denouncing the goals of *Brown* and insisting that they can make a *Plessy*-like plan work better in the schools. Such views have been expressed by African American mayors of several major cities whose school systems have declining white minorities in the mid-1990s. This is exactly what occurred in the late 1880s after the Jim Crow system had been fully institutionalized.

When the courts slam the door to meaningful access to an integrated society, those leading minority institutions must project a positive view, and the only short-term policy that seems feasible to many is to accept the basic racial structure of the society and to affirm the capacity of their own community to resolve its own problems. In fact, black and Latino educational leaders, administrators, and policymakers in resegregated school systems today are often in much the same situation as black spokesmen at the end of the Reconstruction.

At the end of Reconstruction, the black leader most respected as a "responsible" leader by whites was Booker T. Washington. In his 1895 Atlanta Exposition speech, Washington argued that pursuing issues of racial discrimination and inequality would lead nowhere, that blacks should make the best of what they had. Washington's program called for skillfully trying to obtain some resources from state officials by reassuring white leaders that blacks would accept the existing structure of inequality and that they only wanted to improve themselves within their own sphere. Progress must be, Washington said, "the result of severe and constant struggle rather than an artificial forcing."[59] He assured his audience that blacks had no interest in crossing the line of racial separation. Washington recounted in his autobiography that "papers in all parts of the United States published the address in full, and for months afterward there were complimentary editorial references to it." President Grover Cleveland hailed Washington's ideas as did many other political leaders.[60] Washington would continue to be a favorite of white philanthropists for decades, controlling or directing much of the charitable money coming into the South.

Washington's great critic, W. E. B. DuBois, however, argued that while the compromise Washington had set forth in his Atlanta address had consolidated Washington's position as the recognized leader of black America and had obtained some aid for black institutions, there had been, at the same time, consolidation of the institutions of white control. DuBois said: "[Washington's] doctrine has tended to make the whites, North and South, shift the burden of the Negro problem to the Negro's shoulders and stand aside as critical and pessimistic spectators."[61]

Once blacks accepted the racial system and absolved whites, they could easily be blamed for the resulting inequalities. After Reconstruction, then, blacks were forced to take responsibility for outcomes that would almost inevitably be unequal given the inequality of resources and opportunities on opposite sides of the color line. The resulting inferiority of many black institutions was blamed on blacks in ways that reinforced racial stereotypes and acceptance of racial separation and subordination.

In urban education today there are many signs that whites are again, in DuBois's words, standing aside "as critical and pessimistic spectators." In fact, many policymakers are using the continuing failures of central city schools to urge strategies of state takeover of local schools from the local minority administrators or boards, or abandoning public education altogether.[62]

Today, the inequalities within metropolitan school districts are profound. And, once again, it is increasingly common to find leaders who inherited failing, segregated school systems being blamed for their problems. Once racial and class separation are accepted as legitimate and leaders affirm the possibility of "separate but equal", they will then be blamed for the school system's failure. A classic manifestation is the extremely short terms served by leaders of urban school districts, many of them African American.[63] Often, these leaders are threatened with humiliation for low school achievement scores while authorities refuse to recognize the social and economic crises that overwhelm schools segregated by race and poverty.

Today, the whole country may find itself in a situation much like that of the South during the time between *Plessy* and *Brown*. There were only a handful of vocal critics in the South for decades after *Plessy*.[64] The Southern system was initially challenged from the outside. Today, however, there is no outside force, like the combination of civil rights, intellectual, labor, and religious groups that supported change in the South and fought the battles that ended the state-mandated apartheid system in the South. Today, the entire country is affected, and any reassertion of the values of *Brown* must come either from protest within the structure of segregation or from affirmation of *Brown*'s vision by those communities that are still desegregated. Political and intellectual leaders could, of course, also play a very positive role if they chose to examine carefully and then challenge the decisions reinstating segregation.

This makes it all the more important that there be an independent appraisal of the shift toward "separate but equal" before a new status quo becomes so deeply entrenched that it will simply seem natural and questions will be ignored. We are perilously close to that point now.

A Future at Risk

The Southern experience under *Plessy* suggests that segregation is not an unfortunate aberration but a powerful and stable system, very difficult to change from the inside and apt to get little attention from academics or educational leaders.

The history of *Plessy* shows segregation and inequality not only as the dominant approaches to U.S. minority education, but as strongly self-perpetuating policies. There is no assurance that the schools confined to racial isolation under *Milliken I* twenty years ago, or under the resegregation decisions of the 1990s, will not be as difficult to change as those that operated under the Jim Crow system of 1896 to 1964.

Each generation is a prisoner of its own experience, viewing its dominant ideas and politics as the natural result of the growth of knowledge. Since judges are not social researchers and are chosen through a political system that reflects the values and beliefs of their time, it should not be surprising that unexamined assumptions dominant in politics tend to creep into judicial decisions as if they were self-evident facts. The resegregation decisions made in our federal courts are the natural products of five national administrations elected on anti–civil rights platforms. Since the Nixon administration, the Republican party has received only about a tenth of the black vote.[65] Presidents Nixon, Reagan, and Bush all pledged to roll back civil rights enforcement and specifically criticized urban school desegregation.

But the situation we confront today is different from the period following *Plessy* in some important respects. The reforms of the 1950s and 1960s did change society in some enduring ways. For example, there is a substantial minority middle class with significant electoral power, though that is threatened by continuing legal battles over voting rights and representation, and strong attacks on affirmative action policies that helped the rise of the minority middle class.

The rise of black and Latino political power was answered by a resurgent white anti–civil rights backlash that captured the Republican Party and has now reshaped the courts and national policy. Open racism, however, is not acceptable in either political party or among the public. Allegations of black cultural and social structure inferiority have resurfaced.

The public discussions of the 1990s reflect quiet but severe erosion of *Brown*. Local administrators never say they are instituting segregation; they talk about moving beyond "physical desegregation" or "racial balancing" or "numerical integration," as if there were some new kind of desegregation in which schools were not really desegregated. What these leaders are actually seeking is a way to pursue "separate but equal" without admitting it in a brave new Orwellian era of segregated "desegregation."

Although no one calls for the mandated segregation that followed *Plessy*, the future of urban education is at stake. We risk making permanent the highly unequal structure of opportunity that confines millions of children to segregation and inadequate schools in declining parts of metropolitan America where three-fourths of Americans live. The limited but crucial progress of the last half century is threatened.

We have a system of residential segregation in most of our metropolitan areas that often approaches the level of segregation produced by the old apartheid laws. This system, together with the policies and practices of the school systems, produces highly segregated and increasingly unequal education for most minority students. Under our existing laws, this segregation is legal unless local or state officials are guilty of official actions to segregate. The resegregation decisions would make even desegregation orders short-lived and ineffectual, and would legitimate sending minority students back to inferior schools after a few years without any showing that the harmful effects were cured.

Segregation tends to be self-reinforcing, creating increasingly deep inequalities and generating enduring stereotypes and ideologies to legitimize them. All kinds of practices and expectations grow up within segregation. Seven decades of "separate but equal" under

Plessy were probably the best documented social policy experiment in American history. The Supreme Court spelled out what we had learned in the ringing words of *Brown*. Yet, step by step, many leaders have returned to the old beliefs. The issue is serious enough and the parallels with *Plessy* so obvious that the most searching debate is needed before committing the nation once again to the propositions that separate can be made equal and that state and local school officials will enforce that equality.

CHAPTER THREE

The Growth of Segregation
African Americans, Latinos, and Unequal Education
Gary Orfield

Segregation grew in the early 1990s. For the first time since the Supreme Court overturned segregation laws in 1954, southern public schools returned to greater segregation. Southern segregation grew significantly from 1988 to 1991 and segregation of African American students across the United States also increased. Latino students remained in an unbroken pattern of increasing segregation dating to the time national data was first collected in the late 1960s.[1] These trends surfaced even before the Supreme Court opened the door to large-scale resegregation. Those decisions were likely to accelerate the trend.

National data show that most segregated African American and Latino schools are dominated by poor children but that 96 percent of white schools have middle-class majorities. The extremely strong relationship between racial segregation and concentrated poverty in the nation's schools is a key reason for the educational differences between segregated and integrated schools. One of the most consistent findings in research on education has been the powerful relationship between concentrated poverty and virtually every measure of school-level academic results. Schools with large numbers of impoverished students tend to have much lower test scores, higher dropout rates, fewer students in demanding classes, less well-prepared teachers, and a low percentage of students who will eventually finish college. Low-income families and communities can provide much less for children and their schools have much weaker links with colleges and good jobs. Segregated schools are far more likely to face intense social and personal problems related to poverty.

Such problems include: low levels of competition and expectation, less qualified teachers who leave as soon as they get seniority, deteriorated schools in dangerous neighborhoods, more limited curricula, peer pressure against academic achievement and supportive of crime and substance abuse, high levels of teen pregnancy, few connections with colleges and employers who can assist students, little serious academic counseling or preparation for college, and powerless parents who themselves failed in school and do not know how to evaluate or change schools.

Poor children face a variety of family problems that make their way into the classroom every day and deeply affect the school environment. Poor families are more likely to move frequently for lack of rent money, disrupting school continuity. Children of jobless parents are more likely to encounter violence, alcoholism, abuse, divorce, and desertion related to joblessness and poverty. Poor children are much more likely to come to school sick, sometimes with severe long-term problems that limit their ability to see or hear in school. Students in concentrated poverty communities and schools often grow up without experience preparing them to function effectively in the middle-class settings of college or well-paying jobs.

In contemporary debates, desegregation plans are often ridiculed as reflecting a belief that there is "something magic about sitting next to whites." In fact, however, a student moving from a segregated African American or Latino school to a white school is usually moving from a school of concentrated poverty with many social and educational shortcomings to a school with fewer burdens and better resources to prepare students for college or jobs. Attendance at an integrated rather than a segregated city high school greatly increases the probability that an African American or Latino student will finish college, even if both students start college with the same test scores.[2] Black disenchantment is most likely when the desegregation plan is not able to provide access to strong middle-class schools for black children, a particular problem in plans in older central cities with few remaining middle-class families—cities that have been cut off from suburbia by *Milliken I.*

Resegregation in the Late 1980s

The proportion of black students in schools with more than half minority students rose from 1986 to 1991, to the level that had existed before the Supreme Court's first busing decision in 1971.[3] The share of black students in intensely segregated (90-100 percent minority) schools, which had actually declined during the 1980s, also rose. The consistent trend toward greater segregation of Latino students continued unabated on both measures. During the 1991 school year, they were far more likely than blacks to be in predominantly minority schools and slightly more likely to be in intensely segregated schools.

Since there has been little effort to desegregate Latino students, they will be far less affected than blacks by many of the changes analyzed in this book. However, any discussion of the future of segregation in U.S. schools must keep in mind the trends affecting what will be the nation's largest minority community.[4] The Latino share of U.S. enrollment has more than doubled since 1968. Current legal trends are dismantling the tools that could be used to provide desegregated education in middle-class schools to Latinos.

Another segregation measure, the exposure index, provides a second way of describing the changes. The average share of whites in the school attended by a black or Latino student fell. This reversed a trend toward greater integration for African Americans and continued the trend toward increasing segregation for Latinos.

The Relationship Between Race and Poverty

A student in an intensely segregated African American and Latino school was fourteen times more likely to be in a high-poverty school (more than 50 percent poor) than a student in a school that was more than 90 percent white. Ninety-six percent of segregated white schools have a majority of middle-class students.[5]

Among all U.S. schools reporting free lunch data in 1991, 13 percent were "high poverty" schools with more than half poor students who get free school lunches because they have low family incomes. Another 18 percent had between 25 percent and 50 percent poor students. Half of U.S. schools, on the other hand, had less than 10 percent poor students. Two-thirds of the schools with less than one-tenth students in poverty had 90 to 100 percent white students. At the other extreme, among the 5,047 schools with 90 to 100 percent African American and Latino students, 57 percent were high-poverty schools.

Free lunch data is the only available measure of school poverty generally available from U.S. schools. It is based on federal standards of family poverty needed to obtain lunch subsidies. Some states do not report this data at the school level. It is also likely to be an underestimate of poverty levels because some eligible children do not apply, some schools do not have lunch programs, and high school students often refuse to participate because of embarrassment. These factors mean that the segregated schools are probably significantly more impoverished than these data indicate. Later chapters will show the high poverty levels in resegregated schools.

Race and Poverty

One of the fundamental problems in thinking through possible remedies for metropolitan educational inequality is the complex interaction of issues related to race and poverty. To a considerable extent, concentrated school poverty is a problem affecting minority students only. In our studies of metropolitan areas, for instance, white high schools with concentrated poverty were rare.

In other words, the existing patterns of income distribution and residential segregation make it almost impossible to disentangle the problems of race and poverty in American schools. Though there are millions of poor whites, they have more residential options. They are much more likely to be only temporarily poor (as a result of divorce, health problem, or job loss) and to be able to continue living in a nonpoor area.[6] White schools are overwhelmingly middle-class schools. Even in central cities with large nonwhite school majorities, whites tend to be in schools with less poverty than are Latinos and African Americans.

In metropolitan Los Angeles, for example, high schools with more than 80 percent white students averaged less than 3 percent low-income students; predominantly minority high schools, in contrast, averaged 33.3 percent low-income students.[7] And in metropolitan Chicago, the correlation between minority percentage and low-income percentage for elementary schools was .895 — so high that, for statistical purposes, the two measures are virtually indistinguishable.[8]

Race and poverty are confounded politically as well as statistically. The Fourteenth Amendment and the civil rights laws prohibit unequal treatment of racial minorities in public institutions, but they provide little, if any, protection against unequal treatment of the poor. In the housing market it is illegal to exclude families on the basis of race but perfectly legal to use lot size, zoning, and other local legal powers to exclude all housing affordable by any but the top five or 10 percent of families in terms of income. Many of the inequalities in schools, however, derive from the concentrated poverty that is the result both of historic and contemporary job discrimination and housing segregation.

Unfortunately, the framing of the issue in racial terms often leads both blacks and whites to conclude that desegregation plans assume that black institutions are inferior and that black gains are supposed to come from sitting next to whites in school. But the actual benefits come primarily from access to the resources and connections of institutions that have always received preferential treatment, and from the expectations, competition, and values of successful middle-class educational institutions that routinely prepare students for college. Segregated schools are unequal not because of anything inherent in race but because they reflect the long-term corrosive impact on neighborhoods and families from a long history of racial discrimination in many aspects of life. If those inequalities and the stereotypes associated with them did not exist, desegregation would have little consequence. The fact that they do exist means that desegregation has far more significance than those who think of it merely as "race-mixing" could understand.

Regional Differences

Trends in segregation and concentrated poverty differ from region to region across the country. The much clearer legal requirements imposed on the South and the fact that the racial composition of school districts made desegregation more feasible within single districts there meant that much more progress was achieved in the South and that black students there became more integrated than blacks in other regions. This was true even though the South had by far the largest share of African American students in its total enrollment.

The fact that enforcement was concentrated in the South and desegregation was never achieved in some of our largest and most influential cities may help explain the belief that desegregation cannot work. Leaders in intensely segregated and visible cities like New York, Washington, and Los Angeles often assume that things are worse in the South and that desegregation was an unfortunate failure. Both African American and Latino students, however, continue to face the most intense segregation in the Northeast. Millions of African American children in the southern and border states attend schools that are still well-integrated decades after the first court orders. Understanding regional differences is essential when examining current realities and future choices in desegregation policy.

The seventeen southern and border states that had state-mandated segregation until 1954 continue to make up the most integrated region for blacks. Southern black students are only half as likely to be in such intensely segregated schools as black students in the Northeast. Latinos are least segregated in the Midwest, among the regions with significant Latino populations. Latinos in the West, the region with the highest share of Latino students, however, are significantly more segregated than Southern blacks.[9]

Blacks have more contact with whites in schools in the South than in any other region. More than half of all blacks in the United States live in the South. The exposure index shows that blacks in the southern and border states are in schools, on average, where almost two-fifths of the students are white. The Northeast and Midwest, which have much larger white majorities, provide much less integration for blacks. Latinos experience the least contact with whites in the Northeast, the South (which includes Texas), and the West.[10]

The huge changes in school segregation in the South deserve the closest attention since the resegregation decisions threaten them most directly. In 1954 there was legally required apartheid in the region's schools with virtually no students crossing the state-mandated racial lines. That system was 98 percent intact a decade later when Congress enacted the 1964 Civil Rights Act. That act, its enforcement by the Johnson administration, and a series of sweeping Supreme Court decisions over the next six years brought a decisive and lasting transformation. The enrollment of black students in the South went from one-tenth of one percent in majority white schools in 1960 to 33 percent a decade later. There was an even larger change in the proportion of students in virtually all-black schools; almost all Southern black students attended such schools in 1960, but only 34 percent of Southern blacks remained in such intensely segregated schools by 1970.[11] Persistent, stable reform and increasing integration continued in the South until 1988, in spite of the Reagan administration's opposition and the virtual end of federal enforcement activity. School desegregation was unlike the Reconstruction era reforms; there was no rush to abandon this change when pressure was initially lifted.

Contrary to many critics of *Brown*, the South was nowhere near returning to its apartheid pattern before the civil rights revolution; the reversal began forty years later. Given major changes in Supreme Court requirements and debate among Southern school boards about ending desegregation, the increase in segregation shown here could foreshadow much more significant moves toward racial isolation in the future.

Although regional variations in segregation are large, variations among states are even greater. The regional variations reflect, particularly in the case of African Americans, the effects of differences in law and enforcement activity, while variations among the states relate more closely to the impact of particular court decisions, the state's reliance on small or countywide school districts, and patterns of demographic change and immigration.

For more than a decade, the same four states, Illinois, Michigan, New York, and New Jersey, have been at the top of the list of intensely segregated states for African Americans. Segregation is most intense in the largest, older industrial metropolises where the central city and its school districts were hemmed in by independent suburbs a century or more ago and where housing segregation is intense. There were large increases in intense segregation in Michigan, New Jersey, Tennessee, Alabama, Maryland, and Connecticut. The resegregation in the South is beginning to challenge the high segregation levels of parts of the urban North.[12]

The level of segregation for Latino students was high across the country but most severe in the Northeast, in the Chicago area, and in the two states in which a substantial majority of all Latino children go to school—California and Texas. New York State has had the highest segregation for Latino students for a generation. New York led the nation in segregation levels since 1980, leading in all three methods of measuring segregation in 1991. Rounding out the list of the five most segregated states for Latinos are Texas, California, New Jersey, and Illinois. This means that the most important settlement centers for both Mexican Americans and Puerto Ricans have become severely segregated.

Compared to earlier rankings from 1970, almost all states with significant Latino enrollment have become more segregated. The changes in California have been dramatic. In 1970, the typical

California Latino student was in a school with 54.4 percent white students; a decade later the white percentage was down to 35.9 percent, and by 1991 it was 27.0 percent. Blacks in Alabama and Mississippi are significantly less segregated, according to this measure, than Latinos in California.

One reason for the increase in segregation of Latino students is the tremendous increase in the number and proportion of these students in most of the areas in which the group has been concentrated since the 1960s. In all of the states with high Latino enrollments except New York and New Mexico, increases have been explosive, greatly outpacing overall enrollment gains. Latinos experience severe problems in school, particularly in terms of a high school dropout rate that is very much higher than that of blacks. Latinos are more isolated in high-poverty schools than blacks. In the most isolated areas, many students needing to acquire English for college and jobs are attending schools with few native speakers of English.

School District Fragmentation

There is a relationship between district size and severity of segregation. States with smaller districts tend to break up urban housing markets into more segregated school districts. For Hispanics, the relationship between district structure and intensity of segregation is clearer because there are few desegregation plans to offset its effects. Six of the states with fragmented districts had higher levels of intense segregation than any of the states with larger districts.

The effects of small districts are partially offset for African Americans by a large mandatory interdistrict desegregation order in Indiana (for Indianapolis) and substantial voluntary interdistrict plans in Massachusetts, Missouri, and Wisconsin (Boston, St. Louis, and Milwaukee).

The four states that have the most extreme segregation for African Americans—New York, Illinois, Michigan, and New Jersey—are all large states with highly fragmented school districts. These are the states in which segregation is most dramatically reinforced by the 1974 *Milliken I* Supreme Court decision on metropolitan Detroit. Although there are twelve states that have a larger proportion of African American students than any of the four most segregated, the district fragmentation and the absence of significant cross-district desegregation plans produces extreme segregation, even though there was desegregation within district lines.

African American and Latino students who live in towns, rural areas, and in the suburbs of small metropolitan areas are the most likely to be experiencing integrated education. By far the most serious segregation is in the large central cities, followed by the smaller central city communities where *Milliken I* made lasting desegregation impossible.

In the big central cities, fifteen of every sixteen African American and Latino students are in schools where most of the students are nonwhite. In the smaller central cities, 63 percent of African Americans and 70 percent of Latinos attend such schools. About 30 percent of African American and Latino students (almost five times the big city level) attend majority white schools in those smaller metropolitan area cities.[13]

The suburbs are much less segregated than the central cities for black students, although they are far from fully integrated. Two out of five suburban black students in the large metropolitan areas and three-fifths of those in the suburbs of smaller metropolitan areas are in majority white schools. Very large increases in minority enrollment in suburban schools were underway in a number of metropolitan areas by the late 1980s, a trend that may produce severe suburban segregation unless offsetting plans are put in motion, particularly in metropolitan areas with small fragmented suburban districts.

The largest cities had enormous importance for minority students but very little for whites. In 1986, the twenty-five largest central city systems contained 30 percent of U.S. Latino students, 27 percent of blacks, and 3 percent of whites. This unequal distribution of students was a fundamental cause of the nation's most severe segregation.[14]

Why These Trends?

The huge changes in the racial composition of American public schools and the segregation of African American and Latino students over the past half century have often been misunderstood. The great increase in the proportion of nonwhite students has not been a consequence of "white flight" from public to private schools, but rather of basic changes in birth rates and immigration patterns. In fact, there has been no significant redistribution between public and private schools. During the period from 1970 to 1984, there was a small increase in the share of students in private schools, but between 1984 and 1991 public enrollment grew 7 percent while private enrollment dropped 9 percent.[15] U.S. Department of Education projections indicate that between 1994 and 2004 public school enrollment would climb 12 percent while private enrollment would rise 11 percent.[16] Even as many Americans believe there is flight from public schools, many believe that desegregation is something that was tried a generation ago but did not last. Both beliefs reflect the political rhetoric of the 1980s, not what actually happened in the society.

According to the Census Bureau, the number of black students in public schools in the United States increased 3 percent from 1972 to 1992, the first two decades of widespread busing plans. In contrast, Latino enrollments soared 89 percent and white enrollments fell 14 percent. These trends led to many claims that whites were abandoning public education because of resistance to integration. The decline was not, however, the result of whites leaving public schools.

The white drop was not balanced by growth in white private school enrollment. The Census Bureau reports that there were 18 percent fewer white students in private elementary schools and 23 percent fewer whites in private high schools than two decades ago.[17] The proportion of whites in public schools was actually increasing. The underlying cause, of course, was a dramatic drop in the white birth rate. Contrary to many claims by politicians, these overall changes had nothing to do with desegregation. Public schools were actually holding a growing share of a declining group of school-age white children.

In 1992, 89 percent of whites, 95 percent of blacks, and 92 percent of Latinos attended public schools at the elementary level. Even among upper-income whites, only one-sixth of the children were in private schools. At the high school level, 92 percent of American children were in public schools, including 92 percent of whites, 95 percent of Latinos, and 97 percent of blacks. Private high schools were more popular among affluent whites, but served only one-eighth of their children.[18]

White and middle-class enrollments have been shrinking in all of the largest central city school districts for decades. In fact, the total number of white students in the United States fell sharply from 1968 to 1986 as a result of plummeting white birth rates.[19] In 1986, the nation's twenty-five largest urban school districts served only 3 percent of whites.[20] In metropolitan Atlanta, for example, 98 percent of the area's white high school students attended suburban schools by 1986.[21]

There is no evidence that these trends will reverse or that changes in school desegregation plans will reverse these patterns. Middle-class suburbanization is continuing. Census Bureau studies of migration patterns between 1985 and 1990 show that each year "central cities lost 1.6 to 3.0 million residents while their suburbs...gained 1.9 to 3.2 million persons"[22] The overwhelming majority of those who left central cities for the suburbs were white and/or middle class. Central cities were left with increasing concentrations of minority and low-income families. The growth of minority middle-class population is now largely suburban as well, though the suburbs are also segregated, especially for blacks. It would be ironic if *Milliken I*, a decision that was intended to protect the suburbs from unwanted racial change, ended up undermining the ability to cope successfully with vast demographic changes sweeping across the entire nation.

The loss of white and middle-class families and students in central cities occurred in cities that always had neighborhood schools and even in cities that abandoned desegregation orders. Atlanta, for example, decided against a busing plan in 1973 but experienced one of the most drastic losses in white students; similarly, the rapid decline in Los Angeles in the number of white students did not end or reverse itself after elimination of all mandatory desegregation in 1981.[23] The largest cities that never had a mandatory busing plan but experienced large white declines include New York, Chicago, and Houston. Los Angeles bused children for only eighteen months at the middle school level before it returned to neighborhood schools in search of a stability that has not materialized. American cities were changing rapidly long before busing and continue to change where busing stops. Certain kinds of mandatory city-only plans may accelerate the change; others may slow it.

The Feasibility of Desegregation Strategies

While some desegregation plans have proven ineffective in either producing lasting desegregation or creating opportunity for all students to attend quality schools, there is evidence that school desegregation on a metropolitan level is a feasible strategy with major benefits. A metropolitan plan is one in which desegregation takes place both in the central city and in the suburbs. Most of these plans are found in states with countywide school districts where single districts include the central city and much of suburbia. Also, in a handful of other districts, the courts have ordered students transferred across city-suburban boundaries. Experience with such plans shows that the strategy that the Supreme Court blocked in the *Milliken II* case may have been the key to realizing the goals of *Brown*. The first metropolitan desegregation plans were implemented almost twenty-five years ago, and there is now a rich body of experience that permits comparison of their results with city-only desegregation and with neighborhood schools.

Metropolitanwide desegregation is advantageous because it produces by far the highest levels of integration and the most stable enrollment patterns. The achievement of integration is more likely through metropolitan plans than through city-only plans to provide African American and Latino children access to high-achieving middle-class schools, since it provides far more access to suburban schools where most middle-class white students live. Metropolitan plans also establish a framework for interracial areawide concern for and involvement in the same institutions of public schooling.

Separate and Unequal Schools

Contemporary metropolitan educational inequalities are dramatically demonstrated in comparisons of achievement test scores, dropout rates, course offerings, and teacher preparedness. Metropolitan areas are characterized by two-tiered educational systems: one tier serving the mostly white and suburban children of affluent and middle-class families, and the other for the mostly minority and urban students from low-income families and communities.

Inequalities in the Midwest's largest metropolitan region — Chicago — exemplify the big city pattern. (The Chicago and Detroit public schools, because of residential segregation, had the majority of all-black public school students living in the huge Midwestern region from Ohio to Minnesota in 1988.) In 1988, 1,081,000 children were enrolled in public schools in the Chicago metropolitan area, of whom 30 percent of them were black, 13 percent Latino, and slightly more than 50 percent were white. Most attended schools that were intensely segregated. A total of 223,000 black children (69 percent) attended schools that were 90 to 100 percent minority; only 3,350 white students were enrolled in these schools, resulting in a black/white ratio of 70:1. Similarly, 63 percent of the white students—390,000—along with only 5,500 black students, were enrolled in schools that were 90 to 100 percent white—a ratio of 71:1.[24] In other words, more than 60 percent of the children in public schools in the Chicago metropolitan area attended schools where seventy of every seventy-one students had the same skin color. All but one of the 90 to 100 percent white schools were in the suburban communities surrounding Chicago, and 94 percent of the students in 90 to 100 percent minority schools were within the city of Chicago. In the city schools an average of 73 percent of the students were poor (receiving free or reduced-price lunch), compared with 12 percent in suburban schools.[25]

Achievement Inequalities

The intense segregation of minority and low-income students in urban schools is a critical factor in analyzing educational opportunity because it is systematically connected to patterns of low achievement. In virtually every large metropolitan area studied that lacks city-suburban desegregation, low-income minority students and middle-class white students attend schools that are not only separate, but profoundly unequal.

In metropolitan Chicago, the average suburban school had 35 to 40 percent of its students in the top quartile on nationally normed math tests; students in Chicago city schools, in contrast, ranged from a high of 22 percent in the top quartile in the third grade to fewer than 8 percent by the tenth grade. These patterns were very closely tied to race and concentrated poverty. A breakdown of tenth-grade test scores by race and location shows that only 6 percent of the black tenth-graders in Chicago public schools performed in the top quartile nationally, compared with 36 percent of white tenth-graders in the Chicago suburbs. Latino students performed somewhat better than African American students, but still well below national averages and far behind whites.[26] Test scores varied dramatically by income as well. In nonmagnet Chicago area elementary schools with 90 to 100 percent low-income students, only an average of 23 percent of their students scored above the national median in math, compared to 74 percent of suburban students.[27] This means that inner-city children experienced a far lower level of competition and far less stimulation than their equally talented and motivated suburban counterparts.

The same relationships among race, community wealth, and achievement hold in other large urban communities, suggesting that these relationships are systemic and structural. In Ohio, for example, in the state's seventeen large urban districts — characterized by low average incomes, large minority populations, and high proportions of families receiving AFDC benefits — an average of only 43 percent of their students scored at the test's version of the national median on achievement tests in math, reading, and language in grades four, six, eight, and ten. In the thirty-seven most affluent suburbs, in contrast, an average 78 percent of their students scored at the same level. Even suburbs with only average wealth significantly outperformed urban districts, averaging 55 percent of their students scoring above the national median.[28]

The national consistency of these patterns can be seen in the National Assessment of Educational Progress findings, which show that only 19 percent of disadvantaged urban seventeen year olds had "adept" reading skills in 1984, compared to 50 to 55 percent in advantaged suburban communities.[29] The concentration of minority and low-income students in low-performing schools creates a vicious cycle of failure, as these students have little exposure to the culture of achievement that characterizes many suburban schools. Being in a school with a high fraction of the students performing well makes a great deal of difference for teachers who need a critical mass of reasonably prepared students to operate demanding classes successfully, particularly in the upper grades. Low-income and minority students rarely have these opportunities. In fact, because of the resulting wide discrepancy in course content and grading standards between high-poverty and suburban schools, the segregated students often have no realistic conception of what standards they need to meet if they go on to higher education.

Nationally, central city districts have annual dropout rates of 5.7 percent, close to double the 3.2 percent rate of suburban districts,[30] but the differences are generally greater in larger metropolitan areas. In metropolitan Philadelphia, for example, the dropout rate in the city was four times that in the four suburban counties surrounding the city.[31] One study, typical of most dropout studies, of New Jersey urban school districts, concluded that "there are really two school systems in New Jersey — one consisting of most suburban and rural districts, which have relatively low dropout rates and few major academic problems; the other consisting of a much smaller number of big, needy urban districts, many of which have [four-year] dropout rates of from 40 to 60 percent."[32]

Moreover, the differences in dropout rates between urban and suburban districts are not only in the number of dropouts, but in who drops out, and when. In the Milwaukee public schools (MPS), students who drop out tend to do so earlier than their suburban counterparts.[33] In Los Angeles County, 55 percent of African American and Latino dropouts left school by the tenth grade; only 41 percent of white dropouts left schools as early.[34]

Unequal Curriculum

Some may argue that correlations between race, class, and educational success alone are not evidence of unequal opportunity. Data on curricular offerings and teacher credentials, however, provide evidence that the stark differences in achievement are linked to equally stark differences in opportunity.

Low-income and minority students are concentrated in schools within metropolitan areas that tend to offer different and inferior courses and levels of competition, creating a situation where the most disadvantaged students receive the least effective preparation for college. A fundamental reason is that schools do not provide a fixed high school curriculum taught at a common depth and pace. The actual working curriculum of a high school is the result of the ability of teachers, the quality of counseling, and enrollment patterns of students. Schools with high concentrations of well-prepared students offer rewarding teaching experiences and often attract highly qualified teachers in precollegiate subjects. Schools with poorly prepared students in less desirable areas to work may have trouble staffing some courses. Even if teachers offering demanding courses can be found, they may not have enough students to keep a teacher fully occupied. In such circumstances, the classes normally either disappear or are watered down so that they are no longer equivalent to similar courses elsewhere. Even if advanced classes are offered, one key component — challenging engagement and interaction with other excellent students — may be lacking. The practical barriers to excellent precollegiate instruction in high-poverty schools are recognized to be so severe that the accomplishments of one teacher, Jaime Escalante, who taught Advanced Placement (AP) calculus in one

Latino school in California, were celebrated across the United States. He became a hero, though the same course is routinely offered in a great many suburban schools.

As a result of staffing difficulties and high school students' course selections (themselves often the result, in predominantly low-income schools, of inadequate advice from school counselors), low-income urban schools do not offer the same range and level of courses as their more affluent suburban counterparts. The differences in curricula are relatively small in elementary schools, but grow dramatically by the time students reach middle and high school. Middle schools in suburban low-poverty communities, for example, are more than twice as likely as urban predominantly low-income and minority middle schools to offer their students the opportunity to take algebra (25 percent v. 11 percent) and foreign language instruction (30 percent v. 13 percent).[35]

By high school, the differences are more pronounced. Nationally, roughly 34 percent of classes in high schools with fewer than 10 percent minority children are classified as homogeneously grouped, high-ability classes; in high schools with more than 90 percent minority students, only 11 percent of classes are classified the same way. Similarly, wealthy high schools offer three times as many high-ability classes as low-ability classes; high-poverty schools offer roughly equal proportions of each.[36]

Not only do white and wealthy schools offer proportionately more high-ability classes—two to three times as many AP courses per student as low-income, predominantly minority schools—but a larger share of their students take such classes.[37]

Segregated minority high-poverty schools have to spend much larger shares of their resources on remedial courses, special education, dealing with out-of-school problems and crises, managing violence, teaching students in other languages, and other special functions. UCLA Professor Jeannie Oakes also found that 59 percent of all disproportionately minority math and science classes were general level courses, while 85 percent of disproportionately white courses were either academic or advanced-level courses.[38]

The striking differences in course offerings and tracking are compounded by differences in the teaching pools available in urban and suburban schools. Suburban schools, particularly those in communities that are predominantly wealthy and white, report fewer vacancies and fewer difficulties filling science and mathematics positions. For example, 37 percent of principals in high-poverty schools, more than 50 percent in 90+ percent minority schools, and 40 percent in inner-city schools reported difficulties finding qualified biology teachers, compared to only 10 percent in wealthy schools, 15 percent in 90+ percent white schools, and 15 percent in suburban schools.[39]

Young teachers working in high-poverty inner-city schools find the job less rewarding and are more likely to consider leaving teaching. Among many other problems, they report that they are vastly less likely to have the materials they need for their teaching. Among teachers in schools with no poor children, 25 percent of teachers reported that they got everything they needed; another 59 percent said that they got most of the necessary materials and resources. Among those schools with 30 percent or more poor children, only 11 percent of the teachers said that they got everything they needed; another 30 percent said that they received most of the necessary supplies. In other words, 16 percent of the teachers in affluent schools reported significant voids compared to 59 percent of those in the higher poverty schools.[40]

As a result, schools serving poor and minority children often end up hiring less qualified teachers than do advantaged schools. In metropolitan Chicago, suburban teachers were much more likely to have advanced degrees and degrees from more selective institutions than their urban counterparts. Moreover, even within the city, the most qualified teachers were found in schools with the smallest minority and low-income populations, which means that "minority and low-income students tend to be in schools and school districts with less well-prepared teachers and counselors [and] larger class sizes.[41] Research conducted by Jeannie Oakes for the Rand Corporation found a similar pattern for secondary teachers on a national level.[42]

While school success is dependent on many complex factors, it is certainly true that students learn more with better opportunities for learning, whether at school, in the community, or at home. If the schools lack certified teachers, offer few academically challenging courses, and track disadvantaged students disproportionately into low-level courses; if the community is economically depressed, with few libraries, museums, and other out-of-school educational resources; and if a large number of adults with high school diplomas are unable to find adequate employment, disadvantaged students face more barriers and receive less reinforcement to succeed in school.

Segregation is powerfully related to educational inequalities. The most important dimensions of these inequalities—such as the level of competition, qualifications of teachers, and the level of instruction—cannot be readily changed within a context of segregation by race, poverty, and educational background.

Some of the reasons why these issues may become desegregation issues are apparent in the metropolitan Hartford, Connecticut lawsuit against the state government for desegregation and educational equalization. In a typical class of twenty-three students in the Hartford public schools, an average of twenty-one students are either African American or Latino; three were born to mothers on drugs, five to teen mothers; three were born underweight. In addition, eight live in poverty; fifteen live with a single parent; nine have parents with less than a high school education; eight live in households with an excessive housing cost burden, ten are in households where a member is involved in criminal activity; and nine live with parents who are not working and have given up looking for work.[43]

The suburbs have few such problems. If we expect these segregated city schools to provide educational opportunities equal to those of suburban communities, we will have to find support for a long-term policy of treating these schools much better than suburban schools, in terms of resources and assignments of teachers and administrators. Schools that must cope with homelessness, severe health and nutrition problems in communities menaced by gangs, violence, and joblessness face massive obstacles. The only alternative will be to try to open up the suburban schools and their opportunities to city students.

As segregation grows in the country, demographic trends and divisions among school districts point to increasing separation by race and poverty. This isolation is deeply and systemically linked to educational inequality, both in educational experiences and results. It is not likely to be self-correcting since the most troubled are also those with the fewest resources, organizational skills, and political power. Teacher recruitment and assignment practices are likely to increase rather than diminish this gap. To try to provide equal opportunities within segregated schools and districts, school officials would have to set up mechanisms to provide the most resources to the most disadvantaged, who happen to be the most powerless. Given the operation of local and state school politics there is no probability that such money, resources, special programs would stay in place. The depth and severity of the inequalities and their self-perpetuating character help explain why desegregation cases continue to seek ways to reconstruct the basic structures of educational segregation.

CHAPTER FOUR

Unexpected Costs and Uncertain Gains of Dismantling Desegregation

Gary Orfield

When community leaders debate dismantling their desegregation plan and returning to neighborhood schools, the proposed policy changes often appear to promise nothing but benefits. With busing and court oversight ended, neighborhood school advocates believe that educators and students will finally be able to concentrate on teaching and learning. At the same time, neighborhood school supporters hope that the whites and middle-class residents who fled during desegregation will return to schools closer to their homes.

Resegregation usually carries other tempting promises. As school leaders recreate neighborhood schools, they often pledge increased funding and new programs for the segregated institutions. School board members claim that teachers and principals will now have the resources and motivation to help economically disadvantaged African American and Latino children perform at high levels.

This chapter explores some of the basic assumptions that are reflected both in the court decisions and the debates in many cities over the future of desegregation. The examination shows that much of the policymaking is based on premises resting on weak foundations. As communities import such widely shared assumptions into their debate, they increase the probability of choosing policies that will not work.

Neighborhood school proponents, sometimes with the press as unwitting partners, work hard to portray resegregation in a positive light. Educators never mention segregation. As a community moves boldly toward its new "separate but equal" status, general support for the idea appears to be strong. Leaders highlight the complaints of African American parents and politicians about unfairness in the community's desegregation plan and suggest that new programs will solve the problems. It looks as if all the pieces are in place.

Like many seemingly good ideas, resegregation turns out to be much more complicated in execution than in conception. In practice, the initial optimism only temporarily diverts attention from inequality. As the realities of the new "separate but equal" plan emerge, previously silent opposition may crystalize in response to the striking inequalities in the resegregated schools.

Political and legal battles within the community may intensify after segregation is reinstated. This is because resegregation does not solve racial inequalities and school leaders cannot deliver on their promises. In fact, the inequalities may become more extreme in obvious ways. The overall record on providing monetary compensation and special educational programming to segregated schools shows few positive results. Statistics from thousands of already segregated schools across the United States are, with few exceptions, numerical portraits of concentrated poverty and educational failure. What few people in politics, the press, or academia know is that the record on desegregation is much more positive and much more promising than the "separate but equal" policies. Failure may reopen racial wounds in a community.

Perceiving a resegregation case as a battle, school leaders enter the struggle over the future of their desegregation plan with a big advantage. Local and state officials can invest heavily in the court fight, trying to overwhelm adversaries who typically have little money. This compounds the advantages the administrators enjoy from their control of the school district's data and their standing as the leading education professionals in the area. Local elites, as our case studies show, typically give uncritical support to school district resegregation proposals, saying little or nothing about integration.

Thus, decisions to resegregate may be the consequence of an unfair judicial process under which plaintiffs do not have the manpower or money necessary to challenge the school district's evidence or claims. The unequal battles are often waged before conservative judges selected by Presidents Reagan and Bush. This process, in which facts and reality are regularly obscured, increases the likelihood of court approval of superficial alternatives to desegregation that predictably fail to realize their goals.

Thus, if school districts "win" their battle to dismantle, they may only be spending large sums to obtain a policy change whose benefits are at best uncertain. Even winning is not guaranteed, since the courts operate under vague standards and judges have wide discretion in applying them.

The Supreme Court has left many questions unanswered about the circumstances under which school districts may dismantle their desegregation plans; therefore, one cannot predict how a trial judge will rule on the key questions that determine the outcome of the case.

Lawyers and politicians who read the Supreme Court's decisions of the 1990s often tell local school officials that the path is open for neighborhood schools without carefully considering the vast discretion that the Supreme Court has left with the federal judge in the trial court. While the mood of the Supreme Court decisions is clearly in favor of ending court involvement, the Court has also reaffirmed *Brown*. This means there is a good deal less certainty and more risk than appears in a battle for unitary status. For example, it is possible that the trial judge, unconvinced that a school district has complied with an order in good faith, may respond by issuing additional orders for desegregation.

Legal Issues in Ending the Desegregation Plan

Courts grant permission for school districts to resegregate only after officials prove their system to be "unitary"—to have eradicated the continuing effects of their old segregated system. Theoretically, the district has been purified of racism. After being declared unitary, the district is assumed not to be discriminating unless civil rights lawyers can prove that segregation itself was intentional. Even when their actions lead to segregation, such actions may be permitted if districts can offer some other plausible justification for taking the action, such as improving education.

Since the basis for desegregation orders was *Brown*'s conclusion that separate schools are "inherently unequal," one might expect that a finding that desegregation requirements have been fulfilled would require proof of equality. For example, it would be reasonable to expect that education for minority students had become more equal to that of white students in the metropolitan area in terms of achievement test scores, graduation, college preparation, and other educational measures. However, courts have ended desegregation without proof that a district has either provided genuinely equal education or that the racial prejudice that creates the unequal treatment of minority schools and their students has been cured. Courts can terminate plans even when learning gaps between the races have widened. At its worst, a court could reduce desegregation to a brief formalistic exercise—one that provides no redress or remedy for minority children. Under these standards, courts need not consider that the schools to be resegregated are located in communities that are much poorer and more isolated from mainstream society and job opportunities than they were when desegregation began in 1954. Courts are asked to assume that creating more such segregated neighborhood schools would be a reasonable educational strategy though the district never successfully educated children in its isolated high poverty schools, and to assume that the segregation still existing is a coincidence.

A trial may fail to bring to light either the dimensions of persistent racial inequality within a district or the potential inequities of a resegregation plan. When the civil rights side lacks funds, the trial may allow school districts to win on dubious evidence. With the U.S. Justice Department soundly in their camp during the Reagan-Bush years, big city school districts benefited in court from a steady flow of local dollars to legal teams and powerful federal support for resegregation.

In the DeKalb County, Georgia, case that led to one of the Supreme Court's key resegregation decisions, *Freeman v. Pitts*,[1] this large suburban Atlanta school system faced plaintiffs who had hardly any cash and relied largely on volunteer work by a young lawyer just out of a local law school. DeKalb brought in costly expert witnesses to conduct surveys and create evidence about white flight and educational gains that offered the most optimistic school district version of the facts—evidence that strongly influenced the court's finding that the district had done everything feasible to desegregate and was unitary.

The theory of the adversary system of justice is that each side will make its best case, effectively challenge the other's evidence, and help the court discern the truth. However, judges normally have no special training and cannot effectively challenge the evidence produced for the school district unless the problems are pointed out by experts for the civil rights side. Seemingly scientific evidence about local conditions backed up by testimony from local educators and experienced expert witnesses is difficult to counter effectively without money. The most prominent experts testifying on behalf of resegregation now charge $6,000 to $8,000 per week.

When civil rights lawyers in *Pitts* were preparing for the Supreme Court argument, they found that the trial record lacked key data to reinforce their arguments and that the civil rights lawyers had not been able to develop basic issues during the trial. Since the only facts the High Court can consider are those introduced in lower court proceedings, the holes in the record gravely weakened the plaintiffs. The record, for example, had a great deal of evidence produced for the school board by researchers convinced that residential segregation is inevitable in U.S. cities, but very little evidence from the many researchers whose findings about housing integration were more positive.[2] Plaintiffs could not afford to pay for expert consulting, studies, or even serious critiques of the paid defense witnesses.

This imbalance weakens the capacity of the courts to fairly enforce constitutional requirements. The inequities create special obligations for those institutions concerned about the long-term good of the community, namely the press, universities, and local educational and community leaders. Before a community commits itself irreversibly to segregated schooling, such institutions need to examine more closely the local options, what happened elsewhere when similar plans were implemented, and the actual evidence supporting the sweeping claims about the local compensatory plan. Judges also bear a special responsibility given the enduring consequences of their decisions and the unequal resources of the plaintiffs and defendants in these cases. Once the courts wipe clean the historic legal debt of the school district, desegregation cannot be reinstated unless plaintiffs later return to court charging that there has been altogether new violations and then go on to prove intentional segregation, which is extremely difficult to do.

Resegregation Does Not End Legal Battles

Despite the inequities in the judicial system, minority students, parents and their advocates will continue to fight for equal educational opportunities and may well find their way back into court on related issues, especially once the realities of a resegregation plan surfaces, usually in the form of increased racial and economic isolation, unequal academic performance, and negative conditions commonly associated with profoundly impoverished schools. Contrary to what many school leaders hope, the legal battles for access and opportunity will not end, though tactics and goals may change.

Minority parents and their advocates know that success in the economy is linked to getting a good education. The negative impact of inferior education is more severe today than it was when the Supreme Court decided *Brown* more than forty years ago. High school graduates today earn a third more than dropouts and college graduates earn 235 percent as much. Adults with less education are much more likely to be jobless. Recent dropouts are twice as likely as recent high school graduates to be unemployed.[3] As the stakes rise and the data continue to show that segregated schools score much lower on all educational measures, parents and advocates will seek remedies of various types, even after school officials have been freed from court oversight on desegregation. In fact, the conflict may shift to other arenas that require deeper intrusion into the educational process than did the desegregation orders.

For example, after the Austin school board won the right to dismantle desegregation, there was protracted litigation by angry plaintiffs on other fronts. Plaintiffs sued the district over treatment of bilingual teachers, the fairness of its spending decisions, bond issues, and policies restricting access to budget information. Ending desegregation does not necessarily reduce litigation; indeed, it may wake sleeping plaintiffs and spur conflicts in districts where race issues had been settled.[4]

Many older court orders required only student reassignment and courts were usually passive over the years, acting only when conflict erupted between plaintiffs and defendants. But when school districts succeed in ending such an order, they may confront a new style of judicial intrusion. Partly in response to criticisms about the lack of educational components in the early plans and partly because of the impossibility of full desegregation in many central cities after *Milliken I*, most desegregation orders in the last fifteen years have included educational plans as part of the remedy, as the Supreme Court authorized in *Milliken II*. Also, though a unitary status finding in a federal court resolves all the past federal racial discrimination issues, civil rights groups are always free to bring a new suit over new violations. Civil rights groups may also go into state court to determine whether the state constitution and laws create broader desegregation rights than those enforced in federal courts. A turn to state courts was successful in a number of states on school finance equity after the Supreme Court blocked action in federal courts. Many state constitutions contain explicit educational rights; the federal Constitution does not mention education.

When plaintiffs decide to pursue a judicially imposed educational reform, what began as a school district's attempt to get out of court oversight may only bring more judicial intervention to a system that had more or less operated independently over the years. Such educational mandates often alter the court's role from passive overseer to active interventionist into classroom and instructional issues.

Los Angeles is a good example of a district that terminated mandatory desegregation only to face a variety of other legal challenges. Within a decade after Los Angeles dismantled its state court busing order in 1981 (in response to a state constitutional amendment that narrowed desegregation rights), civil rights groups brought both a federal desegregation suit and a lawsuit in state court, *Rodriguez,* charging the district with providing unequal education to minority students.

The federal case was settled, in part because the civil rights groups did not have the millions of dollars they would have needed to prove historic violations in the system. Winning a good remedy would have been difficult, given the formidable barriers created by *Milliken I,* which blocked the city's exploding minority student population's access to suburban schools. Not long after, Mexican American lawyers were back in state court. In the *Rodriguez* case, filed just five years after busing ended, plaintiffs could readily show many of the same patterns of unequal education that had motivated the desegregation battle. The teachers in the Latino and African American areas had less experience, were more likely to be teaching without a credential, and were working in decayed and severely overcrowded buildings, many of which were forced to operate on a year-round basis.[5]

Los Angeles district officials had proceeded under the faulty assumption that their original court victory and subsequent dismantling had ended a long legal struggle. Local voters elected a school board dominated by civil rights opponents, including David Armor, who has testified in many cases that ending desegregation orders would stop white flight and produce a variety of other benefits. The high hopes, however, proved hollow as white flight continued and the pattern of overcrowded education by less qualified teachers for minority schools spread. Richard K. Mason, the school district's lawyer, said that the district was determined to settle the case to avoid another round of "divisive and expensive litigation" producing "social and economic upheaval."[6] In the settlement, the district agreed to transfer money from the schools with less overcrowding and more experienced teachers to the inner city schools—equalizing dollars spent per student in each school—and taking substantial funding and some teachers away from many of the city's remaining middle-class and non-minority schools over a five-year period.[7] The remedy was similar to one ordered for the Washington, D.C., schools in the 1967 *Hobson v. Hansen* lawsuit, a remedy strongly criticized for creating severe instability within the Washington district without producing substantial educational gains.[8]

Civil rights lawyers who have been frustrated in federal courts are also asking state courts for desegregation orders to enforce guarantees of equal education often found in state constitutions. In a Connecticut state case, *Sheff v. O'Neill,* for example, plaintiffs sought a metropolitan desegregation plan that would join the inner-city school district of Hartford with its surrounding suburbs.[9] A coalition of civil rights organizations, including the NAACP Legal Defense Fund, the Puerto Rican Legal Defense Fund, and the American Civil Liberties Union, demonstrated the profound differences between the concentrations of needs of every sort in the declining inner cities and vast resources in the white suburbs, arguing that the differences made educational equity impossible and violated the state's educational obligations. The trial court decided in 1995 that it was unnecessary to decide these issues, adopting the premise that nothing could be done until the suburbs were proved to have intentionally discriminated. As of early 1996, the case was under appeal. State courts have also seen civil rights battles recently in New Jersey, Pennsylvania, and elsewhere.

Expectations vs. Reality Under Resegregation

Battles and divisiveness continue after resegregation primarily because the new "separate but equal" plans cannot live up to their promises. This should not be surprising; what is promised in the throes of struggles to end court orders has never been accomplished anywhere. During the last three decades the country has produced many studies and reports on conditions in big city schools and the record is extremely negative. This record of failure persists in spite of thirty years of large federal programs designed to improve high poverty urban schools, programs including the federal compensatory education program, bilingual education, Headstart, and many others.

Advocates of neighborhood schools have also promised to reverse white flight, but white enrollment decline has continued where their policy was implemented.

Even the expectation that an end to desegregation will reduce costs often disappoints, as some alternatives to mandatory school desegregation turn out to be much more costly than mandatory desegregation. Communities asking for resegregation often make promises for which there is no basis and, thus, face inevitable disillusionment. Since communities decide to give up interracial education on the grounds of those promises, it is extremely important to compare the vision with the results.

Promise One: Improved Education for Minority Students

One of the most persistent urban myths is that someone has a program that makes segregated schools equal. Hundreds of such programs have been announced in urban school districts during the last three decades, but none has broken the fundamental relationship between poor families, impoverished communities, and low academic achievement. In any given year for the last thirty years, any large urban school district had numerous reforms and experiments in operation and a grant office busily applying for whatever the latest idea suggested. Most urban districts have experienced a long series of announcements of major reform packages by new superintendents and state and federal agencies. When each new superintendent comes in, however, he or she finds a basically unchanged pattern and growing community problems.

Each large district can point to one or a handful of schools that defy the odds, usually elementary schools with remarkable principals, involved staffs, and engaged communities. No one knows how to find large supplies of great leaders or, in many cases, even to maintain that school's record after the principal moves on or one of the recurring budget crises devastates the program. The overall pattern is dismayingly predictable after the expenditure of hundreds of billions of dollars on compensatory education. No one has yet demonstrated a remedial program that produces major changes in all subjects across a school district and there is little evidence of successful interventions of any sort after grade school.[10]

This does not mean that there are not beneficial programs—the Johns Hopkins "Success for All" model, for example, shows encouraging results—or that these efforts should stop, but it is extremely unlikely that a given district's latest reform package for a group of newly segregated schools with high concentrations of "at risk" children is likely to solve the problems.

Another fallacy is that education for black students was better before desegregation. Critics often compare their memory of the best of the old black schools with the worst problems in the desegregated schools and assume a decline without examining comparative statistics. White and minority advocates of resegregation often rely on such beliefs. The beliefs are left unchallenged because the dominant political forces are all lined up against the desegregation plan. In fact, since the desegregation era began, minority students have significantly closed the achievement gap with whites and black students have greatly increased their high school graduation rate.[11] These myths have been used to perpetuate antibusing arguments for two decades.

The widely praised Effective School Model, emphasizing strong leadership and internalization of the belief that "all children can learn" as key components, was regularly presented by its originator, Ron Edmunds, as a better alternative to desegregated education. A great many urban school districts adopted this approach in recent decades, including Washington, D.C., and Chicago. Many districts sought school principals who embodied the goals of the model. But none of the districts altered the strong relationship between isolated poverty, low achievement levels, high dropout rates, less demanding curriculum, and low college attendance rates. Part of the problem with relying on the "Effective Schools" Model is that while Edmunds successfully identified key components in more effective urban schools, his model ignores the huge obstacles to translating those characteristics uniformly to all schools. Large-scale replication of these clearly valuable educational conditions is a goal that no one has realized despite decades of trying. In fact, it is no accident that these characteristics of effective schools are more likely to be found in middle-class schools. It should not be surprising that schools and communities that are connected to the mainstream of the society where the parents have already attained educational success are much more likely to have high expectations and working connections to colleges.

Some blame the poor performance of minority students on the fact that whites, not African Americans or Latinos, hold leadership positions in the school systems. But even as African American and Latino superintendents and principals assume leadership in many school districts and implement programs emphasizing high expectations and better instruction in basic skills, urban high-poverty segregated schools trailed badly on the new statewide assessments implemented in the 1980s. This trend manifested itself even in cities that spent substantially more per student than their surrounding suburbs.[12] When minority leadership is limited to segregated high- poverty schools and districts and accountability is imposed in a way that does not take account of these differences, minority educational leaders will often be unfairly portrayed as failures.

Racially segregated schools must often cope with many problems related to the intense and increasing poverty and joblessness of their communities. Schools with 90 percent or more black and Latino students in 1991 were fourteen times more likely than white schools to have a majority of poor children.[13] And the intensity of negative conditions and interminable problems that these children bring to school are not found in suburbs or in schools that enroll a socioeconomic mix. The conditions common to low-income neighborhoods and their schoolchildren—untreated serious health problems, developmental disabilities, hunger, neighborhood violence, more family disruption, lower parent education and participation, and frequent moving to escape threatening conditions— often overwhelm efforts for effective schooling. Teachers with choices tend to avoid high-poverty schools, not because they do not want to help but because they are endlessly assailed with problems they cannot solve, particularly as social policy and job markets change in ways that make low-income families increasingly desperate.

A 1995 federal report on math and science education reported that high-poverty schools are less likely to offer key science and math courses. Principals reported that teachers had lower morale and less positive attitudes toward their students than teachers in middle-class schools. Sixty-six percent of principals in disadvantaged schools, for example, reported that teachers had positive attitudes toward students compared to 82 percent in advantaged schools. Administrators of impoverished schools described the schools as less competitive.[14]

Yet, despite the relationship between poverty, race, and inequality in systems with no desegregation, it is common for people to go so far as to blame desegregation as the principal cause for the educational problems of minority students, extolling the memory of excellent black schools in the days before desegregation.

Was Segregation Better for Blacks?

The memory of good black schools is not entirely inaccurate, but it obscures the substantial educational gains of blacks in the desegregation era. The fond recollection of a very few excellent segregated schools often fails to consider the social and economic realities that confined talented black educators and students largely to a single high school in an urban area. In the days before segregation, middle-class blacks had to live in the ghetto because of rigid housing segregation. The presence of middle-class students from those families contributed to higher standards and positive role models. Educated blacks had few job options except to enter the ministry or to teach in black public schools. As recently as the 1950s, half of all black professionals were educators.[15] Today, however, the black middle class, with far more housing options, has fled many inner city school districts, often for suburban schools and only a small number want to teach.

In the days of segregation, only a small fraction of black students completed high school. The leading black middle-class school in an urban area thus had a far more selective student body than central city high schools have today. The most troubled and disruptive students were often not in school at all.

Today, African Americans with equal talent now have more options; they are today's doctors, lawyers, and business professionals. By the 1980s, African American college students shifted into other fields, with business majors taking first place.[16] Even among those who enter teaching, African Americans are more likely to leave, in part because they are more than three times as likely to be placed in inner-city schools with problems they described as including "teenage pregnancies, drugs, and violence."[17] The great black high school teachers of the past had the kinds of skills that today would put them on college faculties or in a downtown law firm. Academically strong African American students from educationally demanding families have not disappeared, but many are now going to school in suburbs where no black could live when *Brown* was decided. Before deciding to return to the past, it is important to understand that the conditions that made past successes possible no longer exist in most central cities.

The problem of the decline of blacks in teaching has often been blamed on desegregation. There were major declines in employment of black teachers in the South at the beginning of desegregation; the percent of public school teachers in the United States who were black went down from 8 percent in 1971 to 7 percent in 1986. It is also true, however, that the percentage has gone up in many districts with desegregation plans, some of which include specific affirmative action requirements. Unfortunately, the percent of talented young blacks interested in education has gone down dramatically. The problem may be compounded by segregation.

Black teacher employment is greatest in heavily black districts and schools or in integrated districts.[18] Black teachers are much more likely to be concentrated in places where teachers of all races are less likely to stay in teaching—"large urban districts serving high percentages of poor children." Among teachers hired in the same districts, blacks were actually more likely to remain in the profession. Few blacks were hired in the low-poverty areas where teachers tended to remain at much higher rates. In North Carolina, which has a high rate of desegregation, the rate of black teachers remaining in the profession for five years was more than twice as high as Michigan's, the nation's most segregated state for black students in 1991.[19]

Neighborhood school plans put higher fractions of minority teachers in high-poverty schools and ended faculty desegregation requirements. These African American teachers have exceptionally demanding teaching assignments and, therefore, tend to shorten their teaching careers. Where termination of a desegregation order means termination of special state and federal funding, there can often also be large layoffs of minority teachers and staff.

The story of African American education during the desegregation era has some remarkably positive dimensions including an enormous increase in the black high school graduation rate. Forty years ago, less than 50 percent of young black adults were high school or GED graduates, but by 1993, this figure had risen to 83 percent, close to the white completion rate. The U.S. graduation rate for African Americans was higher than the national secondary completion rates for most European societies in the late 1980s.[20] The test score gap between African Americans and whites also narrowed markedly during this period. The gap closed despite the fact that many lower-achieving black students who previously would have dropped out of school stayed in. Scores for blacks were improving despite the fact that poverty, single-parent families, and unemployment were worsening. Since scores for whites showed no similar gains, it is likely that programs targeted on blacks, including desegregation, were related to this progress.[21]

The National Assessment of Educational Progress, which produces the only valid comparison data at a national level, shows that since the early 1970s (the period when busing began) the achievement gap between blacks and whites declined substantially. By the early 1990s, however, the achievement gap began widening again. The SAT average scores show the same narrowing of the gap, even though the percentage of black students taking the exam has increased, which would tend to lower average scores.[22] Desegregation cannot have caused black educational decline, because the desegregation era was a time of major gains, most notably in the South, where the level of desegregation was highest.

Attention in desegregation debates, however, often focuses not on broad patterns but on two extremes: the continuing educational failure of many children living in inner-city ghettos even after desegregation, and the celebrated success of a few well-known inner-city schools and educators. Popular films about Marva Collins's school on Chicago's West Side[23] and Jaime Escalante's calculus class in East Los Angeles[24] illustrate the country's eagerness to celebrate successful segregated education. Certainly leaders of such programs deserve great praise, but their accomplishment is often treated as if it were a model easy to copy rather than an extraordinary accomplishment.

This unbridled optimism is apparent even when success is limited to a single school or classroom. These isolated examples of success are often used to argue against the need for integrated education and for the proposition that every school can pull itself up by its own bootstraps. The perverted logic of the argument is that if any examples can be found of leaders or teachers powerful enough to overcome the problems of segregated high-poverty schools, there is no need to continue efforts toward eradicating the conditions that make such accomplishments so rare. This assumption is like deciding that if one science teacher could build his own computer out of spare parts, our science programs should assume that we can have good science without money for equipment.

The Media and the Acceptance of Resegregation

Once judicial pressure is taken off a school district, the local press tends to ignore the persisting conditions of inequality and isolation, or simply to treat their symptoms as problems of failure at the school level. In some cases, journalists accept without examination what turn out to be exaggerated claims about the success of resegregated schools.

Months after Norfolk, Virginia, returned to racially segregated schools, reporters and editors at the *Virginian-Pilot* and *Ledger-Star* newspaper uncritically accepted school officials' reports of improvement in the segregated schools. The journalists failed to check carefully on whether original promises of the resegregation plan — a reversal of white flight, educational improvement, and increased parental involvement in resegregated schools — actually materialized. Instead, the newspaper declared that "interviews…with educators parents, children and experts show the gamble (to return to segregation) has paid off."[25] Many of the figures and statistics cited were not supported by local data.

The same article documents the drop in the rate of children using a transfer program that allows students to transfer to schools where their race is the majority. Instead of questioning whether officials had effectively advertised the program or offered the counseling and information services necessary to take part, journalists simply repeated the school district's positive spin on the declining use of voluntary integration. The paragraph said: "Use of this option dropped gradually, from about 18 percent…to 10 percent. Officials say better black schools are the reason why."[26] Ironically, however, PTA membership had dropped in these schools and achievement levels remained abysmal.

Nationally, the media has given tremendous attention to the worst cases of school desegregation and to the best cases of compensatory education in inner-city schools. The one high school in the nation experiencing the most violent racial conflict over desegregation in the mid-1970s, South Boston High, was the classic image of the issue on national television. Boston's dramatic decline in white enrollment —the steepest decline of any central city district in the nation—

received relentless press attention. But the press has ignored *increases* in the number and percentage of white students enrolled in some southern metropolitan areas where both the city and suburbs are in a single desegregated county-wide school district.

The press and the pundits who blame the problems of ghetto education on desegregation have neglected to ask two obvious questions. If neighborhood schools kept neighborhoods strong and were better for minority students, would not we find high rates of success in the virtually all-minority schools surrounding us—in Detroit, Washington, Los Angeles, Philadelphia, Chicago, New York City, Newark, and countless other cities? If neighborhood schools offered as many opportunities and as high a quality an education that could be found anywhere, would not the thousands of African American students from Boston, St. Louis, Milwaukee, and other cities stay at their home schools rather than take long voluntary trips by bus to suburban schools every day? These realities are rarely critically explored.

Education, Not Busing: Impacts of the New "Separate but Equal"

After the 1977 *Milliken II* [27] Supreme Court decision, the courts and many cities embarked on an uncertain effort to actually enforce the principle of "separate but equal" by ordering money for special compensatory programs. The results of these efforts in Detroit and other cities were disappointing.

Los Angeles is another large system in which desegregation was rejected and huge sums were provided to remedy the harms of segregation. State law in California provides state funding for 80 percent of court-ordered expenditures in desegregation cases even if no desegregation takes place. After Los Angeles returned to neighborhood schools in 1981 the city received more than three billion dollars from 1979 to 1993 for programs intended to equalize opportunity in minority schools. Because Los Angeles was the first large city where mandatory desegregation was abandoned, its lessons are important ones. Schools remained intensely segregated by race and poverty, and segregation was powerfully linked to educational outcomes. In the mid-1980s, the correlation between the percent of African American and Latino students in a school and its average achievement scores in the greater Los Angeles area ranged from -.85 for writing, -.88 for math, and -.90 for reading—extraordinarily strong and consistent negative relationships. The 1986 *Rodriguez v. Los Angeles Unified School District* case was an effort to deal with some of the obvious inequalities in the resegregated system, even after institution of lower class sizes and "combat pay" for teachers willing to work in some minority areas. College was becoming much more important to making a living in California, but the access of area black and Latino students to college was dropping.[28] The city's percentage of white students continues to fall quickly.

Since the Supreme Court's *Milliken II* decision, a good many cities have experimented with educational remedies for segregation. One of the largest experiments took place in St. Louis. The court order in St. Louis, like that in Kansas City, directed the state of Missouri to spend more than a billion dollars to improve local schools and increase magnet school and suburban enrollment options for local students.

The St. Louis desegregation plan contained four elements analyzed in reports submitted to the U.S. District Court. The 1980 plan combined mandatory reassignments and busing with magnet schools to produce as much integration as possible within the heavily black city system. Schools had a goal of 50-50 integration and large sums of additional money were sent to schools where a shortage of white students made integration impossible. Thus, the plan provided a direct comparison of attractiveness and results for black students in three different kinds of programs. A subsequent 1983 settlement with suburban districts permitted thousands of city black students to transfer to suburban schools.

The 1992 evaluation showed that specialized city magnets attracted the highest achieving African American students, followed by the suburban transfer program. The lowest-scoring black students remained in their neighborhood schools, which got extra money. Although many African American political leaders initially argued that few St. Louis black families would transfer children to the suburbs, families of 14,000 children per year chose this option.

Since higher-achieving black students were transferring to suburban schools, the evaluation studied how the students were doing relative to their different starting points. Only the group of African American students transferring out to suburban schools showed significant academic gains at the high school level, important for college preparation. Their college attendance rate was high and high school dropout rates far lower. Across all grade levels, the results were most positive in the integrated city magnet schools, the top choice for black students. The many millions spent upgrading the African American neighborhood schools, on the other hand, did not lead to any measurable gain.[29]

A court-ordered evaluation of the first eight years San Francisco spent under a 1983 consent decree showed gains for neither the African American nor the Latino students who attended most of the low-income schools that had been given hundreds of thousands of extra dollars each year to improve programs and implement initiatives planned by each school's own staff. Under San Francisco's plan, large additional budgets went to targeted low-income schools. In a multiracial district with few whites and several disadvantaged ethnic groups, it was possible for students to be "desegregated" by, for example, transferring from a low-income black school to a school where the largest group of students were impoverished Latinos. Many poor families probably made such transfers because the schools were nearby.[30]

Studying the academic gains for students who actually remained in a school for several years, the report showed that unless the school was also completely reorganized (a practice known as "reconstitution") the money seemed unable to change outcomes. The only clear gains found in low-income schools occurred when a new principal and teaching staff committed to philosophical principles of integration and intensive reform were running the school. In order to hire the new staff at the schools, it was necessary to suspend rules and requirements laid out in the union contract and consider applicants from across the country eager to work in a newly energized school.[31]

Both students transferring to the reconstituted schools and those students who transferred to high-achieving middle-class integrated schools that received no extra money showed significant gains.[32]

The San Francisco study was the first court-ordered examination that assessed the effects of various types of schools by following students for several years rather than just looking at short-term school-level scores. The evaluation suggested that far more than the provision of large new resources or widespread choice would be necessary before segregated urban schools could offer disadvantaged urban student even some of the opportunities for gains found in high-achieving middle-class schools. The study found that students making the various choices were similar in terms of their poverty levels, but that they moved much further from their starting point in the better schools.

The research, accepted as valid by school district leaders, suggested that concentrated poverty schools are extremely difficult to change and that drastic methods may be needed to produce significant gains.

There is little in the studies of these individual school districts or in the general research on compensatory education to suggest that even a costly compensation plan implemented in a sophisticated school district is likely to produce marked educational improvement. In trying to change education for students in schools of entrenched poverty with long-term failure and staff burnout, very profound institutional change is probably needed.

Certainly what is known about urban school reform does not support any assumption that historic inequalities would be resolved by a few years of an add-on plan designed by the local school bureaucracy and never independently evaluated. Such plans come and go with each new superintendent and the average urban superintendent lasts less than three years.[33] Big claims, bitter criticism, new leader, and more big claims followed by bitter criticism is the typical urban school district cycle. Some of the most celebrated examples of urban school "triumphs" turn out to be little more than creative manipulation of misleading test score data.[34]

Courts often assume that there is a known cure, that the professionals will do it, and that the court can contribute most by simply getting out of the way. Often, however, they are turning power over to someone who has never solved such problems who will not be there the next year, and who cannot bind future boards and administrators.

Desegregation critics argue that liberals have supported spending vast sums for desegregation over the past several decades—money that should have been invested in educational reform. Civil rights groups respond that gaining access for isolated minority children to better schools is an educational reform. In any case, the truth is that the two biggest federal education programs, Title I and Head Start, are compensatory programs aimed at schools and communities with disadvantaged children. As these two programs grew during the past three decades, the small federal aid program for desegregated schools —the Emergency School Aid Act— was eliminated in 1981 after only nine years of operation on a much smaller scale. Title I, for example, received $6.7 billion in the fiscal year 1995 budget.[35] There is no significant federal desegregation aid program and only a few states—mostly under court orders—provide desegregation funding.

Many local boards have significant desegregation budgets, but much of that money, in the more recent plans, actually pays for educational programs and magnet schools, not busing. Local and state governments also spend large sums fighting legal battles to permit resegregation. Desegregation has been a low priority in education spending, and compensatory programs with no proven record of success have received many times as many dollars.

In contrast to the incessant and often skeptical evaluations of desegregation, Title I (called "Chapter I" during the 1980s) was not seriously evaluated for almost thirty years and after many billions of dollars were spent. The July 1993 report by Abt Associates on the first systematic national evaluation showed no evidence of net benefits for Title I students in the first year of the five-year study. The study also produced dramatic evidence on educational differences related to concentrated poverty and suggested that compensatory education was not strong enough to offset those striking negative patterns. The Abt Associates study showed that eligible low income students receiving Title I services in high-poverty schools performed at lower levels than similar students receiving no compensation but attending less impoverished schools.[36] Students receiving benefits still had a multitude of problems: "...Chapter 1 children are more likely to be retained in grade, to be absent from school, to be suspended, and to receive lower grades in reading/language arts/English and math. They are also more likely...to be judged poorly by their teachers on a wide range of educationally relevant dimensions."[37]

Teachers surveyed for the study said the children lacked respect, could not follow rules or instruction, and did not have the capacity to work independently or concentrate.[38] Though there are many causes of such problems, it was clear that this central federal educational program was not solving them or even making a significant difference. Given this record, courts and communities should critically examine claims that compensatory programs alone can provide equal opportunities. The lackluster Title I performance was evident even though school districts that receive federal money for compensatory education are subjected to far more extensive supervision than courts typically provide under desegregation remedies.

Unfortunately, courts often incorporate an unfounded belief about the educational benefits of segregation into their decisions about whether to return to segregation. After the Supreme Court, in *Dowell*, returned the case to the lower court for it to decide whether to let segregation in the city stand, the district court judge expressed his faith in the "separate but equal" programs installed in resegregated schools. In praising the "Effective Schools Program" in Oklahoma City's resegregated schools, District Court Judge Luther Bohannon cites test score gains in the schools as proof that the city's "separate but equal" plans work. The judge concluded that the Effective Schools Program shows that district did not resegregate with an intent to discriminate against African American students.[39]

The apparent gains to which Bohannan points are suspect; substantial charges of test score inflation have surfaced against the school district and its former superintendent, Arthur Steller.[40] Thus, the resegregated schools did register improvements over time. Yet subsequent investigations suggest the increases in Oklahoma City might have been achieved by lowering the percentage of students taking the exam — by exempting an extremely large portion of children from the testing requirements.[41] Compared with similar urban districts, Oklahoma City, had the second-smallest share of students taking standardized tests.[42] Lowering the percentage of test-takers is a well-established way to increase scores.

Though there are some successful segregated schools across the country, no district has produced equal education on a large scale within segregated African American or Latino schools. Because of vast differences in resources and parent-education levels — products of earlier discrimination in education and employment — segregated schools must cope with negative peer group effects and the absence of the clear paths to success that students and parents in middle-class schools take for granted. These problems become even more intense in secondary schools as influence of the family and the school recedes relative to peer group and neighborhood influences.[43]

Promise Two: Whites Will Return Under Resegregation

There is a ubiquitous belief about "white flight" that motivates school districts and courts to end desegregation. Local leaders attribute a district's rising proportion of minority students to an exodus of whites who left because of school integration. School leaders and courts often believe that once desegregation plans end, this white flight will cease and whites may return in substantial numbers. In many dismantling cases, school districts hire experts to offer court testimony in line with this white-flight theory. Courts sometimes rely on this testimony.

When trying to dismantle desegregation, district officials argue that they have taken every practical step to create desegregation, but that remedies have failed because of white flight. It is clearly a mistake, however, to blame the decrease in the proportion of white enrollment entirely on a desegregation plan. Local officials, incorrectly thinking that the district's enrollment was stable before desegregation, often have little understanding of the actual changes in their community with regard to birth rates, the pattern of white suburbanization, and the spread of black ghettos that existed long before their busing plan.

Federal courts have often adopted simplistic theories of demographic change. For example, in *Riddick v. School Bd. of Norfolk*,[44] the federal judge attributed much of the white enrollment decline to desegregation without considering the large declines in white enrollment occurring in other cities without busing.[45]

Research refutes this theory. If white enrollment decline were caused by busing, then cities with neighborhood schools would have stable enrollments; but there are very big white enrollment losses there.[46] From the mid-1960s to the mid-1980s, for example, DeKalb County, the district released from desegregation obligations under the *Pitts* decision, lost white enrollment more rapidly than all but three large U.S. districts. But DeKalb had neighborhood schools; the only "desegregation" the county ever had was when the county closed a handful of black schools decades earlier when it was 95 percent white. From that point on the system had neighborhood schools, but the enrollment shifted from 95 percent white in 1967 to 49 percent white by 1986.[47]

In reality, DeKalb's white decline was caused by huge housing changes resulting from massive black flight from Atlanta and a steering of white home buyers into other parts of suburbia. Black leaders in the city of Atlanta had accepted the proposal of white business leaders to drop their busing case in 1973 in exchange for administrative control of the school district, with the expectation that neighborhood schools would help hold white families. Contrary to expectations, there was a dramatic white departure from the neighborhood schools and an exodus of middle-class blacks to DeKalb, where resegregation continued to spread under another neighborhood school system.[48] Atlanta eventually became more than nine-tenths black.[49] When compared with the other leading central cities, Atlanta experienced the biggest increase in the proportion of black students, rising from 41 percent in 1967 to 92 percent in 1986. The city's children not only experienced severe racial segregation but also intense, concentrated poverty as the black middle class followed whites to the suburbs.[50]

Chicago, with neighborhood schools and no history of mandatory busing, fell from 41 percent white students in 1967 to 12 percent by 1988. Houston also avoided busing and dropped from 53 percent white in 1968 to 16 percent by 1988. Some of the central cities with mandatory busing plans experienced less rapid transitions and held larger white enrollments.[51]

Debates about plans should start by recognizing that the nation's urban school districts, whether they have busing, voluntary transfers, or neighborhood schools, have all had declining white enrollments for decades. We are still building new all-white suburbs and continuing to accommodate minority population growth primarily by expanding residential segregation nearer the metropolitan core. These housing trends, our changing birth rates, immigration patterns, and other factors produce white enrollment declines in cities no matter what happens in the schools. The effect of a school plan is not to create or stop these trends but, at best, to modify them.

After Los Angeles dismantled its mandatory plan in 1981, its white enrollment continued to decline. This occurred even during the first year after dismantling—the time one might expect whites to return. The Los Angeles system has become overwhelmingly nonwhite with neighborhood schools. In parts of the San Fernando Valley, where antibusing fervor was intense, many of the white neighborhoods that fought most fiercely for neighborhood schools now have virtually all minority schools. One of the studies done for the court in Los Angeles showed that the city had had no stable substantially integrated white and black schools before desegregation; neighborhood schools tended to go through a total transition in a few years.[52] In the 1980-81 school year when busing ended, Los Angeles had 24 percent whites; in 1990 it had 14 percent. In contrast, St. Louis, which had a mandatory plan with suburban transfer options, held a stable percentage of white enrollment throughout the 1980s.[53]

The fact that school systems with segregated neighborhood schools often experience large white declines does not mean that white flight from busing never occurs. There are certainly kinds of plans that accelerate loss of white enrollment and others—equalizing desegregation across all or much of the metropolitan housing market—that may slow it substantially by ending any racial incentive for flight since all schools are similarly integrated and none are threatened with resegregation. The least stable plans are those that involve mandatory desegregation in heavily minority central cities surrounded by unaffected white suburbs. Ironically, this is precisely the kind of plan the courts were requiring because of the limitation in the *Milliken I* decision, reinforced by the 1995 *Missouri v. Jenkins* decision. Virtually no attention has been given to the fact that some communities with mandatory city-suburban busing are actually gaining white students. For example, the metropolitan Raleigh, North Carolina (Wake County), district enrolled about as many students as Washington, D.C., Cleveland, or San Francisco, but had a 38 percent gain in the number of white students from 1976 to 1993 while the percentage of black students fell from a 30 percent peak to 26 percent in 1993, thus indicating white flight *into* this highly desegregated district in one of the nation's most rapidly growing local economies.[54]

The white-flight issue reflects a long-standing, general problem with judicial treatment of demographic change. In the 1974 Supreme Court *Milliken I* decision, the Court rejected the lower courts' conclusions that dwindling white enrollment made a plan limited to the city unable to maintain integration over the long term.[55] The Supreme Court rejected Justice Thurgood Marshall's conclusion that a plan limited to an overwhelmingly black and declining city could exacerbate segregation. On the other hand, courts have viewed the spread of housing segregation as a justification for ruling that desegregation is futile and ending it. Since the mid-1970s, courts have tended to ignore housing issues as a reason for broader desegregation requirements. Courts rely on housing segregation, however, to justify the dismantling of existing school desegregation plans on the grounds that school desegregation is futile in the face of residential segregation.

Promise Three: Continued Protection for Minority Students

In resegregation cases, school districts present themselves as organizations free of discrimination, deeply committed to educational progress for minority children. They promise to deliver better education. They ask that the court not only permit resegregation and let them implement their own programs, perhaps with a court order requiring state government to pay, but assume that no accountability or independent assessment is needed. The general assumption is that a bureaucracy promising to do something no other city has accomplished should simply be trusted to do it.

Local Control

The Supreme Court's resegregation decisions emphasize the inherent value of local government control of public schools. Local government control first took precedence over desegregation with the 1974 *Milliken* decision. Subsequently, the Court's 1995 *Jenkins* decision limited the extent of educational reform for Kansas City, Missouri, and authorized an end to the state's funding of educational reform measures in the schools. The Court said that courts must not engage in "usurpation of the traditionally local control over education."[56] Ironically, however, the local school board supported the order the Court struck down. The local control the Court endorsed actually gave the local district less power because, without state money, the city may now be forced to shut down its magnet schools.

When minority administrators first assumed power in many big cities in the late 1960s and early 1970s, there was great optimism. Many believed that the fundamental problem in inner-city systems resulted from the inherent racism of white leaders and institutions. This problem would be cured, optimists believed, once African American or Latino leaders and teachers took control of administrative offices and classrooms. This argument seemed plausible at the time since there was still a substantial tax base in many big cities, and state and federal spending on education was on the rise. In fact, education spending in central cities would rise sharply during the next decade. At the time, a large share of the African American middle class was still living in the central cities.

Twenty-five years later, things looked very different. Rapid suburbanization of both middle-class residents and jobs weakened the central city by cutting into its tax base, its political power, and its ability to compete with even weak suburbs for investments or new residents who had any choices. No one had predicted a generation ago that the African American middle class would depart for the suburbs in such high numbers. As the middle class fled, more poorly educated families, particularly Latinos and Asian refugees, made the overburdened city home. Reductions in state and federal transfer payments following the antitax movement beginning with California's Proposition 13 in the late 1970s compounded the problems. During the 1980s, federal housing and job training programs took giant cuts and the federal role in education was sharply reduced. As cities lost power in state legislatures and states cut their taxes, the burden on increasingly poor local taxpayers to pay for city schools increased. Inner-city areas were increasingly occupied by welfare-dependant families but the reduction of welfare payment levels, cut by almost half from the 1970s to 1990, and the freeze in the minimum wage tended to make poor families even poorer and to increase the number of families who worked and remained poor.

It was clear that after two decades of minority leadership in city schools, the race of the superintendent, school board, or administrators did not alter the systemic problems in the city. By the 1990s, many of these school systems faced even greater challenges amid state and federal funding cutbacks as the suburbs consolidated their control of state legislatures and Congress. Minority superintendents, in turn, were being hired and fired as quickly as white superintendents.

Even big city mayors found it was good politics to run against their own school systems. It was much easier, they found, to blame the unions, the bureaucracy, and the childrens' families for the district's poor showing on tests than to acknowledge and correct either the systematic inequality for disadvantaged children or the lack of adequate money and personnel resources to provide an equal education.

Minority as well as white politicians have become less supportive of urban school districts in the last decade. Cleveland's African American superintendent, Sammie Campbell Parrish, faced incessant criticism from the city's African American mayor, Michael White. In 1995, after the school system failed to win referenda that would have resolved a fiscal crisis, Parrish resigned in frustration. After attacking plans for racial integration and criticizing the system bitterly, White also blamed Parrish when the federal court turned over control of the deteriorating system to the state government.[57] The ideal of racial solidarity and the hope of transcending inequality through empathy have been badly battered by several decades of experience.

Amid huge cuts in the New York City school budget in 1995, New York City Mayor Rudolph Guiliani continually assailed School Chancellor Ramon Cortines. After a frustrated and angry Cortines issued his resignation, five of the seven school board members identified the true source of the system's problems. The members argued that "to far too great an extent, this city's school system has become a scapegoat, required to address the results of the city's other ills—poverty, homelessness, the absence of other programs to assist children and families."[58]

Urban superintendents rarely even serve long enough to implement any significant change. A 1992 Twentieth Century Fund task force reported that "constructive board-superintendent relationships have collapsed almost entirely in many large cities. In 1990, 20 of the 25 largest central city school superintendencies were vacant. Most big-city superintendents did not last three years on the job, and, as a result, fewer qualified candidates apply for these posts."[59]

Despite the well-documented problems with local politics and the systemic problems of deterioration within cities, the next new leader, or program, is often viewed as the cure. The Supreme Court's embrace of local control only reinforces the notion that there is a simple solution to what are very complicated problems rooted not in the schools but in the cities in which they are located. The Supreme Court assumes we have healthy viable localities able to solve extraordinary social problems if only the courts stand back. In fact, we have an increasingly unworkable system in which the central city institutions have constantly growing responsibilities—including a very disproportionate share of the responsibility for resolving racial inequities—but a constantly shrinking share of resources, power, and leadership.

Not only did the Supreme Court resegregation decisions offer no guarantee of effective "separate but equal" programs; they did not guarantee continuation of even ineffective symbolic efforts. Austin's school board resolution about its resegregated elementary schools illustrates this problem. Identifying some special programs, the board promised "to provide these educational efforts for a period of five years to ensure that students in the sixteen schools named herein have the finest education available in the Austin Independent School District."[60] Nothing was said about what would happen in future years, however, since that board could not bind boards chosen in future elections.

There is never enough money to satisfy all needs in any school district. All school districts face strong competition for funds, desirable programs, facilities, and the best teachers. Normal politics produces budgets and administrative decisions slanted in favor of the communities with the most power. Administrators and boards tend to reward communities with resources, skills, and access because it is this constituency that can most damage the reputation and community support of school officials by using communication skills and their ability to mobilize the electorate.[61] In the long run the weakest communities almost always lose. Resources flow toward power like water flows downhill. Money, good teachers and administrations, and special programs are always scarce and there is always competition for these resources. Assuming that the most powerless communities with the most disadvantaged students and families will receive equal priority over the long run is like assuming that water will flow uphill. Actually, of course, because concentrated poverty schools have much greater burdens, they need much more than equal resources to have any chance at equal outcomes.

It is not that communities trying to dismantle always fail to acknowledge such political realities. It is common, in fact, for school leaders — often with considerable fanfare — to set up commissions or watchdog committees charged with ensuring that extra resources and other projections do flow to less politically powerful constituencies. However, such committees are often powerless themselves; members lack basic research skills required to analyze data or to assess the state of equality in a district. In many of the districts we have examined, school district officials failed to provide the monetary or personnel support citizen's groups would need to conduct substantive investigations. In general, school administrators resist any independent agency with staff able to make independent assessments. If commission members do publicly criticize the district for its policies or practices, school officials characteristically dismiss the criticisms, labeling the charges as unscientific or invalid. In several communities, we have found that such committees—some of them critical of their respective school district, some of them not—are eventually abolished, usually with little attention from the press.

This cycle of appointment and abolition is particularly striking in Oklahoma City, *Board of Education of Oklahoma v. Dowell* (1991), which paved the way for other school districts to return more easily to segregated schooling. *Dowell* returned the case to local district court so that the judge could apply the Supreme Court's more lenient standard in deciding whether or not the district should be released from court oversight. In his 1991 decision, freeing the Oklahoma City public schools from court oversight, Judge Luther Bohannon pointed to the district's establishment of an Equity Committee as insurance that educational equality would be guaranteed.[62]

Because Judge Bohannon had refused to hear any new factual evidence, his decision was made without knowledge that the very Equity Committee he had used as justification for resegregation had been abolished the year before. The school board, in fact, had abolished the committee immediately after an Equity Committee report concluded that the resegregated schools were unequal. Although an Equity Committee has since been reestablished on paper, with members appointed by school committee members, as of 1995, a majority of school board members had failed to appoint members to the Committee. Equity Committee members reported in 1995 that attendance by members had been so sparse that it could not even establish a quorum required to hold meetings.[63]

Tiana Douglass, Oklahoma City's former Equity Committee Chairwoman, reported that the district had been uncooperative in providing important data and that members were not properly skilled to conduct adequate research. In an interview, Douglas said, "Although many of us on the Committee are professionals, and professionally trained, we have neither the time or resources to do this kind of research. And so you're reliant upon the information and the resources that can be provided by the school district…in terms of…information, data, money, that kind of thing, we were just pretty much on our own."[64]

Similar watchdog committees were abolished in other cities that had either been freed from court oversight or that had established policies that reduced desegregation. For example, Norfolk, Virginia; Austin, Texas; and Charlotte, North Carolina, removed such committees that had been established to oversee funding distributions and various other equity measures. As was the case in Oklahoma City, members of these groups complained about unclear responsibilities, inadequate resources, and their lack of appropriate research skills.

Promise Four: Declining Costs

Another basic justification for ending court orders is to end what is often described as a drain of dollars away from educational functions. Experience suggests, however, that school districts should not enter into unitary status proceedings expecting to save money in the long run. Desegregation plans are criticized for their costs, though two things are usually ignored in the debate over those costs. First, much of the money spent on desegregation may not be district money, but additional funds that come from state or federal governments due to desegregation rulings. Since most desegregation plans adopted over the last fifteen years include educational reform and special choice schools and programs, part of this desegregation money is actually supporting education reform. Second, alternatives to mandatory desegregation are often expensive. This is especially true if a district offers a substantial voluntary approach to desegregation or major reform of inner-city schools. Busing costs are often reimbursed under state formulas. Having transportation-funded permits experiments with citywide magnet schools and special programs. Some states provide funding for desegregation-related expenses on their own initiative; others do so under court orders or consent agreements, in which a judge can order a state government to provide money for educational changes. California, for example, has provided billions of dollars for desegregation orders. State governments in Missouri, Wisconsin, Massachusetts, and Connecticut fund voluntary interdistrict transfer programs that permit students to transfer across city-suburban boundary lines. Ohio, Indiana, and Georgia are among the states that provide dollars under *Milliken II* orders or consent agreements.

One of the reasons costs do not decline is that most districts want to preserve some choices for integrated education or magnet schools. Most want to keep open the option of integrated education at least for students who might choose it voluntarily through a magnet or transfer program. The political debates and court decisions rarely acknowledge the fact that voluntary approaches tend to be more costly and no more stable. Voluntary busing without a court order may not be eligible for state reimbursement.

Busing for mandatory plans often costs less per student because children are picked up from one neighborhood and dropped off at a single school. Those children who live in the neighborhood of the receiving neighborhood and are assigned to that school can often walk there. Voluntary transportation plans, on the other hand, employ the most expensive type of mass transit, picking up students from all parts of the district and delivering them in small numbers to schools all over the district. Magnet schools, for example, may enroll no students who walk to school. Asking parents to provide transportation will not work because that limits the choice option to those with money or time for transporting their children. If a district requires parents to provide transportation in a system where many minority families cannot, the plan has a foreseeable racial impact in denying choice to a large share of the minority community.

If school leaders adopt a plan that relies on magnet schools that replace mandatory assignments, they can expect costs to rise significantly. For example, when Indianapolis implemented a less coercive "controlled choice" plan inside the city district, there was an increase of 158 extra busses. Ironically, more choice may equal more busing, implying higher costs.[65]

Not only are there higher transportation and program costs in magnet systems, but this approach also builds in constituencies for maintaining those costs. A recent national study of magnet schools shows that the schools cost about ten percent more than regular non-magnet schools.[66] Creating a new magnet school often requires costly new equipment, modification of facilities, and retraining costs for teachers.[67] Once magnets are established, it is difficult for officials to close the schools even if they are unusually costly.[68] This is because attractive magnet programs tend to draw the best educated and most affluent families who believe their school to be superior and will fight to preserve it.

The More Promising Strategy: Extending Desegregation and Working Toward Integration

Since there are unanticipated perils on the road to neighborhood schools, it is appropriate to review what is actually known about desegregation. What are its successes and failures, and under what conditions is it most successful? A second question is equally important — how do we get to real integration? Civil rights advocates saw "desegregation" — enrolling black and white students in the same school — not as an end in itself but as a step on the path to successful integration. Integration was to be a condition of equity, mutual respect for individuals and cultures, a setting that emphasized the positive features of diversity in which students and staff could develop the capacity to work fairly and effectively across racial and ethnic boundaries. What do we know about the steps needed to move toward integration? What will be their impact on children and communities?

These are complex questions and issues around which there has been considerable academic and political debate. Much of the debate about the value of desegregation turns on the strength of the relationships between desegregation and measures of educational achievement. A central part of the conservative attack is their claim that test score gains are too small to justify the policy of desegregation.

Before getting into that debate, it is important to emphasize a few central facts that are indisputable. Most African American and Latino students are segregated by both race and income, a segregation that is most intense in the metropolitan North and West. Their schools have much lower average levels of academic achievement than white schools. The educational differences are strongly related to the concentration of poverty in those schools. If the courts were to order desegregation wherever segregation keeps minority students in schools with inferior levels of competition and performance, there would be massive mandatory desegregation. There is no doubt that desegregation generally moves minority students to schools with better levels of competition, particularly when the area covered by the plan still includes many middle-class students. In such cases, the central policy problem should be defined as one of making certain that minority children obtain full access to those better opportunities.

In fact, however, conservative critics have turned the question of desegregation's impact on its head. They argue that if desegregation does not rapidly provide such access and rapid gains in test scores, then desegregation has failed and should be abandoned. Since there are very few educational reforms that show unambiguous short-term impacts on test scores, such a standard would defeat almost any proposal. (None of the major conservative reform proposals of the past generation meets this standard.) Because desegregation is an effort to transcend a basic social cleavage, it often requires difficult changes within schools before its values can be realized. It needs to be evaluated over a longer period.

Most studies of achievement in desegregated schools are analyses of test score data from the fall to the spring of the first year of desegregation. These studies have been analyzed and classified in a variety of ways. Desegregation critic David Armor argues that the gains are too small to be significant. Robert Crain, a desegregation expert at Columbia University, described the average gains as more significant, arguing that it was essential to sort out the studies to understand the story. In an important study with Rita Mahard, Crain found that desegregation that started at the beginning of elementary school and lasted throughout the school years had larger benefits, as did access of minority students to suburban schools.[69] Janet Schofield has done the most recent major summary of the research literature. She found that there were significant but relatively modest test score gains, especially in reading and English. Schofield noted considerable evidence of benefits in college and later life that relatively simple techniques to have students work together across racial lines may significantly increase the benefits of desegregation.[70]

The most coherent body of supporting evidence for desegregation, however, rested on an entirely different way of defining the harm of segregation and the gains from desegregation. In work dating back to the late 1970s, a group of researchers then at Johns Hopkins—JoMills Braddock, James McPartland, Robert Crain, and others—said that test scores were an inadequate measure. The real goal of desegregation for minority students, they said, was to change their life chances by moving them into an opportunity system much more likely to lead to success in American society. These researchers defined segregation as isolation from mainstream opportunities—a self-perpetuating process with lifelong and intergenerational effects that institutionalize inequality. Desegregation and integration were seen as ways of breaking out of the isolation into a full range of middle-class opportunities affecting higher education, employment, and choice of community in which to live and bring up one's children. "Because there is ample evidence that test scores and grades in school do not explain much of the variance in later income or status," researcher Mark Granovetter argued, "it is very important to study those effects "directly."[71]

This research, described as "perpetuation theory" in a recent analysis by Amy Stuart Wells of UCLA and Robert Crain produced considerable evidence supporting the argument that desegregation plugs students into a different network tied to greater lifelong opportunity. There was a marked difference in college success, for instance, among students who graduated from desegregated schools,[72] and a documentable tendency for students who attended desegregated schools to be much more likely to settle in interracial neighborhoods. Analyzing twenty-one studies, the authors concluded that there are indeed many ways in which desegregation can help black students break out of self-perpetuating isolation and inequality.[73]

Why a Dismantling Battle May Be Unwise

If local leaders and community organizations realize that the glittering promises of neighborhood schools have not been met and that desegregated schools can produce real gains, they may be prepared to consider whether to abandon the goal of ending their plans.

Many districts have set out quietly to nullify the desegregation goals of *Brown*, thinking that their district is only reflecting public opinion and believing sincerely that they know how to make separate schools equal. The case studies in the following chapters suggest that these are radical oversimplifications of fateful and possibly irreversible decisions.

Does the Public Really Want Separate Schools?

It would be the ultimate irony if political leaders were to pursue a policy that resulted in failure and divisiveness because they believe that public attitudes on desegregation are far more negative than they actually are. Because race is such a central and sensitive question in American life and the society is suspended somewhere between an overtly racist past and a future of enormous social and political change, it is often easy to miss the complexity of public opinion and the real changes that occurred as a result of the civil rights movement. Reviewing public attitudes on desegregation over a third of a century, it is clear that the picture is far less negative than our politics would suggest.

Busing has been under attack for so long that political leaders often believe that neighborhood schools enjoy great support within a community. A move in the direction of neighborhood schools is often considered politically safe, particularly when visible minority leaders express their disappointment about persisting inequalities. Busing is often described as a failed social experiment, one that even blacks have turned against. In fact, public opinion data show that there is deep support of integration. Few people see busing as a severe educational problem, and support for busing has grown since Ronald Reagan's presidency. Positive views are strong among families who have actually experienced busing.

The way the question is asked affects the answer. If a survey question were to ask "would you support taking money spent on forced busing for racial balance and spending it instead on improving educational programs?" there will, of course, be a large majority favoring school improvement. But if the public were asked "do you favor sending black children back to inferior segregated schools?" the response would likely be different. Politicians and, often, the press, have been asking the first question, which assumes that desegregation does not improve education but compensatory programs do.

The national desire for integrated schools usually goes unmentioned in desegregation debates. This may be related to the way that the press approaches the issue. After decades of politics dominated by opposition to social change, the vocabulary of the conservative opposition — including "forced busing" and "quotas" — have been accepted by the press as neutral descriptions rather than politicized codewords. When journalists call the Harvard Project on School Desegregation, they often talk about "forced busing," but rarely about the enforced segregation that had persisted for decades in their city and proven in a trial court. Reporters often begin questions with statements such as "why do these policies continue when even blacks have turned against them?" not knowing that large majorities of black families whose children are bused report very satisfactory experiences. Imagine a parallel query from a reporter covering the abortion debate: "Why do doctors who murder unborn children continue to do this job when even Christian women believe it is immoral?" Public opinion is much more nuanced and much more positive than a cursory review of press articles would lead one to believe.

A national Gallup Poll in 1994 found that 87 percent of Americans believed the Supreme Court's decision in *Brown* was right, a 24 percent increase since the peak of the civil rights movement. Change in the South was even more dramatic. In 1954, 81 percent of Southerners thought the Supreme Court was wrong in mandating desegregation. Although the South experienced far more coercion and is more desegregated than other regions, only 15 percent of Southerners in 1994 said they thought the *Brown* decision was wrong.[74]

A growing majority, 65 percent of the public and 70 percent of blacks, said integration "improved the quality of education for blacks"—a large increase since the beginning of busing in 1971. Forty-two percent of Americans also believed that "integration has improved the quality of education for whites." Fifty-six percent said in 1994 that efforts for desegregation should be intensified. Eighty-four percent of blacks supported more efforts.[75] A 1993 Connecticut poll showed that 63 percent of the public believed that "children who go to one-race schools will be at a disadvantage when they grow up and must live and work in a multiracial society."[76]

Opposition to busing among both whites and blacks, often described as growing in the 1990s, actually peaked in the years following the first Supreme Court busing order in 1971; when asked at that time, only 18 percent of the public said they favored busing. (Forty-five percent of blacks supported the policy, but only 17 percent of Northern whites and 10 percent of Southern whites favored it.)[77]

A decade later, at the beginning of the Reagan Administration, a Gallup Poll showed that 72 percent of whites still opposed busing though black support was up to 59 percent, including 73 percent of Southern blacks, the group experiencing by far the most integration.[78]

Though the press often reports that African Americans are increasingly skeptical of busing, surveys show a different trend with black support rising after the mid-1970s. The General Social Survey showed that 53 percent of blacks opposed busing in 1975; opposition was down to 38 percent by 1986.[79] The press has given a great deal of attention to the election of African American mayors who favor neighborhood schools, suggesting that this reflects a shift in black public opinion. This type of coverage, however, illustrates the media's tendency to view the "black community" as a monolithic entity where one speaks for all. The media would never report that white opinion had changed because a few white mayors announced new positions; there should be equal care in reporting black attitudes. As is true of their white counterparts, black politicians may or may not reflect community views. Since the electoral stronghold of black politicians is often in segregated black communities, those officials may be particularly unreliable barometers on issues of racial integration where they face a personal conflict of interest since most are elected from segregated areas.

The percentage of Americans who saw busing as one of the most serious problems facing our schools has declined rapidly since the late 1970s. In recent years, few people listed busing or desegregation as one of the nation's serious educational problems; a 1994 Gallup Poll reported that only 3 percent mentioned such issues as integration, segregation, and racial discrimination as leading national problems. Such issues ranked far behind the problems of money, drugs, discipline, violence, and academic standards.[80]

Families whose children had been bused were solidly positive in a series of surveys. In 1978, 63 percent of black and 56 percent of white parents of bused children said that their childrens' experience had been "very satisfactory."[81] By 1989 attitudes of families had become even more positive, with 64 percent of whites and 63 percent of blacks whose children had been bused saying that the experience was "very satisfactory."[82]

Since the 1960s, most Americans have been critical of busing while strongly favoring integrated schools, as if it were possible to have both. However, when courts order busing, it is because they see it as the only means of achieving integration. Polls rarely ask the public to make the choice the courts face between segregation or busing.[83] A January 1992 *Boston Globe* national poll asked Americans whether they would support busing if it were the only way to integrate schools; in response, whites supported busing by a 48-41 majority.[84] Twenty years earlier in 1972, at the peak of the busing conflict, polls found similar reactions; although only 21 percent said that they favored busing in general, many more were supportive if it was the only way to achieve desegregation.[85]

When asked to choose between busing and segregation, African American and Latino support for busing was overwhelming. This was true in both the early 1970s and the 1990s. In 1992, 79 percent of African Americans and 82 percent of Latinos favored busing if there was no other way to achieve desegregation. When asked the more difficult question "would you be willing to have your own children go to school by bus so the schools would be integrated?" whites split evenly, African Americans said yes by a 76-21 ratio, and Latinos agreed by a 60-18 ratio.[86]

Many of the survey questions about busing are not relevant to the contemporary desegregation orders. For example, they ask about totally mandatory student transfer plans, though actual desegregation plans for the past fifteen years have been combinations of mandatory assignments, magnet schools, choice, and major elements of educational reform. Choice and magnet schools have been extremely popular in recent national polls but people often do not realize that most magnet schools were created as parts of desegregation plans.

If policymakers took seriously the structure of public opinion, they would search for ways to achieve the dual goals of desegregation and reduced busing. The policy most congruent with those values is school desegregation with more choice, clearer educational requirements, and less mandatory transportation. This is exactly the direction of policy evolution in desegregation plans since 1980. The other compatible policy is an increased emphasis on housing desegregation to produce integrated communities, which could have integrated neighborhood schools without busing.[87]

The contradictory tendencies in public opinion help explain the experience of several school districts where dismantling desegregation plans turned out to be far less popular than expected. In 1991, the Jefferson County (metropolitan Louisville, Kentucky) school superintendent proposed a dismantling of elementary school desegregation eleven years after the district was released from court supervision. Little controversy was expected, since the change had been endorsed by the school board's only black member and other community leaders. Shortly after the proposal was announced, community groups demanded a delay. The teachers union protested.[88] It was soon joined by the local human relations commission, the regional National Conference of Christians and Jews, and the city's newspaper.

Black leaders were divided. A black school board member supporting dismantling said, "...we don't believe anymore...that sitting next to a white kid is going to make my child any more academically astute."[89] Several other elected African American officials declared that separate schools would still be unequal.

Lyman Johnson, a civil rights pioneer, challenged assumptions about the treatment black students would receive in the resegregated schools. "Why do these people suppose that we can trust white people?" he asked. "What history proves that we can trust them?"[90] A survey of metropolitan area residents found 36 percent of those responding were opposed to termination of the busing plan. There were fifty-two people who thought education would be better in white schools after resegregation for everyone who thought education would be better in black schools.[91] Seventy percent of blacks opposed the dismantling proposal. Fifty-three percent of blacks said that under a resegregated system, the quality of education would be better in the white schools, but less than one-fiftieth (1.8 percent) expected the education would be better in the black schools. Perhaps most significant, those who thought education had improved for black students under the busing plan outnumbered those who saw deterioration by a 6:1 ratio.[92]

Pressure for an end to busing was not coming from the Jefferson County parents of children who were bused. More than four-fifths of black parents of bused children (81 percent) said that the experience had been satisfactory; among white parents 53 percent found busing satisfactory while 46 percent did not.

The attitudes were a striking contrast from the early days of Louisville's busing plan, implemented with great strife resulting from the sudden merger of city and suburban systems and massive transfers of students. Only one white in twenty favored the busing plan during the first two years. Although three-fifths of blacks were favorable in the first two years, there was considerable black opposition to the plan.[93]

In Louisville, the actual experience changed community attitudes. The division in the community that emerged after the 1991 dismantling proposal eventually resulted in a compromise that included a magnet school choice plan for the elementary grades with a guarantee from the school district that mandatory reassignment would be resumed if necessary to maintain integration. When it began in the fall of 1992, the compromise plan was successful in maintaining elementary school integration. The once well-regarded local superintendent whose resegregation proposal ignited the controversy left his job. A similar pattern developed in Charlotte, North Carolina, in 1995.

The surveys certainly do not show that busing is a popular policy with the general public. The policy is seen as far more successful by those who have actually experienced it. The widely discussed shift of black opinion to opposition to desegregation never actually occurred; in fact, it appears that black opinion moved in exactly the opposite direction.[94] (This does not mean, of course, that there may not be strong local opposition to a particularly ineffective or unfair plan, such as busing black children from one poor and ineffective central city school to another.) The press, by highlighting the views of black critics for the last twenty-five years, has contributed to the clearly incorrect impression that there was a shift in opinion throughout the black community. If local educators and school officials assume that these press accounts are correct, they may greatly underestimate the political and social costs of reopening the battle between "separate but equal" and desegregation.

From Resegregation to Integration

This chapter raises questions regarding many common assumptions about resegregation. Assumptions of both courts and local policy-makers often turn out to rest on flawed foundations and inaccurate generalizations. The findings suggest that there may be far fewer gains and much higher costs than have been previously recognized from the return to segregated neighborhood schools. Expecting equality to come from unchecked local control amounts to betting that "separate but equal" can now work because race is no longer a problem. Turning to choice as a cure-all amounts to assuming that we have good solutions to the ways in which markets often end up recreating and reinforcing inequalities.

Rejecting efforts to dismantle does not mean that old plans cannot be improved and the degree of judicial control diminished over time. Jurists and educators may, however, be much more likely to find the path to greater local control, educational quality, and public support by keeping their eyes on the prize of *Brown* rather than by turning again down the blind alley of *Plessy*.

The scope of the errors in the basic assumptions raise extremely serious warning flags about the irreversible changes being considered. "Separate but equal" policies have not worked in the past and do not appear to work in the present because of the many forms of unequal opportunity and resources still attached to race in U.S. society. In fact, large learning gaps between black and white students persist or even grow with resegregation. There is no evidence that transferring funds from busing to educational compensation has ended or reduced racial inequalities. Results from districts that have dismantled their plans have been bitterly disappointing as the case studies in the following chapters illustrate.

Resegregating schools does not end white flight, which began long before busing and continues long after. National statistics show that declines in white enrollment have continued in school districts that had always had neighborhood schools and in those that returned to them.

Ending a busing order often does not reduce racial tensions. In many cities, tensions over the issue were low until the possibility of resegregation was reopened. Nor does resegregation eliminate the possibility of future legal confrontations. The initial battles that lead to desegregation orders arose out of local frustration over manifest inequalities. When neighborhood schools are restored, manifest inequalities surface again as soon as the first test scores are published. Plaintiffs will continue to search for new avenues and legal levers to address the problems.

The fact that costs of resegregation may be higher does not mean that the status quo is a good one or that we do not need to make changes to accomplish the goals of desegregation and answer the legitimate complaints. Many desegregation plans are seriously out-dated, reflecting the demography of a generation ago. They may be unfair in the way the burdens are allocated or because of the reseg-regation of students at the classroom level in nominally desegregated schools. A school district may not be offering enough seats for its most popular magnet programs, thus creating needless racial competition. A plan may combine two disadvantaged groups of students in the same school. There may be no serious accountability in terms of methods to obtain actual gains for minority students. Local educa-tional leaders may have done nothing to train teachers about effective techniques for multiracial classes. These problems are not inherent in desegregation, but they do require much better solutions if the poten-tial benefits of desegregation are to be realized.

A desegregation order is sometimes thought of as the conclusion of the process. But, actually, it is only the beginning of a long set of changes needed to produce fair and equitable integrated schools.

Changing the issue from resegregation to successful integration could move both school officials and civil rights leaders to concede that major improvements are possible and needed. The community case studies strikingly demonstrate how seldom these possibilities are seriously explored. Most of the debate and many fateful decisions still turn on beliefs and fears that have little basis in fact.

CHAPTER FIVE

Broken Promises
Resegregation in Norfolk, Virginia
Susan E. Eaton and Christina Meldrum

In 1986, Norfolk, Virginia, became the first school district in the
nation to be given federal court sanction to dismantle its desegregation plan and return to racially segregated elementary schools. The
Norfolk decision was the Reagan administration's first big victory in
its effort to dismantle desegregation plans and restore neighborhood
schools. Many politicians and educators hailed the ruling, which permitted the deliberate creation of ten nearly all-black elementary
schools, as a triumph of common sense.

The Norfolk decision seemed logical because at the peak of the
conservative Reagan era, it appeared that "everyone knew" school
desegregation had failed, that white families fled from the public
schools when desegregation was mandated, and that minority children
would be much better off back in their own "neighborhood" schools.

Despite the historical significance of Norfolk's resegregation, little
national attention has focused on the results. Once the federal court
decision was handed down, journalists, the court, and local policymakers seemed content to consider the case closed and made no systematic effort to look at the results of resegregation.

Although few noticed, none of the promises attached to the
return to neighborhood schools came true. All the community and
court's assumptions about the potential benefits of undoing the city's
busing plan have turned out to be incorrect. Norfolk's return to segregated neighborhood elementary schools has been neither the
panacea for white flight nor the cure for low parental involvement
the court had expected. From an educational standpoint, the plan
designed to improve achievement for black students in newly "resegregated" schools has failed. In fact, academic achievement has worsened overall in these schools and the gap between segregated and
better integrated elementary schools has grown wider. Similarly, the

academic achievement gap between black students in the segregated schools and black students in better integrated schools has also grown wider over time.

Educators who believe students might be better served by an out-right end to desegregation and a return to neighborhood elementary schools should consider seriously the lessons from Norfolk, which suggest just the opposite. These findings should inform the debate about desegregation policy at a time when claims about the superiority of segregated neighborhood schools are winning favor among some politicians, including a substantial number of black mayors. The frequent claims about the value of segregated neighborhood schools, meanwhile, have gone more or less unchallenged by the media.

The Historical and Legal Setting

The complex, interrelated historical and legal issues involved in the Norfolk case stretch back four decades. Like all southern communities, Norfolk has a history of intentional racial segregation.

In 1954, the year the Supreme Court declared illegal the intentional segregation of public schools, Norfolk's schools were segregated under state law. Despite the clear message sent by the Court in *Brown v. Board of Education*, by 1956 the state of Virginia had still made no attempt to integrate its schools. On the contrary, the state legislature enacted an official policy of massive resistance to racial integration.[1]

In response to the resistance, black Norfolk parents in 1956 sued the school board in *Beckett v. School Board of the City of Norfolk*, seeking access for their children to white schools.[2] In February 1957, the district court ruled that the school board could no longer refuse to admit students solely on account of race or color.[3] The school board avoided complying with the injunction by offering a variety of excuses for denying the applications of the 151 black students who had applied for access to the white schools. U.S. District Court Judge Walter E. Hoffman ordered the school district to reconsider the applications; the school district agreed to admit just seventeen of the students and requested a delay in the admission process. The appeals court, however, affirmed Hoffman's decision and ordered that all transfer requests be granted. Virginia Governor J. Lindsay Almond Jr. responded to the 1958 court order by closing the schools slated for integration[4] in order to avoid desegregating them.

The civil rights lawyers continued to challenge the segregation under a renamed 1970 lawsuit, *Brewer v. School Board for the City of Norfolk*.[5] Finally, after much legal wrangling, the school board agreed to implement a desegregation plan. But civil rights lawyers challenged the school zones proposed in the desegregation plan, saying the zones would preserve segregation because the zones corresponded with segregated neighborhoods. Norfolk then implemented a limited desegregation plan. Not until 1972, after the Supreme Court's *Swann* decision that authorized busing as a remedy, did a federal district court issue an order for a revised mandatory plan that provided free bus transportation.[6] The 1972 plan affected 24,200 white students and 24,600 black students.[7] The plan relied on mandatory student assignments and a program that allowed students to transfer from schools where their race was in the majority to schools where their race would be in the minority.[8] Under the initial desegregation plan, only one of thirty-nine elementary schools was more than 70 percent black.[9]

This was a considerable change from 1955, when the city maintained twenty-one all-black elementary schools and twenty-one all-white elementary schools.[10] Even in 1969, under the more limited plan, Norfolk still had eleven schools that were more than 90 percent black, eighteen schools more than 90 percent white, and three schools between 13 percent and 40 percent black.[11]

From 1972 to 1975, Norfolk remained under court supervision and complied with the desegregation order. In 1975, at the request of the school board, U.S. District Court Chief Judge MacKenzie determined that the school board, after only about four years of mandatory desegregation, had eliminated vestiges of racial discrimination from the schools and had thus earned "unitary status." "Unitary," in the case of desegregation, might best be understood as a "single" system in contrast to "dual"; dual implies that a district maintains two types of schools—in this case, "black" and "white."

The order read, in part, as follows: "discrimination through official action has been eliminated from the system...this action is hereby dismissed, with leave to any party to reinstate this action for good cause shown."[12]

Neither school leaders nor plaintiffs could have anticipated the significance of this ruling, since "unitary status" was not an established legal concept in 1975. No party took any legal action in response to the order at that time, perhaps because civil rights lawyers assumed that action to reinstate segregation would automatically be considered unconstitutional. Norfolk did not attempt to change any aspects of the previous desegregation order until 1981.

Looking for a Way Out

On 11 September 1981, the Norfolk school board, tired of administering a mandatory transportation plan, took its first official step to end busing for desegregation. In a meeting that was closed to the public,[13] school board members addressed the issue for the first time, starting a contentious battle over whether to go to court to try to end the busing plan. (The Rev. John H. Foster, one of three blacks on the school board, was not present at this meeting. Foster was not in Norfolk on the night of the meeting and believed that the school board was on vacation. Foster said he was not informed that the school board would be discussing a proposal to end busing.)

Two years later, in a 5-2 vote, the school board approved a modified student assignment plan that would end busing of elementary school students, thereby creating ten schools that were nearly all black. Under the plan, three schools would be more than 70 percent white.[14]

According to Thomas Johnson, the school board chairman who instigated the move, school officials had several reasons to end busing. These justifications included the observation that schools seemed to be resegregating anyway and the strong perception among some whites that their neighborhoods were now integrated enough to create integrated neighborhood schools. Johnson also said that his belief that the U.S. Justice Department under Ronald Reagan would support the effort to end busing further encouraged him to initiate the court battle.[15] Johnson said, "I realized that the DOJ [Department of Justice] might go along with a plan to end busing. I wouldn't have done it if I thought I would have to fight the U.S. Government."[16]

The rationale behind the new plan—officially called "Proposal for a Voluntary Stably Desegregated School System"—was drawn largely from the controversial findings of David Armor. In anticipation of a court battle, the school board had hired Armor to write a report documenting the problems that would be caused by continued racial integration in the city schools. A social scientist specializing in studies of white flight for school districts resisting desegregation, Armor was well known for his anti-busing stance, having been elected as an anti-busing member of the Los Angeles school board. His report suggested, among other things, that Norfolk's busing program had caused white flight from the city and its schools. Ending desegregation, Dr. Armor contended, would retain whites who otherwise would leave and it would attract other white families back to the city.

The board's proposed assignment plan was challenged by parents of black schoolchildren in *Riddick v. The School Board of the City of Norfolk* in 1986. But the district court judge, John MacKenzie, approved the new assignment plan, accepting the defendant's explanation that the proposed neighborhood school plan would ameliorate white flight and also increase parental involvement in the schools.

The plaintiffs in *Riddick* appealed to the Fourth Circuit Court of Appeals, and the U.S. Department of Justice became actively involved in the *Riddick* case on behalf of the Norfolk school board. William Bradford Reynolds, then chief of the Justice Department's Civil Rights Division, filed a brief in favor of Norfolk's effort to dismantle desegregation. That the Justice Department, once the primary enforcer of desegregation rights, would oppose desegregation did not come as much of a surprise. Indeed, Reynolds had previously said in speeches and before Congress that busing was a failed social experiment, publicly encouraging school districts to get out of mandatory desegregation plans.

In the Norfolk case, Reynolds argued that, because Norfolk had been granted unitary status, it should be treated exactly like a district that had never discriminated. Unitary status, Reynolds argued, meant that so long as the district meets the constitutional standard of showing that actions in question are rationally related to a governmental interest, the school board should be allowed to return to segregated neighborhood schools.[17]

The Fourth Circuit Court of Appeals accepted the school board's plan for neighborhood schools. Civil rights lawyers appealed to the Supreme Court, but the Court, in 1986, refused to hear the case. In the fall of 1986, Norfolk ended its busing plan for elementary school students, creating ten nearly all-black elementary schools and three disproportionately white elementary schools.

The 1975 "unitary status" declaration played a crucial role in this decision. The fact that Norfolk was "unitary" was held to erase Norfolk's discriminatory history, thereby allowing the court in the

Riddick case to evaluate the school board action by a lenient standard. Had Norfolk never been declared unitary, Norfolk's resegregative action would have had to be treated by the court as a historically discriminatory district. This would have placed the burden of proof upon the city school board to prove that its action would not impede creation of a desegregated or "unitary" district. Since the district was knowingly creating segregated schools, it seems logical that a court would have viewed the action as impeding desegregation.

But as a unitary district, the school board needed only to prove that its proposed return to segregated schools was "rationally related" to "legitimate" government interests, with the interests in this case being an end to white flight and an increase in parental involvement. This placed an enormous burden on civil rights lawyers who, under this standard, were forced to prove that the latest plan for resegregation constituted a new instance of intentional racial discrimination. Of course, laws that are overtly racially discriminatory have been purged from the books and astute, modern-day officials know better than to make public comments that could be used as evidence of discriminatory intent. The court legally presumed that school district actions were a nondiscriminatory effort to improve education, even though it was clear the actions would produce racial segregation.

Research and the Court's Assumptions

The logic leading to the *Riddick* decision was informed by questionable social science research about the causes of declining white enrollment in the district.

The judge concluded that because of busing, Norfolk lost 6,000 to 8,000 white students. The court's conclusions mirror those offered by David Armor, whose 1982 report submitted to the court, stated: "…about 8,000 white students appear to have been lost because of mandatory busing policies."[18]

However, later analyses by Leslie G. Carr and Donald J. Zeigler of Norfolk's Old Dominion University test Dr. Armor's predictions about the number of white students who would have continued to leave the schools if busing remained intact and the number who would return if busing were to end. Their research concludes that Armor's predictions have all turned out to be inaccurate.[19]

This finding is significant because the court's principal justifications for ending busing were that the move would reduce white flight and lure white students back into the city, thereby making integration more viable — or in the federal court's words: "so that the school administration will have considerably more white students for the purpose of integrating the system than it would have if the present plan [busing] continues in operation."[20]

Armor estimated that between 1969 and 1981, Norfolk lost 19,000 white students from the K-12 grades.[21] About 42 percent of that loss (about 8,000 students), he said, was because of busing.[22] Projecting this 8 percent annual rate of loss into the future, he predicted that the school system would lose an additional 8,000 to 10,000 white students and would therefore be 75 percent black by 1987 if busing were to continue. This led David Armor to conclude that busing would resegregate the school system.[23]

Making an alternate estimate on the lower end, David Armor also calculated a smaller loss. With about 13,730 whites in the school system in 1981, a loss of 600 students a year would amount to about 2,400 students over four years, or a loss of 4.4 percent annually with an overall loss of 17.5 percent.[24]

The next year, Armor responded to criticism of his methods and submitted to the school board a revised report with a second, lower-end limit to his predictions of 3 percent white loss if busing were to continue.[25]

Carr and Zeigler tested all these predictions in two subsequent analyses and found Armor's predictions about how big white losses and gains would turn out to be substantially in error.

White Loss

Armor predicted that Norfolk's 41 percent white system would have only 32 to 36 percent whites by 1985 if busing were continued.[26]

But Carr and Zeigler show that the decrease in white enrollment decline "abruptly moderated" in 1982 and reversed direction in 1985 while busing continued.[27] At the K-5 level, enrollment of white students did decline in 1982 when 419 white students — or 6 percent — were lost. However, between 1982 and 1985, while busing was still in place, there was a gain of 266 white students, or about 4 percent.[28]

White Return

In considering these rates of loss and return for grades K-5, where busing ended, Armor predicted an annual gain of 7 percent in the white K-5 student population.[29]

But Armor's critics found that in the first four years after busing ended, the annual gain in white students at the K-5 level that resulted *from the end of busing* was 2 percent or less. After a few years, the decline of whites resumed.

Carr and Zeigler conclude:

> The irony in the Norfolk case is that there actually was no white flight in the schools by the time the [district] court ruled on the case in 1984 or through the appeal period that ended in 1986....There was an immediate and significant increase in segregation when busing ended. Since then, the small gain in white students, which appears to be dwindling, has had no discernible effect on the trend toward increased segregation.[30]

The Carr and Zeigler report spurred a detailed rebuttal from David Armor, who defended his original prediction that white flight would end once busing stopped. His rebuttal posits an "anticipatory" theory, claiming that the stabilization was spurred by anticipation of neighborhood schools in reaction to the school board's 1983 decision to try to end busing. Armor argues that parents probably anticipated an end to busing and therefore felt safe to enroll their children in the schools. Although Armor offers no empirical evidence to support this theory, he argues that it is whites who would be most likely to return to the city schools between the time the school board decided to end busing and when the court granted the policy change in 1986.

In reality, however, it seems highly unlikely that white parents would assume that busing would end, since at that time no school district in the United States had been permitted to end desegregation and return to segregation. It was also clear that the litigation would last for years in the courts.

Armor later complained that Carr and Zeigler ignored his modified predictions and claimed the actual 3.2 percent increase in white return "falls within the range" of his 1983 forecasts,[31] which reported a low-end limit of 3 percent. (While Armor's predictions appear straightforward, they are difficult to test and analyze, because Armor made his predictions about white loss and white return based on the K-12 population, assuming that busing would end for all grades. Armor made these calculations and assumptions independently, even though the school board in Norfolk had never proposed a full-scale end to busing, but was considering an end to busing for elementary school students only. Because of this, the predictions need to be adjusted so changes on the K-5 level can be considered independent of the overall K-12 population.)

But once Carr tested Armor's lower 1983 predictions, he found those, too, to be significant overestimates. Using an adjustment technique suggested by Armor himself, Carr tests Armor's minimum estimate of a loss of 6 percent, or about 300 white students per year in grades K-5 if busing were to stay in effect from 1981 to 1985. Explaining how to adapt his predictions of white loss and white return, Armor simply splits his overall predictions in half. (Thus, over this four-year period, 1,200 white students—or 17 percent of the 1981 K-5 white enrollment of 6,899—would be lost, according to Armor.) But Carr shows that the percentage of elementary white students did not decline at all during this time. In fact, the enrollment increased by four percent in grades K-5 during this period while busing was still intact.[32]

White Return

Carr concludes that Armor exaggerated estimations of the rate of white enrollment gain that would occur in the system after busing ended.

According to Carr's analysis, if one rejects Armor's anticipatory theory, Armor's predictions are radical overestimates. But even if one grants Armor his theory, the predictions are still significant overestimates. Specifically, Armor's minimum prediction for white return in grades K-5 between 1982 and 1987 is about 1,000 students over these *five* years.[33] Armor then goes on to point out that the white gain was 1,136 from 1982 to 1989, arguing that this number is within his prediction. However, 1982 to 1989 is a *seven*-year period, not the *five*-year period of 1982 to 1987, which the original predictions covered. Adjusting the original calculations for a seven-year period (1982-1989) increases the original prediction by 400 students. The actual number of 1,136, as Carr points out, falls below Armor's minimum projection of white return over seven years: 1,400.[34]

Demographic prediction is an imprecise science, involving projections of trends resting upon assumptions that can change and prove to be inaccurate. Under different circumstances it might be unfair to hold predictions to such rigorous standards. However, this type of demographic prediction should be rigorously examined because it has been used as the basis for taking away students' rights to a desegregated education.

Do Neighborhood Schools End White Flight?

In *Riddick,* the court reached a paradoxical conclusion. Essentially, the court sought to halt resegregation through white flight by ordering resegregation. Judge MacKenzie reasoned that if the district did not end busing, white flight would grow so extreme that the district eventually would be left without enough whites to integrate with in the future. So, he concluded, in order to have any kind of integration over the long term, busing, which created desegregated elementary schools, must end.[35]

But in practice, the end of mandatory desegregation in the elementary schools sharply increased racial segregation and failed to trigger a significant increase in white enrollment. The order produced a plan that created ten schools in which more than 90 percent of the students were black.[36] This returns these schools to racial compositions that existed before the district took any action to eradicate its previously segregated school system. Additionally, within three years, two other elementary schools, Norview and Poplar Halls were more than 70 percent black. Ingleside and Coleman Place Elementary Schools grew to 69 percent black.

Meanwhile, the neighborhood school plan has allowed the district to create and maintain disproportionately white elementary schools as well. In 1993, Bay View was 76 percent white; Ocean View was 67 percent; Taylor was 63 percent; Calcott was 60 percent; Tarralton was 57 percent; and Sherwood Forest was 59 percent.

Each of these schools was far above the district's overall white enrollment of 34.5 percent.

School Board member Lucy Wilson characterized the current situation: "The irony is that the school system is much more segregated now than it ever was under the busing plan. We now have eleven schools that are about 95 percent black so the practical reality is that we have returned to segregation."[37]

Resegregation has also caused severe concentrations of poverty in the segregated schools. This is significant because concentrated poverty is related strongly to low academic achievement and high dropout rates. In a majority of the segregated schools, more than 90 percent of students are poor.[38]

The end of busing clearly did not reverse or stem white flight or enrollment declines. In spite of the well-publicized initial gains in white enrollment after busing ended, the percentage of white students at the elementary level dropped five percentage points from the most recent high of 42 percent in 1989 to 37 percent in 1993.[39]

At the elementary school level, the overall white enrollment in numbers actually *increased* during the final four years of busing. It rose from 7,911 to 8,073, an increase of 2 percent. After neighborhood schools, however, white enrollment has actually *decreased* from 7,461[40] in the first year to 6,547 five years later, a decrease of 12.2 percent.[41]

Small declines were also apparent at the middle-school level where busing was retained. However, the proportion of white students increased slightly at the high school level, where busing continued.

In its decision, the court of appeals noted that the stabilization in white enrollment between 1980 and 1983 might have been caused by the changes in the number of people housed in areas set aside for U.S. Navy personnel. Even if Navy housing patterns did, in fact, contribute to the stabilization between 1980 and 1983, stabilization continued from 1983 to 1985. The district court did not use data from these years, and therefore never tried to explain or consider this continued stabilization in making its decision.[42]

White enrollment increased even in half of the predominantly black schools where white flight was assumed to be most common. These increases in white enrollment were apparent in six schools — Diggs, Roberts Park, St. Helena, Tidewater, Tucker, and Willard. Though white enrollment declined in six of the twelve high-minority schools, taken as a whole, black loss was larger than overall white loss, both in total numbers and in the percent of loss in the final three years of busing. This is significant, because busing had been blamed for white flight from the schools. Since blacks were also leaving, and at much higher rates, it is clear that reasons other than the schools' integration policies were affecting the trend of enrollment loss. During these years, about 4.4 percent of white enrollment was lost in the predominantly black schools and about 10.6 percent of the black enrollment in these schools was lost, suggesting that when there was flight, it was biracial.[43]

Is Busing Really to Blame?

The court also failed to consider reasons other than busing that might have influenced the decisions of middle-class residents to leave Norfolk and its public schools.

Particularly, the concentration of middle-class housing in the suburbs probably contributed to a loss of students from middle-income families, both black and white. Norfolk's relatively high crime rate may also have spurred middle-class families to choose other communities. Urban middle-class flight has occurred nationwide, even in cities that do not have mandatory busing. The court also ignored the long-term national trends of white migration to suburbs and black migration to cities.

Limited Housing Stock: A Barrier to an Integrated Norfolk

Norfolk has a disproportionate share of low-income housing. The city simply has fewer non-low-income single-family homes available than do neighboring communities such as Virginia Beach and Chesapeake. The growing number of middle- and upper middle-class families, no matter their race, settled in communities other than Norfolk. Because Norfolk provided low-income housing, families with low incomes, disproportionate numbers of whom are black, settled in the city. Statistics below also suggest that families who lived in Norfolk and who wanted to move into larger homes as their incomes rose may have left Norfolk for Chesapeake or Virginia Beach.

During the years of busing, Norfolk builders constructed far fewer middle-class homes than suburban builders in neighboring Chesapeake and Virginia Beach. During the 1970s, for example, Norfolk built an annual average of 226 single-family homes, Virginia Beach built 2,072, and Chesapeake built 847.[44] Thirteen of every fourteen new homes were built outside the city.

Norfolk city planning officials determine "fairshare distribution" in various price ranges by calculating the overall number of homes, and then determining what percentage share of homes each city or town had. For example, in 1990, suburban Virginia Beach had twice its fairshare distribution of homes worth more than $200,000 and only one-fourth its fairshare distribution of homes worth between

$60,000 and $80,000.[45] Virginia Beach had less than 25 percent of its fairshare distribution of housing worth less than $25,000.[46]

In contrast, Norfolk had just about 60 percent of its fairshare distribution of homes worth more than $200,000.[47] Perhaps most significant, the city had 140 percent of its fairshare distribution of homes worth less than $25,000.[48] The number of people in the metropolitan area grew, the poor were concentrated in the city, and the middle class were overwhelmingly concentrated in the suburbs.

These housing patterns resulted in Norfolk's attracting a disproportionate percentage of low-income residents. In 1990, the city had about 138 percent of its fairshare distribution of persons whose incomes were less than 50 percent of the median income. Chesapeake had only about 76 percent of its fairshare distribution of this group, and Virginia Beach had about 60 percent.[49]

Dean Paul T. Schollaert of Illinois State University also challenged the white-flight model in his testimony before the court. Schollaert's studies show not only that middle-class whites were leaving Norfolk, but that middle-class blacks were leaving as well. Schollaert showed that the *proportion* of middle-class blacks were actually leaving Norfolk at much higher rates than middle-class whites.[50] Since blacks would not be expected to leave a city because of an increase of blacks in their schools, one can see there are other factors at work besides racial integration that cause people to leave a city.

Other evidence in the Norfolk case suggests that middle-class flight is, and has been, a trend in all cities, not just those with mandatory busing. Several expert witnesses for the plaintiffs, Dr. Schollaert, Dr. Reynolds Farley, and Dr. Robert Crain, cited research showing that as cities age, the population of the inner city, and therefore the city school enrollment, typically decreases.[51] Demographer Reynolds Farley and sociologist Robert Crain both cited Chicago, Kansas City, and Baltimore as examples of cities that experienced large losses in white population without busing.[52] Later data show large white enrollment declines in cities that have neighborhood schools.[53]

Higher relative crime rates in cities such as Norfolk are another plausible explanation for people's decisons to leave the city or to settle elsewhere.

Although the population in 1970 in Norfolk was roughly twice that of Virginia Beach and three times that of Chesapeake, the crime index total for Norfolk in 1971 was more than three times greater than for Virginia Beach, and six times greater than for Chesapeake.[54] There was a much higher crime rate in Norfolk even when one accounts for differences in population. By 1980 the population in Norfolk and Virginia Beach were nearly equal, while the total crime index for Norfolk was one-third higher than Virginia Beach.[55]

Was It Busing or the Lack of Buses?

Assuming that busing did contribute to the decline in white enrollment in its early years, part of the problem may have been the lack of adequate buses in the program's first year. In busing's first year, the district faced severe transportation difficulties. Children were left stranded at bus stops. The city's bus company, Virginia Transit Service, responded to a federal price freeze on transportation by refusing to provide the extra services required by the busing plan. Although the district needed transportation services for 20,000 students, the bus company provided services for just 12,000, according to the deputy superintendent at the time.[56]

"We lost about 5,000 children through the first four or five weeks of 1971,"[57] former Deputy Superintendent John McLaulin recalled, referring to the problems associated with transportation.

During this first year, Norfolk lost its greatest percentage of white students, many of them "no shows." The lack of buses may have contributed to white flight.

McLaulin has said he believes that the transportation problems caused many parents who otherwise had not been concerned about busing, to enroll their children elsewhere. "Those who had said I am going to give it a try and see how it works, and then every day for two to three weeks had to go and pick up their kids, said, 'the hell with it; I am not going to mess with this.'"[58]

The court did not even consider the impact of the transportation problem.

School Satisfaction and Parents Reasons for Leaving Norfolk

Implicit in the court's conclusion that neighborhood schools would end white flight was the belief that parents would have a more positive attitude about a school system that had neighborhood schools.

In his 1982 report, David Armor had asked survey respondents to answer the following question, first assuming that busing would continue, and then, to answer it a second time assuming busing were stopped:[59]

> Suppose you had a friend or new co-worker moving into the Norfolk area for the first time and this family asked you about elementary schools for their children. Assuming their income level and feelings about education are about the same as yours, would you advise them to live in Norfolk and send their children to public school, live outside Norfolk and send their children to public school in another district or send their children to private or parochial school?[60]

Based on the responses to his survey, Armor predicted that 89 percent of white parents and 80 percent of black parents would recommend the public schools if busing were to end. Armor predicted an increase in parent satisfaction.

But a later survey conducted at the Institute for the Study of Minority Issues at Old Dominion University concludes just the opposite. The survey reports that the percentage of parents who did recommend the public schools to friends or coworkers when busing ended was lower than Armor had originally predicted in 1982.[61] To complete the survey, the researchers duplicated the above-quoted question that Armor asked of respondents.

The later Old Dominion survey, conducted in 1987 after busing actually did end, showed that white parental support was 17 percentage points lower and black support was 15 percentage points lower than Armor predicted.[62]

As part of the Old Dominion survey, researchers also interviewed parents who said they had considered private school for their kindergarten-age children, but who, in the end, chose public school. Only 9 percent of the parents stated that the end of busing was the "main" reason for their choosing public school. The most popular reason given was the "high cost of private schools" (36 percent), followed by the "quality of education" in the public schools (19 percent). The survey also shows that 91 percent of parents surveyed who transferred a child from public to private school in 1986 gave some reason other than busing.[63] This survey indicated that parents' perceptions, both positive and negative, were based on a variety of factors and in neither case was busing the central issue. Another prediction relied upon by the court proved severly flawed.

Evaluating the Compromise Plan

During the *Riddick* trial, Norfolk School Superintendent Gene Carter claimed that a new "school effectiveness" program would narrow the achievement gap between white and black students.[64] The program was to include a preschool and an alternative school that offered individualized instruction. Multicultural education was supposed to promote interaction between the races. The program also sought to increase student achievement by involving more parents through conferences and new parent information centers.[65]

Despite the fact that target schools receive more money per student, have more library books, smaller classes, and better educated teachers,[66] test scores for students in the target schools have remained low. The academic achievement gap between the races and between students who attend target schools and nontarget schools has increased after 1990. Scores in target schools, meanwhile, have decreased. Black students in the better-integrated schools score higher on standardized tests, on average, than black students in the resegregated target schools. The data used to examine school district promises is not ideal for purposes of evaluation, and, for that reason, this chapter should not be viewed as a comprehensive statistical analysis of school district performance. It is important to remember, however, that this data is at least as good as that used by courts and by policymakers when they reach conclusions about neighborhood schools or desegregation policies.

Thus, the purpose of this section is not to prove that education was superior before neighborhood schools or that busing had any effect on educational quality. (Such analyses would require data that is simply not available from the Norfolk schools.) Rather, this section tests the promise that achievement and educational quality would improve for black students in the target schools.

Declines on the SRA Measure

Findings in a 1993 study by Vivian W. Ikpa of the University of Central Florida suggest that, on at least one measure, achievement test scores for black fourth graders declined after the elimination of busing for integration.[67] Ikpa compared scores on the Science Research Associates Assessment Survey Series (SRA) of black and white students in 1985—when there was busing—to scores the year after busing ended. The study controlled for school racial composition, teacher and student expenditures, instructional materials, substitute and teacher salaries, the age of school buildings, teacher education levels and library size.[68]

The mean SRA score for black children declined from 52 to 47 in the first year of resegregation.[69] The achievement gap between black and white students increased after the elimination of busing from 15.9 in the busing year to 18.3 in the first year of resegregation.[70] Ikpa's findings show that "school level" characteristics, such as racial composition and the other variables, account for only about 8 percent of the variation in test scores.[71]

Ikpa concludes that "given these findings, policymakers should reevaluate the costs and benefits of maintaining segregated schools. Segregated educational settings may serve to retard the development of children."[72]

The Iowa Test of Basic Skills: Declining Scores, Widening Gaps

Data from other tests confirm findings that achievement remains low in target schools. The most recent data, from the 1993-94 school year, indicate that percentile ranks for third graders on the Iowa Test of Basic Skills declined in eight of the ten segregated target schools since 1989. Percentile ranks for fourth graders declined in six of the ten target schools. Bowling Park school, however, did substantially better than the other target schools, and the district often points to this one school as a symbol of success of the entire resegregation plan.[73]

Students in target schools failed to reach the national average for both grades in every school with the exception of Bowling Park fourth graders. Students in the more integrated nontarget schools consistently scored above this national average.[74]

Most significantly, the gap between achievement in the target schools and in the nontarget schools has increased over the years.

Among all the schools, seven had decreases, one remained the same, and two had increases in scores. None had reached the 50th percentile average.

At the fourth-grade level, four schools had increases in scores and six had declines. Only one school, Bowling Park, met the national average.

Students in target schools score consistently low compared with their counterparts nationally and compared with students in non-target schools in Norfolk. Of course, aggregate scores of students in predominately low-income schools are usually relatively low for a variety of complex reasons, including family- and neighborhood-related issues.

But these data demonstrate that students in target schools have much lower levels of academic competition and opportunity. More significantly, the in-school strategy that pledged to improve achievement for black students in target schools did not even bring them close to the average achievement levels of students in nontarget schools.

Although the average fourth-grade achievement of blacks and whites taken together decreased for a while after busing ended, overall, black students' scores on the Iowa Tests increased by more than twenty points during busing, while white students' scores increased by nearly twenty points.[75] Armor attributed the increase in achievement to the Competency Challenge program that was designed to increase test scores. But this explanation is inadequate because scores of both blacks and whites began improving before the start of that program.[76]

Differences Between Black Students in Target Schools and Black Students in Nontarget Schools

Norfolk school officials in 1994 argued that there are no differences in achievement between black students in the segregated target schools and black students in the more integrated schools.[77] However, according to scores on the Iowa Test of Basic Skills, this is not true. In fact, the performance gaps between the black students in the segregated target schools and those in the better-integrated non-target schools have become wider over time. Gaps in third grade increased from four points in 1990 to ten points in 1993. By grade four, the gaps increased from one point in 1989 to twelve points in 1993. In addition, scores for blacks in integrated schools, while still below the national norm, have remained relatively stable while scores for blacks in segregated schools have worsened.

Literacy Tests: High Rates of Failure in Segregated Schools

Results on basic literacy tests reveal a sizable gap between the percentage of students passing in the segregated target schools and that of students in the nontarget schools. In all subject areas in every grade, students in target schools, on average, did far worse than their counterparts in nontarget schools on those state-required tests.

Under the Virginia Literacy Testing Program, the state requires that before students earn eventual promotion to the ninth grade, they pass basic exams in writing, reading, and math. Students take the test in sixth grade. The program also administers tests to students in the fourth and fifth grades to determine which students may be in danger of failing the required sixth-grade test.

On the fourth-grade literacy predictor test in the segregated schools just 34 percent passed reading and 63 percent passed writing. But in the other schools, 66 percent passed reading and 81 percent passed writing.[78] The gaps persist but diminish slightly, under the fifth-grade pretest, with 60 percent of target school students passing the math portion of the test compared to 79 percent of students in regular schools. On the reading portion, 60 percent of target school students passed, compared with 73 percent of non-target school students. On the actual sixth-grade test, the gaps between target and nontarget students are still apparent. Specifically, in reading, 49 percent of students in segregated target schools passed, compared with 76 percent of students in non-target schools. In writing and math, the passing rates in segregated target schools were 57 and 61 percent, respectively. Comparably, in non-target schools, the passing rates for writing and math were 70 and 82 percent.

Majority-to-Minority Transfer Program

As part of the plan to end busing, the school board continued its optional transfer program that allowed black students from schools where their race constituted at least 70 percent of the school population to transfer to schools where their race was in the minority.

The school system did not recruit the district's 900 white students in the three schools with white populations of over 70 percent in 1986 because school officials assumed white students would not take advantage of the plan.[79]

Thus, the transfer program places the burden of integration solely on black children. Despite this obvious imbalance, the court approved the majority-to-minority (M/M) transfer plan as a viable method of voluntary integration. This model is precisely the type of freedom of choice plan that proved unsuccessful and was a basis for the Supreme Court decisions requiring the use of mandatory transportation to achieve racial integration in schools. Freedom of choice plans, historically, have had low rates of participation in the South— often with only one or two percent of either race participating.[80]

In Norfolk, the program has done little to further integration because so few students participate in it. The number of students participating is significantly below the optimistic projections that may have influenced the court's decision to accept the plan. The court cited Dr. Armor's predictions that 10 to 15 percent of eligible students would transfer in the first year and 30 to 40 percent would transfer in the second year.[81] Dr. Armor based his predictions on his 1982 survey in which he interviewed 850 parents with school-age children in Norfolk.[82] However, Armor failed to consider the experience of other transfer programs in the country, which, in general, have had much lower participation rates than he predicted.

Although both the court and Dr. Armor accurately predicted the participation rate for the program's first year, they greatly overestimated the number of students who would transfer after five years. Specifically, in 1986-87, of 5,011 eligible black children, 711, or 14 percent, used the option. The number of students transferring rose by only 2 percent after five years. In 1990-91, of 4,338 eligible black students, 698, or 16 percent, used the option.[83] About 10 percent of eligible students used the transfer program in the 1992-93 school year, according to one report.[84]

Parental Involvement

The court expressed the hope that an end to busing would trigger an increase of parental involvement in the schools. The court had concluded that parental involvement was "essential to the health and well-being" of a school system.[85] The evidence, the court asserted, "was absolutely clear"[86] on this point. The court's conclusions about the decline in parental involvement caused by busing appear spurious.

The court noted that PTA membership had declined from about

15,000 to 3,500 "as a result of cross-town busing."[87] The only basis for this conclusion was testimony from a handful of parents and then Superintendent Albert Ayars. At the trial, parents said it was harder to get involved in their children's schools because of the distance between home and school. Ayars said that based on his experience, he believed more parents would get involved if busing were to end.

Other knowledgeable people's opinions differed, however. According to Dr. Lucy Wilson, one of two black school board members in 1981 and school board chairwoman in 1993, "Parental involvement was a smoke screen. Sure, there were parents who did not attend schools because of the distance, but they were probably few."[88] Former school board member Dr. John Foster, who is black, emphasized the importance of parental involvement, and his opinion was quoted in the court decision as justification to end busing. But Dr. Foster was actually opposed to ending busing. "Busing was a secondary issue for me," Foster said in a recent interview. "I'm concerned about parents getting involved, but I don't think busing had much effect on it."[89]

As it turns out, parental involvement, as measured by PTA membership, declined in the first six years of neighborhood schools in most of the predominantly black target schools. Although general volunteer hours did increase, this is not an indication of parental involvement. Volunteer hours include nonparent community volunteers and do not measure simply the number of parents involved in the school but the overall hours contributed. In other words, it would be possible for one or two people—even nonparents—to be contributing large amounts of time, causing the number of volunteer hours to rise, while the rest of the parents remain isolated and uninvolved.

Although PTA membership did increase in most of the nontarget schools, PTA membership decreased in six of the ten target schools. Overall, PTA membership in the target schools declined from 1,944 members in 1985 to 1,374 members in 1992-93, a decline of about one-third. Specifically, Bowling Park lost 138 members, Jacox lost 166, Monroe lost 72, Roberts Park lost 75, St. Helena lost 110, and Tidewater lost 237.[90] This decrease was not an artifact of decreased enrollment at the target schools. In fact, enrollment in these schools increased by more than 100 students from 1985 to 1992.

In press reports and interviews, school officials have consistently dismissed this phenomenon, saying that these numbers are misleading.[91]

Their argument is that poor parents were always the ones least likely to get involved in schools and that the end of busing has simply concentrated those poor parents in certain schools, leading to an overall drop in involvement. Their explanation unfortunately contradicts their earlier contention in court that resegregation would increase parental involvement. The end to busing must have had a negative effect on the all-black target schools because, as school officials admit, it led to a decline in parental involvement. It is obvious that a policy that simply seeks to put a school closer to students' homes is not a cure for low-parental participation. Reasons for low rates of parental involvement are varied and complex; reversing the negative trend would require systemic policies and programming that take more than only school location into account. In this case, the diagnosis appears to have been wrong, and the resulting prescription ineffective.

Indeed, research on parental involvement does not lead logically to the conclusion that increasing parent participation requires an end to integrated schools. Two consistently successful methods, in fact, could be implemented easily by a district that has busing. The first strategy, identified by researchers at Johns Hopkins University, centered around reading packets that students worked on at home with their parents.[92] Second, schools that distributed parent newsletters also saw an increase in parent involvement, the Johns Hopkins researchers found.[93]

There was even evidence within the Norfolk school system of a successful strategy that increased parental involvement during the busing years. The principal of Bowling Park Elementary School, Herman D. Clark, was successful at involving parents through telephoning and visiting them at home to convince them that they are crucial to their children's education.[94] Frank Hassell, who counsels, advises, and visits with children and parents who live in the public housing projects and attend the target schools, also believes that low-parental involvement has less to do with distance to the school and more to do with the feeling of intimidation experienced by low-income black parents at schools. "School can be a very cold and intimidating place for poor parents. The parents assume that they are looked down upon, and they don't feel welcome. They don't think that they have anything to offer to their children's education. The distance of the school does not matter much when the parents feel this way."[95]

Findings from a national survey on parent involvement might help explain the trend in Norfolk. A 1987 survey of U.S. schools, the School and Staffing Survey of the National Center for Education Statistics, reported that predominantly minority schools and schools with heavy concentrations of minority teachers had far lower numbers of parents volunteering in the schools. This may well reflect the fact that such schools have far higher concentrations of parents with less education and lower incomes. Among schools with more than three-fourths minority students, only 8.7 percent of the schools reported twenty or more parent volunteers. The highest number of volunteers per school came not in all-white schools, but in schools that were between 5 percent and 50 percent nonwhite. According to the survey, almost a fourth (23.2 percent) of the schools that were between 5 percent and 20 percent minority had twenty or more volunteers and a fifth of the schools where 20 percent to 50 percent of the students were minorities, reported at least twenty or more volunteers.

In an analysis of these trends, researcher Michael Bernard offers an explanation that may very well apply to Norfolk: "There are a number of possible explanations.... Schools with high proportions of minority enrollment generally are located in areas whose residents have relatively low incomes. As a result, parents may be less likely to have either the time or the energy to engage in volunteer activity; there may be fewer intact families and fewer parents overall to participate."[96]

Thus, one of the court's primary justifications for ending busing —that it would enable parents to play an active role in their children's education—seems to have been misguided. This is particularly dismaying in light of research that shows that other methods of improving parent involvement had the potential of being successful.

Housing and Recycled Segregation

A more thorough consideration of the connection between segregated housing and schooling in Norfolk suggests the presence of the intentional segregation that is illegal under *Brown v. Board of Education*.[97]

As the city of Norfolk began clearing slums in the 1950s through the 1970s, it also created racially segregated housing projects, concentrated in the southern section of the city for the 9,416 black households that had been displaced.[98] Many of these projects were, by law, built purposely as racially segregated projects.[99] The school

system was deeply involved in this housing policy; its officials participated in discussions about the locations of housing projects and the
schools to serve them and knowingly built their schools to service
those officially segregated housing projects.[100]

The pattern of these segregated school assignments is identical to
that made possible and sustained by legal, intentional segregation
and "state action" in public housing and was sustained by public
housing site laws and regulations. It is reasonable to hold government
officials responsible for the continuing effects of segregated housing,
because today these neighborhoods and housing projects are still
occupied primarily by members of only one race. However, no one
has been held accountable for the housing segregation. Forty percent
of the students attending target schools live in these housing projects,
illustrating that the vestiges of the original state action.[101] In a
number of other school desegregation cases, housing segregation
was viewed as a contributing cause and patterns like these were
ruled unconstitutional.

In five of the ten target schools, more than half the students live
in segregated public housing. Public action determined that these
children would live in this housing and attend segregated elementary schools.[102]

Despite this clear connection between housing and school segregation, *Riddick* ruled that it "defied logic" to suggest that the school
board is responsible for the fact that "racially identifiable schools are
located in close proximity to those projects."[103]

Norfolk's Response

School officials continue to defend their return to neighborhood
schools on several grounds. In a written response[104] to a draft of this
chapter, officials stressed that after the return to neighborhood
schools, the portion of white elementary school enrollment increased.
As has been said, that is true. In the first few years after then end of
busing, white enrollment did increase. However, as of 1993, there has
been an overall decline (of 12.2 percent) in white enrollment at the
elementary level since the end of busing. School officials, however,
argue that this overall decline, manifest in the school district's enrollment figures from 1993, was caused by the Gulf War, which sent high
numbers of residents of this Navy town to war. It is important to

remember, however, that the Gulf War was relatively short-lived, lasting about three months. Further, it is most probable that one parent remained in Norfolk and continued to enroll their children in the local schools.

The end of the Gulf War did not result in any significant increase the following year; in fact, white enrollment, according to the school district's own response, declined in 1993-94 by .64 percent. Enrollment declines may very well be related to factors outside the school such as economics, housing preferences, and job relocations. If this is true, it was inappropriate for the court to blame the previous substantial white enrollment declines on busing, especially during the Vietnam war.

School officials claim that since the end of busing at the elementary school level, there has been a decrease in racial isolation. But this is simply untrue. Of course there are much higher levels of racial isolation since the return to neighborhood elementary schools. In 1985, before the end of busing, just 11 percent of Norfolk black children were in schools that were more than 75 percent black; in the 1993-94 school year, 41 percent of all black students were in such schools.[105] Officials go on to claim that the return to neighborhood schools prevented the district from "tipping" toward an all-black system. But this analysis falls apart because, again, the white enrollment began and continued to stablize during the final years of busing.

School officials also claim that test scores have remained more or less stable in Norfolk, even as higher numbers of economically disadvantaged students enroll in the district. While our reading of the data suggests otherwise—that there have been variations in test scores—we are not trying to establish stabilization. The school district did not promise stabilization; it promised that black students' achievement levels would improve and that the achievement gap would be narrowed. Clearly, this has not happened in Norfolk, based on the data supplied to us by city school administrators.

In an effort to prove that achievement levels are acceptable in Norfolk, officials there also point to an analysis conducted by the Virginia's state Department of Education in December 1993. This analysis, suggests that, in taking the percentage of economically disadvantaged students into account, the Norfolk schools, overall, were scoring better than one would predict based upon a regression analysis model.[106] However, this does not mean that Norfolk's *black* students are performing better than would be predicted, or that *black students in segregated schools* were scoring well or better than would be expected. This is because the regression analysis model considers the average performance of all students in the district. Therefore, there is no way to tell whether higher than average scores or passing rates among white students, higher than average black scores or a combination of both produced a performance in Norfolk that was better than might have been predicted. This model offers no information about relative scores by race and is therefore not useful for answering the question of whether the neighborhood school plan resulted in—or is even correlated with—improved achievement for black students in those schools.

The Verdict on the Norfolk Decision

The assumptions and predictions made by the court in *Riddick*, which sanctioned resegregation in the elementary schools in Norfolk, Virginia, have proved inaccurate. Today, Norfolk's black elementary school students are intensely segregated and there has been no substantial return of white students to the district. Although the court assumed that busing caused white flight, an abundance of evidence suggests that both black and white residents probably left the city for reasons other than just the desegregation plan. The court assumed that the school system would have become resegregated had busing continued. But actually, the population had begun to stabilize five years prior to the end of busing.

The evidence shows that the prediction that continued busing would have led to complete resegregation was unfounded. Projections about white flight and white return, upon which the court relied, have proved inaccurate. The actual segregation that exists today, and which was caused by a return to segregated neighborhood schools, is much more severe than that which could have possibly occurred if elementary-level desegregation and the stable population trends of the final years of desegregation continued.

The school board's programs to improve the segregated schools and promote voluntary desegregation options have also been a disappointment. The court assumed that about 40 percent of eligible black students would use the majority-to-minority transfer program after five years, but only 16 percent actually used it in 1990 and only 10 percent in 1992.

Although the court asserted that the elimination of busing would increase parental involvement, the end of racial integration actually brought an overall decline in PTA membership in the segregated schools. This trend suggests that the policy of putting schools closer to students' neighborhoods is not in itself a cure for low-parental participation in schools.

Finally, while the court justified its decision to allow resegregation by suggesting that the school board was implementing programs to improve student achievement in target schools, the programs did not improve achievement for black students. Test scores for these black students remain extremely low; the achievement gap between target and nontarget schools is wide and, based on some measures, is growing wider.

In addition, the new school assignments reflect patterns of segregated housing — a fact that should have been scrutinized by the court. Many of the children attend segregated schools because of official policies of housing agencies in an earlier time that promoted housing segregation.

The lessons from Norfolk suggest that dismantling desegregation carries false promises. In Norfolk, undoing integration did not bring white people back to urban areas, did not increase parental involvement among the poor, and did not provide evidence of an equal educational opportunity or increased achievement for black students.

In Norfolk, the only clear results of the city's abandonment of school desegregation and its subsequent return to neighborhood elementary schools have been severer racial isolation and an increase in concentrated poverty, both of which have consistently been associated with poor school performance and inequality.[107] Meanwhile, two generations after *Brown v. Board of Education* declared intentionally separate schools "inherently unequal," the students relegated to Norfolk's nearly all-black schools have lost their right to a racially integrated school system.

CHAPTER SIX

Still Separate | Still Unequal

The Limits of *Milliken II*'s Monetary Compensation to Segregated Schools

Susan E. Eaton Joseph Feldman, and Edward Kirby

Not long after the Supreme Court, in *Brown v. Board of Education*,[1] outlawed segregated schools, the job of racially integrating those schools proved not only politically unpopular but difficult in a practical sense as well. As the post-World War II trend of white suburbanization persisted in the 1960s and 1970s, many urban school districts were enrolling growing proportions of minority students. For the school districts whose pool of white students was small and shrinking, racial integration was becoming all but impossible to achieve.

In 1973, this trend of white flight led a federal court in Detroit, Michigan, to approve a controversial remedy for the intentional segregation proven in the lawsuit, *Bradley v. Milliken*.[2] It concluded that unless school officials included white schoolchildren from the neighboring suburban districts in Detroit's desegregation plan, racial integration simply could not be achieved. After all, the city schools were already about 71.5 percent black. Concluding that "metropolitan" busing was the only logical option, the court ordered a city-suburban school desegregation remedy.[3]

However, a year later, in 1974, the Supreme Court in *Milliken I*[4] overturned the federal court's rulings to reject the metropolitan remedy by a 5-4 vote. The Court's opinion stated that the scope of a desegregation remedy must be determined by the scope of the Constitutional violation. In other words, the Court said, Detroit's suburbs should not be forced to participate in a remedy unless the communities could be found guilty, themselves, of intentional segregation, or unless it could be shown that state action created the pattern of all-white suburbs and a predominantly black Detroit. The court did not consider the degree to which illegal housing action contributed to the region's intense residential segregation reflected in the schools.

The Court cited what it called the "local control" of public schools, claiming that such an important tradition should not be violated for the purposes of racial integration. In coming years, *Milliken I* would make it all but impossible to achieve racial integration within predominantly minority school districts.

The *Milliken* ruling forced the Detroit case back to the lower federal district court, which still had to find a way to remedy the intentional segregation in Detroit. Since it was clear that racial integration would be nearly impossible to achieve within the city over the long run, the court considered alternative remedies proposed by the school board.

If the Supreme Court would not guarantee the long-term integration that a metropolitan remedy would have ensured, the school board and the district court reasoned, then the courts should at least guarantee that minority children in the inner city receive a quality education to remedy the educational deficits traceable to segregation. After all, in most urban districts, not only were minority students victims of racial separation, but their academic achievement levels were also far lower than those of their white counterparts. In the second phase of *Milliken v. Bradley (Milliken II,* 1977),[5] the Supreme Court followed this line of reasoning in allowing for the provision of additional monies to "restore the victims of discrimination to the position they would have occupied in the absence of such conduct."[6]

Milliken II said:

> Children who have been thus educationally set apart from the larger community will inevitably acquire habits of speech, conduct, and attitudes reflecting their cultural isolation. They are likely to acquire speech habits, for example, which vary from the environment in which they must ultimately function and compete, if they are to enter and to be a part of that community...Pupil assignment alone does not automatically remedy the impact of previous, unlawful educational isolation; the consequences linger and can be dealt with only by independent measures.[7]

The decision meant that special compensatory education programs could now be included in desegregation remedies. Now school authorities could allocate additional educational resources to remedy the educational deficits of isolated minorities when that isolation could be traced to enforced segregation and discrimination. Perhaps the most far-reaching aspect of *Milliken II* was its declaration that states found guilty of prior discrimination must pay for remedial educational programs.

Since 1977, school districts across the nation have used *Milliken II* provisions to install state-sponsored compensatory educational programs for minority students in racially isolated schools. A critical examination of *Milliken II* programs is necessary because the programs have played an increasingly prominent role in desegregation remedies since 1977. This is partly because the demographic patterns evident in Detroit in 1974 have become more pronounced. School districts in the nation's central cities and some older suburbs enroll large proportions of minority students, while surrounding suburbs remain predominantly white. As patterns of isolation persist, racial integration of the type envisioned in *Brown* has become increasingly difficult to achieve. This pattern has forced school officials and courts to rely on *Milliken II* programs to supplant rather than supplement true racial integration.

This chapter examines four school districts to determine how and why *Milliken II* and similar programs were put in place and how they were designed, funded, evaluated, and treated by the federal courts. This is not a comprehensive statistical data analysis but a compilation of four case studies that together illuminate repeated patterns, problems, and weaknesses at the policy implementation level. Indeed, the data required to conduct a sophisticated statistical analysis was simply not available from local school districts. In most cases, the data presented here are at least equal to what courts, school leaders, and others used in their own discussions and judgments about the programs and policies studied here.

Nor is this chapter an evaluation of classroom-level activity nor a judgment about the general quality or competency of the school districts or administrators studied here.

The fundamental limitation illustrated by these case studies is that the compensation programs have evolved not as permanent changes in opportunity structure, but as temporary, supplemental add-ons that are not linked to any systemic effort to redress harms of segregation. It appears that the primary function of the remedies is *not* "to restore victims of discriminatory conduct to the position they would have occupied in the absence of such conduct,"[8] but, rather, to serve a way for school districts and states to sustain a temporary and superficial punishment for discrimination. We find many illustrations of this underlying philosophy.

Neither school officials nor the courts are attempting to define or interpret the Supreme Court mandate in order to apply it to their particular district. As a result, the compensation is often implemented without corresponding plans for overcoming effects of segregation; it is being used like extra money for things the district wanted to do anyway.

Districts do not seriously evaluate the supplemental educational programs and thus have no way to tell whether the programs are actually benefiting children. District policymakers do follow directives that specify how long programs should last, how much can be spent, and in which schools the programs must be placed. Rarely, however, is there an identifiable meaningful outcome at the end of this experimental strategy for equality or even a real effort to establish a standard for evaluation.

A fundamental weakness of this strategy is that the extra funding to segregated schools is not guaranteed to last. The programs suffer from impermanence because they often depend upon tenuous political support and politicized local or state budget processes. Thus, the programs can easily be removed by courts or school districts even when there is no proof that the programs have done what they were supposed to—improve conditions for minority students. That the programs' survival depends upon a thin web of political support and budgetary possibilities is particularly troubling because these schools serve communities that are traditionally weak players in local politics.

For all of these reasons, the programs are simply an inadequate means to fulfilling *Brown's* mandate. *Milliken II* and *Milliken II*-type programs have not evolved as systemic changes to the unequal opportunity structure *Brown* sought to eradicate, but as transitory extras of questionable utility.

Some of these problems may be traced at least partially to the nature of the *Milliken II* ruling. The *Milliken II* standard "to restore victims of discriminatory conduct to the position they would have occupied in the absence of such conduct" is vague compared with past Supreme Court rulings that set clearer standards for racial desegregation.

For example, in *Green v. County School Board of New Kent County*,[9] the Court established standards—or indicators—for measuring a school system's success in creating a desegregated school system.[10] But the Court never established indicators by which to judge the effectiveness of compensatory education programs allowed by *Milliken II*. Ironically, with courts taking their customary "hands-off" approach, the parties found guilty of discrimination—the school district and the state— were allowed to judge the effectiveness of their own remedies.

These problems are compounded drastically by the Supreme Court's 1995 ruling in *Missouri v. Jenkins*.[11] In *Jenkins*, the Court considered a lower court order in Kansas City, Missouri, that had required test scores to improve before the district and state could be freed from court oversight. In a 5-4 decision written by Justice William Rehnquist, the Court said the lower court ruling was inappropriate because the court had failed to specify exactly how past discrimination and segregation had resulted in low test scores. Post-*Jenkins*, lower courts will need to specify exactly what educational deficits are traceable to segregation and discrimination and what results will be required as proof that the deficits are remedied. If the specification is absent, *Jenkins* gives courts license to return school districts to local control, thereby releasing the state and the district from paying for the remedial programs.

Jenkins also takes *Milliken I* a step further. While *Milliken* hindered *mandatory* metropolitan desegregation efforts, *Jenkins* struck down Kansas City's *voluntary* metropolitan school desegregation plan under which school officials had improved urban schools in an effort to attract suburban transfers.

As a nation, we need to reexamine historic decisions, such as *Milliken I*, against metropolitan desegregation. Despite the legal limitations, the evidence presented here suggests that the goal of racial integration should not be abandoned in favor of the seeming attractiveness of educational compensation remedies. Metropolitan desegregation remedies provide a more permanent structural change in the promotion of equity by allowing students the opportunity to attend schools that are neither racially separate nor overwhelmed by poverty. However, the legal obstacles to obtaining such plans are formidable, especially since the *Jenkins* ruling against even voluntary incentives.

Of course, mere numerical integration made possible by metropolitan desegregation should never be an end in and of itself. But we might do best to *combine* structural changes such as integration *with* educational compensation plans that are well designed and rigorously evaluated.

There is no reason to set up a false dichotomy between desegregation and educational compensation, as racial integration and high-quality schooling are not incompatible opposites. They might best be seen as supportive characteristics in equitable institutions. In fact, it was never the explicit intention of the Supreme Court that

Milliken II remedies be used *instead of* integration, but the original plan provides *Milliken* relief as part of a plan for integration.

Curiously, our findings have led some readers to interpret our draft reports of our research as a conservative call for ending extra funding to urban districts. But the message of this chapter is very different. We argue that monetary remedies, alone, are not nearly far-reaching *enough* nor sufficiently focused to remedy the lingering effects of segregation. Not only should educators be using the remedies in more productive ways, but because of inherent limitations, the supplemental funds should be spent in conjunction with permanent structural changes, such as integrated schools. We do expect that educational remedies, when used well, usually as part of a more systemic strategy for equity, surely will improve students' opportunities for learning. Where racial integration is impossible to achieve, policymakers should use the recommendations offered here at least to ensure that educational compensation remedies are as accountable and effective as possible. Although originally perceived as a much less intrusive remedy, such remedies to be successful would require reaching much more deeply into the operation of school districts. The districts studied here are Detroit, Michigan; Little Rock, Arkansas; Prince George's County, Maryland; and Austin, Texas.

Detroit, Michigan
History and Background

The landmark *Milliken* case and *Milliken II* arose in Detroit, the first city in which *Milliken II* remedies were implemented.[12]

U.S. District Court Judge Robert DeMascio, hindered by the *Milliken I* decision, was unable to achieve substantial integration. As the core of his plan, he ordered nine "educational components" taken from the defendant school board's proposed plan.[13] Under DeMascio's order, these components would be placed in all schools, regardless of their racial composition. Although most school districts have come to interpret *Milliken II*[14] as a prescription for state-supported programs solely for racially identifiable minority schools, this was never the explicit intent of DeMascio's Detroit program. DeMascio was clear that the educational components were for all schools, whether they were segregated or integrated. DeMascio also ordered a small-scale intradistrict plan for student integration.

The components included a remedial reading program, a counseling and career guidance program, more testing and monitoring of student achievement, a plan to improve relations between the races in the schools and community, a new student conduct code, vocational education, extracurricular activities, and bilingual/bicultural and multicultural studies. DeMascio ordered the state to pay half the annual cost of four of the nine components.[15] The school board would pay the balance, through its publicly funded budget and federal grants. DeMascio also appointed a citizens' monitoring commission, directed by a small professional staff, to oversee the programs and to make reports to the court, the parties in the case, and the public. The court ordered that the state Superintendent of Public Instruction seek out state educational experts to "collect and analyze all data...submitted and to provide sufficient staff to supervise the work of the monitoring committee."[16]

In 1977, under *Milliken II*, the Supreme Court upheld the lower court's remedy, thereby validating the concept of educational compensation as an acceptable component of a desegregation remedy.

By 1981, however, six years after the components were ordered, and with no evidence that the remedies had met the required mandate to correct the educational deficits of minority students, the court directed defendants and plaintiffs to negotiate an agreement that would end the remedy by 1989. After twelve years the court relinquished control over the city schools. This meant that school officials were free to terminate the special educational programs and were now under no obligation—financial or otherwise—to provide any compensation to the black students. Some programs were removed immediately; others dwindled in size or became part of the school system's regular offerings. But the most significant point is that there is no guarantee that any *Milliken II* programs will remain in the schools. The school board is under no legal obligation to keep any programs in place.

The experience in Detroit illustrates the tenuous political process that can hinder effective implementation and monitoring of educational components. In the broader sense, the question of how programs affect students was not the primary concern of policymakers, defendants, and court officials. Rather, the primary questions were what programs to fund and how long to pay for them. This relative inattention to student performance probably came from viewing educational compensation as an obligation to provide temporary relief rather than as a systemic, comprehensive plan that might have some hope of "restor[ing] the victims of discriminatory conduct to the position they would have occupied in the absence of such conduct."

Implementation

The Detroit plan was set up in the public schools by Detroit educators and subcontracted professionals such as local university officials and educational consultants. Presumably, the court approved the educational components as programs likely to eradicate the past effects of segregation. However, the court failed to articulate any clear standard, goal, or measure by which to judge the educational success or failure of the components.

The assistant superintendent at the time, Stuart Rankin, said the plan consisted of educational programs policymakers were interested in implementing anyway, with or without desegregation. Those who selected the programs probably thought that they looked to be the most promising.

In this sense, Rankin said, the remedy was not viewed primarily as an attempt to reach a legal mandate but as a way to get funding for programs that the district otherwise would not have had the money for. Rankin said, "With the education components we took the opportunity to [fund and] do the things that we wanted to do in the school system...and we didn't expect the components would be sufficient to overcome the urban pathos in Detroit."[17]

A few years after implementation began, several events hindered the evaluation and monitoring of the educational components. First, the stipulation agreement drawn up prior to court withdrawal required only that the programs be funded for an arbitrary number of years negotiated by parties; it did not require a showing of educational results. Earlier, an adversarial relationship had developed between the court-appointed monitoring commission and the school board, which effectively prevented assessment and resulted in the monitoring commission being disbanded.

In response to a March 1979 monitoring commission report that cited deficient implementation of educational components, Judge DeMascio found that "the Detroit Board has knowingly failed to implement the remedial programs ordered by the court in 1975. The evidence presented at the July 23, 1979 hearing on the Monitoring Commission Report fully supports our conclusion."[18]

Eleven months later, in August 1980, the chief judge for the

Eastern District of Michigan replaced DeMascio with a three-judge panel for reasons unrelated to the educational components in Detroit.[19] This panel, following a dispute between plaintiffs and defenders over the amount of funding for the educational components for the 1980-81 school year, immediately encouraged the two parties to reach a settlement to end educational components.

In a speech at the University of Michigan in 1989, Judge Avern Cohn, the junior member of this panel that supervised the case alone in its last three years, said the panel had lacked "long-range" views about the Detroit remedy:

> I'm not sure any of the judges had a particular goal in mind," Cohn told the audience. "...other than to see that the Constitution's commands were observed and then to shape a proper remedy and see that the remedy was implemented or complied with. I doubt any of us were very philosophical or had any long-range views...Judges are frequently the last to know about the total environment in which a case exists. We only have, by and large, what the lawyers give us and generally in any particular case in court there is a much larger world surrounding it that we don't know very much about.[20]

Judge Cohn explained the court's reasoning for seeking an end to the case, stressing that after the implementation of the remedy, the court was not an appropriate body to manage the educational affairs of the school district: "The court's thinking was that courts can not perpetually keep it [school district] under its authority and it seemed to the court that it had to look to a point in time when the school district walked on its own...being free of judicial supervision."[21]

Parties in the case followed the court's directive and negotiated a settlement ending educational components by July 1988. The settlement agreement also established a payment schedule for the defendants, the State of Michigan, and the Detroit Board of Education.

Judge Cohn characterized the agreement as one that "seemed like a fair bargain...the state would fund these components for a period of time and then the school district would be on its own...the court could not hold the state perpetually liable...sooner or later one expiates his or her own guilt."[22]

The Stipulation Agreement itself, said Arthur Jefferson, the city school superintendent at the time, resulted from political negotiation not from a calculated strategy to meet the Supreme Court mandate. He characterized the settlement primarily as a way to retain state funding for as long as possible:

The Detroit Board position was that we wanted the state to pay for [*Milliken II* programs] as long as possible...It was really a political decision more than an educational decision. We wanted [to continue the funding] longer [than the state did] and we settled for 7-8 years beyond 1981...The State's position was that they wanted to cut their losses as quickly as possible.[23]

One of the major obstacles to implementation and evaluation of the education components in Detroit was the contentious relationship between the court-appointed monitoring commission and the elected school board, which soon degenerated into a bitter public contest of wills. Soon after implementation, the monitoring commission began issuing reports critical of the board's performance. The board, in turn, simply denied the conclusions. After the three-judge panel began overseeing the case, the report-counterreport pattern continued, squashing all hope for a constructive working relationship.

Such unproductive and highly publicized exchanges contributed to the dissolution of the monitoring commission by the three-judge panel. Originally, the court required that it operate until 1988,[24] but in 1984, the court found that the tension between the school board and the monitoring commission was counterproductive:

We are of the opinion that our oversight responsibilities under the remedial orders and the manner in which courts usually operate to enforce such orders might distort the political processes which govern elected boards of education in Michigan.... The environment we mentioned earlier is an inevitable result of the creation of the Monitoring Commission as an arm of the court to report on the implementation of the educational components.... Certainly there could have been no expectation that the Detroit Board would always agree with the Monitoring Commission. The Detroit Board is elected by the voters of Detroit. Its responsibilities are defined by law. Under the laws of Michigan, the State Board of Education and State Superintendent have ample oversight authority. We believe that under present conditions the Monitoring Commission intrudes on the normal processes we mentioned above. This intrusion, however necessary in the past, is no longer necessary today.[25]

While this order would be the subject of two subsequent appeals, it was left intact until the case was closed in 1989.[26] The district court ended its oversight of the educational components because of the political obstacles it believed had emerged in the relationship between the monitoring commission and school board. In so doing, the judges essentially passed the important responsibility of oversight to defendants in the case. In using the words "intrusion" to characterize the oversight process, the court implied that the very defendants found guilty of discrimination could now be trusted to treat plaintiffs fairly.

The state was looking forward to freedom from financial liability. Anecdotal evidence also suggests that while the district was benefiting from state funds through the case, by 1987, it, too, was looking forward to freedom from judicial oversight.

Between 1975 and 1984 when it was finally disbanded, the monitoring commission had conducted extensive evaluations of how, when, and whether programs were being *implemented*. However, it was disbanded before it was even given a chance to evaluate *outcomes*, which might have indicated whether the programs were enhancing student achievement or being used correctly by educators. The commission had planned to begin such evaluations as noted in a 1984 report.[27]

The monitoring commission did, however, have a chance to review results of the reading component in the high schools by examining test scores on the Michigan Educational Assessment Program (MEAP) and other surveys. Its 1984 report said rising MEAP scores did suggest some improvement, but additional commission evidence, including subsequent test score declines in some schools and negative reports from some school leaders, reveal that reports of success were not necessarily widespread, accurate, or guaranteed to last: MEAP scores increased from 1980 to 1983 in twenty-three of the city's twenth-four high schools; in the 1983 school year, however, only twelve high schools showed improvement over the previous year and eleven others reported declines.[28]

With regard to the MEAP test, the commission identified inconsistencies in testing policies and programs. The reported percentage of students tested on the MEAP ranged from an obviously impossible high of 105 percent for one high school to a low of 60 percent for another high school. The monitoring commission reported that informal interviews with school personnel showed some schools to be more diligent than others in testing students who were absent on the original test day.[29]

According to this 1984 report, in only seven schools did high school English and social studies teachers surveyed in 1984 perceive their own schools as having improved since 1981 in the teaching of reading and communication skills. Teachers in nine schools reported that their schools' effectiveness in these areas was declining. According to teachers, only two high schools deserved a "B" rating in this area, thirteen deserved a grade of "C" and three high schools were rated "D" or worse.[30]

In monitoring inputs, the commission performed its own studies and reviewed other studies commissioned by the school district. Its final report in 1984 found that while some components, such as reading and bilingual education had been implemented in compliance with the court order, other components, most particularly, a new code for student conduct had not. Its reports also reveal a pattern of inconsistency. Some schools complied with implementation while others did not.[31] The board of education, again, countered these claims in its own status reports.[32]

It is still unclear what type of evaluations were conducted by the school board and the state superintendent of instruction before and after the dismantling of the monitoring commission in 1984. Despite repeated attempts made over the course of a year, we were unable to obtain any additional documentation or evaluations from either the school district or the state. The court did require that the school board conduct yearly evaluations of components and that these evaluations be reviewed by the state superintendent of instruction.[33] In any case, it is unlikely that evaluations conducted during this time would be particularly useful because the stipulation established no standards of performance or indicators of success against which to judge the programs.

The overall effect of the educational components upon students in Detroit is unclear. No systematic evaluations of the effect of programs on students were ever conducted because the monitoring commission was dissolved and the court never ordered any. The panel of three judges that took the case in 1980 proved reluctant to intervene in the management of educational components. So it is doubtful that the court would have enforced any modification of components based on evaluation of outcomes anyway.

The case was closed in February 1989. That year, each of the parties to the case, including the plaintiff NAACP, signed the Final Judgement for Unitary Status. As a result, the Detroit Board of Education and the State of Michigan are no longer legally accountable for any effects of past segregation, the current isolation of minority students, and the remaining inferiorities in the city schools. During their twelve years in existence, Detroit's *Milliken II* educational compensation remedies cost about $238 million.

Blatant educational inferiorities remain in the Detroit Public Schools. Today, school officials acknowledge the current poor condition of the system, stating that the *Milliken* programs might have had some positive effect but conceding that the programs simply did not prove to be the systemic remedy needed by urban Detroit.

Former School Superintendent Arthur Jefferson stressed that any shortcomings of *Milliken II* programs should be seen in the context of the *Milliken I* decision. This, Jefferson believes, prevented the district from winning a metropolitan remedy that held more promise for helping minority children:

> You have to consider the situation we were in. This case, this attempt at a plan that involved the suburbs had gone to the highest judicial body in the nation and we had lost.... To even think that it [*Milliken II* programs] was going to be possible to eradicate those problems caused by segregation in a decade? That's impossible. We have to consider whether a district's programs can really overcome the effects of segregation within a segregated district....When we lost, [with *Milliken I*] of course we knew it [*Milliken II* remedies] couldn't overcome the problems the same way a metropolitan remedy would, but that's what we had to work with.[34]

Jefferson believes that the programs probably had some overall positive effect on students. "My feeling is that they did do some good. My feeling is that while the condition of the Detroit schools is nothing to stand up and applaud, it probably would have been worse without that [*Milliken II*] relief."[35]

Milliken II relief, Judge Cohn acknowledges, was an inherently limited form of reparations that could not live up to the Supreme Court's expectation that remedies could return minority students to the position they would have enjoyed if racial separation and discrimination had never occurred.

"These monies were insignificant when considered in light of the school district's budget," Cohn said, "and were insufficient to serve as an incentive for real change."[36]

In the 1993-94 school year, the educational deficits of Detroit students were still apparent. In 1992-93, for example, Detroit students, on average, scored well below the state average on the Michigan Educational Assessment Program. Detroit fourth and fifth graders were twice as likely to fall into the low category on the math test and the city's seventh and eighth graders were three times less likely to meet the satisfactory standard in math. By the tenth and eleventh grades, Detroit students were nearly seven times less likely than statewide students to meet the satisfactory standard in math. In reading, Detroit seventh and eighth graders were half as likely than students statewide to reach the satisfactory standards. By the tenth and eleventh grades, Detroit students were less than half as likely to reach the satisfactory standard in the Michigan Educational Assessment Program.

While gaps between urban districts such as Detroit and other school districts occur for a variety of complex reasons, this achievement gap does suggest that blatant inequities remained after the removal of the *Milliken II* remedies.

Little Rock, Arkansas
Background and History

In 1982, school officials in the predominantly black Little Rock school district sued two nearby predominantly white school districts. In the lawsuit, Little Rock officials sought consolidation with the Pulaski County Special and North Little Rock school systems in order to create a system that would be 61 percent white and 39 percent black.[37] Little Rock officials considered this strategy the most effective for countering the effects of prior segregation. U.S. District Court Judge Henry Woods, in turn, approved the consolidation remedy. But the Eighth Circuit Court of Appeals overturned Woods, in 1985, ruling that consolidation was unnecessary, even though the court conceded that the proven constitutional violations were a result of interdistrict policies.

After the regional plan was rejected, the parties in the Little Rock School District (LRSD) case finally negotiated a six-year student assignment plan in 1989 that included interdistrict and magnet schools and provided *Milliken II* relief to largely all-black "Incentive Schools" that had been difficult to integrate because of their isolated location. These schools were called "Incentive Schools" because officials believed that the special programs and extra funding would provide incentive for white students to transfer there. Under the plan, these segregated schools, which enrolled about 20 percent of the black student population, would get twice the amount of money per student as other elementary schools, "for compensatory education and desegregation expenses."[38]

District Court Judge Henry Woods initially rejected this plan on the recommendation of the court's Special Master Aubrey McCutcheon, who wrote:

> Lack of detailed planning and programming for the Incentive Schools is another critical deficiency of the LRSD plan....Neither parents nor teachers could possibly know what to expect in the Incentive Schools from reading the plans....The availability of "double funding" is meaningless if the programs on which the money is spent are not designed and implemented to achieve educational excellence.[39]

Woods offered a more fundamental criticism claiming that, "approval of the LRSD long-range plan would have resulted in progressive segregation of elementary schools over a six year period."[40]

But the Court of Appeals, concluding that the Constitution does not forbid all-black schools, overruled Judge Woods and approved the district's Incentive School plan in 1990. (The Incentive Schools, which reflect the *Milliken II* strategy, are only part of a larger desegregation strategy that will not be evaluated here.)[41]

The court of appeals expressed the hope that the *Milliken II* programs would improve the educational environment in the Incentive Schools so dramatically that white students would choose to transfer into them, thereby creating integration.[42] The Incentive Schools were informally termed "super magnets" because they received more money than the district's magnet schools; the school district, in turn, pledged to recruit white students for the Incentive Schools.

That *Milliken II* programs were temporary, disjointed programs is manifest in the lack of attention to planning, design, and follow-through in the Little Rock Incentive School remedy.

Implementation

The final tally of Little Rock's *Milliken II* programs, known as the settlement plan, was revised several times and not approved until May 1992, though the money began flowing into the district in 1989. The school officials and attorneys who crafted the plan devoted about one-third of the its 240 pages to an itemization of more than 100 programs to be placed in the Incentive Schools. These programs ranged from new science labs to additional teachers and classroom aides.[43] Most characterized the plan as a conglomeration of expensive techniques and programs, rather than a coherent, goal-oriented strategy for ameliorating the educational problems of minority students.

As director of the state department of education, Dr. Ruth Steele helped develop the plan. Later, Steele became superintendent of the Little Rock district and thus was in charge of overseeing the *Milliken II* programs:

> We made the assumption that if you put enough aides in a room, or if you put enough computers in a room, or if you put enough of this, that, or the other, you can achieve an outcome, instead of thinking about the outcomes that you want to achieve, then backing yourself up to what outcomes for your individual class you need...that will lead you toward the ultimate outcome....That kind of thinking was not done.[44]

The educational remedies were developed without specific goals attached to them. It was simply assumed that the assortment of programs would somehow solve the low achievement and academic inferiority in the heavily minority schools. Chris Heller, attorney for the LRSD, conceded that the *Milliken II* program lacked a clear vision: "One of the problems...is there wasn't a real unifying theme to all this. I think it was a product of a lot of different people operating... and maybe without regard to how much we would be bombarding these kids with and whether or not it could be coordinated in some useful way."[45]

In the face of considerable expenditures, the district's evaluations, at this early stage, have focused primarily on inputs rather than educational results. In fact, the monitoring schedule contained in the desegregation plan emphasizes only the dates when programs should begin and says nothing about the need to measure success.[46]

Three years before the programs were approved in the settlement plan, the financial agreement between the parties required the state to pay the LRSD $73 million over ten years for desegregation and educational compensation remedies. Consequently, a key problem with the plan is that its funding and educational components were considered separately by two distinct committees. As a result, there was no realistic assessment of what educational programs the district could afford financially. Not only were the agreement and the plan developed separately, but those who created programs were told to design the programs without considering costs. The negotiators of the financial settlement assured program designers that there would be enough money, even though the financial negotiators had little knowledge of what programs the planners were creating.

In the end, program designers had to accept the $73 million, although educators knew the funds would be inadequate.

> The staff people were back trying to figure out what it would all cost while negotiations were going on with a whole different set of people.... [W]hat [district administrators] tell me is when the negotiators came back from the table with the amount that had been settled upon, the first response from the staff was, "This isn't enough money to pay for the plan," and the superintendent said, "It'll just have to be enough, it'll just have to work, we'll just have to make it work. This is basically a plan that the Little Rock school district cannot afford to implement...the district can't afford it, simply cannot afford it.[47]

Through its Office of Desegregation Monitoring (ODM), the court has kept track of the implementation process. Horace Smith, associate monitor for ODM, has this to say about the evaluations: "The Little Rock plan was measured by implementation, not by outcome, and that was because of the way the plan was designed.... We really got caught up in just meeting deadlines...evaluation is based more on 'Did you do it?' as opposed to 'Was it successful?'"[48]

As of 1994, the school district had spent three-fourths — or about $55 million — of the $73 million settlement monies,[49] with few evaluations other than those determining whether the programs exist.

Another financial uncertainty exists. Under the settlement agreement, the state agreed to loan the district $20 million for educational programs. This loan will be forgiven if the district raises test scores of black students districtwide so that their composite scores are at least 90 percent of the composite scores of white students by the year 2000. If the district fails to improve scores, it must pay the loan back, with interest.[50]

As of 1993, two years into the plan and four years into the financial agreement, the district had spent $12 million of its $20 million loan. Most of this money has been spent in the segregated Incentive Schools, even though loan forgiveness hinges upon improvement in black students' scores districtwide. And even though loan forgiveness is to be judged on test results, the district has administered four different standardized tests to measure achievement over the last five years. This makes achievement comparisons difficult, if not impossible.

So far, test scores indicate that despite the increased spending, the school district is not approaching the goal of improving black students' scores. The aggregate scores of black students have not risen significantly districtwide; further, it seems the achievement gap between black and white students may be getting larger, putting the district in danger of failing to meet the specified target for loan forgiveness.

In the 1991-92 school year, the gap between black and white student scores on the Stanford-8 Achievement Test increased by three points for fourth graders, decreased by one point for seventh graders, and increased by two points for tenth graders.[51]

In the Incentive Schools, which received the most funding and extra programs, the scores of black students dropped in the 1990s. A monitoring office report discussed this problem:

> There is no consistent incentive school test performance configuration from 1988 through 1991, with test scores showing a seesaw pattern for the most part....However, a preliminary review of the [Stanford Achievement Test] results is very discouraging: overall performance of incentive school students between [1992] and [1993] has dropped significantly.[52]

District Court Judge Susan Webber Wright, replaced Judge Woods. She has found the district too slow to put its own plan in place. She was particularly dismayed that the school district had failed to develop a budget detailing exactly how money was being spent. If the LRSD "were a corporation," Wright said, "I would put it in receivership."[53]

> Since the time of victory by the Little Rock School District in this case, when the Court of Appeals granted almost every facet of relief requested by Little Rock, the Little Rock School District has shown a tendency to drag its feet and act as if it had lost, rather than won, the litigation which it instituted....It was your plan that you agreed to; you got it approved by the Court of Appeals; and I must enforce it. Let me make this clear: while the District Court has some latitude in modifying the plan, the Court of Appeals has identified elements of the plan which it deems essential and which, under present circumstances, are not within the prerogative of this court to modify.[54]

Wright asserted that the district failed to fulfill more than a dozen provisions of the court orders. With regard to Incentive Schools, she said the district failed to "engage in documented, sustained and vigorous recruitment" of white students. In addition, Wright complained, program specialists had not been hired at every Incentive School and the Parent Council had not monitored or reported on Incentive School activities as required by the court.[55]

Although Wright can enforce implementation of the plan as written, she can approve modifications, "only to a limited extent."[56] The plan, then, may remain virtually unchanged, even if it fails to redress the effects of past segregation. The "essential" elements to which the judge referred include double-funding for Incentive Schools and the effort to eliminate the achievement disparity between the races. All but one of the Incentive Schools still had a nearly all-black student body in 1995.[57]

In its January 1995 report, the ODM chastised the district for its lack of effort in desegregating its schools.

> In its desegregation plans, the LRSD committed to the tough job of recruiting white students in numbers that would allow its schools to be desegregated within the range the district set up for itself. Unfortunately, the LRSD does not have a history of vigorous and sustained recruitment; thus, it has largely failed to meet its recruitment goals and obligations.[58]

The district is bound to these specific programs at the segregated schools, regardless of whether the extra programs, as designed, succeed in helping students. The court, in fact, scolds the district for failing to actively recruit white students who might help integrate the segregated schools. As some informants suggested, inaction on this point might stem from a lack of commitment to desegregation. ODM Associate Monitor Melissa Guldin characterized the goal of integration as being "way down the list [as a] secondary goal of the Incentive Schools...the enhancements were really to [say] 'we're making you go to these segregated schools, so we're going to give you a lot of neat things to do while you're there.'"[59]

The events in Little Rock suggest that the District Court may have been correct both in its initial recommendation for a consolidation plan and its criticisms of the ambiguity inherent in the planned educational compensation remedies. The Court of Appeals, on the other hand, may have been overly optimistic about what some monetary extras would be able to accomplish in segregated schools. Policymakers in Little Rock never devised a clear strategy to reach educational goals; program designers did not even know the amount of funding available, and evaluations were inadequate, putting the segregation "remedy" in a financially precarious, politically vulnerable position. Today, a separate but theoretically "more than equal" remedy is in place and is approaching the financial day of reckoning with no measureable educational gains.

Prince George's County, Maryland
Background and History

The *Milliken* school program in Prince George's County, Maryland, is part of a larger voluntary desegregation plan in this suburban, predominantly black school district, with 113,000 students, outside Washington, D.C.

The school district has operated under a court-supervised desegregation plan since 1972. In 1985, in an effort to end a busing plan that could not cope with the rapid demographic change, school officials instituted a magnet school program that was designed to achieve integration by attracting whites to black schools and blacks to white schools.

However, in crafting this desegregation plan, school officials believed it would be impossible to integrate some schools because of their geographically isolated locations and large minority populations. As compensation, school officials and plaintiffs agreed that extra money would be funnelled to these segregated *Milliken* schools. The school board agreed to provide this extra compensation in exchange for the NAACP's promise that plaintiffs would not challenge the racial imbalance in these schools.[60] At the *Milliken* program's inception in 1985, 10 of the district's 174 schools were designated as *Milliken* schools; the next phase, in 1986, added eleven more schools. Former School Superintendent John Murphy, the architect of the plan, credits the segregated schools with great success, stating:

> The greatest academic gains occurred in the *Milliken* schools. Now to ask me to put my finger on the one specific thing that made it happen, I couldn't do it…but to give you a guess…I believe that it was the structure that was built into the lives of these kids.…There were responsibilities that they had to meet, there were guidelines that they had to follow relative to their behavior patterns, and for the first time in their lives somebody was giving them some structure and I think that that helped these kids to perform a lot better in the classroom.…[61]

School officials have also created a new category of schools called "interim *Milliken* schools," also known as "model comprehensive" schools. These twelve schools have special designations because they are not in compliance with racial balance guidelines and therefore receive extra funding. However, these schools do not receive as many extras as the original *Milliken* schools. This new category of school has not been sanctioned specifically by the court and there were no court hearings held on the new designations. However, plaintiff attorney

George Mernick said that in light of changing demographics that make it more difficult to achieve integration, plaintiffs have no plans to challenge the new categories.[62]

This case study illustrates the vague, unchecked nature of *Milliken II* educational reforms. School officials here make no attempt to define, articulate, or prove they have met the Supreme Court mandate to restore "the victims of discriminatory conduct to the position they would have occupied in the absence of such conduct." Instead, school officials simply announced their own success and offered no proof to back up the claims of overall excellence. Meanwhile, the use of extra money to provide "equity" at some schools has triggered charges of "inequity" from other schools that are growing more segregated without additional compensation.

As the dwindling pool of white people in Prince George's County makes integration more difficult to achieve, the "extra money" remedy will inevitably run its course as budgets tighten. School officials, as the recent budget process proved, will simply not be able to afford to provide all racially disproportionate schools with extra monetary relief.

Implementation

The 1985 Memorandum of Understanding negotiated by the school board and the NAACP required only that the district demonstrate that *Milliken II* programs existed. There is no mention of any measurement of success.

Compensation relief to the segregated *Milliken* schools includes all-day kindergartens, teachers who specialize in reading and math, computer labs, strategies to improve parent involvement, media specialists, reduced class sizes, after-school tutoring, high-quality field trips, and other special programs.

But the settlement fails to address questions about the rationale for including certain components, the educational philosophy behind the programs, and what results would indicate that the programs had been successful in remedying the negative educational effects of segregation. In 1987, an informational booklet disseminated by the school system defined the educational goals for *Milliken* schools this way: "The *Milliken II* program...offers additional staffing and enriched resources for students who attend a school with limited integration. The program is specifically designed to enhance the quality of instruction and the potential for achievement among all students attending the school."[63]

In fact, all of those interviewed describe the purpose of *Milliken* schools in similarly vague terms. Edward Felegy, the superintendent, said, "the additional resources of the *Milliken II* program are intended to enrich the educational experience of these students...so there is an educational goal...one closely linked with educational outcomes...."[64]

The Committee of 100, the citizens' court-appointed monitoring group, repeatedly asked that the school system be more explicit in its goals for *Milliken* schools. But this committee was never intended to be a watchdog for plaintiffs in the case.[65] The plaintiffs have not been active monitors. In 1987, the Monitoring Sub-Committee of the Committee of 100 said that "required ratio racial categories of students must be met along with the improvement in the academic performance of the students,"[66] but it could not enforce this policy.

The school system did develop "school improvement plans" for each building but not districtwide data measuring the success of *Milliken II* programs.

In 1989, school officials did conduct a study comparing the achievement of black third graders in the *Milliken* elementary schools to achievement of students in the regular elementary comprehensive schools that received no extra compensation. The study showed that achievement gains for black third graders in the *Milliken* schools were larger.[67] *Milliken* third-grade students moved from the 57th to the 63rd percentile on the California Achievement Test between the third and fifth grades. Black students in comprehensive schools remained in the 58th percentile from third to fifth grade. Certainly, the larger gains of *Milliken* students are worth noting and should be an impetus for conducting more studies; these gains, however, do not provide us with enough information with which to evaluate the program. It may be true that the extra resources and programming in the *Milliken* schools did produce results. However, questions remain. Since this study of elementary school students was released six years ago in 1989, there has been no other study of the effect of the *Milliken* program. Further, the results from this 1989 study mirror other evaluations that show that compensatory measures usually register their largest effect in the elementary school years and that initial gains tend to diminish as children move through school in later years.[68]

Questions have also been raised about the reliability of the research; for example, the 1989 study used only a single measure to evaluate students. Obviously, the evaluation would be more reliable if multiple measures had been used and if a longitudinal analysis had been conducted that measured the same students over time.

It should also be noted that this version of the California Achievement Test may not be an accurate measure of general progress over time, because the national norms for the tests were established in 1976-77[69] and remained unchanged in subsequent years. The test was administered in 1989, after national elementary achievement had risen nationwide; therefore, the test results may very well be misleading. This phenomenon has made it easy for many school systems to claim improvement over time, when, in fact, the old norm to which they are compared may be far below the current norm.[70] Despite these criticisms of dated norms, officials continued to cite CAT scores as evidence of success. As late as 1993, district officials cited CAT scores as sufficient "concrete evidence" to conclude that education had improved as a result of the *Milliken II* programs.[71] It should be stressed that this criticism of dated norms *does not* discredit or negate the school district finding that black students in *Milliken II* schools registered larger gains than black students in regular schools. It simply throws the more general claims of improvement over time into question.

The State of Maryland stopped using the CAT in 1988 and replaced it with a criterion-reference test, which, unlike a norm-reference test whose standards derive from comparisons between students, evaluates how well students perform on the material on the exam. Prince George's County administrators did design for the *Milliken II* and magnet schools a more comprehensive evaluation that would conduct sophisticated analyses and use measures tailored specifically to study certain programs. But because of budget limitations, the evaluation proposal was never approved by the Board of Education. In 1994, administrators were designing a simpler version of the evaluation. As of April 1994, the evaluation proposal had not been approved.

Though there is little evidence that the supplementary programs have improved educational quality, representatives from non-*Milliken* schools, many of which are also growing segregated, requested a share of extra money as well.

In response, Superintendent Felegy had included extra money for the nonmagnet comprehensive schools in his 1994-95 budget request, but the requested $5.4 million was cut by the school board. The elimination of extra funds for the neighborhood schools followed an intense lobbying effort by a church-based civic group, the Interfaith Action Committee, which wanted extra dollars for nonmagnet schools.

It seems that *Milliken II* programs, although developed to provide equity, have, in the view of many, created a new kind of inequity. So, as the percentage of white students declines, school officials may find it even more difficult to achieve court-ordered integration at their other non-*Milliken* schools. It seems highly likely that there will be pressure to increase the use of *Milliken* funds. But both school and county governments in 1994 faced a serious financial crisis that threatened to reduce funding. The increasing demand for money probably cannot be met. Unfortunately, as racial integration becomes less feasible, the monetary remedy is rapidly becoming the only option school leaders are pursuing.

Austin, Texas
Background and History

It is common for school officials under desegregation orders to claim that they could better help their students if courts were not involved in school affairs. This case study of Austin, Texas, focuses attention on a district that has a history of intentional segregation but was declared "unitary"[72] by the federal court and, as a result, released from its duty to desegregate. Soon after its release from court control, school officials dismantled their busing plan for elementary schools and returned to neighborhood schools. The district then put extra money into some of these newly segregated schools, thereby creating programs much like those found under traditional *Milliken II* plans. Austin did not create these compensatory programs under legal mandate, but did so as part of an independent district-designed plan to try to ensure that segregated schools were offered equal opportunity.

Austin was first found guilty of intentional racial segregation in 1970, when the U.S. Court of Appeals found that the district had discriminated against African American students through segregative school assignments; in 1979, this court found that the district had also discriminated against Latino students. In response to these findings, the district started a mandatory busing plan for African American secondary school students in 1972; in 1980 a busing plan was extended to include Latino students.[73] The 1980 consent decree required the school district to build an integrated junior high school in the eastern part of the city. In exchange, plaintiffs agreed to give the school board until the autumn of that year to design and implement a crosstown busing plan. Construction of a new junior high school had been a demand of the NAACP during negotiations that began in 1978.[74] The demand was significant because the closing of segregated black schools in 1972 had left the African American community without a secondary school in their neighborhood for about eight years.[75] The consent decree also included a requirement to continue a program that allowed students to transfer from schools where their race was the majority to schools where their race was a minority.[76]

In 1983, just three years after a desegregation plan had been established for all students, the Austin Independent School District (AISD) filed a court motion for unitary status. This status would imply that the system had satisfied its duty to desegregate under the law. The NAACP and the Mexican-American Legal Defense Fund objected. Following negotiations, however, plaintiffs withdrew their objections; under the agreed-upon stipulation plaintiffs would be entitled to court hearings over boundaries[77] and a new junior high school would be completed. In June 1983, the court dismissed the case "with prejudice," meaning plaintiffs could have the case reopened at any time if they charged that there had been a new violation. Just three years later, the court granted the school district complete release from court control. In the eyes of the court, the unitary ruling essentially erased the school board's history of illegal segregation.

In April 1987, a year after court oversight had ceased entirely, the Austin School Board began implementing its five-year "Plan for Educational Excellence." The plan redrew attendance zones, more than tripling the number of segregated minority schools from six to twenty. The school district designated sixteen of the most intensely segregated schools as "Priority Schools," which would receive extra money and programs.

Former board member Abel Ruiz said that many schools that should have been compensated for high levels of segregation were not. The decision to provide extra money to just the sixteen schools that were more than 80 percent minority was not based on any research or comprehensive needs assessment. Rather, Ruiz asserts, the decision to fund just sixteen schools was the result of politics and financial considerations. A coalition of three minority board members on the seven-member board had agreed to support the Priority

Schools Plan *if* all schools where more than 65 percent of students were minorities were provided with special services. This would have provided extra services to about twenty-five schools. However, the board refused to support that plan. One of the minority members even switched sides to vote with the majority in favor of the plan that assisted only sixteen schools, according to Ruiz. "The board voted for the services but they went ahead and limited it as a dollar amount.... What happened was then they just said, 'well, we can only spend *x* number of dollars on it, so whatever we can do for $4 million, that's what we'll do,' and that's how sixteen came about...a lot of schools that should have received services didn't."[78]

In response to the neighborhood school plan, civil rights lawyers again charged that the AISD's new attendance zones discriminated against Mexican American and black children. But since the school district had been declared unitary—or, in the eyes of the court, free from the vestiges of discrimination—the court shifted the burden of proof to the plaintiffs. They had to show that the school district's action was a new act of intentional discrimination against minority students. If the district had not been declared unitary, it is likely that school officials would have had the burden of proving that their plan would not undermine the goal of achieving a unitary—or desegregated—school system.

The standard actually used in the case, which required civil rights lawyers to prove that the action in question was motivated by discrimination, is difficult to meet, since contemporary school officials rarely make public statements admitting to intentional discrimination. In addition, school officials cited the "Priority Schools" designations as evidence that the district was committed to providing educational opportunity to minority children.[79] The district court sided with the school district and upheld its plan to return to neighborhood schools.

Under the new "Priority Schools" plan, Austin school officials pledged to allocate extra money to the schools and to create *Milliken II*-type programs for the students. In 1987-88, the Priority Schools received twice what the other schools received and in the years thereafter, one-and-a-half times the amount other schools received. The district's Plan for Educational Excellence detailed the special programs that would be included in these schools, including such things as reduced student-teacher ratios, parent-community involvement, and a preschool program. For each of the ten components, there was a stated goal, rationale, and procedure for implementation. However officials removed independent oversight of the programs and offered no guarantee that the programs, as first devised, would last because their continuation hinges upon political support from the local school board.

The Austin plan is significant because it demonstrates that giving school districts local control over compensatory measures is clearly not a permanent solution. Internal evaluations do show some improvement over time within Priority Schools. But even with the extra funding, special programming and freedom from court requirements, Austin's segregated Priority Schools are still unequal on several measures to schools that are more integrated. Equally significant is that there is no guarantee that this extra effort to make segregated schools equal will continue. The board promised "to provide these educational efforts [in Priority Schools] for a period of five years to ensure that students in the 16 schools named herein have the finest education available in the Austin Independent School District."[80] The resolution, however, never indicated what would happen to funding and programming in the segregated Priority Schools once the "period of five years" was up.

Implementation

The implementation and progress of the five-year Priority School plan was studied each school year from 1987 to 1991 by the system's Office of Research and Evaluation. Its final report shows that after five years, only the lower student-teacher ratio appears to have had a direct, measurable effect on students. And this positive effect, it said, occurred only in the kindergarten and first grade. Evaluators used test scores to determine that some schools demonstrated overall improvement, but none had reached the level the district had hoped for.[81] Specifically, the district set up "Priority School Standards" it hoped the schools could achieve. These standards included student average daily attendance of 95 percent or higher; teacher absences of less than five days; fewer than 10 percent of students scoring within the bottom quartile on the Iowa Test of Basic Skills; and "parent agreement" that the school is "effective"(but "effective" was not defined). School officials, however, stress that other elementary schools, and not just the Priority Schools, also have had difficulty in meeting these ambitious standards.

According to the fifth-year evaluation, principals at ten of the six-teen Priority Schools reported that student achievement at their schools had not improved over five years.[82] Such statements from principals are especially discouraging because it is reasonable to assume that principals try to present their schools in a positive light to their supervisors and to the public at large. On the other hand, some standardized test scores indicate that achievement at Priority Schools has improved over the years.

If the goal of the Plan for Educational Excellence is really to provide Priority Schools with the "finest" education available, the most telling measure of success is not whether Priority Schools are improving, but how educational opportunity, achievement, and school climate in the Priority Schools compares with academic performance at other elementary schools in the district. After five years of the Priority School programming, achievement levels at the racially segregated Priority Schools lagged behind achievement levels at the more integrated elementary schools, and improvement, overall, is not consistent. After five years, achievement and other measures show Priority Schools are still lagging behind other elementary schools.

Specifically, the five-year evaluation notes that Priority School students registered steady improvements on aggregate median percentile ranks on the Iowa Test of Basic Skills each year from 1987 to 1992. Improvements for grades one through six ranged from 6 percentile points in grades three and six to 17 percentile points in grade two. Percentile ranks are based on 1991 norms. But according to data from the 1991-92 school year, the most recent year for which data is available, students in Priority Schools score much lower than other students on standardized tests despite the extra funding.

Priority School students failed to meet the national norm (above the 50th percentile) in every grade except grade two. Students in other elementary schools consistently met this standard. Gaps between the two types of schools ranged from 13 points in grade two to 33 points in grade four.

Similar achievement disparities are evident in scores on state-mandated tests. The Texas Educational Assessment of Minimum Skills (TEAMS) tested students in math, reading, and writing. The TAAS, a criterion-referenced test that replaced TEAMS, also evaluates skills in reading, math, and writing and bases its assessment of district-level performance on the percentage of students reaching the "mastery level on the exam."

Since scores are provided for only two years, this data are not adequate for establishing definitive trends. Students in the regular schools were always more likely than Priority school students to pass TEAMS or score at the mastery level. Gaps between the schools ranged from 14 to 21 percentage points on the TEAMS and from 9 to 25 points on the TAAS.

Another indicator of school quality is that the number of teachers requesting transfers from their schools is higher in Priority Schools than it is in other elementary schools. In the 1991-92 school year, 21 percent of teachers in Priority Schools requested transfer, compared with 14 percent in other elementary schools.[83]

Compared with other districts studied here, school officials in Austin have conducted a fairly comprehensive evaluation of Priority Schools. However, the results might be more objective were an agency independent of the Austin School District rigorously monitoring and evaluating the compensation programs. In 1987, the AISD did create a seven-member Priority Schools Monitoring Committee, composed of community members who were to audit programs and report findings to the school board and administrators. But the group was never given adequate instruction and assistance in conducting evaluations and was dissolved in 1991 after five years. The committee had no independent staff and had to rely on the school district for data. Loretta Edelen, a former committee member, discussed this situation:

> It was pretty much an open-ended type of thing, in a way, just going by the guidelines that were in that Plan for Education Excellence in terms of viewing the schools and preparation of the report. What we basically did when we went into the schools was to kind of visit with them and whatever interested parties they wanted to bring in. Some of the schools, for instance, had parents that came, some had some of their teachers and some of their counselors, so it varied with the school in terms of the kinds of presentation that we received, but we were trying to go in and find out where they were with the whole process and in terms of meeting their goals, what kinds of things they were falling short on.[84]

Reports from the committee contain little, if any, statistical evidence to confirm or deny the value of specific programs. Findings of the committee were rarely used in policy-making decisions according to some committee members, one of whom, Blanca Garcia, said:

Last year, we requested more of a working meeting with the board of trustees [the school board], because there were a lot of new school board members who were not members when this agreement came about and so they had a lot of questions; they didn't know what was going on. Then, we had a new superintendent and he was confused and so we wanted to meet with the superintendent and the board of trustees to sit down and tell them, "Look, these are the problems with these schools, and these are the reasons that we're getting low test scores and why our kids are not learning, why our kids are not achieving, and why we have such a high rate of dropouts in the minority community in AISD." That never occurred. The superintendent didn't want it, and the majority of the board didn't push for it. In fact, the board of trustees had a work session on Priority Schools and the monitoring committee was not even advised or invited to attend.[85]

When studies were released by the school district, the public—in this case, parents—found it difficult to interpret the findings, according to some informants. Test scores and other measures often were not translated into an easily understandable form, said Joseph Higgs, who works with parents in his role as president of Austin Interfaith, a community organization of thirty interdenominational congregations, with black, Mexican American, and white members.

Almost none of these parents had any idea what the achievement data was for the Priority Schools. They kind of knew that their kids weren't doing as well as they wanted them to, but they didn't know how their school did relative to other schools or relative to the Priority Schools, how the Hispanic or black kids did relative to Anglo kids in the district, the difference between a norm-referenced and a criterion-referenced test…parents don't know what the difference is and [they wonder], "What does it mean that my kid's passed this test?" [and] "What does it mean that they got a 40 percent on this test?"[86]

In most *Milliken II*-type programs the court would establish a monitoring committee to oversee the plan. But in the absence of effective court supervision, it is unlikely that a school district, on its own, would choose to appoint a powerful external body. The superintendent, in 1993, notified the internal Office of Research and Evaluation that it should scale back its evaluations in light of budget cutbacks. This cutback may mean that many important evaluations will not be conducted, among them an analysis of achievement disparities between different races and ethnicities in Priority Schools.[87] There has been no evaluation that specifically analyzes and assesses the benefits of Priority Schools since 1991.

Another complication emerges from the Priority Schools designations. Sixteen schools were originally identified in 1987 as "racially identifiable" because more than 80 percent of their students were racial minorities. But as of 1993-94, twenty-six schools were more than 80 percent minority,[88] and no accommodations had been made for these schools. The lack of a court presence in Austin means no independent body will ensure that these schools are examined, evaluated, racially integrated, or provided extra money.

Funding and rigorous critical evaluation to ensure results, then, depends upon support from a school board that has the potential to change with every election, that has a history of intentional segregation, and that is, to some extent, accountable to fickle public sentiment. As Bernice Hart, a member of the school board in 1993 explained, "You can't commit one board to something another board did."[89] Blanca Garcia, the former Priority Schools Monitoring Commission member, characterized the current situation:

> I think that the new members felt that this was a plan that was initiated by someone else and the commitment was there for five years....I don't think they intended to keep the spirit of the ten components [of the plan] as it was written. I think that they feel like yes, there is a need to fund the Priority Schools to a certain extent...I don't know if they're going to go beyond that.[90]

The Austin school district did recognize the special academic needs of students in segregated schools and agreed to try to meet those needs for five years.

Later, in 1994, school officials reduced funding to the Priority Schools by about 5 percent so as to provide other high-poverty Schools, Tier 2 schools, with extra money. The 5 percent reduction resulted in an average $8,000 loss per Priority School. There are twenty-five Tier 2 schools which receive some extra funding but not as much as Priority Schools.[91]

Shortcomings of *Milliken II*

It is beyond the scope of this chapter to determine whether educational compensation remedies can ever meet the Supreme Court's mandate to "restore the victims of discriminatory conduct to the position they would have occupied in the absence of such conduct."[92] But in the districts studied here, we see some troubling patterns indicating that the mandate has not been met.

Design and Funding

In each district studied, policymakers implemented educational components without providing an explanation of exactly how such programs would eradicate the harmful effects of prior intentional segregation. It seems that programs were selected because they were believed to be beneficial in and of themselves and not because the programs specifically fit the needs of the students in a particular district. There is little evidence to suggest that policymakers engaged in thorough analyses of what specific effects these programs might have on students. The remedies tended to be viewed as a supplemental temporary program rather than a redress for structural inequalities.

Policymakers do not seem to be addressing such questions as: *How will smaller class sizes benefit our students? In what ways will proposed reading programs affect our students' literacy skills, prospects for enrolling in upper-level classes, and opportunities after graduation?*

The funding and continuation of a program was determined arbitrarily through funding limits or a scheduled date of termination. Little Rock's $20 million incentive loan from the state may have been an attempt to use funds as an incentive for positive outcomes, but district officials concede that it is unlikely that the district will achieve its goal, especially since the district had spent more than $12 million with no success.

Detroit provides a clear example of arbitrary funding; the provision of money was based not on whether the programs were successful but on the outcome of a politicized bargaining process.

In Austin, funding for segregated Priority Schools is not guaranteed. It will depend upon political support and fluctuating budget allocations and has already decreased. In Little Rock, the design of programs was not even related to what they would cost. Program design and budgets were crafted independently of one another.

Courts have not forced districts to substantiate their program selections or plans; they have been willing to accept these programs, their funding, and the termination of their funding without assuring their effectiveness. And Austin shows that these programs would not necessarily be more successful in the absence of court oversight. On the contrary, there is no guarantee or clear commitment to maintaining special programs in Austin, which is free from court control.

Evaluation

School officials have failed to evaluate rigorously the effects of various educational compensation measures. In some instances, there have been extensive studies to demonstrate the *existence* of programs, but nothing more. Policymakers seem to disregard such questions as: *What have been the actual effects on students of a particular program? What are the specific opportunities created for a student who is receiving benefits from a particular program?*

In many cases, evaluations were not comprehensive or, as in Prince George's County and Austin, were carried out by internal school district offices. When considered at all, standardized test scores were the principal data used to determine effectiveness. Test scores might say something about student achievement overall or about the level of academic competitiveness in the district, but these tests are not designed to measure the effectiveness of a given program or curriculum. There was never any scientific link made between test score results and educational components. As the Committee of 100 in Prince George's County said, "…performance indicators, when they are limited to test scores, are only a small piece of the puzzle when evaluating the effectiveness of a desegregation program as it pertains to the students as a whole person. The findings should not be used as an indication, by themselves, of the success or failure of a school system."[93]

Oversight

Courts have not held school districts accountable for evaluations. Court oversight has been characteristically weak or short-lived. When monitoring groups did make recommendations, school boards were not required to follow or even consider the suggestions; for example, monitoring groups in Detroit and Prince George's County offered repeated criticisms and recommendations, but, as the courts, and sometimes the plaintiffs played passive roles, the district could ignore the stated problems without repercussions. In Detroit and Austin, monitoring commissions were even disbanded. While in the Detroit case, the court may have viewed the commission as counterproductive, it took no action to appoint a more effective and independent monitor. Instead, the court in Detroit appointed public authorities, the defendants in the case, as overseer. The same problems emerged in Austin, where the monitoring body had no real power, unclear responsibilities, and was eventually dissolved. The internal evaluation office in Austin did evaluate its Priority Schools, but it is unclear what type of evaluations will be conducted in the future.

In Little Rock, the supervising judge did scold the district for non-compliance, but the agreement requires that components must continue in their current form, regardless of whether they help students. Officials in Little Rock cannot move in any direction because they are bound to fulfill the court-approved program requirements.

Ways to Improve *Milliken II* Programs

The court's most crucial tasks are first to identify carefully the educational problems resulting from the lingering effects of segregation and, second, to select programs and methods that hold the most promise for correcting them. District court judges typically lack specialized training in education. Therefore, independent educational experts should be appointed to formulate remedies in consultation with the school district; they should establish a set of specific, measurable educational goals. Prior to program design, the court must require the school district to submit detailed budgets. The Court should then direct the parties to negotiate over agreements on the issues raised in the reports and then hold hearings on the recommendations before signing new consent agreements or ordering changes in the local desegregation plan.

A panel of professional, independent monitors, trained in statistical methods and accountable to no one but the court, should be appointed. Plaintiffs should always have a role in choosing members of an evaluation and monitoring team. This panel's primary responsibility should be to analyze the educational results of *Milliken II* programming. Court orders should require evaluations of specific outcomes. "Contingency plans" should describe what school officials should do if evaluations show poor, average, or good results. The most effective means of assessing programs' effectiveness are longitudinal analyses with adequate controls; total dependence on a single indicator—such as a standardized test—is unreliable and not always informative. Evaluators should conduct comparative long-term longitudinal studies of student groups receiving compensatory services and groups of students who do not receive the services. (Prince George's County did conduct such a comparative study, but it was limited to an analysis of a single indicator, the California Achievement Test, and it measured progress over just two years.)

Evaluations should always be presented in an understandable form to policymakers and the public.

Continued provision of *Milliken II* money to a particular program should be contingent upon the demonstrated gains of the children and favorable evaluations of the children. There should also be measured progress toward equality and narrowing racial gaps. School districts and courts should resist the temptation to regard the *Milliken II* remedy, once designed, as a "finished product." The district, court, and monitoring arm must anticipate and institutionalize a systematic process of revision and modification. Evaluations should not be seen as ends in themselves but as means to differentiate effective programs from failures. The court should take advantage of its political insulation and should not hesitate to discontinue or replace ineffective programs.

Beyond *Milliken II* Remedies

It seems that courts and school officials have come to view *Milliken II* strategies as temporary financial obligations of the plaintiff class. From this perspective, the essential goal of *Milliken II* programs is not to eradicate the harms of prior intentional segregation by eliminating achievement gaps between the races and by increasing opportunity. Rather, the remedies have become a way for school districts and states to endure a short and superficial punishment for prior intentional segregation. School districts are allowed to abandon remedial programs after an arbitrary number of years even when there is no evidence whatsoever that the educational deficits of minority students have been eradicated.

Certainly, there are things that can be done to improve the design, implementation, and possibly the results of educational compensation programs. School districts and courts who use *Milliken II*-type programs should take steps toward improvement as outlined here.

But until there is a guaranteed cure for the myriad problems that stem from racial and economic isolation and the continuing effects of intentional segregation, *Milliken II* remedies may simply give "separate but equal" another chance. Though they may be viewed as the only viable "desegregation" option, the evidence in these case studies makes it clear that educational compensation to segregated schools is no substitute for systemic structural changes, such as successful racial integration.

This is not to say that educational components cannot ever have positive effects if they are conceived, managed, and implemented properly. On the contrary, it may be that a combination of successful racial integration *and* well-designed, permanent, accountable, and effective educational compensation measures offers the best chance for equal opportunity and the most promising way to meet the Supreme Court mandate.

For the many school districts whose pool of white students is small, racial integration is likely to occur only by including predominantly white communities in desegregation plans. Even though the 1974 *Milliken I* decision made it difficult to achieve such city-suburban plans, school officials, civil rights lawyers, and courts should continue to explore alternative avenues to racial integration.

In 1994, twenty years after the Supreme Court decision in *Milliken I,* Justice Thurgood Marshall's prophetic dissent rings true:

> Our nation, I fear, will be ill-served by the Court's refusal to remedy separate and unequal education.... Desegregation is not and was never expected to be an easy task....In the short run, it may seem to be the easier of course to allow our great metropolitan areas to be divided up each into two cities—one white, the other black—but it is a course, I predict, our people will ultimately regret.[94]

CHAPTER SEVEN

Desegregation at Risk
Threat and Reaffirmation in Charlotte
Alison Morantz

In the 1970s, as most of the nation's school systems continued to ignore racial segregation or only made token changes, the Charlotte-Mecklenburg schools, after the Supreme Court *Swann v. Charlotte-Mecklenburg* decision, embarked on an effort to achieve real integration. Charlotte became the first school district in the nation to implement a mandatory student reassignment plan across a metropolitan region. From the mid-1970s through the mid-1980s, Charlotte was lauded as the "city that made desegregation work."[1]

In the mid-1980s, a confluence of local and national trends — rapid demographic transition, dissatisfaction with particulars of the busing plan, and a growing concern with educational quality — triggered a movement to alter the status quo. In 1991, the school board ushered in a new era with its selection of Dr. John A. Murphy as superintendent. Murphy, a controversial, corporate-style educational leader, resolved to upgrade the quality of education in the district by phasing out mandatory busing and phasing in a new plan that would rely primarily on magnet schools and busing that was either "voluntary" or shared evenly among all parents. The new superintendent's skepticism about desegregation ignited a major community debate.

During the 1990s, desegregation in Charlotte hung in the balance. During those years, the number of racially unbalanced schools has increased as has the degree of racial imbalance. However, in a 1995 school board election that many viewed as a referendum on integrated schools, Charlotte voters reaffirmed their commitment to desegregation. Integration advocates won a strong majority on the board, a telling example of community support for integrated schools.

The Evolution of *Swann* and the Era of Mandatory Busing

In 1960, the Charlotte and Mecklenburg County school systems were consolidated into a single district composed of the urban core and the surrounding suburbs (CMS). This fortuitous consolidation meant that desegregation would not be threatened by white flight from the city. Nor was the district constrained by the *Milliken* decision, which made it difficult for courts to compel students to be bused between separate city and suburban districts.

The symbolic beginning of school desegregation in Charlotte was September 1957, when fifteen-year-old Dorothy Counts became the first African American student to break the color barrier at Harding High School. Counts's pioneering effort marked the beginning of a decade of token integration, in which desegregation proceeded incrementally as the district retained its essentially segregated character. Following the Counts case, the district fashioned a "freedom of choice" plan that allowed black students to transfer to all-white schools. But the plan was not effective; by 1964, only 21 of Charlotte's 109 schools contained students of both races. Of these, fifteen had less than a dozen blacks.

The *Swann* case sought to eradicate the segregated system. The case began in January 1965, when a local civil rights lawyer, Julius Chambers, filed suit. In April 1969, federal District Judge James B. McMillan ruled that the board's freedom-of-choice plan had not fulfilled its "affirmative duty" to desegregate the system, and ordered the board to submit a "positive plan...for effective desegregation" by 15 May 1969. The Supreme Court affirmed McMillan's order on 20 April 1971,[2] which was implemented later that year.

By the summer of 1974, the judge and school board had devised a mutually acceptable scheme for mandatory busing. The plan used four strategies. First, the district was divided into geographic zones that would maximize the available pool of students of each race. Second, at the elementary level, the district used a complex system of "pairings" or "two-way busing" to achieve desegregation. As part of the elementary pairings, inner-city minority students from an urban residential zone would typically be bused to the suburbs for kindergarten through third grade to attend school in a white suburban neighborhood. White children in grades four, five, and six from that school would be bused to the central city to attend school in the minority students' neighborhood. Pair by pair, the district managed to ensure that the majority of its elementary schools fell within within 15 percentage points of the racial composition of the district as a whole—40 percent black, 60 percent white.

But in some cases, the minority student population was too large to be fully accomodated by the local "paired" 4-6 grade school, while youngsters in the suburban white neighborhood were not plentiful enough to fill the local k-3 school to capacity. To correct these imbalances, a third strategy was devised. As part of "satellite assignments" or "one-way busing," inner-city minority students were bused to the outlying suburbs for their entire elementary school career, thereby relieving overcrowding in their neighborhoods while filling up underused schools in affluent white suburbs. Finally, the plan created five magnet or "optional" schools to attract a diverse mix of students from across the district. A year after the Student Assignment Plan went into effect—11 July 1975—Judge McMillan noted his satisfaction with the district's efforts in his final order, entitled "Swann Song." Although Judge McMillan subsequently issued some minor orders, his "Swann Song" ruling of 1975 removed the case from the active docket and marked the end of the era of extensive court intervention.

The CMS system's 109 schools include 76 elementary schools, 22 middle schools, 11 senior high schools, and 9 special programs. In the fall of 1974, all schools in the district—except Hidden Valley Elementary, which was excluded from the court order—opened with a student body between 17 and 45 percent black.[3] By 1977, enrollment in 6 schools was above 52 percent, but the school board revised the plan in 1978 to bring the racial proportions in these schools closer to the district average. This technique of annual revisions, used to improve racial balance in schools with large black populations, would continue into the following decade. From 1980 to 1986, the school board adopted minor changes every year to relieve overcrowding and to equalize student ratios. During this period, no more than five schools had a population with more than 52 percent black students.[4]

Meanwhile, the community improved levels of residential integration. The "index of dissimilarity," or the fraction of residents who would have to be reassigned to achieve perfect integration, can be used to measure the degree of residential integration in metropolitan areas. (A score of one indicates total segregation, while zero denotes perfect integration.) In 1970, Charlotte's dissimilarity index was 0.69; by 1990, the index fell to 0.61.[5] In terms of student enrollment, white flight, and enrollment decline, instability during the 1970s was followed by racial stability and modest enrollment growth during the 1990s. Overall enrollment began rising substantially in 1980; in the early 1990s, the percentage of blacks in the district stabilized and is expected to decline. In other words, the district was experiencing a growth in the proportion of white students that was projected to increase.

The Late 1980s: A Fraying Consensus

During the mid-1970s to the mid-1980s, integration in Charlotte was viewed as "the proudest achievement of the century," with a consensus that integration played an important role in improving educational quality, fairness, and race relations in the district as a whole.[7] Through the early 1980s, then, the prevalent view was that busing and desegregation went hand-in-hand with academic achievement, equity, even economic prosperity.

In the middle and late 1980s, however, the prointegration consensus began to fray. New sources of tension and instability undermined support for the status quo. Although not all the sources of discontent were directly related to the busing plan, they helped foster a willingness among school board and business community leaders to overhaul the school system and mandatory assignment. The Reagan administration had launched broad-based attacks on the use of busing for racial integration; the resurgence of antibusing sentiment in Charlotte mirrored the prevailing national political mood. The issues that helped undermine support for the busing plan can be divided into three broad categories: demographic change and instability, educational quality, and equity.

Demographic Change and Instability

As noted, Charlotte-Mecklenburg schools experienced a period of white enrollment decline, declining enrollment, and instability during the 1970s, followed by one of racial stability and growth during the 1980s. Since the late 1980s, growth has been primarily due to an influx of white, middle-class families settling in the southern and eastern fringes of the county. Consequently, the pattern of districtwide racial change—which became increasingly black in the 1970s and then stabilized in the 1980s—has changed again. The 1990s is a period of dramatic expansion, with total enrollment in the schools projected to increase more than 25 percent by the end of the decade.

During the 1970s and 1980s, Charlotte's Chamber of Commerce spearheaded an aggressive drive to attract new businesses to the county and cement Charlotte's position as a leading center of distribution, financial, legal, and other services. In 1988, in large part because of the success of Charlotte's efforts, businesses seeking to relocate chose North Carolina more frequently than any other U.S. state.[8] A huge number of affluent white newcomers from the north and midwest began to settle in the southern and eastern fringes of the county. One-fourth of all Mecklenburg residents moved into the county in the last five years.[9] Many of these northerners moved from areas that had had no experience with racial integration.

Approximately 50 percent of all black students live within the central city section of the school district; white students are dispersed throughout the suburban areas.[10] School leaders expect demographic growth will be highest in the southeastern and northern edges of the county. These high-growth areas have the smallest concentrations of black residents.

In the late 1980s, these emerging demographic trends began to undermine the consensus in favor of the mandatory assignment plan in two respects. The rapid—and racially bifurcated—demographic shifts in Mecklenburg County vastly complicated the task of maintaining racial balance in the school system. As Frye Guillard observed, "a rigid, immutable formula—devoid of annual tinkerings—was a contradiction in terms in a city of rapid growth and demographic change." The 1992 report of an outside expert concurred that "instability has been the hallmark of the assignment process."[11] The plan was forced to rely on continuous adjustments to remain functional and, therefore, could not offer parents a very wide scope of choice with respect to school assignments. In early 1988, the recently hired superintendent, Peter Relic, held a series of community forums on the proposed changes to the assignment plan. The forums were monopolized by recently relocated parents who used the opportunity to express their opposition to the pupil assignment plan and to busing in general. This constant adjustment and resulting frequent school reassignments became an important source of community discord.

Second, white newcomers typically raised in segregated white communities placed little if any importance on integrated education. They were thus unwilling to make any sacrifices (real or perceived) to preserve desegregation in Charlotte.[12] Although it is difficult to find evidence directly corroborating this assumption, it was universally held among those interviewed, many of whom offered a wealth of personal and political anecdotes to illustrate the claim.

A 1994 sociological study of Charlotte found that middle-class (usually white) newcomers to Charlotte placed a negative value on integrated education, as they linked it with inferior educational quality.[13] Stopping to deliver a brief campaign speech in Charlotte in October 1984, President Ronald Reagan decried busing as a practice "that takes innocent children out of the neighborhood school and makes them pawns in a social experiment that nobody wants.... And [that] we've found out...failed."[14]

Although Reagan's comment was met with a stony silence, the view he espoused gained credibility and momentum as the decade progressed. In the 1986 school board election, a right-wing Christian fundamentalist made neighborhood schools the centerpiece of his platform and won a seat on the nine-member board. In 1988, four pro-busing incumbents were defeated. Of the four new board members, two expressed their willingness to explore alternatives to mandatory busing; one explicitly declared her opposition. Although opponents of busing failed to gain a majority on the board in the 1990 election, by the early 1990s the antibusing point of view had gained a visible foothold in the ranks of the school board leadership.[15]

Educational Quality

A second source of tension during the 1980s was the growing perception that the schools were not providing what was referred to as "quality" education. The district's first attempt to address disappointing academic performance was in June 1978, when the superintendent, Jay Robinson, received the results of new state competency tests, which measured minimum competency skills to be acquired at the elementary level. The results indicated that fully 80 percent of black students and 40 percent of white students in the eleventh grade failed either the math or reading components. Robinson's response was to enforce more stringent attendance and disciplinary policies.[16]

Between 1978 and 1985, Robinson's policy appeared to be effective, as scores on the California Achievement Test—especially black students' scores—began to rise dramatically.[17] Yet it is unclear whether these apparent gains represented real educational improvement. The test used in this case, the CAT, was not renormed until 1986.[18] Generally speaking, test scores are likely to rise in proportion to the age of the norms being used, both because of improving achievement nationwide and teacher familiarity with the tests. Nevertheless, whether the alleged gains were real or illusory, the perception that education was improving and that the interracial achievement gap was narrowing fostered a sense of pride and optimism among district residents for the first half of the 1980s.

By the middle of the decade, however, this perception began to change. Several local observers suggested that the loss of public confidence in the schools began to accelerate after Robinson resigned in 1986.[19] On the basis of empirical data alone, the cause for this dramatic fall in public confidence is difficult to ascertain. But dissatisfied newcomers played a key role in convincing the community as a whole that the educational system was in dire straits. This perception of widespread educational failure matched a nationwide perception of national failure that had been inspired by the biting, largely rhetorical, *A Nation At Risk*, released with fanfare in 1983.[20]

In November 1987, the Chamber of Commerce formed a Task Force on Education and Jobs at the behest of several top executives of relocated business firms. Complaining about the poor quality of the local labor force, the relocated business elite urged the Chamber to help dismantle the race- and class-desegregated educational system, which they believed to be impeding educational success by lowering educational standards.

Roslyn Michelson and Carol Ray found that two factors contributed to the Chamber's decision in the late 1980s to investigate the quality of education: the formation of the Task Force on Education and Jobs and the Chamber's realization that something must be done to appease irate newcomers.[21]

Real or not, the system's educational failure was all but taken for granted by the time Superintendent John Murphy was appointed in 1991. In its brochure describing the new assignment plan, the district summarily condemned the quality of education with the blunt assertion that: "the overall state of education in Charlotte-Mecklenburg is not good. Measures of student outcomes are reflected by relatively low national test scores, too few students participating in advanced courses, and an unacceptably large gap in achievement between black and white students."[22]

In principle, however—unless one accepts the extreme view that the presence of low-income and minority students in a given educational setting would preclude effective educational reform—overhauling the educational system and overhauling the busing plan were two different issues. Joe Martin, school board member and prominent businessman in the county, said that he personally favored the option of "maintain[ing] the busing plan but simply mak[ing] the schools better." Yet, Martin said that

> the argument that carried the day though was that we had passed the time when we could [maintain the busing plan because] we had lost so much confidence that you had to do something different just to restore confidence....In the mid-1980s we had failed to recognize that educational quality was the issue and not integration. Had we done things then to improve the schools, we would never have gotten to the point of needing magnet schools or anything else. We got stuck, deafened by our civic pride, and didn't do what we needed to do to make the schools better.[23]

Humbled by the widening consensus that the schools were failing in their educational mission, the business elite was eager to extend a political olive branch to the disaffected newcomers. Relaxing the mandatory busing plan—the primary focus of resentment—seemed the logical choice.

Fairness

The third set of factors that undermined the integration consensus in the 1980s centered around the plan's perceived inequity or lack of "fairness." The most frequently cited of these inequities was the disproportionate burden placed on the youngest black children. Both of the two methods of mandatory assignment, school pairings and satellites, illustrate this inequity. In "two-way busing" or school pairings, kindergarten through third grade were typically located in black communities, while grades four through six were almost invariably situated in white areas. The fact that only black children were bused in the earliest grades was perceived as an unjust feature of the pairing strategy.

Meanwhile, the use of satellite zoning or "one-way busing" placed the burden of busing almost exclusively on black students. The report of an outside expert, Michael Stolee, noted that "most, if not virtually all, of the satellite zones which have been created for the purpose of school desegregation are located in black residential areas," so that "any given black child is much more likely than any given white child to be assigned to a school outside of his residential area."[24] In 1991, a total of 2,562 African American elementary schoolchildren or roughly 15 percent of all black elementary students were bused to schools away from neighborhood schools for their entire K-6 career. In contrast, only 293 white students—or roughly one percent of all white elementary students—were bused away from home for all six elementary grades.

In addition to the disproportionate burden it placed on black students, the plan also failed to promote the stabilization of integrated neighborhoods. According to Louise Woods, a member of the Committee of 25 (the school board desegregation advisory committee), as communities became integrated, they were rarely supported in a timely fashion with a neighborhood school. Instead, old busing patterns were usually maintained, so that the community's children were bused elsewhere as part of pairings or to satellites. Meanwhile, Woods said, black children from remote satellite zones often continued to be bused into integrated communities. All of these practices, Woods said, tended to discourage families from living in integrated neighborhoods and created cases in which naturally integrated "schools were becoming racially imbalanced by virtue of busing."[25]

A 1992 phone survey of Mecklenburg County residents conducted by KPC Research in Charlotte for the district staff suggests that by the early 1990s, dissatisfaction with the current plan had reached a critical mass within the white community. Out of 416 survey respondents, 63 percent said that the present busing plan should not continue. The district failed to provide separate statistics for white and black respondents, and only 93 black people were questioned. Fifty-five percent of survey respondents went even further, saying that busing to integrate schools is "not an effective procedure." The district also reported that 86 percent of survey participants wanted more choice in selecting the schools their children would attend, and 65 percent indicated their willingness to send their children to magnet schools.[26]

A poll conducted by KPC Research for the *Charlotte Observer* in Septemeber 1993 (with 425 randomly selected respondents) yielded somewhat different results, perhaps due to the different phrasing of questions. When asked to characterize their "feelings about busing for integration," 53 percent described themselves as somewhat or very much opposed, while 38 percent were somewhat or very much in favor (the remaining nine percent answered "don't know.") Fifty-eight percent of white respondents, 42 percent of black respondents, and 48 percent of all parents were somewhat/very much opposed.[27]

The New Superintendent: John A. Murphy

By the spring of 1991, the confluence of destabilizing forces helped foster a mood of crisis within the school board. Joe Martin, then chair of the school board's superintendent search committee, described the sense of urgency that led to the school board's ultimate selection of Murphy as the superintendent: "What we were facing was a loss of civic confidence in public schools, and we felt we needed to do something rather drastic to restore that confidence.... [Murphy] is not into consensus, not into team. He is into results. And he is flat out going to get his results, so he was much higher risk than the other three [candidates for the position]...."[28]

Murphy, who took office on the first of July, began his tenure by infusing an air of grand drama into his new educational reform agenda. Just one month after his appointment, he staged a back-to-school rally in the Charlotte Coliseum, attended by approximately ten thousand school employees and elected officials, and painted a dire picture of the district's educational performance. Emphasizing poor student performance and the interracial achievement gap, he resolved to make educational improvement the district's number one priority. In December 1991, Murphy convened a high-profile "World Class Schools Panel" composed of ten educational experts whose recommendations were subsequently collected in a fourteen-point document. In his first year, Murphy unveiled his educational reform package: bureaucratic restructuring, curriculum reform, a phasing in of new criterion-referenced tests, and performance accountability measures.

During his first year, Murphy began to develop a new, primarily voluntary desegregation plan to phase out the mandatory assignment plan. The decision to implement a magnet plan, Murphy claimed, had not been a foregone conclusion when he was hired. He recalled that Board members had originally expressed an interest in magnet schools and were "under a great deal of pressure from some elements in the community to return to neighborhood schools." Nevertheless, Murphy emphasized that it was the perceived poor instructional quality—not the desegregation plan *per se*—that Board members cited as their primary concern. He said that at town meetings he had held after his arrival the most frequent complaint was dissatisfaction with dislocations caused by busing and that those complaints convinced him that parents wanted to see an end to busing.[29] Woods, the League of Women Voters Member, however, disputed Murphy's account. At all three town meetings she attended, Woods said, parents expressed concerns mainly about discipline, instructional quality, and equity of resources. Complaints about the busing plan *per se*, she said, were few and far between.[30] (The district, unfortunately, made neither transcripts nor tape recordings of the meetings.)[31]

Martin said that although the desire to appease white resistance "was a factor" in Murphy's hiring, the motivation was: "not that cynical. If nobody had been complaining, we wouldn't have done anything…the whole community, black and white, was getting tense over the attack on busing. And so…it was necessary to do something, to say 'we're going to get over that so we can do something we should have been doing in the first place, which is improve the schools.'"[32]

Whatever the initial intentions of the school board, it is clear that soon after Murphy's arrival, the business community viewed magnet schools as the key to rallying the community behind the educational reform agenda.

Stolee's Plan: The Theory

The principal architect of the new magnet plan was Dr. Michael Stolee, Professor of Administrative Leadership at the University of Wisconsin at Milwaukee, an expert in producing "technical blueprints" for desegregation policymakers. By early 1992, the broad contours of the "Stolee Plan" had begun to take shape. Stolee recommended that the plan "be gradually changed from a mandatory plan with little voluntarism to a voluntary plan with few mandatory facets."[33] In other words, the magnet plan would gradually sever the mandatory busing linkages between inner-city neighborhoods and suburban neighborhoods, which had been "paired" to maintain racial balance.

The district proposed three strategies for maintaining integration. The new plan resolved to make the establishment of "stand-alone schools for neighborhoods and areas which are naturally racially balanced" its first priority. No particular stand-alone schools were specified in the first year of the plan, however, nor did the plan specify precisely *which* areas were to be considered "naturally racially balanced."

The second declared strategy of the new assignment plan was to develop "midpoint schools" as a more equitable strategy for student assignment. The concept of the midpoint school was straightforward: schools would be built equidistant from black and white residential areas, so that black and white students drawn from both areas would share equally the burden of bus rides.

The third, and most controversial, voluntary desegregation strategy was the creation of magnet schools. The goal of each magnet school was to attract enough black and white students to approximate the 60 percent white/40 percent black racial balance of the district as a whole. In its application for federal grant money submitted 25 February 1993, the district specified that magnets would be used only in areas that could not be desegregated through other means.[34]

This official characterization of magnets as a "strategy of last resort," however, appeared to contradict Murphy's own long-term goals for magnets, as he had stated elsewhere. In a March 1993 article in *Phi Delta Kappan*, Murphy was reported to have said that his "long-term plan" was "to create 113 magnet schools" — in other words, to transform nearly every school in the district into a magnet school.[35] Thus, in the first year of the new plan, the true function of magnet schools was subject to conflicting interpretations. The official version was that magnet schools would take a backseat to stand-alone and midpoint schools; yet Murphy's statements elsewhere seemed to belie this peripheral role, implying that "magnetization" would one day encompass every school.

The five-year plan, tagged "Student Assignment Plan: A New Generation of Excellence," was divided into three "phases" lasting from one to two academic years. For each phase, the plan specified in theory which schools were to be de-paired, converted into "midpoints," or transformed into magnets.[36]

In addition to the intrinsic benefit of greater parental choice, the district cited three advantages of the proposed magnet plan: enhanced elementary school "continuity," fewer separations of siblings within different schools, and increased parental involvement.[37] The district also asserted that the plan would be "more equitable" than the previous mandatory assignment plan in three respects. First, it would bring about "a reduction in the distance students are bused to assigned schools." Second, it would lead to "an increase in the number of black students who attend schools closer to home." Third, it would "increase the number of schools that are racially integrated, both in the percent of students attending and in the extent to which they are involved in high educational outcomes and activities."[38] To convince critics of good faith of his attempt to maintain desegregated schools, Murphy informed the *Charlotte Observer* that "if requests for admission to magnet schools did not result in integrated schools…he would use mandatory busing to achieve racial balance."[39]

Prior to the school board's vote on the five-year plan, several prominent black leaders objected to its immediate implementation on the grounds that they felt it would "continue to bus black students farther and more frequently than white students." Murphy countered their objection with the assertion that the plan would instead "give black students more opportunity to attend neighborhood schools."[40] In March 1992, the Board of Education unanimously adopted the magnet plan and agreed to begin phasing it in during the 1992 school year.

The same month, the school board appointed the Committee of 25, a group of parents, community leaders, and interested citizens. The watchdog group was instructed to evaluate the efficacy of the new plan in two respects: its impact on busing and desegregation trends (with particular emphasis on the promotion of integrated neighborhoods), and its effects on the equity of resource distribution.[41]

Dwindling Oversight: The Rise and Demise of the Committee of 25

In October 1993, the school board asked the Committee of 25 to conduct research on each of its tasks and to report its findings to the board. On 19 July 1994, the Committee of 25 presented its two summary reports to the school board. The Committee reports argued that the new desegregation plan—contrary to its stated goals—had fostered an increase in racial imbalance and inequities between schools. "There was a non-reception of the reports," Annelle Houk, an active League of Women Voters member who attended many of the Committee meetings, said of the school board's response: "They had a very tightly controlled meeting where only two people from the Committee of 25 were permitted to speak at all...and only three questions [from each Board member] were permitted after the presentation....It was a non-communication was what it was. It got the thing out of the way of the board."[42]

Two months later, on 16 September 1994, the school board voted 4-3 (with the chairman, William Rikard, abstaining) to disband the Committee of 25. The sudden dissolution seemed to come as a shock to the community at large, evidenced by a flurry of startled and critical letters to the editor in the *Charlotte Observer* the following week. But it came as no surprise to the members of the Committee of 25.

The Committee of 25 had not been the only independent community group systematically evaluating the new plan. The League of Women Voters (LWV) also devoted considerable time to analyzing the effects of the plan and issued its own series of reports in February 1994, which were as rigorous and data-intensive as the two issued by the Committee of 25. Citizens for Integrated Education (CIE), the Black Political Caucus, PTA committees, school-based coalitions, and other community interest groups also issued occasional reports assessing desegregation trends and promoting the cause of integrated neighborhood schools. Nevertheless, during its two-year existence, the Committee of 25 was the largest, most prominent and well-connected community oversight group in Charlotte-Mecklenburg, whose express function was the evaluation and analysis of the magnet plan.

Susan Burgess, a board member who opposed the Committee's dissolution, commented after the vote, "They're our insurance policy that we're not going to create a dual school system of haves and have-nots with magnets. If our magnet program cannot stand the scrutiny of a watchdog group, then we should all be concerned."[43]

Evaluating Charlotte's Plan

The degree of specialized knowledge required to grasp fully the technicalities of any desegregation plan is beyond the reach of all but its most intimate practitioners. Charlotte's current plan in its transitional form — a "hybrid" form containing magnet, "midpoint," "paired," satellites, and neighborhood school elements — is daunting in its complexity. A systematic analysis of the remedy, encompassing all schools, is beyond the scope of this chapter. Therefore, its goal is to examine the available summary data and secondary sources in order to address two questions.

First, what have been the trends in desegregation in Charlotte since the magnet plan was installed? Second, how fairly has the magnet plan distributed costs and benefits among black and white patrons?

Desegregation Trends

Like nearly all older Southern desegregation plans, Charlotte's plan only desegregates black students. For the purposes of this report, the Court's designation of "white" encompasses not only caucasians, but also all minorities other than African Ameicans. The percentage of "other" minorities was nearly 5 percent in the fall of 1994, two-thirds of whom were Asian. (The situation of "other" students will not be addressed here.)

Has the new plan been an effective desegregation strategy? The answer is yes and no. The district's most impressive achievement is the maintaining of integration in magnet schools. With few exceptions, schools that were converted into magnet schools became and remained racially balanced after 1991. When one surveys desegregation patterns in the district as a whole, however, a very different pattern emerges. The number of racially imbalanced schools has been growing steadily since 1991. Moreover, the *degree* of racial imbalance in most of these schools has also increased. The district's projections consistently under-estimate the degree of racial imbalance in both black-imbalanced and white-imbalanced schools, frequently by wide margins.

The term "racially imbalanced" requires some clarification. The proportion of black students in the district was stable at 40 percent. If the school system were perfectly racially balanced given that racial proportion, each school would contain 40 percent black students and 60 percent white students. However, neither the district court nor the Supreme Court required perfect racial balance. Mathematical ratios were to be used only as a "starting point" in developing a desegrega-tion order. Specifically, any elementary school whose percentage of black enrollment was no more than fifteen percentage points above the proportion of black elementary students districtwide and any sec-ondary school with no more than 50 percent black students were in compliance with the court order.[44] Even after the district court stopped intervening in the plan, these guidelines were maintained.

In keeping with the court's guidelines, all elementary schools above 55 percent black, and all majority-black middle and high schools, will be considered "black-imbalanced." For our purposes, it is also useful to look at schools that have unusually high concentrations of white students. Consequently, "white-imbalanced" will be used to mean less than 25 percent black at the elementary level, and less than 30 percent black at the secondary level. Although the Court never defined "white-imbalanced" schools as being out of compliance, this category has been widely used in Charlotte.[45]

Desegregation in Magnet Schools

The basic premise of magnet schools is that they can generate enough voluntary applicants of all races to attract an integrated student body. In 1992, the district received nearly 13,000 applications (50 percent from white and 46 percent from black families) for 3,995 spots in magnet schools—more than three applications for every magnet seat. Twelve new elementary magnets, six new middle school magnets, and three new high school magnets were opened in 1993.

The data suggest that magnet schools have been successful in attracting diverse student populations and improving their own racial balance. There were several exceptions to this rule: one new magnet school at each level had insufficient white enrollment in 1994, and one middle school had too few black students.

Another important measure of magnet school desegregation is within-school desegregation. As is shown in our studies of Prince George's County and Montgomery County, when only a fraction of students in any given school are enrolled in a magnet program—or when different groups of students are enrolled in different magnet programs—individual magnet programs may be out of balance even though the school as a whole is balanced. The district has repeatedly stated its intention to avoid this situation in its magnet schools.

In two of the three Academically Gifted magnets, black enrollment in magnet programs was more than 25 percentage points lower than their representation in the school as a whole. The situation in the International Baccalaureate magnets, a special program that awards high school degrees recognized all over the world, is less uniform. In two of the four International Baccalaureate schools, black enrollment nearly matches black enrollment in the school as a whole. In the remaining two programs, however, African American students are dramatically underrepresented. Because the district did not provide the necesssary data, there was no way to evaluate whether the degree of within-school segregation that occurred in 1993 decreased the following year.

General Desegregation Trends

Overall, segregation is on the rise in Charlotte. The number of racially imbalanced schools rose in the early 1990s, and these schools have tended to become more racially imbalanced over time. The first community group to identify this trend was the LWV. On the basis of their detailed analysis of school-level enrollment data from the fall of 1991 to 1993, the LWV concluded that "the system appears to be continuing to drift toward blacker and whiter schools. Across the three-year period, with few exceptions, the whitest schools got whiter and the blackest schools got blacker whether they were elementary, middle, or high schools."[46] The district countered the LWV's study by citing its own study, which revealed that "the percent of black students currently enrolled in predominantly black elementary schools decreased from [32] percent to [31] percent [between 1991 and 1993] —a clear reversal of the earlier trend. Those are the facts."[47] The LWV was considering overall racial balance, but the response from the district was dealing with predominantly black schools. Both of these measures tell only part of the story.

Neither the LWV's method of analysis nor the district's technique will be used in this chapter, for different reasons. On the one hand, the "clear reversal" alleged by the district is not borne out by more recent data. In the fall of 1994, the percentage of black elementary students enrolled in predominantly black schools held steady at 31 percent.[48] Moreover, the district's single indicator method does not take into account the *degree* of racial isolation in majority-black schools over time. The LWV's method, in contrast, charts racial balance trends in every school in the system, which raises important issues that go beyond the scope of this study. In the analysis that follows, racial trends are evaluated only in schools which have been either black-imbalanced schools or white-imbalanced (as defined earlier) since 1991.

The data indicate a clear increase in both the number of imbalanced black schools and the percentage of black students attending such schools, at all three educational levels. The number of imbalanced white schools also rose markedly at both the elementary and middle schools, although it declined in the high schools. The district's pro- jected enrollment figures for 1994 underestimated both the number of imbalanced black schools, and the percentage of black students attending them, often by wide margins. District projections also underestimated the number of imbalanced white schools at the elementary and middle school levels.

Detailed, school-by-school study of desegregation trends in racially imbalanced schools reveals several important trends. First, every school but one that was black imbalanced in 1991 remained so in 1994, unless it was converted to a magnet school. This trend held at all three educational levels. Second, at the elementary level, every black-imbalanced school but one increased its black percentage over the three-year period, often by a dramatic margin. Finally, the number of elementary schools that became imbalanced grew by more than half from 1991-1994. The growth of white elementary schools was nearly as pronounced. Forty percent more schools were imbalanced in 1994, and two-thirds of the original group increased their proportional white enrollment. The number of additional schools that became imbalanced by 1994 was more than 40 percent the size of the original group.

Is the Increase in Segregation Caused by Demography?

The district's attack on the LWV's report claimed increased segregation was actually the result of housing changes for which they have no repsonsibility. This claim was elaborated later the same year in a CMS document entitled "Demographic Changes in the Charlotte-Mecklenburg Community."[49] This line of argument has been used repeatedly by the district and therefore will be examined in detail.

In its report, the district uses 1980 and 1990 census data to make a claim that segregation was produced by neighborhood change.[50] In each of the census tracts studied, the percentage of black residents was either steady or rising in 1980 and fertility rate of black residents was higher. A rise in total black population over the decade was reinforced by a modest decline in white population. Thus, the district concluded that "the increase in the percentage of black students attending predominantly black schools is mostly a result of black population growth in attendance areas that are already either integrated or predominantly black."[51]

On the basis of one census tract analysis, the district made parallel claims about white suburban growth. There, the white growth far surpassed black growth. On the basis of these two studies, the district concluded that "demographic changes are contributing to the reduction in integration in many CMS schools."[52]

There are several important flaws in the district's argument. First, as the report itself concedes, the "census data do not allow for direct comparisons to be made between the years in question."[53] The use of 1980 and 1990 census data to analyze racial balance between 1986 and 1991 is a poor match. There are various other methodological problems. In some heavily white residential areas, an increase in black population might be expected to increase integration in CMS schools by facilitating the creation of a "stand alone" school serving an integrated neighborhood. Clearly, a much more sophisticated analysis of school-level racial balance and demographic changes is needed to establish an unambiguous linkage between residential trends and school desegregation.

Even more important than the empirical weakness of the district's claim is the reasoning behind it. The district has argued that "there is no evidence that CMS policies or practices are responsible for the increase in the percentage of black students attending predominantly black schools... [this trend] is mostly a result of black population growth in attendance areas that are already either integrated or predominantly black."[54] Yet the Supreme Court's ruling in *Swann*, as well as Charlotte's experience of the last two decades, undermines the legitimacy of this view. In a district with extensive busing and magnet schools, one would not expect racial trends in majority-black schools to be strongly linked with demographic trends in their immediate proximity. Indeed, a basic purpose of a good desegregation plan is to break this linkage and avoid the rapid expansion of ghetto schools as segregated housing expands. There is evidence, in fact, that widespread school segregation increases housing segregation, suggesting that segregation in schools might be contributing to housing segregation, not vice versa.

The general picture of desegregation trends that emerges from these analyses provides grounds for concern. Magnets, for the most part, have been successfully integrated, although there is significant within-school segregation in some programs. By one narrow measure, the percentage of black elementary students in majority-black schools, there has been a recent leveling off. However, using the standards established by the Court, the percentage of black students in black-imbalanced schools has risen not only at the elementary level, but also at all three levels. The overall trend is toward an increasing number of racially imbalanced schools. There are also increasing levels of segregation throughout the system. This pattern holds for both black-imbalanced and white-imbalanced schools (with the exception of white-imbalanced high schools). The district's projected enrollment figures for 1994 typically overestimated the degree of racial balance in both black- and white-imbalanced schools at all three levels, frequently by wide margins.

In a report released in December 1994, the LWV claimed that the district's decision to build a new high school and elementary school in the mostly white southeast edge of the county boded ill for desegregation in the county. The two schools, they predicted, would be white imbalanced and would further exacerbate the resegregation trend.[55] If continued, the long-term implication of these trends is that over the next decade, the system as a whole will become less integrated, with more schools diverging from the racial balance guildelines and schools at either end of the continuum becoming easily identifiable as "black" or "white." If the outer suburbs and parts of the city develop such racially identifiable schools, it is likely that aspects of the dual school system will be re-created and that residential integration will be destabilized.

Equity

In its original blueprint for change, "Student Assignment Plan: A New Generation of Excellence," the district concluded that the long-term goal was "to be more equitable than the current pupil assignment system."[56] Using a wide range of criteria, the plan has not succeeded in meeting this goal. Both the number of students bused and the average number of bus miles an average pupil rides to school have increased since 1991, although trends in mandatory busing overall, and for black and white students, are unknown.

Fairness in Busing

In its grant application to the U.S. Department of Education's Magnet Schools Assistance Program, the district stressed its intention to reduce "forced busing" in Charlotte-Mecklenburg, as well as the total miles students are bused to assigned schools:[57] "Given that a key desired outcome [of the magnet plan] is the reduction of school pairings and a reduction of mandatory busing, the number of paired schools and the numbers of students who are mandatorily bused (including the length of the bus ride) will be compared from year to year. Data from *transportation records* will be used to supplement this analysis."[58]

Many local education activists shared the view that de-pairing of elementary schools had led to an increase in mandatory busing for black students, without a comparable increase for white students. The de-pairing of these schools under the magnet plan reportedly created a situation in which white students would remain in a suburban neighborhood school for their entire elementary schooling, while black inner-city students would be bused to the outlying suburbs as satellites all six years.[59]

To determine the accuracy of this view, detailed data on the degree of busing under mandatory assignment, and under the current magnet plan, would be required. We requested data on the total miles and/or number of students bused at each educational level since 1991, but the district said that transportation data were not broken down by race, or by "voluntary" and "mandatory,"[60] even though this was the original intention of their federal grant. For that reason the picture is incomplete. But the North Carolina State Department of Public Instruction does provide data that gives a rough synopsis of recent transportation trends. From 1988 to 1991, the extent of busing seemed to be decreasing slightly or leveling off, as measured by the percentage of students bused and average number of miles an average student is bused to school. In 1991 and 1992, however, this trend was reversed in both respects. The percentage of students bused increased slightly, and the average miles bused per student rose substantially, during the first two years of the new plan.[61]

Reflecting the view of many people interviewed, the LWV report also contended that under the magnet plan, "most white children are bused only voluntarily while many, if not most, black children are bused involuntarily."[62] Since available transportation data are not broken down by race, there is no way to assess the validity of this claim. However, another set of closely related data may be used as an approximate measure. As described earlier, the term "satellite" in CMS refers to one-way mandatory busing.

Under the new magnet plan, the distribution of satellite assignments or "one-way busing" has increased or maintained the degree of inequity. In both years, black children continue to represent a highly disproportionate share of satellite assignments. While the number of black children in satellite assignments increased by 1,303 during the three-year period, the number of white satellite children increased by only 115. Although white students composed a larger fraction of all satellite students in 1994 than in 1991, this statistic is misleading because there are 50 percent more white than black elementary students in the district as a whole.

Thus, each black elementary student's likelihood of being bused increased by 5.1 percentage points, while each white student's chances increased only by 0.3 percentage points. There was a modest rise in the number of both black and white students assigned to midpoints. Although midpoint assignments for 1994 affected more white students in absolute numbers, the likelihood of participation was higher for blacks than for whites.

The key distinction between satellites and midpoints is that satellites involve "one-way busing" while midpoints involve "shared busing." In other words, a satellite (usually black) will be bused to a given school each year of attendance, while the students who reside in the community (usually white) can attend the same local school. A midpoint school, in contrast, is located equidistant from a predominantly black and a predominantly white area, so that *both* the white and black student populations are bused every year but for shorter distances.

Equity in Magnet "Shadow Zone" Assignments

When schools were de-paired, it was almost invariably the inner-city halves of the pairings that were converted into magnets. Admission to magnet schools is conducted by application. When a school is converted to a magnet, students living in the vicinity and/or students who formerly attended the school must submit an application for admission. Those students who do not apply or are not admitted to the nearby magnet are assigned to a different school, often as part of satellites. The Stolee Plan specified that in each magnet school, up to 75 percent of the total seats available to each race would be reserved for those who live in the neighborhood "shadow zone" of the school—"first the safe walk zone, then the former attendance area."[63]

Many of those interviewed contended that in practice, a disproportionate share of black students were displaced from their neighborhood school (that is, assigned elsewhere) when it was converted into a magnet. The Committee of 25 Pupil Assignment Report states:

> Once a school is depaired...we know that a number of children are displaced by the magnetization of their neighborhood school (that is, they are in the former attendance area of their nearby school but are reassigned elsewhere). It appears, however, that displaced magnet satellite children [residing in the inner city]—who thus far are overwhelmingly black—are typically bused for up to 13 years while white children are more likely to attend the depaired predominantly white neighborhood school [in the suburbs]....[64]

To substantiate this assertion, the Assignment Report documented that a total of 1,156 black children (excluding two satellites) were displaced from magnetized schools, in contrast to only 19 whites.

In its response to the Pupil Assignment Report, the district conceded that "when schools are magnetized, black students are more likely to be displaced than white students," but defended this phenomenon on several grounds. First, "given that the schools that were furthest out of compliance with integration guidelines were magnetized as a means of integration, and that these schools were located in primarily black communities, it is inevitable that some black students would not be able to attend the magnetized schools." The district's response also points out that magnets located in white suburban communities are likely to displace fewer students than in central city black areas because they tend to be less densely populated, average school capacity is larger, and 60 percent of seats are reserved for white students (compared to the 40 percent reserved for African Americans).[65]

In its review of the Pupil Assignment Report, the district specified that a total of 3,335 seats in central city K-12 magnet schools were reserved for black students residing in magnet shadow zones.[66] If it could be shown that 75 percent of the spaces reserved for African Americans in each central city magnet were actually being filled by students residing in the shadow zone, it would be reasonable to conclude that the district has "minimized" the displacement of black students. So far, however, the district has not provided any school-level data on "shadow zone" enrollment.

In a letter to the district, Louise Woods, former Committee of 25 member, pointed out the importance of this omission:

Stability and fairness for children around magnet schools needs to be addressed by the REALITY of the number of children who attend the magnet from the surrounding area, not the general rules which may not relate to the population of students around the school. For example, students who live near [Academically Gifted] schools are automatically eliminated from 4-6 placements if they do not qualify. Our information, such as the large numbers of additional satellite children...suggests, in fact, that in many magnets, few children from surrounding areas attend even if there are no qualifications for admission...particularly in areas where the population is transient, lottery selection may not be, as other systems have found, the best way to reach these students.[67]

Stand-Alone Schools and Integrated Neighborhoods

According to the district's pupil assignment blueprint for action, the first strategy to be used to desegregate the district is "establishing stand-alone schools for neighborhood and areas which are naturally racially balanced."[67] Both the LWV and the Committee of 25 have claimed that the magnet plan had not only failed to encourage, but had actually hindered racial stability in integrated neighborhoods. As of 1994, all magnets were located in areas already racially imbalanced.

Second, the Pupil Assignment Report argued that magnet schools have drawn away substantial numbers of students from integrated areas. The Pupil Assignment Report evaluated this phenomenon at the kindergarten, elementary, and middle school levels. In all three cases, it was found that the schools most affected by loss to magnets were in naturally integrated areas.[68]

Although described by the district as a "last resort" strategy, magnets had in fact superseded the establishment of stand-alone schools in integrated neighborhoods as the priority desegregation method. This concern was voiced by all three community groups involved in monitoring the plan—the LWV, the Committee of 25, and the CIE. As of fall 1994, only one elementary school, Idlewild, could be considered a "stand-alone school in an integrated neighborhood," serving only the population of the adjacent area.

Estimates of the number of neighborhood schools that their racial mix could be "stand-alone" schools varied widely between the district and other sources, and even between different documents produced by the district. Much of the confusion stemmed from the fact that "naturally integrated neighborhood" was never clearly defined by the district, nor was it clear precisely *which* schools were considered to be candidates for "stand-alone schools"—a situation noted in the Committee's Pupil Assignment Report. Documents produced by the CIE and Committee suggest that the relevant criterion should be a population of between 25 percent and 55 percent black (mirroring the school system's in-compliance guidelines), and that areas undergoing rapid demographic transition should be given preference.

The district, however, stated that for a school to "stand alone," serving an integrated neighborhood, African Americans must account for between 25 and 45 percent of the student population. Moreover, the district specified three additional criteria: "must *not* be moving quickly toward predominately one race or the other; must *not* require changing the boundaries of a large number of other schools to create the new boundary; and must be stable in school-age population—no growth or decline." The district included a list of nine elementary schools that could "stand alone" if their satellites were removed, and indicated that three would "stand alone" by 1995-96. The district also indicated that the remaining six could "stand alone" the following year, once their satellites were assigned to an "Education Village."[69] In contrast to the district, the Committee of 25's Pupil Assignment Report observed:

> From our best projections, it appears that there are at least 24 elementary schools and ten middle schools presently located in naturally integrated areas which could have a racially balanced attendance area without satellites. They could have continuity from elementary, through middle, to high school. It should also be possible to create integrated community schools in at least six other elementary schools."[68]

These conflicting accounts seem to indicate that the district has clearly established neither the definition of "naturally integrated neighborhoods" nor the criteria necessary for the establishment of "stand-alone" schools. The advantage of stand-alone schools is not only that fewer students are bused, but also that the integrated neighborhood reinforces the school experience and gives recognition to the accomplishment of an integrated neighborhood.

Summing up the Evidence: Theory Versus Practice

Desegregation in Charlotte, by nearly all measures, has declined modestly under the magnet plan. Although racial balance in most magnets has improved, segregation within some magnet *programs* is substantial. The percentage of black elementary students in predominantly black schools has recently leveled off, but the use of the "in-compliance" standards established by the Court yields a very different picture. The number of imbalanced schools has increased at all three levels, as has the degree of racial imbalance *within* imbalanced schools.

The district's projected enrollment figures for 1994 underestimated the degree of racial imbalance in all imbalanced schools that actually occured that year. Upon examination, the district's claim that any increase in school-level racial imbalance can be attributed to adverse demographics is not convincing.

In several important respects, the magnet plan appears to have worsened the inequity that had existed under mandatory assignment. In both relative and absolute terms, many more black elementary students are enrolled in satellite assignments, compared to a very small increase of white children in these schools. The district's oversight and monitoring committee reported that mandatory busing has increased under the magnet plan, mostly at the expense of black students. Data to examine these issues fully was not made available. The concept of naturally integrated neighborhood schools has not been developed. The fact that the establishment of magnets in integrated areas was apparently not considered, and that the very definition of the term remained in doubt after three years, implies that it was a low priority in the district, belying its supposedly high priority in the plan.

Looking ahead, what are the prospects for maintaining a desegregated school system? The factors working in desegregation's favor are considerable. Most important, Charlotte's merger into a countywide system gives it a unique practical advantage. Its favorable demographics, including a stable white enrollment, and the county's long history of substantial community support for integration cannot be underestimated.

In the summer of 1994, school board member Arthur Griffin attempted to generate support for a low-income housing initiative that would encourage the formation of integrated neighborhoods, particularly in high-growth suburban areas on the fringes of the county. Subsidized housing initiatives, especially "scattered site" projects, had been tried with considerable success in Charlotte during the early 1980s.[71]

On the other hand, the forces that might undermine the maintenance of desegregation seemed at least as formidable. Demographic changes are rapidly undermining school desegregation by concentrating black and white residents in different regions of the county. In a political sense, they are "erasing" historical memory because the business elite, traditionally a key locus of decision-making power, will be increasingly dominated by white newcomers who have not experienced desegregated schools and place little, if any, value on integrated education. The future of desegregation would be determined by school board elections and the selection of school superintendents.

The magnet plan seemed to be undermining support for desegregation by fostering a perceived opposition between desegregation and educational improvement. It appears that in Murphy's own ideology, court-ordered busing was single-minded in its focus on achieving racial balance and necessarily ignored the goal of educational quality. In an op-ed piece in *The Washington Post*, Murphy expressed his viewpoint that

> the sole focus of court-ordered busing is numbers that look good—the right number of students of each race in a school....The numbers that count are test scores, measures of the gap between black and white students, enrollments in higher-level classes and college, suspensions, expulsions and dropouts. Progress...is more difficult to measure than simply loading students on buses and achieving the right racial proportions.[72]

The implication is that desegregation and educational improvement are on opposite sides of an ideological continuum, one concerned solely with "statistics of color," the other concerned with education, the "true purpose of integration."

In an op-ed response, Annelle Houk criticized the implication of Murphy's argument:

> What John Murphy wrote...may foreshadow where he is leading Charlotte-Mecklenburg.... Busing is about moving students from separation to an equitable integrated education. If African American students do not learn effectively where they are bused, the failure is not in the buses. Murphy knows that the flaws of integrated education are not in busing itself. Otherwise, why would he recite a litany of discriminations that—even in Charlotte-Mecklenburg—accompany busing and stunt the learning of African American students?... These abuses seriously flaw the implementation of busing. However, they are injustices of administration that cry out for correction rather than justify abandoning busing.... excellence in education and equity in integration are not mutually exclusive. Both are essential. Charlotte-Mecklenburg must never choose between them.[81]

Integration Reaffirmed
Charlotte in the 1995 Election

The election in November 1995 for the Charlotte-Mecklenburg school system marked a clear rejection of Superintendent Murphy's decision to accept increased segregation under a magnet school plan. The leading candidate, who won by a large margin, for the three districtwide seats was board member Susan Burgess, a forceful advocate of desegregation. In its editorial on the election results, the Charlotte Observer pointed to her "vigorous advocacy for parent voices and integrated schools." Second place went to an African American incumbent, Arthur Griffin, Jr., who was also a critic of Dr. Murphy. The election system was also changed to include six members elected from voting districts within the county for the first time. Only one of the seats went to a strong supporter of neighborhood schools. One of the newly elected members was Louise Woods, who had been a leader of the LWV's critical study of local moves toward resegregation. The Charlotte Observer also highlighted incumbent John Tates's massive win against "what looked like a strong challenge from neighborhood schools advocate Will Webb."[74]

Superintendent John Murphy, the most active critic of desegregation policies among the educational leaders in the cities we studied, seemed to be riding the wave of the future in supporting the efforts of some Charlotte business leaders to end the county's desegregation policy. The day after the new school board was sworn in, he announced his resignation. In spite of an active search, including widely publicized discussions with Kansas City school officials, he ended up without a new superintendency and worked for a housing developer.[75] Much like a former metropolitan Louisville, Kentucky, superintendent, Murphy discovered that the widely discussed disenchantment with integrated education is a gross oversimplification and that advocating seemingly popular resegregation strategies can polarize a community. In Charlotte, the consequence was a reaffirmation of support for integrated schools in the district with the nation's first big city busing plan.

CHAPTER EIGHT

Slipping Toward Segregation

Local Control and Eroding Desegregation in Montgomery County

Susan E. Eaton

On an October night in 1975, the Montgomery County school board passed its first official policy designed to support desegregation in its public schools, the Quality and Integrated Education Policy (QIE policy). Its passage helped build Montgomery County's reputation as a progressive moral leader in social policy and education.

At the time, school board member Roscoe Nix, who later became the outspoken president of the county's NAACP chapter, spoke proudly of the school board's moral commitment and backbone in standing up to community opposition to the desegregation effort:

> We believe in an inclusive society and we intend to do something about that....I am proud of the fact that we are not attempting to appeal to that which is fearful, but to appeal to that which is good.... This may not have satisfied everyone, but avoids playing on fear and appealing to the beast in people. Quality education and integration are not mutually exclusive goals."[1]

Many community political leaders and community activists in Montgomery County, a district of 114,000 students adjacent to Washington, D.C., were optimistic about the policies and later about the magnet schools that grew from the effort, saying they had found a route toward integration that was far preferable to mandatory plans.

Montgomery County was able to avoid court-ordered mandatory desegregation because unlike many of its southern neighbors, officials there have never faced a desegregation lawsuit. They avoided such plans because in 1977 officials started a small voluntary magnet school program that followed the 1975 school board policy. After the adoption of a magnet school policy, educational leaders put in place more locally controlled desegregation policies that were never challenged in court. By 1983, the district had a policy requiring the school board to consider correcting racial imbalances once a school's minority composition differed more than 20 percentage points from the racial composition of the school district as a whole.[2]

It is informative to focus on the results in Montgomery County, as many courts and politicians are increasingly putting faith in this type of locally controlled plan that assumes school boards will work on their own to prevent segregation and inequitable policies. And if locally controlled desegregation offered and monitored only by local officials could resolve the problem of segregation, Montgomery County could very well have been the place it would happen. This is because the county has many favorable preconditions that increase the likelihood of successful locally controlled desegregation efforts.

The county is wealthy,[3] supportive of public education, has a solid middle-class enrollment, and a history of progressive ideals and activism. The county is generally liberal in ideology. Most residents vote Democratic, suggesting that there might be higher relative community support for policies designed to create integration and reduce inequality.[4] Perhaps most important, Montgomery County still has a substantial white student population—the schools were about 58 percent white in 1995—which makes racial integration viable.

But the proud local goals of 1975 quietly shifted away from integration over time. By the mid-1990s some Montgomery County schools, including some of the magnet schools, have become more segregated.

In spite of its touted voluntary integration policies, the county's schools have, overall, become more isolated, with measures of segregation and concentrated poverty increasing sharply from 1988 to 1994. Not only are larger proportions of the county's minority students concentrated in high-poverty, disproportionately minority schools, but larger proportions of white students are isolated in disproportionately white schools. These trends are apparent even when controlling for the racial change that has occurred in the district over time, meaning that the segregation cannot be attributed solely to large-scale racial changes at the district level.

The locally controlled policies and voluntary programs neither triggered sufficient action to create better integrated schools nor spurred policies or programs to prevent the spread or exacerbation of concentrated poverty. Even policies expressly intended to promote integration ended up increasing segregation in some schools. The evidence from Montgomery County suggests that "local" unchecked voluntary efforts that lack clear, enforceable guidelines and permanent status probably will not reduce racial isolation and create equal access over the long term.

Nearly two decades after his hopeful proclamations in 1975, Roscoe Nix expressed disappointment. "I don't think that this county can live up to its progressive image now.... The policies and programs do not foster integration. If you look at the elementary schools, the middle schools, the high schools.... you have intense isolation."[5]

Programs and Policies in Historical Context
Magnet Schools and the Original QIE Policy

Since 1977, Montgomery County has used two distinct magnet school models in an attempt to desegregate areas of the county that at one time were considered most vulnerable to segregation.

Elementary magnets are based upon the choice concept, with parents requesting transfer to specialized schools located in areas with large proportions of minority students. The school district's stated policy is that, in most cases, a child will be allowed to transfer into an elementary magnet school as long as space is available and as long as the transfer does not increase segregation. Meanwhile, some elementary students are automatically assigned to the magnets because they live in the school's neighborhood. Elementary magnet programs include communication arts, computer literacy, French, Spanish, reading and language arts, science and math, an academy program that emphasizes interdisciplinary instruction, and Gifted and Talented programs. At the elementary level, entire schools—rather than just programs within schools—are usually transformed into what is commonly called a "dedicated" magnet.

Admission to middle and high school magnets is competitive, with a selection committee choosing students who must have a good record of past school performance and favorable teacher recommendations. The programs in these schools are small, usually of about 100 students, and operate independent of the larger comprehensive school in which they are located.

Magnet schools are situated primarily in one of two "clusters,"[6] —Blair and Bethesda-Chevy Chase—just across the Washington, D.C., line in the county's southeastern section, where the minority population was originally concentrated. All ten of the elementary schools in the Blair cluster are magnets. Four of the seven elementary schools in the Bethesda-Chevy Chase cluster are magnet schools. One elementary school magnet was recently placed in Maryvale Elementary School in the outlying Rockville cluster. The county's three secondary level magnets are in the Blair cluster.

The seventeen-year history of magnets in Montgomery County should be discussed within the context of the rapid demographic change that has affected the region during the last two decades. As mirrors of their community, the public schools reflect the profound shifts in population. Both the portion of minority students[7] and the percentage of students living in poverty have risen dramatically in Montgomery County over the last two decades.[8] In 1970, just 8 percent of the school population were members of minority groups. That percentage grew rapidly, reaching 18 percent in 1978. By 1988, about 34 percent of the county students were members of minority groups. In the 1993-94 school year, 42.3 percent of students were members of minority groups.[9]

Until the mid-1980s, growth in the minority population was concentrated in the county's southern section, which fed students to schools in the "Blair cluster." The only other minority concentrations at that time surfaced nearby in the heavily white, racially polarized Bethesda-Chevy Chase cluster.

During the 1970s, the Rosemary Hills Elementary School in the affluent, mostly white Bethesda-Chevy Chase cluster was about 30 percent African American. This represented a sizable disproportion since, at the time, about 5 percent of the district's students were African American. The PTA at Rosemary Hills had filed a complaint with the federal government and had threatened to sue the school board over the increasing segregation. To avoid the PTA lawsuit and, as school leaders tell it, to fulfill a desire for integrated schools, the seven-member school board in 1975 adopted the desegregation policy to guide it in meeting its goal of "quality and integrated education."

Though hailed as a great beginning in the struggle toward integration, the original QIE policy, was really little more than an informal guide for school officials. The policy required no action to eliminate racial segregation in schools; it required only that the school board consider taking action if a school became racially imbalanced. With no monitor or firm guidelines, the policy's effectiveness hinged on school board action.

However, political events in the 1970s and early 1980s did provide the impetus for school leaders to use the QIE policy to foster integration. In 1974, the Office of Civil Rights within the U.S. Department of Health Education and Welfare (HEW) investigated the district at the request of the Rosemary Hills PTA. HEW, which during the Nixon administration did not favor mandatory school desegregation, found the county in compliance with federal law. Despite the favorable ruling, the investigation nonetheless forced the topic of racial integration onto the political agenda. Montgomery County's NAACP chapter was an outspoken participant in school board discussions during this time.

In this political climate, school leaders developed plans for integration. But because there was never a lawsuit, officials embraced the least disruptive, most politically palatable forms of desegregation. Harriet Tyson, a former board of education member and an architect of the magnet plan, articulated the school board's sentiments at the time:

> We couldn't politically bus in parts of the county...and for whatever reasons of political wisdom or cowardice, we decided...to take advantage of the naturally occurring differences in the schools that were in that part of the county....We put out brochures that described the characteristics of each of these schools...and encouraged people to choose schools based upon programs.[10]

Magnets seemed especially appropriate for the Blair area because the board of education was hesitant to break up the established Blair community and wanted to avoid school reassignment. School officials reasoned that the only way to create desegregation without disrupting the families living in the area was to somehow attract more whites.[11]

School officials sought a slightly different remedy in the Bethesda-Chevy Chase cluster pairing the increasingly African American Rosemary Hills Elementary School with the predominantly white North Chevy Chase and Chevy Chase Elementary schools. Under the plan, Rosemary Hills enrolled kindergarten through second graders and the other schools housed the higher elementary grades. (These schools eventually were developed into magnets.) This remedy did require some busing but the average trip was only about 2.5 miles.[12]

In 1983, school officials expanded magnet programs to the three secondary schools in the Blair cluster, to the remaining three elementary schools in the Blair cluster, and to four of the elementary schools in the Bethesda-Chevy Chase cluster.

Diminishing Attention to Desegregation

The weaknesses of both the magnet program and the locally controlled desegregation policies are manifest in the pockets of segregation that have developed in the district under its permissive policies.
However, school officials publicly stated that these patterns are the
result of housing patterns, not the result of school policies.[13]

Barron Stroud, director of the school district's QIE program, said
that the changing legal standards in Supreme Court decisions suggest that school officials are not legally responsible for correcting
racial imbalances in schools when those imbalances can be attributed to demographic change. (Those decisions and the housing-
related issues they raise actually apply only to school districts who
have complied with all requirements of a federal court order for several years. This justification, which is becoming quite common
among school districts trying to dismantle desegregation, is discussed
more fully in chapter 11.)

At it has evolved the QIE policy, in 1994, is no longer intended to
desegregate or to prevent segregation. Rather, its stated purpose is to
prevent other school policies and decisions from worsening the
segregation that does exist and is spreading. But this chapter shows
that school polices are not always implemented in a way that reaches
this goal.

In 1989, the school board voted not to take any action to decrease
the intense segregation at Broad Acres Elementary School, which, in
1993, was about 83 percent minority, with about 94 percent of students
living in poverty.[14] In addition, county school officials in 1991 moved
the heavily white French Immersion program out of the heavily minority Oak View School to Maryvale School, reducing white enrollment at
Oak View dramatically—from 42 to 6 percent in just one year.[15]

These actions and failures to act represent a shift in philosophy for
the board, which, as recently as late 1988, had paired two elementary
schools in the Kennedy cluster in an effort to reduce segregation.

Policies in 1994
The Amended QIE Policy, Diversity Profiles, and Educational Loads

The centerpiece of the civil rights policy in the county is still the QIE
policy, most recently amended on the anniversary of *Brown v. Board of
Education*, 17 May 1993. The policy supports action to "promote diver-

sity so that the isolation of racial, ethnic, and socioeconomic groups is avoided and the full benefits of integration are achieved." It points to particular values arising from school integration that "foster racial and cultural understanding" and "expands postsecondary opportunities for diverse populations."[16] It sets no specific requirements for creating integrated schools or preventing the spread of segregation. The focus of the policy is on improving academic performance and targeting schools for additional monetary aid.

In May 1993, the school board eliminated the specific desegregation standards in the QIE policy. The district replaced the standard with a new formula designed to assess the "diversity profile" of each school in order to determine which schools might be in danger of becoming segregated.[17] Under this policy, officials use a statistical formula to determine (1) the degree to which the population of each racial and ethnic group differs from the population of that ethnic group in the school district as a whole and (2) the rate of change in that ethnic group during the last four years.[18]

School officials use the results in making future decisions about where to build schools, where to draw attendance boundaries in the future to reduce overcrowding, and whether to grant student requests to transfer to schools outside their neighborhoods.[19]

After eliminating the specific 20 percent rule, Montgomery County Public Schools (MCPS) officials also developed a need determination formula in 1993 designed to provide information so school officials can funnel extra money or educational resources to segregated schools with high numbers of disadvantaged students. Schools with the most need are labeled as having large "educational loads" and are tagged for potential extra benefits. In 1994, the need determination conducted by the school department showed that schools with the greatest concentrations of poor children and the most segregation are also the schools defined as having the largest "educational load."[20]

In instituting this policy, school officials essentially concede the strong link between concentrated poverty and severe need but contend that it is not necessary to reduce the intensity of those two school characteristics. The educational load policy does not trigger any action to reduce the isolation contributing to a school's special need status. Officials cited two principal justifications for these policy changes. First, they said the original QIE policy, which red-flagged a school for examination once its minority population became disproportionate, stereotyped minority schools as inferior. Second, officials said they wanted a policy that reflected their commitment to achievement by funnelling extra resources to schools in an effort to help schools reach high standards.

It should be noted, however, that integration standards as they existed under the former 20 percent differential standard need not stigmatize high-minority schools. On the contrary, many of the district's segregated schools are disproportionately white. School officials could have cited these schools as being out of compliance and crafted policies to encourage the transfer of minority students.

Some school officials acknowledged this. Anne Briggs, director of facilities management, noted that some high-minority schools are running out of the space needed to accommodate white transfers. Yet little attention has been paid to integrating all-white schools in the county.

"You see a lot of these schools in the upcounty [northern] area that are almost all-white," Briggs conceded. "That's the other end of the policy that maybe we should be taking a look at."[21]

The Transfer Policy

MCPS allow students to transfer from their assigned schools under certain circumstances. Officials contend that the regulations guiding this policy promote desegregation by rejecting transfers that would exacerbate segregation. The district attempts to explain the rules of policy transfer to parents in the "School Transfer Information Booklet," a complex thirteen-page single-space document setting forth rights and conditions.

The document provides no information about the educational quality or options available at a school to which a parent might want to transfer his or her child. There is no counseling center through which a student might be able to receive such information and help in understanding transfer possibilities. Nor does Montgomery County provide transportation for transferring students.

However, school officials consistently pointed to their controlled transfer policy as one that supports integration efforts and cite it as an example of the district's continuing commitment to racial integration.[22]

What Are the Results of Locally Controlled Policies?

The following sections employ several standards to measure segregation and poverty in the Montgomery County school district. The measures document changes from 1988 to 1994 in the percentage of students in schools that were disproportionately minority, disproportionately white, predominantly minority, and the percentage of students in schools where the percentage of at least one ethnic and racial group was disproportionate.

The section also considers changes in the percentage of students attending schools where there are high levels of concentrated poverty.

Later, we review transfer request data made to and from three schools to determine whether officials have, as they have claimed, denied transfers that work against racial balance.[23] An exhaustive review of transfer requests is beyond the scope of this chapter.

Racial/Ethnic Disproportion

The first measure we consider applies the Montgomery County Board of Education's recently rescinded guideline that considered a school racially imbalanced once the minority population differed more than 20 percentage points from the minority population in the district as a whole.

In this chapter, "minority" is defined as the combined percentage of African American and Latino students. Asian students, who in Montgomery County are not significantly segregated or disadvantaged, are counted as neither minorities nor whites.

Since the combined percentage of African American and Latino students was 30 percent in 1993, a school is defined as "racially or ethnically disproportionate" once the combined percentage of the African American and Latino populations is smaller than 10 percent or larger than 50 percent. The calculations for 1988 are based upon the minority composition at that time, which was 23 percent African American and Latino.

The share of students in disproportionately minority schools more than tripled in five years. In 1988, only 10 percent of students attended such schools. But by 1993, the figure rose to 31 percent.

Thus, if the 20 percent differential standard were still in place, we would see far more schools being tagged for possible action to correct racial imbalance. Yet, it appears that even when the standard was in place, it failed to trigger significant action on the part of school officials, as many schools that were racially imbalanced in 1988 remained so in 1993.

Increases in racial imbalance are also apparent when the 2 percent differential standard is applied to each ethnic group, as opposed to the overall "minority" compositions. At the time the 20 percent differential was passed, the system was essentially biracial. This standard allows us to consider the level of segregation for Latino students as well.

In 1988, 20 percent of students attended such schools, and by 1993, that share had increased to 27 percent.

The next measure breaks down the racially imbalanced schools into two categories—disproportionately minority and disproportionately white.

These particular measures show that even when taking demographic change into account, racial isolation in schools increased for all racial groups from 1988 to 1993. Curiously, even as increasing numbers of African American and Latino students enrolled in the district, white students were increasingly likely to be enrolled in disproportionately white schools.

In 1988, 20 percent of African American students were in schools that were disproportionately minority. That figure increased to 24 percent in 1993. Among Latino students, 24 percent were in disproportionately minority schools in 1988, with an increase to 28 percent by 1993.

In examining trends in disproportionately white schools, we see similar increases in isolation, even when accounting for districtwide racial change. In 1988, 12 percent of all white students attended disproportionately white schools, but by 1993, 16 percent of white students attended such schools.

Predominantly Minority

This section employs a simple measure to determine the increase in predominantly minority schools since 1988. Schools are defined as predominantly African American or Latino if more than 50 percent of students are members of either group.

This "predominantly minority" measure is limited as it does not allow us to take into account the racial change in the county schools over the five years. Nevertheless, it is a standard measure and an important part of the full picture of desegregation trends in the county.

As one would expect, the percentage of students in predominantly minority schools increased since 1988 as more African American and Latino students enrolled in the district.

In 1988, only 6 percent of MCPS students overall were enrolled in predominantly minority schools. As for African American students, only 13 percent were enrolled in predominantly minority schools in 1988, compared to 24 percent in 1993. Only 14 percent of Latino students were enrolled in predominantly minority schools in 1988, but by 1993, that share had increased to 28 percent.

Montgomery County's black and Latino students are still far more integrated than African American and Latino students in the nation as a whole. In the 1991-1992 school year, 73 percent of Latino students were in predominantly minority schools nationwide, 66 percent of all African American students were in predominantly minority schools nationwide.[24]

Concentrated Poverty

Because of the strong correlation between race and poverty, the segregation of racial minorities almost always concentrates poverty in neighborhoods and schools.[25] Concentrated poverty has long been correlated with low academic achievement and inferior school environments.

Concentrated poverty is defined here as at least 40 percent of the student population being poor. Poor is determined as the percentage of students qualifying for reduced-price meals. (This measure of 40 percent equalling concentrated poverty has been used frequently in studies of poverty.)[26] The 40 percent standard represents approximately twice MCPS' districtwide elementary school average.

From 1988-1993, there was a dramatic increase in the percentage of students in high-poverty schools for every group but white students.

Latino students were five times more likely than whites to be in high-poverty schools. African American students were more than three times more likely than whites to be in high-poverty schools. And while the percentage of whites in high-poverty schools stayed more or less steady, moving from just 7 to 8 percent over five years, the rates for minority groups skyrocketed. For African American's the rate rose from 11 to 25 percent and for Latinos the rate jumped from 14 to 40 percent in just five years.

Nineteen schools, all of them elementary schools, had enrollments where more than 40 percent of the students were poor. About 16 percent of all MCPS students attended such schools in 1993. In 1988, only six schools had such high concentrations of poverty.

Poverty, overall, did increase over the five years in elementary schools, thereby increasing the likelihood of concentrated poverty.[27] (About 17 percent of the elementary school population qualified for free and reduced lunch in 1988, rising to 21 percent in 1993.)[28] Thus, poverty overall increased about 4 percentage points but student exposure to concentrated poverty increased at a much more dramatic rate, especially for black and Latino students. This means that increases in poverty levels in MCPS are compounded because they are confined mostly to the poorest, segregated schools while other schools remain unaffected.

Are Secondary Magnet Schools Desegregated?

Although desegregation is the stated goal of secondary magnet schools, the schools as organized reinforce patterns of racial stratification.

The selective programs, while they do draw whites, often do not contribute to desegregation in the larger school, whose racial and ethnic compositions remain segregated. Minority schoolchildren do not have the same degree of access to the "school within a school" magnet programs that are so attractive to white students. This has been a controversial point for many years. In 1990, Yale University psychologist Edmund Gordon, hired by the school board to study minority student achievement, criticized this trend: "The students of color are not enrolled in the magnet programs and must witness daily the gross inequities between their experience and those of their White magnet-enrolled counterparts. The 'school-within-a-school' model must be seriously examined."[29] The district made no changes in response to this report, which they had commissioned.

The influx of white students into the separate magnet program makes the school appear, on paper, to be better balanced racially. For example, without the magnet program, Blair High School would be 38 percent African American and 26 percent white. With the program, it is technically 33 percent African American and 31 percent white.[30] But this school-level racial "balance" can be a smoke screen, because the magnet program's racial composition is predominantly white and Asian and the larger school is predominantly African American and Latino.

Director of Enriched and Innovative Instruction, Wayveline Starnes, stressed that magnet school students take only four classes in which they are separated from the non-magnet students and are actually integrated for many of their other classes, such as physical education.[31] But a 1990 MCPS internal Department of Educational Accountability (DEA) report found that magnet students did not mix with regular school students and the programs had no "integrative effect" on the school as a whole. The racial composition of classes in the regular secondary school remained unchanged, the report said, because schedule configurations limited opportunities for magnet and non-magnet students to share classes. When magnet and non-magnet students did mix, it was usually in advanced classes where white and Asian non-magnet students mixed with white and Asian magnet students.[32]

According to the DEA report, "When seen from the viewpoint of the school as a whole, the influx of high achieving magnet students and the introduction of a block of courses attended largely by them has the effect of producing less overall classroom integration throughout the school.... Racial separation between classrooms follows directly from student racial differences in academic performance."[33]

Gordon, the Yale researcher, cited comments from students who complained about the segregation:

> The division between magnet programs and regular programs was a very big issue in some schools....The segregation of the magnet program from the rest of the general curriculum was very disturbing to many students....
> First of all, Latino and African American students complained about not having access to information about the magnet program which may keep someone from looking into the possibility of attending a magnet.
> ...Students in the magnets felt uncomfortable with the separation issue, but students not in the magnet program seemed to be hit the hardest. One student said, "The magnet students get the best of everything and we get nothing. I just feel like I'm not even wanted here," to which many other students nodded in agreement....It was common among non-magnet and magnet students to label themselves as smart or stupid according to their participation in the magnet and consequently, seemed to justify this segregation and inequality on the basis of talent and merit.[34]

The separate nature of the secondary magnets has contributed to a perception of inequity shared by some community members and MCPS staff members. Roscoe Nix, the former president of the county NAACP and school board member, offered a sharply critical view of secondary magnets. Secondary school magnets, he said, are "restrictive and elitist....What this program has done, is to create an elite, exclusive program to which minority students do not have equal access....In my mind, the program the way it exists now should really be abolished. It benefits a very small group of students and excludes many more."[35]

The DEA reports show that secondary school magnets have been successful at attracting whites, therefore creating more integration than there would be without them.

While the competitive programs are luring whites into predominantly minority areas, it may be at the cost of using admission standards that exclude significant numbers of African American and Latino students from the elite, well-regarded program(s) and separate students by race within a school.

Are Elementary Magnets Desegregated?
The Blair Cluster

Nine of the ten elementary school magnets in the Blair cluster are racially imbalanced, with more than 50 percent of students African American or Latino.

Eight of the ten Blair magnets have enrollments in which the percentage population of at least one racial or ethnic group differs more than 20 percentage points from the racial composition of the district. In six of the ten, more than 40 percent of the students in the schools live in poverty.

In six of Blair's ten magnets, more whites transferred out of the schools than into the schools in the 1992-93 school year.[36] Thus, the district's transfer program effectively compounded rather than alleviated segregation in six of these schools.

Bethesda-Chevy Chase

In the Bethesda-Chevy Chase cluster, just one of the four magnet schools would be considered racially imbalanced based on the standards applied earlier. None of the schools have high levels of poverty.

Within the cluster itself, however, there are striking differences between two closely situated schools. Rock Creek Forest school is 56 percent minority while nearby Westbrook, which is not a magnet school, enrolls 84 percent white students.

The distinct demographics of the two cluster areas might explain why the Bethesda-Chevy Chase cluster was more successful than

Blair in achieving integrated schools. For one, Bethesda-Chevy Chase cluster includes and is closer to affluent white areas. The conversion of a 5,000-resident-subsidized housing project into a middle-class development with higher numbers of white residents might also have been partly responsible for increasing white enrollment in the schools in the Bethesda-Chevy Chase area.

A Limited Role for Elementary Magnets?

School officials acknowledged that magnets have not been able to create substantial integration in all schools. But some officials stressed that elementary magnets have been important vehicles for creating at least some degree of interracial contact and diversity in many schools that otherwise would be even more segregated.

It is for this reason, said Wayveline Starnes, that the magnets should be retained:

> Have magnet schools been the perfect solution for Montgomery County? No.... But there are schools that have been able to hang onto a very active White population that really fights for the school and stays involved. In that way, I think that magnets, while they aren't achieving racial integration on most measures, are making sure that some of these schools don't become completely segregated.... They haven't achieved the type of racial integration we had been hoping for in the beginning, but maybe we were expecting too much at the beginning."[37]

In many cases, it is clear that there would be even higher levels of segregation if there were no magnets or no desegregation strategy. Starnes and other officials stress that part of the problem is that space at magnet programs is limited and that the schools cannot take in any more transfers without displacing students who already live in the schools' attendance zones. But it might also be possible to offer magnet options at some of the heavily white schools and recruit students from the heavily minority neighborhoods for transfer there. School officials have not pursued such options.

Flaws in Policy and Programs

The county has tried to achieve racial balance in the elementary magnets by making them attractive enough so that students from outside the cluster area will want to transfer to them. Under district policy, transfer applications to magnets that would exacerbate racial isolation or hinder integration efforts either in the magnet or the school from which the student wishes to transfer, will be denied. But, as evidence shows, school officials failed to deny magnet transfer requests that hindered integration at least during some earlier years.

The study of transfer requests to magnets conducted by the school system's Department of Education Accountability shows that many of the approved transfer requests to magnet schools actually worked against desegregation. The study found that among transfer requests between 1983 and 1985, about 86 percent of transfer requests in Blair and 85 percent of those in Bethesda-Chevy Chase were approved. Of those, 38 percent of the transfer requests in Blair and 30 percent of those in Bethesda-Chevy Chase had a negative effect on the racial balance of a school.[38]

"[G]iven the 86 percent approval rate...the current administrative practices produce essentially an open market condition," the report said.[39]

The DEA report showed that, overall, transfers did not improve racial balance in the Blair cluster elementary schools from 1981 to 1985. In fact, the transfers exacerbated imbalance in five of the ten schools in the Blair cluster.[40] In two schools, Pine Crest and Piney Branch, the incoming transfers had no effect on racial balance.[41]

On the other hand, the transfers had a small but "positive effect" on the racial balance of schools in the Bethesda-Chevy Chase cluster.[42] Although transfers to the Bethesda-Chevy Chase cluster usually had a positive effect during these years, in two of the schools, Rock Creek Forest and North Chevy Chase, racial balance worsened because of demographic changes.[43] According to the report, "Transfer effects in (Blair) elementary magnet schools go against racial balance about as often as they contribute to racial balance...while in B-CC the transfer effects on school racial balance are consistently positive."[44]

A more recent examination of transfer requests to Blair elementary magnets for the 1992-93 school year shows that six of the ten magnet schools lost white students as a result of transfers. In other words, the number of white students approved for transfers into the predominantly minority magnet schools was smaller than the number of white students who were allowed to leave those schools.[45] This shows not only that the magnet program is not powerful enough to attract high numbers of white students, but that in a majority of magnets, whites are more likely to flee the schools than come to them.

An earlier but more comprehensive review of MCPS magnet transfer requests by George Washington University Professor Jeffrey Henig suggests that if desegregation is a goal in a magnet plan, parental choice should be controlled. Henig analyzed more than 450 requests made in 1985 for transfer into MCPS elementary magnets. A bivariate analysis of transfer requests by race showed that white families are most likely to seek transfer into schools where the percentage of minority students is relatively low. African American and Latino parents, however, were more likely to seek transfer to schools where there were higher proportions of minorities. Minority families sought to attend schools in neighborhoods where incomes were relatively lower and where more people were poor.[46]

These findings are consistent with the DEA study indicating that many magnet school transfers hindered rather than fostered racial balance. Henig's study might lead one to speculate that families might feel more comfortable putting their children in school with members of their own race and ethnicity and economic class. But, more significant, the data suggest that unregulated parental choice that allow these trends to manifest themselves may result in segregated schools.

Henig concludes:

> Montgomery County provides a conducive environment for choice: its wealth and lack of severe urban problems means that school officials have more room for innovation than do their counterparts in many struggling school systems, and the absence of a history of court-ordered busing and severe racial polarization increases the likelihood that parents will be free to evaluate schools on the basis of their programs, resources and performance instead of the racial and class composition of their students and the neighborhoods in which they live. Even in this conducive environment, giving freer rein to parental choice would seem to have done little to diminish the potency of racial and class factors in structuring the school environment.[47]

Henig shows that at least in the years his research covered, the school system failed to inform adequately parents about magnet options. Equal information is generally seen as the first necessary prerequisite for equity in a voluntary choice program. Henig based his findings on a survey conducted by the MCPS DEA that showed more than one-third of elementary school parents—the constituency at which the transfer program is aimed—were not even aware that magnet programs existed.[48] The findings were based upon a telephone survey of 1,083 parents. Responses to a survey question revealed that about 35 percent of the parents had never "heard the term 'magnet school' or 'magnet program.'" Even more dismaying is that 36 percent of the parents with students *in magnet schools* had never heard the term "magnet school or magnet program." This ignorance on the part of parents with children in magnet schools might be explained by the fact that some students, by virtue of where they live, are automatically assigned to magnet programs and these parents may not be aware that their neighborhood school is a magnet school. Latino parents were least likely to have heard the term "magnet school" or "magnet program," with 59 percent saying they had never heard either term. White parents were the most well informed, with about 28 percent saying they had never heard the terms.[49]

Neighborhood and School Stabilization
Did Magnet Schools Prevent White Flight From Schools and Neighborhoods?

In conceding that racial integration has not been achieved in many magnet schools, most school officials stressed that racial integration, per se, is no longer the primary purpose of magnet schools. Rather, they said, the magnets' primary purpose is to stabilize the population of the southern area clusters. School Superintendent Paul Vance articulated this view: "They [the magnets] have been important tools for integration in that they really reclaimed a lot of the White, middle-class presence that had been draining from that area....They are an important stabilizing force."[50]

The question of whether secondary school magnets stemmed white flight or stabilized neighborhoods is difficult to answer. Answering the question conclusively would require a longitudinal study of how many families who live in a given area would have left or put their children in private schools over time if it were not for the magnet schools. To date, no such study has been conducted. This section will review the existing data to determine the degree to which the population in the schools and neighborhoods in the Blair and Bethesda-Chevy Chase clusters have stabilized. One can only speculate about the degree to which the magnet schools may have caused or contributed to this stabilization.

The Blair Cluster

White enrollment in the Blair elementary schools has been stable for nearly a decade. Specifically, 1,530 white students attended the elementary schools in 1988 and 1,534 white students attended those same schools, five years later, in 1993.[51] This is a positive, significant development because many areas with high concentrations of minorities tend to destabilize, with the white population decreasing and the minority population increasing. A 1986 report by the MCPS DEA documented the limitations of magnets effect on racial balance and the low transfer rate. But it also concluded that by 1985, racial balance had stabilized in Blair's elementary schools.[52]

However, this does not mean that the percentage of white students will remain the same, even if the number of whites remains stable. This is because the white transfer rate may not be strong enough to offset the larger number of African American and Latino students who are assigned to Blair-cluster elementary schools and who will move into secondary schools in the coming years. The African American and Latino enrollment in Blair's elementary grades is increasing, while the white population, again, remains the same. Even though the population of whites has remained stable over time, the Blair magnets would have to attract increasing numbers of white students for the schools to maintain that stability. Alternatively, the cluster would have to be expanded or more minority students would have to decide to transfer out of the area. It is clear that the successful stabilization of the white population, while a significant accomplishment, is not sufficient to counteract the population shifts occurring in the cluster area that contribute to school segregation.

These trends have already begun to manifest themselves at Blair High School and the middle schools in the Blair cluster. Since 1988, the proportion of white ninth through twelfth graders has declined from 37 percent to 31 percent in 1993. The percentage of African American students has stayed the same, but the percentage of Latino students has increased from 15 to 19 percent in 1993. The percentage of Asian students has increased just 1 percentage point from 12 percent in 1988 to 13 percent in 1993. The percentage of white students at Eastern Middle School declined from 39 percent in 1988 to 33 percent in 1993. The percentage of African American students during this time increased from 28 percent to 29 percent. The percentage of

Latino students also increased, from 20 to 23 percent. The percentage of Asian students increased from 13 to 14 percent.

At Takoma Park Middle School, the percentage of white students declined from 42 percent in 1988 to 37 percent in 1993. During this time, the percentage of African American students rose from 31 to 32 percent, the percentage of Latino students increased from 14 percent to 15 percent, and the percentage of Asians rose from 13 percent to 15 percent.

Racial balance trends in elementary and secondary schools cannot tell us whether or not the secondary magnets actually have *affected* the stabilization of neighborhoods by retaining whites and middle-class residents, because school enrollment data include not just neighborhood residents, but residents from outside the cluster area as well. The magnet school enrollment at secondary schools and elementary schools is, to at least some degree, an indicator not of stabilization of the white population in the neighborhood, but rather, of the attractiveness of the schools to students outside the neighborhood. To determine neighborhood stabilization, it is necessary to consider population trends outside of the schools.

The most recent report from Blair showed that the percentage of white Blair-cluster *residents* in grades 9 to 12 declined at a faster rate than the county average. The percentage of white students living in the area declined 34 percent between 1985 and 1989, compared to a countywide drop of 27 percent.[53]

Unless more affordable or mixed-income housing is opened in other areas of the county or formal transfer programs with transportation are developed for minority students to predominantly white schools, Blair cluster will continue to enroll a highly disproportionate number of minority students and disadvantaged students.

Bethesda-Chevy Chase Cluster

Desegregation in the Bethesda-Chevy Chase cluster has improved remarkably since 1975, when an intensely segregated, high-poverty school—Rosemary Hills—sat in the middle of a predominantly white and affluent area. In recent years, racial balance has improved even more and schools that were once heavily minority have evened out considerably.

Since 1985, the minority composition in the cluster magnets has improved dramatically, from 18 percentage points above the overall county average to just 3 percentage points.[54] Since 1988, the number of white students attending magnets in the Bethesda-Chevy Chase cluster has increased by 33 percent.[55] There is little question that the population in this area has been stable. What is not as clear is how much effect the magnet schools had on achieving this stabilization.

As early as 1986, DEA concluded that other factors, such as housing, birth rates, and changes in school assignments, had more of an effect on racial balance, in both Bethesda-Chevy Chase and Blair than did the transfers to magnet programs.[56] Housing shifts also have contributed to the most recent racial changes and stabilization apparent in the Bethesda-Chevy Chase area. In several interviews, school officials noted that the large, dilapidated 1,122-unit, 30-acre[57] Summit Hills low-income housing complex near the Washington, D.C., line had housed several hundred mostly minority students since the 1960s. The Summit Hill complex, officials said, became run down and, eventually, gentrified, bringing in mostly white young professionals, many of whom commuted to Washington, D.C., to work.[58] This change is reflected most prominently in enrollment figures from the Rosemary Hills elementary school, which is now 67 percent white.

Even school officials were quick to credit the changes in racial composition to the changes at the Summit Hills complex.[59] "The change you see there is really because of housing," said Wayveline Starnes, the director of enriched and innovative instruction. "Magnet schools could not have produced changes that dramatic."[60]

It is certainly plausible that magnets helped retain whites in the neighborhoods, thereby preventing higher levels of residential segregation. But the most accurate conclusion might be that magnet schools were one of several factors that stabilized or improved the racial balance in the two neighborhoods.

Analysis of Transfer Requests

In Montgomery County, parents are permitted to request transfer from an assigned school. During the years considered here, district policy required that transfers that would exacerbate segregation at schools where the minority (black and Latino) population differed more than 20 percentage points from the district average be denied.[61] In 1991, the minority population was 28 percent.[62]

Citing these controls, school officials have claimed repeatedly that the transfer policy is an initiative that contributes to racial integration. In July 1994, however, district officials said they had never analyzed the results of the policy and thus did not know if it was having a positive effect on racial integration.[63]

The school district does not provide transportation for students who wish to transfer from schools.[64] According to a July 1994 U.S. Department of Education study, Montgomery County's lack of transportation for transfers is unusual, especially at the elementary and middle-school levels. According to the study, 72 percent of school systems that offer elementary transfer choice options also provide free transportation. Also, 57 percent of all middle schools and 48 percent of all secondary school districts provide transportation for transfers.[65]

The evidence suggests not only that the county's "controlled" transfer policy is not far-reaching enough to have any measurable positive effect on racial balance, but also that transfers may be having a negative effect on racial balance. Therefore, the very policy that school officials have publicly cited as working in favor of integration has failed to do so in transfers to and from at least three of the county schools most vulnerable to increasing segregation. The three schools considered here are Greencastle, Glen Haven and Broad Acres elementary schools.

Greencastle Elementary School

Greencastle is located in the county's Paint Branch cluster, in the eastern section of the county. In 1991, Greencastle Elementary School was 42 percent white, 44 percent African American, 6 percent Latino, and 8 percent Asian. The percentage of white students at the school declined from 51 percent in 1988 to 34 percent in 1993. The percentage of African Americans increased from 33 percent to 52 percent during those years, while the Latino and Asian populations have been relatively stable.

According to school district data, there were twenty-three transfer requests for transfer from Greencastle for the 1992-93 school year. Of those requests, fifteen were approved, six were denied, and two were withdrawn. Of the fifteen approved:

- nine worked against desegregation, mostly at Greencastle, the sending school, primarily because white students were allowed to leave the increasingly minority Greencastle for such schools as nearby Galway and

Burtonsville, where higher percentages of the students were white;

- four worked in favor of desegregation, primarily because African American students from Greencastle chose schools with smaller percentages of African American students and where the racial compositions of those receiving schools were not disproportionately minority;

- two had no effect on desegregation.

There were twenty-seven requests for transfer into Greencastle school for the 1992-93 school year. Of those, twenty-three were approved. One was pending and three were denied. Of the twenty-three requests approved:

- twenty-one worked against desegregation, primarily because African American students transferred to Greencastle from schools that had lower (not disproportionate) percentages of minority students;

- two worked in favor of desegregation when white students transferred from schools with higher percentages of white students.

Glen Haven Elementary School

Glen Haven Elementary School is located in the Einstein cluster, in the southeastern section of the county. In 1991, Glen Haven was 35 percent white, 37 percent African American, and 17 percent Latino. From 1988 to 1993, the percentage of whites in this school declined from 45 to 37 percent. The percentage of African Americans, in the school increased from 29 to 36 percent, and the percentage of Latinos rose from 13 to 18 percent during those years.

There were twenty requests to transfer from Glen Haven in the 1992-93 school year. Of those, fourteen were approved and six were denied. Of the fourteen approved requests:

- eleven worked against desegregation at either the sending or receiving school. This occurred either when whites at Glen Haven left for schools with higher percentages of whites or when minority students left Glen Haven to attend schools that had disproportionate percentages of African American or Latino students;

- three worked in favor of desegregation at either the sending or receiving school or both.

According to school district data, there were twenty-three requests to enter Glen Haven in the 1992-93 school year. Of those, eleven were approved, eleven were denied, and one was pending. Of the eleven approved:

- eight worked against desegregation, one worked in favor of desegregation, and two had no effect on desegregation.

Broad Acres Elementary School

Broad Acres Elementary School is located in the southern end of the Springbrook cluster, in the county's southeastern section. In 1991, Broad Acres was 4 percent white, 37 percent African American, 41 percent Latino, and 18 percent Asian. The percentage of white students at the school declined from 7 percent in 1988 to 3 percent in 1993. The Latino population increased from 32 percent in 1988 to 52 percent in 1993. In 1989, the county school board voted *not* to take action that would have reduced the segregation and concentrated poverty at Broad Acres.

There were seven requests for transfers from Broad Acres for the 1992-93 school year. Five of these were approved, one was denied and one was listed as pending. Of the five approved requests:

- All five worked against desegregation at the receiving school because minority students left Broad Acres to attend another disproportionately minority school.[66]

According to school district data, there were fourteen requests made for transfer to Broad Acres. Eleven of the requests were approved, one request was denied, one was withdrawn, and one was still pending. Of the eleven approved requests:

- eight worked against desegregation because African American or Latino students transferred into Broad Acres;

- three had no effect.

The net effect of transfers was negative.[67] The transfer policy that has been cited by school officials as proof of a progressive, effective desegregation strategy has worked against the goal of desegregation to and from each of the schools examined. School officials have argued that their definition of segregation now differs from the standard used above and that they have recently employed a more complex formula to determine when a school needs transfer controls.[68] Nevertheless, during the time that the 20 percent standard was in place, it appears that school officials ignored the standard and approved transfers that hindered segregation efforts even at Broad Acres, the county school where segregation is most extreme.

Clearly, no matter what standard of segregation is applied, if the transfer policy really is designed to support integration, as school officials have repeatedly claimed, then transfers should have been controlled at Broad Acres where only 4 percent of the students were white in 1991.

The transfer policy as employed by the school district in these three schools hindered desegregation efforts by facilitating white flight from racially and ethnically changing schools and by allowing minority students to transfer into schools that were already disproportionately minority.

Achievement Trends

After reviewing an incomplete working draft of this chapter, school officials criticized this analysis, complaining that it focused on the less relevant issue of integration, while ignoring what officials referred to as "the continuing success of our educational policies in addressing racial and ethnic disparities in academic achievement."[69] School officials argued to the press and in correspondence that they should not be criticized for their desegregation policies, since minority achievement showed such tremendous improvement. Saying their attention was rightly focused more on achievement than on desegregation, they charged that we should be acknowledging their superior accomplishments in improving minority student achievement.

But when we examine achievement data in response to the criticism, the available data provide a much more complicated and far less positive picture of achievement than that offered by school officials. Test score data are, of course, always limited in usefulness. And the data supplied to us by the school district are neither complete nor detailed enough to conduct a comprehensive analysis of school performance. But since school officials claimed the existing testing data showed success, evidence for the claim will be examined here.

It is actually extremely difficult to determine conclusively whether the school district has successfully narrowed the achievement gap between African American and white students and between Latino and white students. There are several reasons for this, mostly related to limitations and problems with the available data. According to the data that do exist, the gap between white and African American students and between Latino and white students has narrowed on basic skills tests, but when other measures are considered, gaps have even widened in some cases and persist on the most recent measures available.

The Success for Every Student Plan

In January 1992, the Montgomery County Board of Education adopted the "Success For Every Student Plan" (SES). The plan was built, in part, on the findings and recommendations made by Gordon, in the 1990 Study of Minority Achievement. The plan called for a concerted effort to raise student achievement and reduce racial gaps in academic achievement in the county. The report emphasized the need to improve math performance, acknowledging that math "continues to be the largest separating factor in student success among some students." Math was described as "the gateway subject that helps to determine success in future academic study."[70] The plan set many goals for academic improvement and promised to watch the outcomes. The report did not cite segregation of minority students by race or poverty as problems. One passage in the policy called for "reducing the isolation of ethnic groups and language minorities by increasing the diversity in staffing, classroom compositions and schools to reflect more accurately the society in which we live," but none of the specific strategies spelled out any way to reduce segregation.[71]

In December 1993, school officials released the Second Annual Report on the outcomes of the SES plan. The report summary said that "disparities still exist but less so now than two years ago in many of the outcome areas." School officials stressed the steadily improving passing rates on the state's minimum competency test, The Maryland Functional Test. The district reported progress for African American and Latino students on some measures, but the report did not show narrowing gaps on some of the most important measures. In some key areas, in fact, gaps between white and minority students increased because as minority students made progress, the white students were making much more progress, thereby widening further already large gaps.

A July 1994 report from the Board of Education-appointed Advisory Committee for Minority Student Education concluded that a review of data and school district practices showed that "...not much progress has been made during the last five years even though plans have been put on paper."[72] In its recommendation, the committee continued, "Our analysis of Success for Every Student proved to be a formidable undertaking. The main reason for this was the lack of data and information....The Advisory Committee's conclusion is that if Success for Every Student is to succeed, more monitoring is essential at the implementation level."[73]

Assessment measures are considered below. The purpose of this chapter is not to link achievement measures to desegregation trends, but to evaluate the district's claim of success in reducing achievement gaps.

Completion of Ninth-Grade Algebra

It is instructive to look at what the district has defined as one of its key goals—increasing the rates of completion of algebra by ninth grade. The completion of algebra at this time has been shown to be a key factor in determining whether a student will attend college.

Overall, in the district, completion rates climbed by 6.3 percent in the three school years from the fall of 1990 through the spring of 1993. For whites, the increase was 8.3 percent. For Asians, the increase was 5.4 percent. Both of these increases came from already high starting points. For African Americans, there was a 5.9 percent increase from a starting point that was less than half the Asian rate. For Latinos, who had the lowest initial rate, the gain was also the lowest, at only 3 percent. Latinos, then, ended up with a completion rate of about 36 percent, compared to 82 percent for Asians and 77 percent for white students.[74]

Whites eliminated one-fourth of their previous achievement gap with Asians, but African Americans eliminated only a tenth of their original gap and Latinos only a twentieth of the original gap. The system made good progress, but the original gap between white and African American students and white and Latino students became even wider.

Enrollment in Advanced Placement Courses

Another good measure of college preparation is the percentage of students enrolled in honors or advanced placement courses. A relatively large share of students in Montgomery County take such courses and that share increased from 1990 to 1993. The overall increase was 3.6 percent to a district rate of 49 percent.

The increase was 5 percent for whites, to 56 percent; for Asians, a 4.3 percent increase to 65 percent; but for African Americans, only

2 percent; and for Latinos, 3 percent. Both African Americans and Latinos ended up at 27 percent—less than half the rate of the other two groups. So, overall, the rates of enrollment were improving, but the gaps between racial and ethnic groups were actually growing wider despite efforts to reverse that trend.[75]

Percent of Students Taking the SAT and SAT Scores

According to data included in the Advisory Committee for Minority Student Education's July report, the percentage of students taking the Scholastic Aptitude Test (SAT) has remained constant in the district, overall, but declined slightly for African American and white students and declined most substantially for Latino students. This test is a necessary prerequisite for the vast majority of four-year colleges and many two-year colleges.

About 74 percent of all students districtwide took the SAT in 1991 and the same percentage took the test in 1993. About 56 percent of African American students took the test in fiscal year 1991 and 54 percent took it in fiscal year 1993; the percentage of Latinos taking the test declined from 48 percent in fiscal year 1991 to 39 percent in 1993.[76] The gap between white and African American students remained stable in these two years, but the gap between Latino and white students widened on this measure.

The committee noted that SAT scores overall increased in the district and also increased for whites (1024 to 1036), Asians (1016 to 1030), and African Americans (798 to 822), and declined for Latinos (918 to 901).[77] The gap between white students and African American students declined on this measure (from 226 to 214 points) and the gap between white students and Latino students increased (from 106 to 135). As seen in other measures cited here, despite the progress of African American students over time, they continue to have the largest achievement gaps between their scores and those of others, as well as the lowest scores on this measure. SAT scores are of limited value because takers do not represent a valid sample of the student population.

Often, SAT scores decrease when larger shares of a population take the test, thereby increasing the chance that low individual scores will lower the overall average. In cases such as this, lower overall scores might very well be seen as a sign of success, as larger shares of students are at least taking the exam that is important for gaining future access to college. However, this appears not to be the case in

Montgomery County, since lower percentages of Latinos took the test over these two years and the percentage of African American students taking the test remained stable.

Maryland Functional Tests

One of the measures, the Maryland Functional Tests, is an examination only of the most basic skills high school students need to earn a diploma and therefore cannot provide information about performance on more challenging tasks. School district performance on the exam is measured only by how many students passed the test, not by a raw score. Thus, the data are limited in usefulness because they fail to document differences between, for example, a student with a perfect score and a student who barely passed. Nor can simple passing rates illustrate how performance on the test translates into classroom skills. The math and writing functional tests have been given by the state since the early 1980s, and the reading test since 1977. The longevity of these tests increases the likelihood that curriculum might have been geared to the exam.

Based on the results from these tests, it is clear that gaps between the racial and ethnic groups have narrowed over time, though math passing rate gaps are 21 and 18 points respectively between whites and African Americans and whites and Latinos. However, it is also important to note that when statistics are examined to show the percentage of students who failed at least one test, the gaps between African Americans and whites and between Latinos and Whites are more apparent and are significantly wider.[83]

The California Achievement Test

Measured overall improvements on the California Achievement Test, administered by the district from 1980 to 1989, were based on outdated norms established in 1977. This means national norms used for comparison were not representative of the actual national norms of achievement that existed the year the test was taken,[79] although general substantial improvements in elementary-level academic achievement had occurred nationwide from 1977 to 1989.[80] Therefore, when this test was given in Montgomery County in 1989, the percentile rankings did not reveal how Montgomery County performed relative to how the nation was performing in 1989, but only now these students performed relative to how students were performing in the nation in 1977. The use of outdated norms provides us with a particularly misleading picture of achievement during these years. The increased percentiles based on 1977 norms do demonstrate that there was improvement within the district over time, but the percentile rankings *do not* demonstrate that the scores kept pace with the improvements that were occurring nationwide.[81]

From 1980 to 1989, African Americans made the largest apparent gains in achievement, but Latinos made progress only in grade three and actually fell behind in grades eight and eleven. While African Americans did make the most progress, overall, their 1989 percentile scores still fell slightly below that of Latinos in grades three and five and matched the ranking in grade eight.

The gap between African Americans and whites from 1980 to 1989 narrowed by between six and nine percentile points depending upon the grade level considered. However, the gap between whites and Latinos widened in every grade level by between 4 and 11 percentile points. The largest achievement gaps under this measure in 1989 were between whites and African Americans in every grade but eight, where African Americans had the same achievement gaps as Latinos.

The Maryland School Performance Assessment Program

The state's mandated criterion reference test, the Maryland School Performance Assessment Program (MSPAP) has been in place only since 1992, so trends cannot be established. In addition, school officials did not have scores that were broken down by race and ethnicity at the school level. This made it impossible to compare achievement trends of African Americans and Latinos between schools. The scores, as released by the state, are broken down by race and ethnicity and then broken down again by gender. Therefore, it is impossible to aggregate the scores back to race and ethnicity to determine how a racial or ethnic group performed overall.[82]

District results indicate the percentage of males and females in each racial and ethnic group[83] who reached the state-established "excellent" and "satisfactory" standard.

Clear and substantial gaps exist between whites and African Americans and between whites and Latinos. Disparities in meeting the satisfactory standard range from a low of 7 percentage points between African American females and white males in reading in grade eight to a high of 43 percentage points between white females and African American males in math in grade eight. White students outscore Latinos and African American students on every measure at every grade level. Clearly, the narrowing gap in basic skills apparent on Maryland Functional Tests is not seen in more challenging measures, such as the MSPAP.

The MCPS' New County Criterion Reference Test

The county also gives its own self-designed criterion reference test intended to measure what the district teaches.

Results from the first administration of this test (in the spring of 1993) in grades four, six, and seven reveal achievement gaps between minority students and white students. Gaps are largest between African Americans and whites in grade four and between Latinos and whites in grade six. This test is delivered to a random sample of students at each grade level and results are reported in terms of what percentage of students met the county-established standard.

These data, too, are limited in usefulness because they show trends only in math and there was no data available for previous years.[84]

Do the District's Claims Stand Up?

Data fail to corroborate the MCPS's argument that racial gaps in educational attainment have narrowed considerably. There has been a convergence in passing rates for a low standard minimum competency test, but such tests of attainment over a low threshold do not provide good comparative information. Clear and large gaps remain on tests of higher order skills and on success rates in important college preparatory experiences.

What Has Local Control Done for Desegregation?

The magnet school program and other locally regulated policies designed to foster racial integration in Montgomery County are unreliable and an ineffective means for achieving desegregated schools. The policies and programs as they are presently designed and administered in MCPS simply have not been effective enough to offset the demographic change that contributes to school segregation and concentrations of poverty. There is also evidence that at least one school policy designed to support desegregation—the transfer policy—has worked against desegregation in some schools.

The eroding commitment to desegregation is manifest not only in the increasing segregation and concentrated poverty that has gone unremedied over the years but also in the official actions that knowingly increased or sustained segregation at two of the most segregated, high-poverty schools in the county, Broad Acres and Oak View elementary schools.

Both the elementary and secondary magnet school models used by the school district are fundamentally flawed. The elementary model has simply been unsuccessful in attracting substantial numbers of white children to heavily minority areas or in offsetting the demographic change that brought more minority students into certain schools. In 1992-93, in six of the ten predominantly minority magnets in Blair, more white students transferred out of the schools than transferred in. The programs have not been adjusted or refined to correct the shortcomings, and formal transfer programs have not been developed that would allow minority students to transfer to other schools and provide them free transportation to do it.

Secondary magnet schools do attract sufficient numbers of white students to a magnet program contained within a school, but this model fails to create actual racial integration. This is because though white students do attend a predominantly minority high school, once inside the school, they end up attending many classes within a smaller, often non-integrated program that is separate in most instances from the larger still mostly black and Latino school and its students. This model undermines the goal of racial integration and equal access because it excludes and stratifies students along racial and ethnic lines. The mission of locally controlled desegregation policies has evolved from its original purposes to create racial integration and abolish segregation to a less reformative one that seeks simply to prevent other school policies from increasing or worsening existing segregation and concentrated poverty. School officials do not expect to counteract or improve conditions and have said publicly that they want to try to sustain the current levels of integration by ensuring that school policies do not worsen the situation. The data show, however, that, in recent years, officials have been unable to live up to even this newer self-imposed mandate.

These basic flaws remain and shifting priorities have occurred, it seems, because the district does not live by any rule or regulation that would require integration efforts either to work or to stay intact.

Consequently, policies born from good intentions were watered down and eventually became powerless to create substantial desegregation in the face of rapid demographic change. School officials allowed segregation and concentrated poverty to increase as community and political pressure diminished after the 1970s.

The Montgomery County experience should prove informative to the many suburban districts across the nation that are facing racial and ethnic change in the 1990s. School officials in these changing suburban districts who desire integrated schools should consider the evidence in this case study before pouring all their resources into unchecked voluntary plans aimed at attracting whites to schools in high-minority areas. This evidence also suggests that mutually supportive housing and school policies designed to create and sustain integration may be the necessary course to take in order to prevent segregation in an area experiencing demographic change.

The Montgomery County experience suggests that failing to institute and stick to strongly enforced desegregation policies will make achieving racial integration increasingly difficult because locally controlled voluntary efforts without clear requirements may be vulnerable to competing political interests and apathy. State lawmakers who want to avoid racially polarized suburban school districts should consider passing statewide legislation that sets standards and requirements for racial or ethnic integration in local districts. Locally controlled efforts depend upon local political will that is diluted easily —through school board elections, the hiring of a new school superintendent, and shifting community priorities that pressure elected officials and educators. The Montgomery County experience underscores the need for federal policies and strategies designed to reduce and prevent rapid segregation of suburban areas undergoing change.

Civil rights litigators who are concerned about racial polarization or concentrated poverty in their community schools should consider lawsuits and should assist in the development and implementation of legislation aimed at reversing those trends; they should not rely upon local, voluntary efforts that do not have the force of law behind them and can be ignored or undone over time.

Finally, school systems such as Montgomery County, which have abundant resources to devise and implement policies for integrated education, should be pressed to do so before racial, ethnic, and economic divisions become more deeply entrenched.

CHAPTER NINE

Money and Choice in Kansas City
Major Investments With Modest Returns
Alison Morantz

In December of 1992, thirty newly elected Missouri state legislators toured Central High School, the showpiece of the Kansas City, Missouri, School District (KCMSD). As part of a court-ordered desegregation plan, the school district had converted most of its schools into magnets with special curricular themes and state-of-the-art facilities. The most expensive and well-publicized of the magnets, the $32 million Central High School, had been designated as a "Classical Greek and Computers" magnet and had been completed only months before the state legislators' visit.

"The first thing they showed us was the swimming pool," recalled Greg Canuteson, a representative from Liberty, an affluent suburb north of Kansas City.[1] "And of course [the school principal] described it as a 'natatorium.'" As the tour proceeded through the gymnasium and the weight training room, Canuteson recalled, the principal described the school's special dietary regimen tailored to athletes. Full-time staff, the principal explained, included a weight trainer, a diving instructor, a Russian fencing instructor, and a gymnastics coach.

Rounding out the tour, the legislators were ushered through a special room reserved for gymnastics, a fully equipped robotics laboratory, an indoor track, and a special wrestling facility.

The Kansas City school desegregation plan represents an extreme case of one popular type of desegregation remedy. During the decades of debate about desegregation strategies, many critics of mandatory plans have often said it would be more effective simply to give extra money to segregated minority districts. In this way, urban schools could be made good enough to lure whites back to the city and hold onto middle-class minorities. After the federal district court rejected the efforts of civil rights lawyers to establish a desegregation plan that would have integrated students from the predominantly white suburbs with students from the predominantly minority city, the court instead ordered an all-out effort to produce desegregation through choice and magnet schools.

Kansas City was given what most educators can only dream of: vast economic resources with which to take on the challenge of improving achievement and creating racial integration by attracting city and suburban whites to city schools through choice. Through the intervention of the federal district court in *Jenkins v. Missouri*, more than $1.5 billion was funnelled into the KCMSD between 1987 and 1995. The judge in the case could be called cautious in his rejection of a mandatory metropolitan plan that would have produced areawide integration. But, he has been criticized as a radical for the range and cost of the education and choice remedy. To fund the costly educational improvements, Judge Russell G. Clark assessed new taxes on district residents, triggering cries of taxation without representation. But the state of Missouri was forced to fund the lion's share of the remedy, sparking intense resistance among voters statewide; there was great resentment of such a disproportionate allocation of scarce state dollars to an urban, mostly minority school district. Nevertheless, when the Supreme Court reviewed the case in April of 1990, it essentially upheld the power of the judiciary to fund the remedy through a property tax increase, even without the consent of the district's voters.[2]

The judge in the case had viewed the extraordinary expenditures as necessary to create an attractive menu of "distinctively different" magnet schools. Each magnet, the theory went, would contain a set of unique, world-class educational facilities to lure white parents from within and beyond the school district boundaries. Unlike the remedy in neighboring St. Louis, the Kansas City plan had no mandatory components: transfers between the KCMSD and adjacent suburbs were encouraged but never enforced.[3] Suburbs, in other words, were not required to participate in any way, though suburban students could attend city schools.

In 1995, a more conservative Supreme Court ruled in a 5-4 decision that the district's goal of trying to attract whites to the city schools was not valid and, instead, that the lower courts should instead focus on the goal of freeing the district from court control and returning schools to the control of local leaders. While striking down this legal underpinning for Kansas City's reforms, the Court also reversed a ruling that cited still low test scores as justification for ordering the state of Missouri to continue paying for "quality of education" programs intended to upgrade the urban schools. In addition, the Court said Judge Clark did not have authority to grant raises to district employees.

The Court returned the case to the district court for more hearings, after which lower courts will need to decide the fate of the suburban transfer program, whether to reduce employee raises to earlier levels, and whether to release the state from its obligation to pay for improvements to city schools.

This chapter does not focus primarily upon the uncertain effects of the 1995 Supreme Court decision. It evaluates the plan and its promises several years after the ambitious program was implemented.

Touted as the solution to both poor achievement and racial segregation, the plan achieved only modest advances in both categories. As tools for desegregation, voluntary magnets alone do not appear to be powerful enough to reverse or even halt white flight. As vehicles for educational improvement, even the most ambitious and comprehensive magnet remedies may accomplish little without vigilant monitoring, skilled administration, and serious oversight.

Despite the apparent limitations of this program, the most devastating, though not unlikely, outcome would be for the district court to abandon, rather than redirect, the remedy at this stage. That choice would leave the city school district with a vast set of court-ordered programs it could not afford to operate.

It is important to remember that this is not the remedy that plaintiffs asked for. The plaintiffs had originally asked that segregated minority students in the city be given access to the already effective white schools in the suburbs. The story of Kansas City should make us reexamine court decisions against remedies that create opportunities for metropolitan-wide desegregation. But whether that remains a realistic strategy is questionable in light of the Court's 1995 ruling in *Jenkins*.

Civil rights lawyers may need to redirect their focus on interdistrict housing discrimination that created school segregation. In crafting legal arguments and remedies, attorneys will need not only to secure funding sources in advance. Plaintiffs who seek educational results or compensation must point to specific ways in which schoolchildren isolated in segregated, predominantly poor schools have been adversely affected by the conditions to meet the new Supreme Court requirements.

The Historical Setting

The state of Missouri is a border state between the North and South. As was typical in the South, the state constitution historically required separate schools for whites and blacks.[4] Six weeks after the *Brown* decision was handed down, the Missouri attorney general left each school district to decide "whether [it] must integrate."[5] For decades after racial integration became the law of the land, the state ceded all responsibility for enforcement to city and county governments.[6] Missouri did not participate in the Southern campaign of massive resistance to integration. But the state did nothing to achieve integration or break down its segregated system. By 1980, the state of Missouri had twice been found guilty by the federal courts of having helped perpetuate segregation.[7]

In the absence of state enforcement, Kansas City officials, like their counterparts across the state, employed a variety of measures to perpetuate the segregated educational system. Attendance boundaries were redrawn to minimize interracial contact.

Between 1950 and 1970, 67,000 white people left the Kansas City Missouri School District and were replaced by black incomers totaling 64,000.[8] These people were moving not only to smaller, mostly white districts within city boundaries, but also across the Missouri-Kansas state line.

The turning point came in 1969, fifteen years after *Brown*. This was the last year in which a majority of the school district's enrolled students were white (although a majority of the school district's *residents* remain white to this day), and also the last year in which city voters approved an educational bond measure. Despite the four times since 1986 that the district has registered a slight annual increase in white enrollment, the percentage of African American students in the district has climbed dramatically to its 1994 level of 75 percent.[9] District voters rejected educational levies nineteen times. In June of 1977, the Missouri Department of Elementary and Secondary Education lowered the KCMSD's state classification from AAA to AA status, a rating reflecting the declining quality of educational facilities and resources.[10]

By 1985, only a few elementary schools of the fifty in the KCMSD were performing at or above the national norms in reading and mathematics.[11] According to district court findings, "substandard conditions" such as "health and safety hazards, educational environment hazards, functional impairments, and appearance impairments" were rampant. "The conditions at Paseo High School," the court noted, "[were] such that even the principal stated that he would not send his own child to that facility."[12]

In 1976, the KCMSD—then 65 percent African American—came under the scrutiny of the Office of Civil Rights of the U.S. Department of Health, Education and Welfare (HEW). The agency was responsible for enforcing the 1964 Civil Rights Act that forbade federal funding to school districts operating segregated schools. In a highly publicized federal hearing, HEW threatened to cut off federal aid unless the district could prove that it was not legally responsible for segregation. In response to HEW's threat, Kansas City's Board of Education established a Community Task Force on School Desegregation to develop a plan to comply.[13] In the end, the task force chose to adopt so-called Plan 6c under which a 50-50 racial balance in most schools would be achieved through the maintenance of several all-black schools.[14] In the ensuing six months, the KCMSD and HEW waged an all-out legal and public relations battle over the validity of Plan 6c. Meanwhile, HEW continued threatening to withhold federal funds.

Although Plan 6c took effect in September 1977, a process with much more far-reaching historical consequences was taking place behind the scenes. The board-appointed task force concluded that in a district that was already 65 percent black, merely redistributing the existing student pool would fail to achieve significant interracial exposure. Several experts on the panel endorsed a "metropolitan" plan, which would have included two-way student transfers between the inner city and the mostly white surrounding suburbs. Only a mandatory busing plan of this type, the experts argued, would achieve an appreciable racial balance and halt the spiral of urban decline. Yet since a metropolitan plan would incorporate students from beyond the KCMSD's jurisdiction, the school board could not order such a broad plan on its own initiative. To do so would require the court's intervention.

Two days before submitting Plan 6c to placate HEW and maintain federal funding, the school board filed suit in federal court against eighteen school districts in Kansas and Missouri, the federal government, and the states of Missouri and Kansas, asking for a metropolitan desegregation remedy.[15] The case was turned over to Judge

Russell Clark. A Democrat from rural Missouri, Judge Clark was assigned the Kansas City desegregation case just three months after he was appointed to the federal bench in July 1977.[16] Preliminary hearings lasted a full year, from 1977 to 1978.

One of Clark's first actions was to force the Kansas City school district to switch sides. Though it had been positioned by its board as a plaintiff in filing the initial suit, Clark named the district as a defendant, anticipating that the KCMSD would be found liable for constitutional violations. At the request of several school board members, a local, private civil rights lawyer, Arthur Benson, agreed to represent the plaintiff schoolchildren. The NAACP Legal Defense Fund, a leading civil rights litigation group, later contributed substantial legal and financial support.

Although it was now positioned as a defendant in the case, the school district worked together with the plaintiffs over the next decade to sustain the case throughout the arduous process of trial and appeals. Thus, the early participation of the school district resulted in a curious alliance—plaintiffs and defendants working together as "friendly adversaries" toward a common goal of integration.

This special partnership between the plaintiffs and the school district is less surprising when one considers that both parties shared a strong interest in infusing badly needed funds into the dilapidated district. There is no question that both parties sought to rejuvenate the district through the implementation of a desegregation remedy.

Many people today see the plan as a way to get money from the state of Missouri, but that view is incorrect because the original plan sought a metropolitan—not a monetary—remedy. If the original goal was simply to obtain as much money from the state as possible, a metropolitan remedy would not have been the most promising strategy. A comprehensive magnet remedy would have been a far more lucrative desegregation method. The fact that the district and plaintiffs originally proposed a metropolitan plan, rather than a comprehensive magnet remedy, strongly undermines this "cynical realist" view of their partnership.

In filing a metropolitan suit in federal district court, the KCMSD plaintiffs carefully crafted their argument to meet the Supreme Court's demanding requirements for city-suburban desegregation.[17] The case developed by the plaintiffs and KCMSD attempted to demonstrate that the suburbs were not only "substantially affected by," but also helped cause the constitutional violations of the state of Missouri. Using an array of demographic and historical data, the plaintiffs argued that the state and local governments worked in concert with federal housing agencies to steer African Americans away from the suburbs and into the mostly black inner city, with the tacit and sometimes overt cooperation of suburban authorities.

Elsewhere, some courts have accepted similar proof as sufficient to fulfill the plaintiff's burden of proof with respect to *Milliken I*.[18] But Judge Clark relied on a narrower interpretation of *Milliken*. He dismissed the plaintiffs' argument on the grounds that he did not believe they had found a "smoking gun" that proved that the suburbs had directly caused segregation. When appealed to the Eighth Circuit, Judge Clark's decision was upheld by a one-vote margin. In his dissenting opinion, Chief Judge Lay argued that Judge Clark's decision had been premised on a "misunderstanding of *Milliken v. Bradley*" and that "the district court thus erected an improper proof burden for the plaintiffs to overcome."[19]

Judge Clark himself conceded that he had considerable latitude on the question of suburban liability. He speculated that had he decided to hold the suburbs liable, the Eighth Circuit "probably would have affirmed me."[20] In the absence of what he viewed as a direct violation, then, it was the judge's own discomfort with applying coercive measures—in this case interdistrict mandatory reassignments—that led to his decision. Although still defending the legal basis for his ruling, Judge Clark admitted that the initial ruling made the task of desegregation far more difficult and costly:

> Based upon hindsight it would have been much much much easier to integrate the Kansas City schools if I had kept them [the suburban districts] in.... So it would not have been necessary to come up with a lot of these plans, and with a lot of the capital improvements....I could have ordered some of the Kansas City school children transferred to the suburban districts, and vice versa...the very minute I let those suburban school districts out, I created a very severe problem for the court and for myself, really, in trying to come up with a remedial plan to integrate the Kansas City Missouri School District.[21]

The real problem in Kansas City, one typical of most American cities, stemmed from decades of white flight, which left the school district predominantly black. This meant, of course, that no amount of student reassignment within the district could produce full desegregation and that the black percentage continuously grew.

After the failed attempt to win a metropolitan plan, the plaintiffs reconsidered their options and decided to propose a comprehensive voluntary magnet plan. The magnet plan was chosen, explained Benson (the plaintiffs' attorney) as the only viable way to attract white students back into the system:

> We had lost the truly widescoped mandatory plan that we were seeking ...so then we looked at our options: well, how do we achieve desegregation in a district that is 75 percent minority? Well, the only way to do that is if we can get the suburban white kids back involved in our plan....So if we are going to do that voluntarily, what will it take to get white kids from the suburbs to come to our schools, remembering that our schools are decrepit, they're underfunded, the class sizes are huge, the classbooks are outdated? We concluded that what we needed to do was restructure the educational system and improve it...[but] we still wouldn't be able to get them to come from the suburbs unless it was different from the suburbs....so we realized we had to make them not only nearly as good as the suburban districts, we also had to make them special...distinctively different. And so that sort of led us to magnet schools.[22]

With the judge's approval, the plaintiffs and school district lawyers began to research the use of magnet schools as a desegregative tool elsewhere in the country. The educational inequity of magnet plans that had been established elsewhere soon became a matter of grave concern. Benson found that magnet plans typically created a "two-tiered system" in which resources and educational gains would be concentrated in magnet schools, while inferior quality and growing minority isolation characterized the remaining traditional schools. The only way to surmount this problem, the plaintiffs and school district experts concluded, was to "magnetize" all schools in the district and thereby avoid the potential inequity.

Throughout the following year, the school district and the plaintiffs' counsel began working on a comprehensive magnet school plan that would convert every senior high school, every middle school, and about one-half of elementary schools in the KCMSD into magnet-theme schools by the fall of 1991. The idea was that world-class facilities and unique educational offerings would impart a high-profile visibility to the magnet schools. This prominence, in turn, would enhance the district's "marketability" to white parents and help attract white transfers.

Legal precedent would have allowed Judge Clark to order a smaller plan. As he acknowledged in his 1986 court order, "[plans which] magnetiz[e] only a limited number of schools in a district…have been approved by the Eighth Circuit Court of Appeals and the United States Supreme Court."[23] Clark chose to implement the proposal of the plaintiffs and the KCMSD, which was unmatched in scope and magnitude. Judge Clark indicated that his decision was based on the desire to avoid the inequity of a two-tiered educational system and to ensure that there were "enough magnets to pretty much entitle every student that wanted to go to a magnet, the right to attend a magnet."[24] As stated in the 1986 court order, the magnet themes "would provide a greater educational opportunity to *all* KCMSD students."[25] Judge Clark's firm commitment to educational improvement for all district students, then, compelled him to implement a daring magnet plan far more comprehensive than plans that existed elsewhere.

Ironically, the attorney general's litigation strategy helped cement the plaintiffs' case. Even though the Eighth Circuit had already held the state of Missouri liable for segregation and discrimination in two other federal cases, the attorney general refused to concede the state's liability. According to Benson, the state's total refusal even to admit any wrongdoing, especially given the overwhelming evidence that the state perpetuated, even enforced, separate and inferior schools for black children, began to alienate the judge after the outset of the trial.[26] Judge Clark himself corroborated this view by characterizing the state's policy of "total opposition" as counterproductive and politically motivated.[27]

The state's next crucial decision, cited as a tactical error by all of those interviewed except the assistant attorney general, was its failure to offer a scaled-down alternative to the comprehensive magnet proposal. The state's legal representatives may have been constrained by their superiors in the state executive branch, who may have been tempted to pursue politically popular strategies even if they had the potential to drain the state treasury. Even after Judge Clark approved immediate implementation of the magnet school concept, the state continued to protest the judge's decision, instead of offering a smaller-scale, more cost-effective magnet alternative. Committed to a comprehensive plan and lacking a credible alternative, then, Judge Clark accepted the school district's plan to magnetize all high schools, all middle schools, and half of elementary schools in the district.

In 1986, once Judge Clark had accepted the full-scale magnet plan, the focus of the litigation shifted. The question was now how to finance the plan. Judge Clark specified that the state would pay between three-fifths and two-fifths to three-fourths and one-fourth, respectively, depending on the type of improvements being ordered. To ensure that the funding would be guaranteed, he made the state and the school district "joint and severally liable" so that if one party was unable to pay its share of the costs, the other party would have to make up the difference.

The problem with this financing structure was readily apparent. The school district, with its current budget, could not pay its two-fifths share. The district had failed to pass a school levy since 1969. The state enacted a variety of additional tax measures, which further impeded the district's ability to maximize its local tax revenue.[28] Unless some new source of local funding were found, the state would end up as the "deep pocket," financing not only its own specified contribution, but also the district's court-ordered share.

Meanwhile, however, the costly magnet plan was taking shape. On his order of 15 September 1987, Judge Clark approved the expenditure of $265 million for "the renovation and construction of approximately 72 schools and six other facilities through the fall of 1996."[29] The plan required the closure of eighteen school facilities and the construction of seventeen new ones.[30] Needless to say, these provisions were costly indeed—the quarter-billion-dollar figure reflected only the building construction and renovation. Additional costs for magnet instruction and programming were to be calculated separately.

In the text of the 1986 order, Judge Clark urged the KCMSD to seek new funding sources, so that the full financial burden of the remedy would not be shifted to the state of Missouri. In 1986 and 1987, the district followed Clark's order and introduced three ballot measures that would have raised taxes to pay the district's share. All three referenda were rejected by district voters.

In April of 1987, Annette Morgan, a state representative from the only affluent corridor of central Kansas City, introduced a bill in the state legislature that would enable Kansas City to finance its share of the costs through three new taxes—a sales tax, an income surcharge, and an earnings tax. "I was laughed off the floor," Morgan recalled.[31] By 1987, then, the plaintiffs and the school district had exhausted every traditional means of generating new local taxes.

In a historic ruling, Judge Clark noted the failure of these conventional methods and unilaterally imposed two tax measures to finance the school district's share of the costs. Property taxes within the school district nearly doubled. A new tax — a 1.5 percent surcharge on Missouri State Income Tax — was instituted for anyone, including nonresidents, who worked or did business within the KCMSD.[32]

Once again, the attorney general's legal strategy failed to prevent the court from making substantial claims on the state treasury. Combined, the property tax and the far more lucrative income tax surcharge generated all of the district's share of costs for the 1987-88 year.[33] If these new taxes were thrown out on appeal, the state would be forced to make up the difference. A "successful" appeal by the state, in other words, would drain more dollars from the state treasury. Nevertheless, the attorney general appealed all of Judge Clark's new taxing measures. On 19 August 1988, the Eighth Circuit Court of Appeals upheld all of the substantive components of the remedy and also the property tax, but rejected the lucrative income tax surcharge.[34] The local property tax thus became the sole source of generating local funds. In 1990, the Supreme Court affirmed the circuit court's ruling.[35]

In April 1993, Judge Clark rejected proposals for making changes in magnet schools, ruling that the measures were too costly. In October 1994, the Supreme Court agreed to consider the state of Missouri's two-pronged argument that improved test scores should not be a prerequisite for Clark to end oversight of the school district and that Clark overstepped his boundaries by ordering salary increases for nonteaching employees of the KCMSD.

In February 1995, the district and the state began negotiations in an effort to end the desegregation case. The negotiations were continuing in June 1995, when the Supreme Court struck what may prove a devastating blow to the desegregation plan, by attacking its central goal of attracting white students from suburban school districts.

The Costs

Costs continued to mount as construction proceeded. As of 31 March 1993, the total cumulative cost of the desegregation plan was approximately $1.15 billion. Of this amount, the State's court-ordered share was approximately $586 million, and the district's share was approximately $564 million. To fund an increase in salaries, the rate was increased 24 percent in July 1990.[36] As anticipated, the local property tax levy did not generate the district's full share of the costs; therefore, the state paid an additional $105 million. Thus of the $1.15 billion total, the state paid about $691 million.[37]

The state uses two measures to calculate per-pupil costs, "current" and "total" expenditures. "Current expenditures" includes instruction and support services, but excludes some types of costs such as capital improvements and capital outlay.[38] "Total expenditures," is an aggregate figure including all spending by the district.[39]

According to both measures, per-pupil costs in the KCMSD expanded dramatically between 1985 (just prior to the court order) and 1992. Current expenditures per eligible pupil increased by more than two-and-a-half times from $2990 to $7819. Meanwhile, the statewide average grew by only about 50 percent (from $2470 to $3683), and the eleven-district average increased by only 54 percent (from $2573 to $3972). When the *total* expenditures per enrolled pupil data are analyzed, similar trends emerge. Kansas City's total spending per enrolled pupil more than tripled during this period (from $3464 to $11,513), while the state average rose by only 56 percent (from $3030 to $4723) and the eleven-district average increased by 65 percent (from $3173 to $5223).[40]

When KCMSD per-pupil costs are compared directly to the statewide average, the disparity is also striking. In 1985, prior to the desegregation plan, KCMSD per-pupil expenditures were 10 to 21 percent higher than the statewide average, depending on which measure was used.[41]

This dramatic trend of increasing expenditures was broken in 1993, when total per-pupil expenditures in the KCMSD fell sharply, from $11,513 to $8917. The decline might have been caused by the fact that rebuilding had been completed at the time. Current expenditures declined to a much smaller degree, from $7819 to $7158. Given this recent decline in KCMSD spending, the disparity between KCMSD and statewide spending has also narrowed. For fiscal year 1993, total expenditures per enrolled pupil were 79 percent higher in the KCMSD; current expenditures were about 90 percent higher.

By 1988, KCMSD costs began to resemble per-pupil spending in St. Louis and two of St. Louis's wealthy white suburbs, Ladue and Clayton. Since 1985, spending in these three districts had been the highest in the state of Missouri. By 1989, Kansas City surpassed St. Louis's expenditure level and has continued to do so through 1993.

Meanwhile, taken as a whole, KCMSD expenditures since 1989 have been roughly similar to expenditures in Ladue and Clayton.

It would be informative to analyze whether KCMSD per-pupil spending for its magnet schools has been similar to national trends. Unfortunately, this type of comparison is not possible for two reasons. First, the district does not calculate per-pupil costs separately for magnets and nonmagnets. Second, reliable national data that would facilitate such a comparison were not found.

One of the first and only studies assessing magnet school costs on a national scale was published by social scientist Kent Chabotar in 1989, using data from 1981.[42] Using a stratified random sample of school districts across the country, Chabotar compared spending in 106 magnets and 588 nonmagnets for 1980-81 and 1981-82. Chabotar found that although magnet secondary schools cost more per student than nonmagnets, magnet elementary and intermediate schools actually cost *less* than their nonmagnet counterparts. Much of the difference, he found, could be explained by "educational economies of scale": magnets' higher fixed cost, when combined with relatively low enrollment at the secondary level, led to higher per-pupil costs; but relatively high enrollment in elementary and intermediate magnets outweighed disparities in fixed costs and thus led to lower per-pupil expenditures. At the high school level, where enrollment did *not* increase, average magnet expenditures in Chabotar's study exceeded average nonmagnet expenditures by no more than 23.9 percent for both years.[43]

Although Chabotar's study is severely limited in scope and applicability, it does seem to suggest that elsewhere in the country, magnet schools are not necessarily very costly when compared to nonmagnet schools. Relying on the limited data currently available, spending in the KCMSD is very high compared to state and local averages; since 1989 it has ranked among the top two or three districts in the state in terms of per-pupil spending. Judged comparatively in historical, local, and statewide contexts, then, per-pupil costs in the KCMSD were moderately high from 1987 to 1988 and have been very high since 1988 to 1989.

Where is the money going? Data from the start of the plan through early 1993 and program expenditures give a very rough, if somewhat deceptive, approximation of the distribution of desegregation funds.[44] Costs related to improving instruction and programming account for about 44 percent of the total desegregation budget.[45] Teacher salary increases account for another 8 percent.[46]

About 36 percent of the total went to the acquisition, construction, renovation, and maintenance of school facilities.[47] Transportation expenditures totaled about 8.5 percent. The remainder could be attributed to various costs such as interest and debt service.[48]

Some local critics believe the plan has overemphasized capital expenditures and costly magnet programming, and paid too little attention to attracting a high-quality teacher pool.[49] To evaluate the strength of this claim, we must examine the court's allocation of funds in more detail. According to the legal counsel for the teachers' union, *Jenkins v. Missouri* was the first desegregation remedy in the country to include salary increases for all district teachers on the assumption that improved quality required better teacher pay.[50]

The court approved a teacher salary package in the original 1987 order. In 1990, the parties reached a settlement that continued salary increases through the end of fiscal year 1992. When the settlement expired, however, the issue of whether and how much to raise teachers' salaries was hotly contested by the state, KCMSD, and the teachers' union. The state charged that the 1990 increase had "virtually no effect on increasing the quality of new hires or decreasing the quality of staff who left the District" and therefore that salaries should be rolled back to 1986-87 levels. The American Federation of Teachers argued that salaries commensurate with the projected average of urban districts nationwide were crucial to retaining and attracting high-quality teachers. The KCMSD, citing the district's "dire fiscal constraints," staked out the middle ground and endorsed a "roughly competitive" compensation plan that was below the national urban average, yet substantially above 1986-87 levels.[51]

Comparative data reveals that salaries in the KCMSD have been competitive with, but not uniformly higher than, salaries offered by nine suburban districts in the greater Kansas City area.[52] In 1995, the Supreme Court struck down the court order requiring payment of salary increases, ruling that lower relative salaries in the urban district could not be traced to intentional segregation.

Monitoring and Oversight

The justification for emphasizing magnet facilities and programs, according to Judge Clark's 1987 order, was to improve minority opportunity and desegregate the district:

[The court] is convinced that the students who are presently enrolled in the KCMSD are entitled to a vindication of past denial of constitutional rights now....First, the carefully chosen magnet themes would provide a greater educational opportunity to *all* KCMSD students....The Court also finds...that the proposed magnet plan is so attractive that it would draw non-minority students from the private schools who have abandoned or avoided the KCMSD, and draw in additional non-minority students from the suburbs.[53]

Beyond this general statement of purpose, however, the court did not specify any exacting criteria for "success" or "failure." The remedy included a complex array of facilities and educational programs tailored to the special theme of each magnet school. Yet Judge Clark indicated no plan standards of improvement for academic achievement test scores, attendance, or dropout rates, nor did he specify any numerical targets for desegregation. However, in 1993, the appeals court affirmed a district court decision ruling that KCMSD had failed to achieve partial unitary status citing test scores were still below national norms. (The Supreme Court reversed that decision in 1995, however.)

In 1985, the court appointed a ten-member Desegregation Monitoring Committee (DMC) to serve as the "arm of the court." The DMC included four subcommittees, each addressing a separate facet of the plan: desegregation, budgeting, education, and voluntary inter-district transfers.[54] The district provided the DMC with monthly and bimonthly reports, copies of all court filings, board actions and agendas, task force minutes, and additional items requested by individual subcommittees. Committee members are paid by the court to consult with district officials and evaluate the district's performance and have also been empowered by the court to hire additional auditors and consultants. With respect to both educational improvement and desegregation, however, the DMC has primarily relied on the data generated by the district. DMC chairperson Dr. Eugene Eubanks said, "I do not believe that the DMC in a meaningful way engages in what I call primary source gathering....We visit schools, we make observations, we generate reports, but we do not administer surveys....We use the district's data in order to gauge their progress in the context of desegregation, and academic improvement as measured by standardized test scores."[55]

In 1993-94, the DMC began to conduct some independent evaluations through three independent on-site evaluators, as well as a consulting firm, to evaluate issues such as potential inequities between magnet and nonmagnet schools. However, Eubanks claims that "the DMC has not been aggressive in pursuing alternative measures of educational performance, in addition to standardized tests," or in influencing the particular types of tests that are used by the district.[56]

The state department of education did not play an important role in either the formulation or oversight of the remedy. According to Diane Vaughan, former director of desegregation services for the Missouri Department of Elementary and Secondary Education (DESE), in the late 1980s, the governor and attorney general discouraged DESE from taking an active role in monitoring the plan and chose to appeal even those components of the remedy that DESE favored.[57] Committed to a policy of blanket opposition, therefore, the state executive branch not only failed to monitor the district's execution of the remedy, but also barred the state educational leaders from doing so.[58]

The Results

In evaluating just how successful the district has been in achieving its dual goals of educational improvement and desegregation, we must remember that it is in every school district's interest to present statistics that showcase its record in a favorable light. It is possible that the testing measures chosen by the district, as well as the types of evaluations used on them, have been influenced by the district's vested interest in demonstrating successful outcomes. Even Dr. Charles Allen, former coordinator of testing for the KCMSD, conceded that "in high-stakes testing environments [school district officials] are attempting to show improvement."[59] Nevertheless, in the absence of independent studies of district performance, we must confine our analysis to the data provided by the KCMSD, since these are the only data available.

The district uses two types of standardized tests that allow comparisons over time, and to other student populations: the Iowa Tests of Basic Skills (ITBS) in kindergarten through grade eight and the Tests of Achievement and Proficiency (TAP) in grades nine through twelve, a national, norm-referenced pair of testing instruments; and the Missouri Mastery and Achievement Tests, statewide criterion referenced tests. The nationally normed ITBS/TAP tests, the centerpiece of the district's testing battery, enable the district to compare ITBS and TAP scores over a variety of groups, years, and cohorts.

Some of these ITBS/TAP comparisons are encouraging. There is some modest but promising evidence that, at least at the elementary level, magnet schools may be doing a comparatively better job of educational instruction than their nonmagnet counterparts. For example, using "grade equivalents," the district tracked the performance over time of four sets or "cohorts" of students at magnet and nonmagnet schools; magnet students (both minority and white) consistently outperformed their nonmagnet counterparts in most academic subjects and years. Even adjusting for three variables that could bias the results (minority status, poverty status, and test score in the initial year of the study), the performance gap that remained in 1992 was statistically significant in eight out of twelve cases, although small in magnitude.[60]

Another cohort study tracking magnet school achievement at the elementary level—this time focusing on a particular group of magnets, the eight "foreign language immersion" schools—also showed a promising trend. The 1988 kindergarten cohort, the first group of students enrolled full-time in foreign-language elementary schools for their entire elementary grades, fluctuated in the earliest grades but by the fifth grade scored well above district averages *and* national norms, with particularly high scores in math.[61] It remains to be seen whether the 1989 and 1990 kindergarten cohorts will duplicate these promising results. Although there is always the possibility of selection bias in magnet school achievement studies, these two cohort studies offer moderate support for the claims that the elementary level, magnet schools in the KCMSD are offering higher quality instruction than nonmagnets and that foreign-language magnet instruction may be achieving exemplary outcomes by both districtwide and national standards.

Analyses of test data that compare grade-level performance over time, rather than following groups of students, raise some formidable methodological problems. Achievement score gains in 1986 and 1992 for grades one through eleven, for example, are difficult to interpret. The KCMSD appears to have made consistent achievement gains in reading and language. Yet this is only part of the story. The apparent gains are based upon national norms from 1985.[62] Since 1985, national norms have risen in all three categories for nearly all grade levels. The available data does not show whether the district has kept pace with or exceeded rising gains in national achievement.[63]

In a separate study, the district has compared 1993 KCMSD percentile ranks on the ITBS/TAP to the nation as a whole, to large city schools, and to high-poverty school districts (low SES). District officials claim that the fairest comparisons would be with the high-poverty group, given Kansas City's urban, high-poverty status. (A higher proportion of KCMSD students receive free/reduced-price lunches than in the large city reference group.) When compared to low SES norms, KCMSD scores in 1993 were much higher than the norm for grades K through five, considerably above the norms for grades six through eight, and roughly similar to norms for grades ten through twelve. In contrast, when compared to the large city reference group, KCMSD averages are only consistently above the norm for grades K through six.

These comparisons are somewhat questionable, however, on two grounds. First of all, it is uncertain to what degree the KCMSD is truly comparable to the low SES reference group. (Riverside, the test publisher that also calculates the norms for the low SES reference groups, uses different criteria for judging socioeconomic status that exclude rates of participation in free/reduced-price lunch programs.) Second, as was the case in the earlier comparison data, the norms used for this comparison (1985) are already eight years out of date, and thus the results of comparing KCMSD's *1993* achievement to national reference groups from *1985* contain an important element of bias.

A growing literature has corroborated earlier findings that various flaws in testing design, particularly the use of outdated norms, call into question the assessment of upward achievement trends in nationally normed tests.[64] Allen, the former coordinator of testing for the KCMSD, conceded that norm-referenced tests in large school districts like the KCMSD must be evaluated with caution. Allen noted that "the nation has been doing better on norm-referenced tests generally [since the late 1970s], and when the norms have been redone nationally, they tend to be a little more difficult with each successive [updating]." Moreover, he suggested that there tends to be "alignment of the curriculum to the test over time, and I would say generally that there's an increase [in test scores] because it is easier to teach to the test." Allen acknowledged that at least part of the KCMSD's rising test score trend from 1986 to 1992 may have been due to teachers' growing familiarity with the tests.[65] Thus, the dimensions of educational improvement remain unclear.

Another set of standardized tests, the criterion-referenced Missouri Mastery and Achievement Tests (MMAT), are administered statewide. Annual test score comparisons can be made at each of four grade levels. For each of the past four years (spring 1990 through spring 1993), district scores have remained from 10 to 20 percent below state averages for all sixteen comparison points. The gap between district and state averages did not significantly diminish.[66]

Educational quality can also be assessed by attendance rates and graduation trends. In Kansas City, these data are either inconclusive or appear to be negative. In elementary schools, average attendance hovered around 93 percent until 1990, but then declined slightly. In middle schools, daily attendance has remained approximately constant.[67] In high schools, attendance fell dramatically from the 1989-90 school year (from 80.9 to 71.6), rebounded to 76.7 in 1991-92, and remained relatively stable the following year.

Graduation rates were also inconclusive. Sixty-two percent graduated in 1984-85, but the rate declined sharply to the 50 percent range where it has since remained. The 1992-93 school year registered a modest upswing (from 43.6 percent to 50.1 percent), but it is unclear whether this short-term rise will turn out to signal a new long-term trend of rising graduation rates.[68]

The primary court-specified goal of the remedy is desegregation. The court specified two methods of increasing desegregation within the district: redistributing the existing student pool so as to maximize interracial exposure in individual schools, and augmenting the proportion of white students in the district as a whole.[69] According to the exposure index, if the district was perfectly balanced, every school in the district would have an interracial exposure index of 25 percent, reflecting the fact that 25 percent of the students in the school were white. The district showed real progress for nonmagnet elementaries.

These data suggest that the remedy has successfully redistributed the existing student population in an advantageous way, slightly increasing the interracial exposure of most KCMSD students (with the notable exception of students at nonmagnet elementary schools) and evening out the racial proportions in individual schools.

When one evaluates the second type of desegregation specified by the court, "to regain some portion of the white students who fled the district and retain those who are still there," the results are much less encouraging.[70] Minority racial isolation has increased since the implementation of the remedy. The district was 73.5 percent minority in the 1986-87 school year, but by 1992-93 had become 74.8 percent minority. The district has argued that the decrease in white enrollment is much smaller than it would have been if the magnet plan had not been implemented. Dr. Mary Esselman, Coordinator of Research for the KCMSD, has estimated what the racial makeup of the district from 1986-87 to 1992-93 would have been in the absence of the desegregation plan.

According to the district, the decline would have been much faster and more dramatic if the magnet plan were not in place. But the methodology used here is somewhat problematic because the projections are not based upon a close examination of changes in minority enrollment in the years immediately before the magnet plan. The most that can be said at present is that the magnet plan may have helped decrease the rate at which white student enrollment declined.

The preceding analysis shows actual and projected enrollment trends, but it does not show how many white transfer students have actually entered the district since the plan has been in place. At the beginning of the program, the number of whites coming in was very small; after the numbers climbed sharply from 1988, they began to level off.

Since the 1991-92 school year, the district has kept track of the student rate of those who remain in the system year after year. The data show that from 1991-92 to 1992-93, about 66 percent of students across all grade levels stayed at least one year after their year of transfer. Private school transfers were much more likely to stay than suburban transfers (76.2 percent compared to 63.3 percent, respectively). Retention rates from 1992-93 to 1993-94 were very similar, with an overall suburban/private retention rate of 65 percent. About 76 percent of nontransfer white students previously enrolled in the system stayed in the district.[72]

What can we conclude about the effectiveness of the Kansas City plan in achieving its twin court-mandated goals of educational improvement and desegregation? Educational achievement data are promising in some respects but the gains are modest. Although there has been an absolute increase in performance for grades K through eleven, it is unclear how students would compare to current national norms. The strongest evidence for dramatic improvement seems to be confined to magnet schools at the elementary level. Statewide criterion-referenced tests provide no evidence that the district's performance is improving, at any level, compared to the state as a whole. Attendance and graduation rates do not reveal any decisive positive trends since the implementation of the remedy.

With respect to desegregation, the evidence is mixed. The plan has made considerable progress in achieving at least one of its court-specified goals, redistribution of the existing student body; measures of interracial exposure have improved. With respect to the second goal—attracting new white students into the district—it is hard to judge the remedy a success. The percentage of minority students in the district has continued to climb very slowly, perhaps at a slower rate than otherwise would have occurred. The district has argued in court that even if the best it has done is to slow the rate of white attrition, this is nonetheless a significant achievement compared to national trends. In many of the eleven districts surrounding the KCMSD, the rate of racial change from 1982 to 1991 has been more dramatic than in the KCMSD, with sharper climbs in minority enrollment.[73] It has also been argued that elsewhere in the country comparable school districts experienced larger increases in minority enrollment during the same period.[74]

But for most local observers, it is not merely the educational and desegregative results of the remedy that have determined its success or failure; it is these benefits *weighed against the cost* of achieving them.

What Now for Kansas City and Beyond?

The Supreme Court's *Missouri v. Jenkins* decision in 1995 put the city's desegregation plan in jeopardy, though it is still unclear exactly how Judge Clark will respond to the ruling.

In its 5-4 decision, the Supreme Court said that because it was not shown that lower relative salaries in Kansas City were a direct result of intentional segregation, that the district court did exceed its authority in ordering the raises. It essentially struck down as inappropriate the underlying goal of the salary increase and monetary payment orders —to make the schools attractive enough so that suburban students would transfer there. Thus, even though the desegregation program is voluntary for suburban students, the Court ruled that mandating government expenditures for this goal is impermissible. Related to this, the Court ruled that it was inappropriate to require that test scores rise before unitary status is granted. Because the lower courts had failed to specify exactly how previous discrimination in Kansas City had lowered student achievement and exactly what would show that the low achievement was remedied, the Court struck down the lower court ruling on this issue. The *Jenkins* decision urged that courts see the ultimate goal as the return of local control to school districts, not the creation of a successful desegregation plan. The Court ruling said the district court should recognize that Kansas City's plan has already achieved many of its goals and "bear in mind that its end purpose is not only to remedy the violation to the extent practicable."[75] but also to restore government control to state and local authorities.

There are many decisions about the case that, at this book's printing, have yet to be made. For example, the judge will need to decide whether to cut salary increases that had taken effect as far back as 1987. What to do with expensive buildings and existing programs will no doubt be a central question now that the Court's pointed language strongly suggests that court control over the district should end.

Even while the issues were pending, white enrollment fell 8 percent in September 1995, the largest yearly drop in a decade. School leaders blamed it on the threatened cuts in the plan.[76]

The weaknesses in the Kansas City plan with the 1995 ruling in *Jenkins* need to be considered together when devising desegregation remedies in the future. In such remedies, the court must oversee and enforce a highly complex series of educational reforms. If the court feels that it must implement a remedy of this sort, it is crucial to consider the long-term implications of any remedy prior to implementation. In *Jenkins*, the district court installed new facilities on a scale so immense that the district would never be able to maintain them on its own. Yet because the district court had not critically examined the remedy from a long-term perspective, this problem did not become apparent until five years into the implementation phase. To be sure, guaranteeing that a comprehensive magnet plan will be financially self-sustaining after the court's withdrawal is a difficult task. Expensive facilities tend to be expensive to maintain. The typical inner-city tax base is barely adequate to support existing school facilities, let alone a state-of-the-art magnet school system.

The irony of the comprehensive voluntary magnet remedy is that although it has been used by the courts to fulfill *Brown*'s desegregation mandate, it may in fact help perpetuate a stratified educational system. Magnets, when used alone, are simply not powerful enough to overcome the economic and demographic trends that have increased the racial isolation of the inner city.

Because of its minimal impact on desegregation, a purely voluntary, comprehensive magnet remedy (in a racially isolated urban setting) should be seen as an ambitious attempt at *educational* improvement. Defining the remedy in terms of educational inputs, however, is not enough. The court should specify what types of improvements are necessary and the specific standards the desegregation plan must meet before it can be dissolved. But certain programs should not be allowed to continue if they do not show educational progress.

Plaintiffs who still see metropolitanwide remedies as the most promising solution to segregation may find their only hope in proving that housing-related discrimination outside the city helped create racial isolation within the city. This is because *Jenkins* strikes down even voluntary efforts toward interdistrict desegregation if they use state monies.

Furthermore, the *Jenkins* decision suggests that plaintiffs and courts must trace educational deficits specifically to intentional segregation or prior discrimination. A central goal of civil rights lawyers, then, should be to prove that segregation and discrimination have been factors in lowering achievement levels, decreasing college-going rates, and affecting other educational achievement measures. Without such proof, courts under *Jenkins* have license not only to deny educational compensation remedies, but also to dissolve remedies before they have had any discernible effect upon the students they are supposed to benefit. If the courts suspend these remedies before they accomplish their goals, courts will only compound the difficulties and break the spirit of educators who are struggling to make the plans work.

CHAPTER TEN

Magnets, Media, and Mirages
Prince George's County's "Miracle" Cure
Susan E. Eaton and Elizabeth Crutcher

In a January 1988 speech to students at Prince George's County's Suitland High School, President Ronald Reagan praised the success of voluntary magnet schools like Suitland and announced he would seek more federal funding for them. "Magnet schools are one of the things Prince George's County is most noted for, one of the great success stories of the educational reform movement," Reagan said.[1] It was a triumph for the large, predominantly African American school district in the Washington, D.C., suburbs. Suitland and Prince George's County, Reagan urged, should be educational models for the nation.

Less than two years after Reagan's speech, powerful Democrats also issued public accolades to Prince George's County's magnet school programs. At another county magnet high school, Senate Majority Leader George Mitchell, House Majority Leader Richard Gephardt, and U.S. Senator Edward Kennedy announced a Democratic plan to "improve and reinvigorate America's schools," citing Prince George's County's magnet program as a model of educational excellence.[2]

Since the program's inception in 1985, Prince George's magnets have also received praise from the national media. Few school systems, and perhaps no large system with such a significant concentration of minority students, received such favorable responses from policymakers and the press in the late 1980s. Democratic and Republican policymakers, influenced by the reported educational accomplishments in Prince George's County, have advocated magnet plans as the optimal tool for voluntarily desegregating school districts and improving student achievement.

The federal magnet school program began in the 1970s as an amendment to the desegregation assistance program, the Emergency School Aid Act, which the Reagan administration eliminated in 1981.

The funding portion of this grant for the magnet school was subsequently revived with the support of U.S. Senator Daniel Moynihan (D-N.Y.) and encouraged by positive publicity about magnet programs such as Prince George's County's. State and federal lawmakers continue to embrace magnet programs in the 1990s, often as alternatives to controversial, politically unpopular mandatory desegregation plans.

This chapter examines the motivations and aspirations that led to the development of the magnet program in Prince George's. Its purpose is to determine whether the repeated and widely accepted claims of success are valid. The evidence in this report strongly suggests that Prince George's reported success and temporarily revived community enthusiasm were more a triumph of public relations than of educational reform. The evidence—and in some cases the lack of evidence—raise doubts about whether the highly touted magnet school program ever achieved racial integration or improved academic achievement.

The Motivations for a Magnet School Program

Bordering Washington to the north and east and adjoining the city's largest African American communities, Prince George's includes a wide diversity of neighborhoods and was the home of the nation's largest African American suburban migration during the 1970s. Enrolling more than 113,500 students in 174 schools, it is Maryland's biggest school system and one of the nation's largest suburban school districts.[3]

Although the least affluent of the major Washington, D.C., suburbs, the county includes the flagship campus of the University of Maryland and many solidly middle-class neighborhoods. In the mid-1980s, the county was among the top 3 percent of U.S. counties in terms of average income.[4]

The county experienced enormous demographic change during the previous two decades. Of the sixty largest school districts in the nation, Prince George's County had the largest percentage increase in African American enrollment concomitant with the largest percentage decline in white enrollment between 1967 and 1986.[5] With African American student enrollment at about 69 percent in 1993, Prince George's is the largest suburban jurisdiction in the nation in which

African Americans make up a majority of the student population.[6]

Housing patterns during this period of African American population growth developed into three bands. The inner band, beginning at the Washington, D.C., border and situated almost entirely inside the beltway, mostly includes all African American neighborhoods. The middle band consists primarily of racially integrated neighborhoods. The outer band — this is the one farthest from Washington, D.C. — is predominantly white.

Prince George's County has operated under a court-ordered desegregation plan since 1972. Suing a historically segregated system that had resisted desegregation for years, the NAACP had little trouble winning a court order after the Supreme Court's 1971 decision in *Swann v. Charlotte-Mecklenburg Board of Education*[7] authorized busing to end segregation. In *Vaughns v. Board of Education of Prince George's County*[8] Judge Frank Kaufman ordered a desegregation plan that reassigned huge numbers of students and included mandatory busing. Under the Supreme Court holding in *Alexander v. Holmes*[9] that said that the "all deliberate speed" defined in *Brown II* had expired and that integration orders must be implemented immediately, the county was forced to desegregate in the middle of its school year.

The desegregation plan was not only vastly unpopular but also eventually failed to create adequate integration because it did not account for the huge changes in racial composition already underway. Many schools were shut down during this period in response to declining enrollments throughout the district. (This was a period of falling enrollment in most U.S. school districts, and in Prince George's, the school enrollment had declined from about 163,000 in 1971 to about 106,000 by 1984.)[10] As racial change continued and school officials failed to make alterations to the original plan, the absurdity of some aspects of the plan became apparent. For example, it was not uncommon for African American newcomers, who replaced a white family in a neighborhood, to be bused away from their predominantly African American neighborhood school to a second predominantly African American school in another section of the county.[11] In cases such as this, the African American community bore an overwhelming share of the busing burden without gaining the benefits of integrated schooling.

Citing the obvious ineffectiveness of the 1972 reassignment plan, the plaintiffs in the original desegregation lawsuit were joined by the

NAACP's national office and had the case reopened. In response, in 1983, the federal district court issued a new desegregation order requiring that no individual school have an African American enrollment of either less than 10 percent or more than 80 percent. This contrasted with orders in other cities that required racial balances that did not differ more than 15 or 20 percentage points from the district average. The school board did file a plan in May 1984, but it did not satisfy the court. A year later, Kaufman ordered an independent consultant, Robert L. Green, to design a desegregation plan. His plan, in the form of what came to be called "the Green Report," recommended large-scale busing, including mandatory reassignment of about 30,000 students and bus rides of up to eighty-five minutes.[12]

It was this controversial report that spurred the community to see magnet schools as a more acceptable alternative. The report sparked broad-based protest in a community that had already been troubled by a desegregation plan that could not maintain desegregation in the face of enormous demographic changes. Plaintiffs and county education leaders quickly saw the benefits of compromise.

Valerie Kaplan, a longtime community activist, characterized the public mood at the time: "When the Green Report was issued, the community went ballistic.... Everyone came together against it. Race was irrelevant. It brought the community together because they found a common cause in ensuring the Green Report was not implemented."[13]

An Alternative Emerges: *Milliken*s and Magnets

In response to community outrage over the Green report, the then newly appointed school superintendent, John Murphy, recommended a more palatable alternative. His plan centered around magnet schools and *Milliken* schools, named after the Supreme Court's 1977 decision *Milliken v. Bradley II*,[14] which permitted courts to order educational remedies for the effects of past segregation.[15]

Under Murphy's plan, though some mandatory busing would be retained,[16] magnet schools would be designed to attract a diverse student body through specialized, unique programs thereby creating racial balance without coercion. In Prince George's, *Milliken* schools are those schools with high minority populations and are usually difficult to integrate because of geographical location. Under the plan, these ten schools would remain segregated and receive extra money or other resources as compensation. Community leaders do not recall any opposition to this plan or mention of an alternative that received significant attention. The NAACP also accepted the plan. Many people attribute the popularity of the Murphy plan not only to a desire to avoid more disruptive busing, but also to the superintendent's political savvy.

"Murphy was very persuasive and he had the established powers supporting him," said Hardy Jones, president of the county's NAACP chapter.[17]

By 1985, the two parties in the suit had worked out a compromise centered around Murphy's magnet school concept. The choice of magnets and *Millikens* as desegregation tools, then, evolved mostly as a reaction to an unpopular proposal. The Memorandum of Understanding compromise, hammered out by plaintiffs and defendants, outlined major elements of a county desegregation plan to integrate schools in order to meet new racial composition guidelines.

Under the plan, it was agreed that magnet *programs* within larger schools, and schools that made a full transformation to a magnet *school*, would result in at least 80 percent of students attending schools that were not less than 10 percent and no more than 80 percent African American by the 1987-88 school year. Eighty-five percent of all students would be attending such schools by the next year. These requirements, the Memorandum states, were to stay in place as long as the African American population at each of the three levels of public school—elementary, middle, and high school—did not exceed 65 percent.[18] (Since that time, of course, the African American enrollment *has* exceeded 65 percent). Originally, magnets were placed in predominantly African American areas to attract white students. Eventually, school officials created "mirror" magnets in white neighborhoods to attract African American students who previously had not had the option of choosing a magnet program.[19]

The agreement also created a community advisory council—the Committee of 100—appointed primarily by school board members, to represent citizens.[20] This committee has played a key role in the monitoring and planning of the magnet program. It provides extensive reports to the court and school board. The Committee of 100 was never intended to be representative of, or a watchdog for, plaintiffs.[21]

As of 1994, fifty-two schools had some kind of magnet program. Twenty schools were "dedicated" magnets; that is, the entire school was transformed into a magnet. "Dedicated" magnets included science, math, and technology schools and "traditional academies" where students were required to wear uniforms, adhere to a strict disciplinary code, and maintain a good attendance record. The remaining thirty-two had magnet programs that operated separate from, but within, a larger, nonmagnet school.[22] There were twenty-one *Milliken II* schools—an increase of eleven from the number that existed in 1985—that receive extra resources and have smaller classes.[23]

There were twelve model comprehensive schools—also known as "interim" *Milliken* schools—that did not have specialized programs but which did have smaller class sizes and received some additional services for students. The school system maintains that these schools should be exempt from racial balance guidelines.

In five other schools, officials have started to implement magnet programs, beginning with preschoolers and kindergarten students. These schools are scheduled to expand and develop over five or six years. In the meantime, these five schools, though defined as having magnet programs, are also given "interim" *Milliken* relief. The school system has exempted them from meeting court-ordered racial balance guidelines.

In July 1994, school officials announced that they would try to get out of their remaining mandatory busing requirements, which currently affects less than 10 percent of county students.[24] For now, the court order requires that magnet schools and programs do nothing more than meet numerical racial quotas. But the mission of magnets, as presented to the community, was more ambitious.

A Broad Mission for Magnets

Beyond the immediate goal of providing an alternative to the mandatory busing, school officials hoped magnets would improve education. Goals for the magnet program were outlined in the district's official booklet, "A School System of Choices":

> First, it facilitates a redistribution of the student population in a manner consistent with desegregation guidelines. Secondly, it is to create qualitatively different educational programs, responsive to the needs and interests of students preparing for the 21st century. Third, the program serves as a creative model for changes and educational improvements which eventually can be diffused throughout the public educational system."[25]

Murphy, the superintendent who introduced the magnet plan, recently restated the dual purpose of the magnets "to integrate our schools and be a vehicle for incremental change."[26] In characterizing the goal of "incremental change," Thomas Hendershot, a school board member, expressed his hope that by demonstrating the "possibilities for public education" the demand for high-level education would grow throughout the system.[27]

One of Murphy's explicit goals was to improve academic achievement. He saw the magnets and *Millikens* as a way to fulfill his promises. "I told the school board point blank to fire me if the school system failed to move into the top 25 percent of the nation by 1990," Murphy wrote.[28]

Four official goals of the magnet program need to be considered. First is the goal of avoiding the *Green* plan, which has clearly been met. Second is the goal of providing unique educational programs. The third goal is to use these unique programs to attract a diverse student body and desegregate the schools. The fourth is to improve educational achievement and educational quality across the system.

While consideration of the goal to create unique programs would require detailed field studies, the selection of programs offered by the schools does seem vast.

At the elementary level, as of 1994, there were two communication programs, one creative and performing arts program, two French immersion programs, three Montessori programs, six math and technology schools, nine programs for the talented and gifted, and six traditional and classical academies.

At the middle schools, there was one communication program, one French immersion program; one humanities and international studies program; a Montessori program; four science, math, and technology programs; two programs for talented and gifted students; and two traditional and classical academic centers.

At the high school level, there was a biotechnology program; a humanities and international studies program, two science and math computer technology centers, four academic centers with professional "career strands," four collaborative programs with the University of Maryland, and one visual and performing arts program.[29] High application rates—in 1993 there were about 6,000 applications for about 3,400 spots[30]—are evidence of considerable success at least in convincing parents and students that the programs are distinct enough from other schools to be worth attending.

Do People Think the Schools Are Desegregated?

There is widespread disagreement about whether the magnet program has adequately desegregated the county schools. Opinions about the success of magnet schools depend upon one's definition of desegregation.

School officials in Prince George's County define desegregation as meeting the court-approved numerical racial balances. Where magnet schools exist as one part of a larger nonmagnet comprehensive school, students in the smaller magnet programs are included in the racial balance count for the larger school. Using this method of tabulation, the requirements have been met. Nevertheless, under this practice, it would be possible for larger nonmagnet—or regular—schools to remain nearly all African American as long as significant numbers of white students attend the magnet program to balance out the count.

In 1994, Edward Felegy, the school superintendent who replaced Murphy, claimed excellent results based upon these numerical standards. "Cumulative results of the enrollments at the magnet schools show success."[31]

On the other hand, those who define desegregation either as substantial interracial contact or integrated classrooms are more skeptical. Some see magnets as "schools within schools," meaning that students in the magnet program have little or no contact with students in the comprehensive, nonmagnet program. The result of this, some contend, is often that integration occurs only within the magnet program. Although formal school policy permits students within the regular attendance areas of the magnet schools to participate in magnet courses, the reality is that only students in the magnet program itself experience integration.

In light of this, NAACP President Hardy Jones, speaking for the plaintiffs, believes integration has not been achieved: "...we have not accomplished the kind of mixing we were talking about to begin with. We still have segregated schools."[32]

The Committee of 100 reports explicitly state that the committee's goals have shifted from desegregation to "equity." Equity in this case is the assurance of equal education for African American children wherever they are, whether in integrated magnet programs or racially segregated schools. Calling the present phase of desegregation, the "Equity Generation," the report states:

The community and the school system have questioned the validity of placing students in a racially diverse classroom with that as the criteria for saying that the school system has achieved equity. The emphasis has turned from the importance of the 10/80 guideline to the output of the students.... [T]he Equity Generation believes that it does not matter who each student is sitting next to in the classroom as long as his/her needs are being met.[33]

For those interviewed, the answer to the question of whether magnets created a desegregated school within a segregated school seems to depend upon whether students in the comprehensive—or non-magnet—program had access to the resources in the magnet schools. From this perspective, then, it seems most school officials view the benefits of the magnet program to be the extra resources they bring rather than their potential for racial integration.

Most school officials are uncertain about whether magnets are now or will continue to be effective desegregation tools. Many of those interviewed cite changing demographics that make achieving racial balance nearly impossible. For example, since 1985, when the magnet program began, the African American student population increased from 59.6 percent to about 69 percent in 1994.[34] The percentage of white students decreased from 34.8 percent in 1985 to 23.5 percent in the 1992-93 school year;[35] in the 1993-94 school year, the proportion of whites declined again, to 21.9 percent. Because of the dwindling pool of white students, some believe magnet schools have outlived their usefulness in achieving desegregation and that within the district, racial integration is simply becoming less feasible.

However, under Superintendent Felegy, the administration appeared more optimistic in 1993. According to Dr. Joyce Thomas, the then special assistant to the superintendent, magnets will always be able to achieve "desegregation" as defined by the court because officials will simply alter the numerical goals of the magnets so that they maintain the court's *ratio* but change the *percentages* to reflect the changing racial composition in the school district.[36] Such modifications are allowable under the court agreement, the Memorandum of Understanding, but the flexibility means that, at the middle and high school level, schools that are nearly 90 percent African American were considered "desegregated" in 1993.

School officials have increased their flexibility in meeting guidelines in a second way. As more schools became segregated because of demographic change, officials created a new category of schools called interim *Milliken* schools. These twelve schools are those that have recently fallen out of balance but continue to receive extra money and resources. The schools receive less than the extras provided to the original *Millikens*. Administrators claim that these schools should not be held to the court's desegregation guidelines because extra money and resources make up for the increased segregation.[37]

This new category of schools is not cited in the original Memorandum of Understanding nor is it officially sanctioned by the court. Plaintiff attorney George Mernick said there was never a court hearing held on the new interim *Milliken* school designations and that, in light of the demographic change that has increased the percentage of African American students, plaintiffs have no plans to challenge the new category in court.[38]

Desegregation Guidelines

The reports to the court filed by the board of education in 1993 state that only one of the county's 174 schools is impermissibly outside the court's racial balance guidelines.[39] School officials have since adjusted the court's 10/80 guidelines. According to the Memorandum of Understanding, the guidelines "are flexible and are to be flexibly administered."[40] The court requires that at least 85 percent of students attend desegregated schools, with the term "desegregated," however, being based upon the current racial composition in the school system.

In elementary schools, a desegregated school was defined in 1993 as one that is between 10 and about 83 percent African American. In middle schools, a desegregated school is defined as one that is between 10 and 89 percent African American. In high schools, a desegregated school is defined as one that is between 10 and 87 percent African American.

The school district reports that 39 of the district's 118 elementary schools would be considered outside the new racial balance guidelines, but officials maintain that all but one of the "imbalanced" schools should be exempt from meeting the guidelines. About 18,236 students attended these schools in 1993. In addition, four of the district's twenty-five middle schools were outside the court guidelines, but again, school officials claim exemptions. About 2,600 students attend these schools, according to enrollment figures. Eight of the district's twenty-two high schools were outside the guidelines but were exempted. About 11,400 students attended these schools, according to enrollment figures.[41] Together, then, about 32,241 students attended schools whose racial balance is outside the established guidelines.

On the other hand, about 81,330 or 71.6 percent of students in the school system are attending schools that fall within the new racial balance guidelines. Mernick, the plaintiff lawyer, said plaintiffs have no plans to challenge the current racial composition of schools in the system.

> In a nutshell, what's going on, is the effort to achieve any kind of mathematical integration has failed.... I don't know if the Memorandum of Understanding...has been violated. It was set up as a target. When you have a school system that is 70 percent Black with most of this population living on the periphery of the area, you are not going to achieve mathematical integration.[42]

Magnets operate at the other schools whose racial compositions fall outside the guidelines but, again, plaintiffs said they have no plans to challenge these racial compositions in light of the rapid demographic change. Of the fifty-one schools whose racial balances fall outside the established guidelines, only one school, Beacon Heights Elementary, does not fit into one of the exempted categories or does not have a magnet operating there. School officials reported that they are "studying possible actions, if any, that could reasonably be taken to return this school within the Court ordered guidelines."[43]

The court standard does not require very much desegregation to begin with. Layers of exemptions make it even easier for school officials to get out of existing requirements.

Schools Within Schools

In September 1993, there were thirty-two schools containing a magnet program or programs.[44] In many cases, the community perception is true that while the magnet programs themselves are often desegregated, as defined by the court, the separate, larger school often remains nearly all one race. In fact, at seventeen of the nonmagnet— or regular—schools, more than 90 percent of students are African American. In addition, enrollment at four of the magnet programs is more than 90 percent African American (two of these schools are 100 percent African American.) These calculations are significant because they show that, depending upon how the individual schools are organized, desegregation at the school building level may not be synonymous with desegregation at the classroom level. Although a magnet *program* may be integrated, it does not mean that the students within the larger *school* are receiving an integrated education. In many cases, a racially balanced enrollment in a magnet program is helping to balance out enrollment counts in the larger school—counts which are then presented to the court.

While magnet programs designed to attract a diverse student body allow the district to claim legal and acceptable school-level "desegregation," the school-within-a-school model can actually end up resegregating either magnet or nonmagnet components.

On a more positive note, there is evidence that there is more racial integration with magnets than there would be without any desegregation strategy. November 1992 data show magnet programs increased desegregation at all schools but one, though these reports do not take into account the separation that could occur under the school-within-a-school model. The amount that magnets increased desegregation ranged from just .4 percent to 29 percent.[45]

Since magnets were implemented in 1985, white enrollment has continued to decline. While percentage declines have been much smaller than they were during the 1970s and even the early 1980s before magnets, the white enrollment decline is slower than it was in the early 1970s and 1980s. African American enrollment continues to rise, though these gains are much smaller than the overall losses in white enrollment.

There appears to be a positive relationship between the implementation of magnets and the slowing overall losses of white enrollment. There is absolutely no evidence that would prove that magnets have retained whites. In recent years, percentage losses in white enrollment have been substantially larger.

Shifting demographics have still made it nearly impossible to achieve full integration. From this perspective, to say that the voluntary magnet school program in Prince George's County has created desegregated schools would be sophistry. Any intradistrict desegregation program in a school system that is approaching 70 percent African American would not be able to achieve racial integration across the district.

Nevertheless, Prince George's County hailed repeatedly for having successfully used magnet programs to create desegregation. This positive image perhaps persists because the racial isolation that does exist has been obscured by adjustments to the court's racial balance guidelines. In addition, the exempting of *Milliken*, interim *Milliken*, and developing magnets from racial balance requirements and the "school within a school" might also veil the level of segregation in the district. These factors have allowed the system to report success to the court, and to the public, while, in reality, an "acceptable" and legal racial balance is clearly not synonymous with the type of racial integration that would bring together nearly equal proportions of white and African American students. What is called "desegregation" in Prince George's County is clearly not what most people would think of when they think of desegregation.

Do People Think Achievement and Educational Quality Has Improved?

Soon after magnets were created, the community rallied around the schools and was quick to believe that grand educational success had come to Prince George's County. President Reagan's assessment of the Prince George's magnets as "one of the great success stories of the educational reform movement" was echoed in two typical newspaper articles describing the improving achievement in the school system. An editorial in the *Baltimore Sun* read: "Prince George's County public schoolchildren are achieving test scores that any racially integrated system in urban American might envy." And, commenting on test scores, the *Washington Post* said, "That type of performance has helped lift the Prince George's schools to the threshold of excellence."[46]

This type of publicity and attention brought pride and confidence to the school system and fueled the perception that all was well in Prince George's County. School administrators, meanwhile, were leading their own campaign that focused on the positive effects of magnets upon school achievement. The campaign, led by then School Superintendent John Murphy, focused on mostly rising California Achievement Test (CAT) scores. The CAT is a nationally normed examination.

The media, the school system itself, and even national political figures continuously praised the district for improving academic achievement based on these scores. For example, a 1988-89 catalog written by the school system that describes magnet options includes an article titled, "Students Continue Rapid Improvement as Schools

Raise Expectations." The catalog asserts that "achievement are [*sic*] most evident in the schools by students in recent results of the CAT."[47]

School officials placed enormous emphasis on these tests. Administrators still recall John Murphy's "Anxiety Room," as his conference room was dubbed. The walls of the room, where other administrators and community members met regularly, were plastered with graphs that chronicled the annual CAT reading and math scores. Each graph was labeled with a principal's name and school.

"Any evidence of slippage was displayed on the wall for all to see," Murphy notes in his 1993 article, "Applied Anxiety: Organizing for Educational Results."[48]

Reports of rising test scores appear to have created the perception that educational quality had improved. Community reports and surveys reflect the positive feeling about magnet schools and achievement. For example, the 1990-91 Committee of 100 report reads:

> The magnet schools have demonstrated that it is possible to achieve integration on a voluntary basis while at the same time improving the quality of education.... Six years of experience with the magnet and *Milliken II* schools provides concrete evidence that equity can be achieved, that meaningful improvement in the quality of education can be accomplished on all levels regardless of the racial or economic class makeup of the students.[49]

In addition, a 1987 survey conducted by the district's Department of Evaluation and Research found 82 percent of principals and magnet school teachers gave their programs either an A or B for improving student achievement.[50]

But the image of a miracle school system seems to be fading. By 1994, people appeared more wary of proclaiming that magnets produced great academic success. This might be partly because Maryland's assessment program stopped using CAT tests in 1989, making it nearly impossible to complete a consistent analysis of trends. Without recent elementary CAT scores, attention has shifted to scores on other tests, on which the record is mixed and these scores never showed the rapid rise of the CAT.

The good publicity that fanned the euphoria now seems to be waning.

An April 1994 *Washington Post* article by the education writer covering the county characterizes the change in mood this way: "The education news of today contrasts with the good news of the mid-

1980s when the most vivid image of Prince George's County Schools was parents enthusiastically waiting on line for days to enroll their children in the county's highly regarded magnet schools."[51]

A January 1994 article by the same writer examining the business community's increasing frustration with the schools reads: "The business community in the county, which only a few years ago was so enamored of the county schools that it paid for an advertising campaign on their behalf is now openly critical of the school system's leadership."[52]

Between 1990 and 1994 the percent of local residents believing the schools were getting better fell from 46 to 15 percent. In a 1994 article analyzing the apparent erosion of support, the *Washington Post* reported: "Board members have long been under fire because of students' poor showing on key performance assessments and crowded schools and limited funds to make improvements in neighborhood schools."[53]

The torrent of positive publicity began to taper off soon after Murphy left the school system in 1991. The less positive perceptions were perpetuated by an intensely critical September 1993 report issued by a twenty-seven-member commission of prominent business leaders headed by University of Maryland professor and former CIA director Stansfield Turner. The report, which called for an overhaul of the way the county schools are governed, read: "Our schools are failing, our children are falling behind, our safety is in question and our quality of life is not at all what we want it to be."[54]

But some school officials, though more hesitantly now, continue to claim that the magnets did improve student achievement. Almost all of those interviewed, including Dr. Louise Waynant, the associate superintendent for instruction;[55] board member Thomas Hendershot;[56] and former board member Sarah Johnson[57] continued to cite the CAT as evidence of success.

Other school officials, including Superintendent Felegy, did not make confident claims about improved achievement. Instead, they stressed that recent financial constraints have prevented the district from accurately measuring success.[58]

But others go so far as to attack the repeated claims of success as misleading. Board Chairman Alvin Thornton characterizes the original claims of superior achievement as "smoke and mirrors."[59] Thornton has been involved with the desegregation effort since the

1980s and was the first NAACP liaison and chief negotiator during the 1983-1985 desegregation settlement conferences. Later, he was chairman of the Committee of 100's monitoring committee.

Thornton said Murphy went too far in trying to improve the system's image by boasting about test scores. "Murphy started believing things were really improving and believing the numbers. He let the community think the achievement was real…and he seemed to think his job was done."[60]

Thornton charges that in terms of achievement, the system has not improved since the magnets were implemented, but that it has more or less remained the same. While Thornton believes the magnets do offer some good educational opportunities to African American students, gaps in achievement between African Americans and whites that existed in 1984-85 still remain. "The fundamental patterns haven't changed; the relationships within the system haven't changed; and there is no such thing as a good magnet program in an average school system."[61]

Did Magnets Bring Improved Academic Achievement to Prince George's County?

The lack of consistent and reliable empirical data and detailed program evaluations means there is little evidence with which to answer the question of whether magnet schools have improved systemwide achievement compared to national norms. In general, the evidence suggests that the claims of improved achievement from magnets were based upon outdated and likely invalid measures. Unfortunately, no firm conclusions can be drawn from the other available test score data. However, since school officials based their claims for success on test score data of the type presented here, this section tests whether the existing evidence can live up to the claims.

The California Achievement Test

The increasing CAT scores upon which the majority of claims of success were based are questionable for the purpose of showing program-related gains. This is because the norms used for this version of the test, given to third, fifth, and eighth graders, were established in 1976-1977.[62] National norms used in a state or district often are established the first year students take a given test and remain unchanged year after year. This means that even when there are nationwide improvements, the district does not use the new improved norms as their basis for comparison in subsequent years. Instead, the district compares its scores to the older — and usually lower — national norms.[63] This makes it easy for school districts to claim "above the norm" when the norm to which they are referring was established several years ago and, in actuality, is probably much lower than the actual norm. For example, every state in 1987 reported that its children were performing "above" the national average.

When the CAT test results were announced in Prince George's County in 1989, the rankings did not represent how the county was performing relative to the nation in 1989 but how it was performing relative to the nation in 1977. The increased percentile ranks do indicate that there was improvement within the district, but the increased rankings do not show that the improvements in Prince George's County kept pace with the improvements occurring in the nation. National scores on some standardized tests for elementary school students have risen rapidly from the 1970s through the 1980s,[64] especially for African American students.

In its 1988 report, the Committee of 100 challenged the school administration's position that the CAT could measure progress accurately:

> The position assumes that it is acceptable to measure student's academic achievement against a dated standard of achievement that does not include contemporary material. Using this standard, most systems have shown significant gains—gains which have not necessarily been reflected in other indicators of an effective school system....[65]

Associate Superintendent Louise Waynant acknowledged that, in some cases, educators have geared curriculum to better reflect the content of CAT standardized tests:

> It depends what you mean by teaching to the test. If you mean teaching the test items or cheating—no, we did not do that. If you mean were we aware of the learning outcomes that were measured—yes, after you give a test for eight years you know the learning outcomes that are measured. They were in our curriculum and they should be.[66]

Finally, while the CAT scores indicate an improvement trend over time in the district, there was always a wide gap between white and African American achievement, a fact that, as one might expect, was not publicized during the magnets' glory days.

Functional Tests

The district's reliance on the CAT ended in 1989 when the state stopped using the measure. The subsequent lack of consistent data at the elementary level increased the district's and the media's focus on state-issued "functional" tests that have been taken by high school students since before magnets began. These test results have been mixed over the years and never equaled the rapid rise in CAT scores. The functional exams test very basic skills in reading, writing, math, and citizenship. Unfortunately, these tests do not provide conclusive evidence about achievement. Scores reflect how many students passed the basic tests, with no indication of how the passing standard might translate into skills or classroom abilities. Under these testing results, it is impossible to know, for example, how many students barely passed the exam and how many students received perfect scores. This test is not one that measures achievement, but one that measures basic, minimum skills.

The most significant functional test passing rates are those earned by ninth graders, since this is when the largest number of students take the test. In later grades, only those students who originally failed the test take it.

The percentage of students passing the tests has always been high, at more than 90 percent, fluctuating just slightly over the years. The system did show a steady rise from 1984 to 1988, but it never again equalled the high passing rate of 95 percent earned in 1988, though it did come close. The percentage of students passing the math portion of the exam has risen steadily, though the gap between state and county rates was seven points in 1983, nine points in 1984, and eleven points in 1991. The percentage of students passing the writing portion increased slightly in 1992 to 93 percent. The county has had mixed results in meeting the state average passing rate for functional tests. From 1990 to 1992, the county fell just below the state average passing rate in reading, well below the average in math, and rose slightly above the state average in writing. Both statewide and in Prince George's County, passing rates have improved over time but the county ranked 22nd among the state's 24 districts in 1995.[67]

The Comprehensive Test of Basic Skills

The Comprehensive Test of Basic Skills (CTBS), the nationally normed test that replaced the CAT, is given only to a random sample of third, fifth, and eighth graders. Officials said that less then a dozen students at each school are usually tested. The data is not broken down in a way that would allow for analysis of performance school by school. Even though the data cannot be used to analyze achievement over time, the 1992 State Performance Report shows that CTBS scores for Prince George's County were low relative to the state average.

Unlike the CAT score rises, these CTBS test results fail to provide the school system with the evidence it needs to prove unquestionable success.

The fact that scores reported here show national percentile ranks 30 to 36 points below the national percentile rank reported by the school system just two years ago on the CAT should call the earlier, higher rankings into question.

Maryland School Performance Assessment Program

The Maryland School Performance Assessment Program (MSPAP) is the state's criterion-reference exam that tests students in third, fifth, and eighth grades. Students are required to demonstrate understanding of reading selections and are required to write extended responses to questions. Students taking these tests also work individually and in groups to solve multistep math problems, conduct science investigations, and demonstrate understanding of social studies concepts.

The standards are determined by an evaluation formula devised by the state department of education. Performance levels ranked from a high of 1 to low of 5. Level 1 is the highest and Level 5 is the lowest.[68]

The percentage of Prince George's County students who reached either the "excellent" or "satisfactory" standard fell below the percentage of students statewide who reached such standards. This was the case in each grade level and subject.

County CRT's

The county also delivers its own CRT tests, but officials claim that since different forms of the tests have been administered over the years, a comparison of achievement over time would "not be appropriate."[69]

Some school administrators claim that students in the *Milliken* and magnet programs had higher relative scores on the county CRT than other students. But the associate superintendent, Waynant, stressed that the test scores have never been adjusted to allow for such a comparison to be made. The school district refused to release the scores.

So, because all the measures of elementary school achievement have varied over the years, or are not available, there is no way to verify improvement in achievement relative to national achievement trends.

Program Evaluations

The absence of comprehensive program evaluations is also troublesome. Such evaluations would determine whether specific magnet programs were beneficial to students. The Committee of 100 has requested more sophisticated evaluations for seven years, since 1987, about two years after magnets began.[70]

In the eyes of some of those interviewed, the lack of program evaluation data suggests was not only an oversight, but also a way of avoiding the reality of program weaknesses. One board member, Marcy Canavan, echoed this view:

> This lack of evaluations is not just because of financial reasons....We have several programs that we spend a lot of money on that sound wonderful that aren't showing any results, but that we don't cut....We need to do more than just a survey of parents. That's not real evaluation, but it's really hard to not like something when the parents are happy. But we have no way of knowing if they have a real reason for being happy or not.[71]

School officials did outline a more extensive evaluation for the system, but funds have not been allocated. The research plan proposed a sophisticated analysis of the magnet program.[72]

The conclusion to be drawn from the data now available is not that students are performing poorly in Prince George's County. The more important point is simply that the Prince George's school system, which has received national acclaim for its "success," has no reliable evidence that would show that there substantial improvement that kept pace with nationwide achievement or that magnet schools improved academic achievement.

Did Magnets Succeed as Public Relations Tools and Reform Agents?

It was hoped that magnets would spread reform across the whole system. Today, the schools are both praised and criticized for their overall impact as reform tools. Many people hoped magnets would invigorate the system by providing examples of innovation, teaching styles or curriculum. Many hoped that these improvements would be shared with other schools, thus enhancing the educational experience for all students. While some believe that this did happen, there is no empirical evidence for it.

Waynant explained that magnets and *Milliken*s were the first to use computers extensively and to improve science curricula. These changes, she said, transferred to other schools. "So, in a sense, the magnets and *Milliken*s have acted as a lighthouse or as an early adopter" Waynant said.[73]

The most commonly cited benefit of the magnet program is that it restored faith in the school system. This enthusiasm benefitted the district in two ways, according to school leaders. First, administrators secured more funding and support from the state government and local businesses. Teachers and parents seemed to renew their confidence in the school system and in the ability of students to meet high expectations. This enthusiasm may have been a result of the advertising campaign launched by then superintendent John Murphy. Joyce Thomas, the assistant to Edward Felegy, the superintendent in 1994, characterized Murphy's campaign: "John Murphy was a master at being able to woo the public. We advertised profusely. Billboards. T.V. shows. We went all over the place."[74]

NAACP President Hardy Jones also said he believed the magnet school concept was a vehicle for changing the school system's negative image among the business community. "Ads were shown for a matter of months that good things were happening. The idea was that magnet schools were going to improve our negative image in the business world...to get business to come here and stay here."[75]

Board member Thornton said that while he does believe reports of academic success were exaggerated, magnets and the advertising campaign were necessary in order to get people outside of the system to see Prince George's County as worthy, and eventually "to attract unprecedented funding by whites."[76] Thornton said, "John Murphy was brought in because he showed an ability to use magnets to stop the hemorrhaging of the white population."[77]

Thornton stresses that the magnets focused "positive public attention on a system that had gone through a period of benign neglect."[78] Business involvement and support, Thornton said, increased during this time. Community support and empowerment increased, he said, as community activists took part in the oversight committee.

Superintendent Felegy also stressed that, overall, the campaign had

had positive effects on the school environment. "...If nothing else, when parents have elected to put their children in the program, they tend to be more interested. When teachers are teaching in a curriculum to which they are dedicated, they'll put their full measure."[79]

However, the enthusiasm, positive image, and improved morale seem to be fading. This waning good feeling may be caused by budget cuts experienced by the system, but generally, the excitement generated by magnets seems to have dissipated. Sarah Johnson, a board member from 1982 to 1992, articulated this common view: "What is happening now is that the magnet program is sort of old hat with the system. There's just not the good feeling about anything right now."[80]

But some officials and community members believe magnets not only failed to improve other schools hurt them. The primary criticism of the magnets is that they drain resources from other nonmagnet—or comprehensive schools—that enroll about 80 percent of the population.

The Committee of 100 Report from 1990 cites this problem:

> [Comprehensive schools] have become synonymous with the term, "poor neighborhood school." Creative principals and teachers were pulled from the comprehensive schools and given the task of creating the magnet and Milliken II schools. Additional funds were provided. In many instances, the more active parents moved to the magnet schools. This left many comprehensive schools with inadequate leadership and inadequate funding.... It is past time to bring the comprehensive schools up to the level of the magnet and Milliken II schools, in terms of expenditure per student."[81]

The Committee of 100 did recommend to the board that it fund the comprehensive schools at the same level as the *Milliken* schools, which spend even more per pupil than the magnet schools do. In 1993, the per-pupil cost of comprehensive schools was $5,097. Magnets additional annual cost per student was $347. The original *Milliken* schools cost $564 more per student and the interim *Milliken*s cost $378 more per student.[82] Jones, the NAACP president, was one of many who complained about the inequities: "There is no money devoted to even enhancing the comprehensive schools because it [the money] is in the magnets."[83]

Felegy had included extra money for the nonmagnet comprehensive schools in his 1994-95 budget request, but the requested $5.4 million was cut by the school board. Extra money for neighborhood schools was eliminated in spite of an intense lobbying effort by a church-based civic group, the Interfaith Action Committee (IAC), that wanted extra dollars for nonmagnet schools. The chairman of IAC's education committee, Howard Bowles, said parents of students who attend neither magnets nor *Milliken* schools were disappointed. Bowles told *The Washington Post*, "They are disenchanted.... They thought so many things were going to happen when they decided to woo white parents back in the county schools."[84]

If the objective was to improve the perception of the school system, it seems the magnets did so successfully for awhile. But these public relations benefits were temporary, as the schools, were being criticized in 1993 and 1994 even by the business community, once a fierce ally. Meanwhile, the schools are being characterized by the media in a seemingly more balanced, but not always positive way. Whether the schools were actually "vehicles for change" is a more complicated, subjective question. But the fact that many view magnets as draining from other schools and creating inequality indicates that, in the long run, the specialized schools did not have unquestionable positive effects on the rest of the system or even upon its overall image.

What Can We Learn From Prince George's County?

Policymakers erred in touting Prince George's County Public Schools as a national model. The widely accepted claims of miraculous success regarding the county's local education reforms have never been substantiated. The claims might have been so widely believed because they were skillfully marketed. But the Prince George's success story probably spread for other reasons. Policies set in Prince George's County could be claimed by both liberals and conservatives. Conservative policymakers may have liked the fact that magnets emphasized the populist "choice" concept and rejected mandatory student assignment for desegregation. Liberal politicians may have seen magnets as an example of the capacity of big public school systems to reform themselves. And in many cases, the press simply increased the visibility and credibility of the local claims.

One of the clear lessons of this case is that the appearance of great success may be more the result of politics and public relations than of educational accomplishments. Such claims need to be much more closely scrutinized.

As for racial integration, demographic change has continued to bring higher percentages of minority students into the schools, making complete integration less feasible. The magnet program has obviously been unable to counteract these trends, though it certainly may have helped in slowing them down. The district's manipulation of guidelines and exemption parameters may also have obscured the high levels of racial isolation in the district. Furthermore, the "school within a school" organization of some magnet schools, while it often desegregates one component of a school, can leave the other, usually larger component, nearly all one-race. The concept of racial integration has ceased to have any serious meaning in Prince George's County.

The Prince George's case may prove informative to the growing number of suburban districts across the nation facing racial and socioeconomic change in their schools. In the face of rapid demographic change, it seems the considerable resources put into voluntary magnet schools may not be enough to create substantial, lasting interracial contact between students.

Systemic housing integration and residential planning may have had more potential in maintaining a desegregated school system in this case. For school districts in which a dwindling minority of white students might make full racial integration difficult to achieve over the long term, educational leaders might be better off considering policies that promote housing integration and residential planning or cooperative efforts with other predominantly white school districts. These strategies may turn out to be more effective than funnelling resources and efforts into intradistrict voluntary magnet plans. There are still large numbers of black and white students in Prince George's County; therefore, possibilities for establishing long-term racial integration still exist. It is time for county school leaders to think about what kinds of integration are still plausible, rather than simply abandoning efforts altogether.

Prince George's had many politicians and other school leaders convinced that the answer to improving achievement and creating good racial integration policies lay in getting the right school leader to corral community support and increase local investment in the schools. In the end, however, such a simplistic solution brought only a temporary public relations remedy that covered up real problems. For anyone who believes that there is a simple remedy for educational inequality, segregation, racial change, and housing and demographic shifts, the evidence from Prince George's should call into question the belief that there is a "miracle cure." These are serious problems that require thoughtful policy and systemic change.

CHAPTER ELEVEN

Segregated Housing and School Resegregation

Gary Orfield

People often visualize cities as if they are collections of stable neighborhoods, but American cities have always been in a state of constant change. Americans are a restless, mobile people. The average family moves every five or six years, and young families move even more often. The story of a family's development and success is often told in terms of a series of moves to better homes and neighborhoods. When the older population in a neighborhood is white and the newcomers are black or Latino, the continuing changes create segregated schools and undermine desegregation plans. All of the communities we have studied confronted policy and legal choices forced by community residential change, and many worried about the effect of school policies on their community's ability to hold its residents. Unfortunately, federal courts often fail to devise rules and policies that work effectively in coping with racial change. In fact, in its resegregation decisions, the Rehnquist Court has used these changes to justify dismantling desegregation, arguing that the spread of housing segregation shows it is futile or counterproductive. Understanding the paths toward viable, lasting school integration requires sorting out the links between schools and housing changes.

The Supreme Court made a good start in describing and beginning to correct the impact of residential apartheid on school segregation in the early 1970s. As the Court turned toward resegregation, however, it radically changed its understanding of housing segregation.

Each of the communities examined in this book face continuous expansion of residential segregation. Even where extensive desegregation was achieved under an old court order, racial integration was threatened by the spread of minority segregation in city neighborhoods and the continuous construction of new all-white suburbs.

Trying to deal with changing communities with a static desegregation plan was often an exercise in frustration. School district officials claimed that there was nothing they could do as segregation spread. Officials asked to be set free of desegregation requirements to reinstitute neighborhood schools. Civil rights groups, on the other hand, argued that school decisions on location, boundaries, transfers, and decisions of other public agencies compounded the segregation, and that courts should hold both school and housing officials responsible.

The Supreme Court entered the era of urban school desegregation with findings that policies affecting school and housing segregation were intimately interrelated. By the time of the resegregation decisions, however, the Court described housing segregation as something separate and mysterious—something that simply happened—and that local officials could do little about. Justice Sandra Day O'Connor described residential change as the result of white flight and "natural, if unfortunate, demographic forces" in 1995.[1]

Serious school segregation today is overwhelmingly caused not by the isolation of students within school districts but by the separation of overwhelmingly minority city systems from overwhelmingly white suburban districts. Three-fourths of the nation's residents and more than 80 percent of minority students live in metropolitan areas. In most states, the metropolitan communities are broken up into many school districts. Residential segregation produces concentration of the African American and Latino students in a small number of districts, thus maintaining segregated education even if authorities try to desegregate within each school district. As long as the spread of residential segregation continues, the schools will constantly face choices among further segregation, continually redrawing plans as the population changes and trying to desegregate with the suburbs.

Trying to cure school segregation without understanding the nature of housing segregation can easily compound the problems. Lasting school desegregation requires either stable integrated housing or a plan that copes effectively with the patterns of spreading housing segregation.

Judicial Theories About Housing

During the past two decades, the Supreme Court and many lower courts have taken spectacularly inconsistent positions on the question of why metropolitan areas are so segregated and whether the schools cause segregation or are simply victims of housing changes. As the Court changed through conservative appointments, the origin of housing segregation has been increasingly described as an innocent result of private choices. When an earlier Supreme Court decided that busing was needed to desegregate cities, it recognized that the violations had deep roots in both school and housing discrimination. When the Court later decided first to limit and then to terminate desegregation, however, it saw housing segregation differently. When it blocked suburban desegregation in the 1974 *Milliken* decision, the Court said housing segregation was something that happened for some unknowable reason. Later, when it approved school resegregation, the Court described residential segregation as a natural force that courts and school districts could do nothing about.

The changing conception of housing, often announced as fact, provided grounds for judicial acceptance of segregated education. The Supreme Court's failure to examine the housing underpinnings of metropolitan segregation in the 1974 *Milliken I* decision made desegregation almost impossible in the metropolitan North. Full and lasting desegregation had become unachievable within increasingly minority city boundaries. Suburbs were protected from desegregation by the courts ignoring the origin of their racially segregated housing patterns.

The *Milliken* decision, which blocked desegregation in the North, *Dowell* (1991), and *Pitts* (1992), permitted resegregation of Southern school districts and embraced changing views of housing segregation. The 1995 *Jenkins* decision said courts must not require policies designed to offset white flight by improving city schools to attract whites.

The great shift of constitutional priorities in *Milliken* from requiring actual desegregation to asserting the primary importance of suburban local control rested on a theory of suburban innocence. The Court ruled that, in order to win a remedy, civil rights groups needed to prove suburban guilt for discrimination or segregation. This meant that findings of guilt in the arena of housing discrimination would have been the only possible way to achieve total school desegregation. After all, many Detroit suburbs had such severe housing segregation that the school districts had virtually no black students to discriminate against. Thus, when the Court excluded all discussion of how the Detroit suburbs came to be among the nation's most rigidly segregated, it guaranteed segregation of Detroit's black students. The

Court said that even though both the city and the state had intentionally segregated black students and the lower courts had found that desegregation without involving students in the suburbs to be unworkable, suburban schools could not be included unless there was proof that they discriminated.

By failing to examine housing, the Court gave neighborhoods that had successfully segregated their housing an exemption from school desegregation requirements. City neighborhoods that had not excluded blacks, on the other hand, faced mandatory desegregation. Fragile, racially changing neighborhoods of the city were punished with a desegregation plan that would almost certainly speed ghetto expansion. Under the plan, the ghetto would expand because desegregation would be concentrated in small areas in transition and all-white schools would be protected from desegregation. This effectively created refuges for whites fearful of minorities moving into their schools.

The Detroit plan produced no significant lasting school desegregation and undermined neighborhood integration. Detroit was the nation's second most segregated metropolitan area a generation after this "remedy." The Detroit schools, 72 percent black the year of the *Milliken I* decision, became 89 percent black by 1986 and remained at that level in 1992. Eighty-six percent of Detroit's black students were in intensely segregated schools with less than 10 percent white students. Only half of one percent (.006) were in majority-white schools.[2] The Detroit experience shows the high stakes in correctly understanding and acting on housing issues.

Segregated urban school systems are built on a base of housing segregation. The vast differences between inner-city and suburban schools help determine where white families with choices will live, as people moving to a new metropolitan area will almost immediately discover from realtors and relocation services. Such services usually show newcomers nothing in central cities or racially changing suburbs. As minority suburbanization grows, realtors also determine where African American and Latino families live. The struggle to integrate schools of urban areas has been an effort to reverse some of the educational inequalities growing out of a comprehensive system of urban segregation in which schools, housing, and employment are racially separate. The system has grown out of public and private forms of discrimination unchecked for many decades. Many effects of that discrimination continue today.

The Supreme Court recognized the interaction of school and housing decisions, in its first urban desegregation case, the 1971 *Swann* decision that authorized busing: "The construction of new schools and the closing of old ones are two of the most important functions of local school authorities," said the Court. "Over the long run, consequences of the choices will be far-reaching. People gravitate toward school facilities, just as schools are located in response to the needs of people. The location of schools may thus influence the patterns of residential development of a metropolitan area and have [an] important impact on composition of inner-city neighborhoods."[3]

The Court's first northern desegregation decision, *Keyes,* arose directly out of issues related to neighborhood residential change. In Denver, residents of the integrated Park Hill neighborhood feared that school boundary changes would resegregate local schools. The residents then initiated the lawsuit that led to a citywide desegregation order.

The ruling declared that Denver's practices had effectively labeled schools by race, affecting the racial makeup of neighborhoods throughout the city's housing market. The Court pointed to school sites and attendance boundaries that undermined integration. The complex interaction between school and housing segregation was a key part of the Supreme Court's reasoning for ordering citywide desegregation on the basis of neighborhood level violations:

> First, it is obvious that a practice of concentrating Negroes in certain schools by structuring attendance zones…has the reciprocal effect of keeping other nearby schools predominantly white. Similarly, the practice of building a school…to a certain size and in a certain location, "with conscious knowledge that it would be a segregated school,"…has a substantial reciprocal effect on the racial composition of other nearby schools. So also, the use of mobile classrooms, the drafting of student transfer policies, the transportation of students, and the assignment of faculty and staff, on racially identifiable bases, have the clear effect of earmarking schools according to their racial composition, and this, in turn, together with the elements of student assignment and school construction, may have a profound reciprocal effect on the racial composition of residential neighborhoods…. We recognized this in Swann….[4]

Protecting the Suburbs

What the Supreme Court recognized in *Swann* and *Keyes,* it forgot in *Milliken,* one year later. Desegregation in Detroit and many other large cities was made impossible. This decision ended the rapid growth of desegregated schooling for black students that had begun in the mid-1960s and blocked efforts to desegregate the soaring Latino population, more than 85 percent of which was concentrated in metropolitan areas.

In *Milliken*, the Court faced an issue full of housing dimensions yet the Court's majority opinion literally ignored housing evidence, although civil rights attorney Nicholas Flannery in his oral argument before the Court had presented the evidence and trial court findings on housing. He argued that "the segregated school practices, operated in lockstep with an area-wide metropolitan policy of confining by housing discrimination...black families to an identifiable core in Detroit...." He cited eight witnesses who testified about "the containment pattern, housing and schools, that was coming to characterize the metropolitan area" and noted that the lower courts had accepted the containment theory.[5]

Chief Justice Burger's opinion, however, asserted that "the case does not present any question concerning possible state housing violations."[6] Justice Potter Stewart, the decisive fifth vote on the case, wrote in a footnote that housing segregation was caused by "unknown or unknowable causes," asserting that "no record has been made in this case showing that the racial composition of the Detroit school population or that residential patterns within Detroit and in the surrounding areas were in any significant measure caused by governmental activity."[7]

The plaintiffs in *Milliken I* had asked the Supreme Court to send the case back to the lower courts because no specific remedy had been approved by the trial judge. Although the Court's majority said that the housing issues had not been raised, the Court asked neither for lower court examination of the housing issue nor for an actual plan from the lower courts before making its decision. Thus, the Supreme Court accepted metropolitan segregation without any effort to find out why the communities were segregated.

By the 1990s, the Court had created, with its theories of housing segregation, a twentieth-century equivalent of the theory of "racial instincts" that an earlier court used to justify *Plessy's* separate but equal doctrine. In *Plessy*, the Supreme Court had portrayed itself as helpless, explaining that "legislation is powerless to eradicate racial instincts...and the attempt to do so can only result in accentuating the difficulties of the present situation."[8] Under the contemporary version of that theory, if housing segregation happens because of some modern version of "racial instincts," then the courts can use similar logic to assert that it is best do nothing since attempts to desegregate schools will inevitably be undermined by the natural "demographic forces" that produce residential segregation.

Ignoring Urban History

Basic assumptions about urban change in many recent decisions are in conflict with research on federal housing policy and the findings of numerous courts about the intentional segregation of subsidized housing. A number of the decisions also require standards of proof for plaintiffs that are impossible.

Few aspects of urban history are clearer than the fact that governments at all levels fostered residential segregation for many years. In most cities it is easy to show that housing segregation was initiated and institutionalized with massive official support, that most minority neighborhoods segregated during the period of overt segregationist policies remain segregated today. Many millions of minority families still live in segregated housing markets, surveys show that this is not by choice.

Segregation has been spreading beyond the borders of older minority communities since World War II. The most recent federal studies of housing market and lending practices show that discrimination continues to be widespread. There is an unbroken pattern of ghetto expansion dating back to the period of overt discrimination, and segregated black communities now extend well into sections of some suburban rings. In many housing markets, most black families have been segregated for generations. The physical isolation of those in the core of the minority communities becomes more extreme as the borders of the ghetto expand and middle-class black families abandon the core.

It is easy to prove that a variety of types of discrimination existed in most housing markets and to show that the segregation they helped institutionalize still continues. Black fears of violence and intimidation in some white communities are still serious obstacles to housing choice. Whites and white realtors almost never look for housing in what are defined as minority communities, and real estate operations are often organized along racial lines. Minority brokers are seldom employed by white offices and rarely get listings in white areas unless racial transitions are well under way. Because most people shop for housing in areas where they have knowledge of housing or acquaintances, the fact that the history of segregation has given blacks and whites familiarity with separate sets of communities and fears about each other's neighborhoods tends to reinforces a self-perpetuating segregation. In these and many other ways, the history of housing discrimination continues to shape communities and, therefore, their schools.[9]

What civil rights lawyers have trouble proving are all the specific linkages between the past and present. Residential segregation was such a pervasive part of the American past that it is built into many institutions, fears, and expectations, but there is no way to prove scientifically just how much of contemporary segregation is directly linked to historic violations. Social science is not capable of accurately measuring the relative influence of the official and private elements of generations of discrimination on the patterns of segregation many years later. To measure the impact of official discrimination alone, it would be necessary to have some cases without private discrimination. To try to measure all the impacts over time, researchers would need to untangle all the beliefs and practices that grew out of the official discrimination and track the relative importance of those factors on contemporary practices. In order to make even very rough estimates of these relationships, it would have been necessary to initiate massive studies generations ago to provide baseline data, control groups, and other essential elements of social research. This, of course, was not done.

Although the courts often impose requirements of specific proof from civil rights lawyers, they often adopt their own theories about housing as if they were simply common sense. Courts also make findings about the causes of segregation on the basis of surveys of racial attitudes conducted for the local officials. Surveys cannot, by their nature, assess the two fundamental legal issues—the degree to which attitudes are a product of the history of discrimination and the degree to which opinions would change under a new policy. The first is a central question in judging the guilt of governmental agencies; the second is crucial for devising remedies that work.

Although surveys are often presented by school districts and accepted by courts as proving the existence of immutable natural private preferences that make lasting remedies impossible, survey data is incapable of proving such a claim. Even if one concedes the validity of fairness of the questions, attitudes could well be shaped by previous illegal housing segregation policies. What opinion surveys can never tell us is how people would respond if they confronted a new reality, if they actually were to live together peacefully in an integrated community and test their fears and stereotypes against that reality. If the Supreme Court had relied on an opinion poll at the time of the *Brown* decision, the fact that 81 percent of white Southerners believed the Court to be wrong would have been taken as a justification for inaction. We would have never known that forty years later, only 15 percent of white Southerners would hold that attitude after two decades of experiencing the nation's most integrated schools.[10]

Sometimes the courts' approach is not to look at any evidence at all but simply to announce that all historic housing violations prior to the 1968 federal fair housing law do not matter, because the law canceled the effects of generations of discrimination. It is as if a court concluded that the national debt had stopped growing because several times in the past fifteen years, Congress has adopted legislation promising to balance the budget. In fact, a finding that discrimination and the effects of past discrimination do not matter ignores the recent national research commissioned by the federal government. The research findings show serious discrimination in housing markets decades after 1968. They demonstrate that the government failed to enforce both the notoriously weak 1968 fair housing law and the 1988 amendments.[11]

The U.S. Civil Rights Commission pointed out in 1994 that HUD was far behind the congressional goal of handling fair housing complaints within 100 days. It had done very little to enforce the goal on a systematic basis. HUD rarely tested for discrimination and developed only about one broad case a year in the entire United States.[12]

Judicial Assumptions That Minimize the Effects of Segregation

Because the levels of segregation remain high and studies show continued discrimination,[13] it is difficult to understand the basis for the court findings that the laws erased the impacts of the long history of state-supported residential apartheid. Though the attitudes, practices, and institutions that created and perpetuate residential segregation developed during that period of overt discrimination and many continue today, the courts often assume that at some point they became detached from their historic roots and became matters of private preference for segregation. A frequent assumption in court decisions is that discrimination existed until the point of a key court decision or passage of a civil rights law. This assumption, which contradicts studies on the implementation of civil rights decisions or laws, is almost always put forward without evidence.[14]

A less extreme version of this judicial approach claims that historic violations have diminishing effects with the passage of time. Thus, over a number of years, discrimination could be safely discounted. In his opinion in the 1995 *Jenkins* case, for example, Justice Clarence Thomas described the way in which "state-enforced segregation recedes farther into the past," as it is replaced by "massive demographic shifts" that are "beyond the practical ability of the federal courts to try to counteract."[15] Although Americans tend to see history as a story of social progress, there is no empirical basis for asserting that racial attitudes gradually improve. The historical record clearly shows, to the contrary, that attitudes and policies change in both directions. Discrimination and exclusion, for example, became more rigid after Reconstruction ended and *Plessy* legitimated segregation.[16] In contrast, the Supreme Court's 1973 *Keyes* decision rejected "any suggestion that remoteness in time has any relevance to the issue of intent."[17]

Some courts raise even more barriers to considering the housing issues. In *Swann*, the Supreme Court had noted that not too much should be put into one case, since a single case "can carry only a limited amount of baggage." This obscure phrase gave lower courts a plausible way to dispose of even extremely serious housing issues. A court can jettison serious housing evidence by claiming that the court will be overburdened by hearing and considering all the evidence on these relationships. Chief Justice Rehnquist employed the excess baggage theory in his decision reversing the Kansas City remedy in 1995.[18]

Plaintiffs sometimes seem inside of a housing maze with no exit: if they present limited evidence, it will be dismissed as failing to establish the required proof of continuing effects of past violations. But if they try to prove the entire intricate history of metropolitan discrimination in a housing market, the argument may be dismissed as presenting more than the courts can cope with.

Atlanta: Examples of Judicial Avoidance

The court decision in the 1979 metropolitan Atlanta desegregation case show how the manipulation of housing issues was used to preclude a remedy. District Judge William O'Kelley decided that the case was too complex for the court to handle, holding "there is just so much baggage a school case can carry."[19] He discarded thousands of pages of proof that the entire racial structure of the Atlanta area was built on many decades of explicit residential discrimination, expressed first in formal segregation laws, then in planned construction of racial borders, in formal agreements between the city's white and black leaders about segregated housing for blacks, and in the administration of many programs shaping housing, transportation, and neighborhood development.

The court, however, wished to avoid forcing what the judge saw as "drastic" change—"to change the residential patterns which exist it would be necessary to rip up the very fabric of society in a manner which is not within the province of the federal courts."[20] The court found eighteen ways in which government agencies had caused housing segregation, including racial zoning laws, segregated relocation from renewal lands, racial designation of schools, and overtly racial public housing site selection. Violations were found both within the city itself and the surrounding suburbs. The court concluded that metropolitan segregation was "caused in part by the intentional acts of government officials,"[21] but treated this as little more than an interesting historical observation. Because a fair housing act existed now, the court ruled, contemporary segregation should no longer be blamed on past discrimination.

Survey data provided by David Armor, the conservative social scientist and former Reagan administration official, was used by the court to claim that "why people live where they do can never be fully explained."[22] The judge spoke of the role of economics, personal preferences, and the "tipping phenomenon."[23] The judge did not consider the possibility that preferences and expectations were themselves vestiges of a history of segregation. Segregation was seen as a hopelessly complex natural force.

The court's Atlanta decision also rejected the linkage of housing and school issues. Since the school districts were not at fault for ghettos and segregated white areas produced by other policies, the court held, school officials should not have to desegregate. The court's approach made it impossible to obtain school desegregation based on intense housing violations. Intense housing segregation, on the other hand, made it impossible to prove, as *Milliken I* required, that all-white suburbs had engaged in school discrimination, since black families could not even live there. At the time of the decisions, metropolitan Atlanta remained one of the South's most segregated urban regions, with a pattern of pervasive educational inequality strongly related to race documented several years later.[24] The courts denied public responsibility for any of this.

When the metropolitan Atlanta case reached the Supreme Court, the Court took the unusual step of affirming the lower court's decision on schools in the Deep South's largest metropolis without even giving a hearing to the parties.[25]

Housing and the Resegregation Decisions of the 1990s

In its key decisions on resegregration, *Dowell* and *Pitts,* the Supreme Court revisited the housing issue but was divided. In the 1995 *Jenkins* decision the five member majority adopted the entire conservative argument, claiming that school policies do not affect housing except when white flight from school desegregation occurs.

The 1992 *Pitts* decision found the Court's majority relying on a variety of techniques to minimize the accountability of public officials for housing segregation. They included switching the burden of proof, assuming that time cured the effects of past discrimination, and accepting the natural preferences theory of segregation. In *Jenkins* the court majority also adopted the white-flight theory.

The Complexity of the Problem

Some of the court decisions evade the issues. The problem that confronts any effort to demonstrate the precise nature of the school-housing relationship is that public and private discrimination, past and present, are woven inextricably together. A single example can illustrate the difficulties of precise analysis. A black family has children in segregated schools because it never looked for housing in white areas—a seemingly clear-cut case of private preference for which no government agency would take responsibility. If, however, the family did not look for housing in white neighborhoods because the wife's parents' house had been vandalized by white neighbors and the police did nothing, causing the family to decide to move back into the ghetto, the decision actually was a result of fears arising from past government actions fostering discrimination. Similarly, if a family lacks the equity to buy a suburban house, this would seem like the most obvious example of economic rather than racial discrimination. But if we knew that the family did not have the wealth of similar white families because they were discriminated against under Federal Housing Authority (FHA) redlining policies that kept them from owning a starter home years ago, the cause would be a continuing effect of past discrimination. If we knew that a community that would meet their needs had rejected a proposal to build affordable housing on racial grounds, another element of official action would be implicated.

Multiplying the issues affecting a single family by hundreds of thousands in a large metropolitan housing, it becomes clear how impossible it is to sort out all the "private" and "public" elements of housing segregation. How much, for example, should the rejection of subsidized suburban housing be attributed to racial fears and stereotypes and how much to economic exclusion? Considering how all these decisions shape minority communities over time and considering the reciprocal effects on white experiences and attitudes, it is clear that past and present discrimination are woven into the fabric of communities in ways that could never be precisely sorted out.

Given that reality, the real legal issue is what assumptions and standards of proof the courts use to reach their conclusions. Those seemingly technical questions powerfully influence whether a community will have segregated schools. In the last two decades the courts have been imposing rules and procedures that lead to conclusions that housing segregation simply happened and that government agencies should not be held accountable.

The History of Housing Discrimination

Resegregation cases require courts to consider whether official actions including the district's implementation of its desegregation plan and decisions of other local agencies contributed to the segregation of neighborhoods and schools. Approving a return to neighborhood schools is much more difficult if the court recognizes that actions of the school board or the public housing authority created more segregation or that school decisions helped spread residential segregation.

The new theories of suburban innocence and voluntary segregation, however, contrast with the findings of many urban historians. Research on the formation and expansion of residential segregation in major cities shows extensive official involvement on many levels. Even in recent times, courts found HUD and local authorities guilty of past and current discrimination.[26] Federal officials enforcing fair housing and fair lending policies freely concede that their efforts have been far too weak to end discrimination.[27] Segregation is related to regulations, laws, practices of officials, and lax enforcement of antidiscrimination laws.

Discrimination by public agencies dates from the black exodus from the rural South triggered by World War I and World War II labor shortages in the North. Public and private institutions worked together to confine blacks to overcrowded, overpriced, and deteriorating ghettos whose inferior city services included inferior segregated schools. Local actions included police toleration of white racial violence against blacks moving into white areas, use of zoning and planning powers to foster separation, planned segregation of subsidized housing, school siting and boundaries, and many administrative practices that fostered residential and school separation.

The first mass migration coincided with the rise of zoning and city planning. Leading cities of the southern and border states including St. Louis, Baltimore, and Atlanta, enacted zoning laws prescribing where blacks could live—official apartheid laws.[28] The Supreme Court struck down such laws, but some cities continued to enforce them.

Although outlawing racial zoning, the Supreme Court authorized court enforcement of private agreements to accomplish the same purpose.[29] In the 1920s, there were neighborhood organizing campaigns for restrictive covenants that attached racial exclusions to deeds on homes. The court enforced the covenants and the federal government, in its home mortgage programs, encouraged their use. After the Court upheld covenants in *Corrigan v. Buckley*,[30] they spread rapidly in areas with significant minority population.[31] Many black communities were almost totally cut off from significant growth by an iron curtain of legally enforceable covenants on all of their boundaries.[32] This created incredible housing demand, massive overuse, a "race tax" on housing prices, and deterioration of housing within the racial boundaries.

Black households confronted with artificially high housing costs and low wages because of job discrimination had no alternative but to double up in housing. Landlords profiting from the housing shortages had little incentive to maintain the property and the resulting decay contributed to the white stereotype that entry of black residents caused decay or "blight." Disinvestment was fostered by policies denying federally insured mortgages to buyers in inner cities and integrated areas. These housing discrimination policies were part of the vicious self-perpetuating cycles that grew up around the ghetto system. Those syndromes contributed to discrimination and flight from integrated neighborhoods long after fair housing laws were enacted.

Not until 1950, did the FHA stop requiring racial covenants in new developments.[33] By that time, the postwar suburban boom was set within a framework of segregation. Massive mortgage financing flowed to FHA and Veterans Administration (VA) buyers in white subdivisions and almost none to older communities or minority home seekers, even black veterans.[34] No significant FHA and VA financing was available to minority families until the late 1960s.

The entire system was one of government-sponsored segregation and a denial of even "separate but equal" opportunities for minority families. The lack of mortgage capital contributed powerfully to the decline of minority and integrated communities and the inability of minority families to enter the housing market under extraordinarily favorable post-World War II conditions that led to huge increases in the worth of the housing investments of millions of families who bought for low prices in new suburban developments and later sold for many times more.

It is not surprising that when urban renewal came along in the 1950s as a strategy to save the downtowns; most of the areas where "blight" was eliminated through "slum clearance" were those of minority communities.[35] With no fair housing rights and no serious plan for replacement housing, leveling black communities to produce new middle-class developments near downtown poured displaced black families into segregated housing markets. This rapidly resegregated neighborhoods and created new ghettos. Suburbs that had small minority pockets often used renewal dollars to level those communities and redevelop the land, sending the residents to live in new housing projects in the inner city. These programs produced a sudden expansion of ghetto communities, serious conflicts with working-class white areas, and reinforcement of stereotypes about the instability of residential and school integration. The new urban freeways built under the Interstate Highway Act in the 1950s and 1960s often resulted in the displacement of more minority communities in a similar manner. The rapid construction of high-rise segregated public housing projects in inner cities compounded the problem; projects were segregated because local politics blocked construction of lower-density subsidized housing in outlying white areas with excellent schools.[36] Subsidized housing site selection doomed generations of children to weak segregated schools.

When the federal approach shifted from building public housing projects to reliance on the private market and nonprofits for subsidized housing in the large programs of the early 1970s, the results once again reinforced segregation and inner-city decay. The low-income homeownership program known as "Section 235," for example, provided subsidies that allowed poor families to purchase small homes by virtually eliminating down payments and subsidizing mortgage interest down to 1 percent. Since the program pumped dollars into segregated markets without challenging their discriminating nature, it enabled many low-income white families to obtain subsidies that they used to leave integrated areas and buy small new homes in outlying white areas. Black buyers, however, tended to end up in old homes in ghettos or racially changing areas. The program reinforced residential and school segregation and helped finance the resegregation of residentially integrated-city communities.[37] In some cities, many black buyers were stuck with old homes with severe deficiencies. The result was the abandonment of a number of black communities, particularly in inner cities, and hundreds of millions of dollars in losses for the government.[38]

Section 8, the next HUD program, begun in 1974, was smaller but relied even more on private developers and owners. Local agencies gave rent subsidy certificates to eligible tenants and landlords rented to tenants who passed their screening. Although there were "affirmative marketing" requirements about advertising, there was no significant outreach by owners for minority tenants for most suburban sites, which filled up with whites. The result was subsidized housing for white families in suburban school districts and reinforcement of minority concentration.[39] President Reagan, in turn, drastically cut back those programs in the 1980s.[40] No significant new housing programs had been enacted by 1996.

Thus, federal subsidized housing programs, administered by local agencies or private owners, intensified residential and school separation decade after decade. One of the clearest patterns of official discrimination in housing has been the selection of segregated housing sites and the assignment of tenants in ways that produced racially defined communities, often served by segregated schools. Many cities went so far as to build schools for projects. Others gerrymandered school attendance districts to keep the project children out of white schools. A 1994 HUD report concludes that the public housing tenants living in the "poorest tracts" are "almost exclusively (91 percent) African American."[41] Most white subsidized tenants lived in low-poverty areas where the proportion of residents living in public housing was one-fiftieth that of the poorest tracts.[42] Black public housing tenants often attend inferior schools almost totally segregated by poverty as well as race. A significant portion of the total black enrollment in some central city school districts live in public and subsidized housing.[43] Norfolk, the first city to resegregate with federal court approval, created some black schools almost totally populated by public housing project children.

Lower courts examining the history of public housing outside of school cases have often found unambiguous discrimination, and they continue to make such findings. In Chicago, where the city council vetoed housing sites on racial grounds for decades, the district court found in 1969 that the site selections and tenant assignments of the Chicago Housing Authority (CHA) were unconstitutional.[44] The court ruled that there was "uncontradicted evidence...that the public housing system operated by CHA was racially segregated, with four overwhelmingly white projects located in white neighborhoods and with 99.5% of the remaining family units located in Negro neighborhoods.[45]

In Yonkers, where the Justice Department brought its first combined lawsuit against both school and housing officials in the same community, the court found that 97.7 percent of public housing for poor people was located in the city's southwest quadrant where about 80 percent of black residents lived. The court ruled that "the desire to preserve existing patterns of segregation has been a significant factor."[46] In other words, housing policy had influenced racial segregation in the city schools.

The Dallas Housing Authority was convicted of intentional segregation in 1989.[47] A HUD-funded study of housing in metropolitan Dallas
had earlier concluded that public housing had "obvious implications
for segregation in public schools," since 97 percent of the units had
been built in all-black areas or areas in the path of transition that
became virtually all minority.[48] The study found that the later HUD
programs, such as Section 8, also contributed to segregation of
minorities and the resegregation of integrated neighborhoods, as did
some of the city's land use and development policies. "Racial isolation in the public schools," the report concluded, "is directly related
to the housing policies which the city of Dallas has pursued." The
U.S. Justice Department later conceded HUD responsibility in Dallas.[49]
Nonetheless, the federal court in Dallas enforcing the school desegregation plan became one of the first to permit resegregation following the Supreme Court's resegregation orders.

Subsidized housing is a small part of the housing market, though
it provides homes for a substantial fraction of the low-income central
city African American families who are so highly segregated in
schools. The much broader effects of the history of housing discrimination are built into a variety of institutions serving the white and
minority housing markets. Sets of attitudes, practices, contacts, and
business specialists grew up around the color line. In the separate
markets there were and are sales and rental professionals often with
offices located on opposite sides of the color line who specialize in
different white or minority areas. There are separate and unequal
capital and mortgage finance markets, which, until recently, rarely
provided conventional mortgage financing in minority communities.

Since all the minority demand for additional housing was concentrated by real estate practices in areas just outside the existing
ghettos, great profits could be made by transferring a new area from
the white to the black housing market. There were specialists in racial
transition ("block busters" and "panic peddlers") who profited from
the process of frightening whites into selling suddenly and cheaply
and then jacking up the price for black buyers with few choices. Such
racial changes tended to be fast and destructive, with entire streets
posted with "for sale" signs. The fear of this process fed the tendencies of white discrimination and harassment of minority households.
White fears of ghetto expansion and black fears of harassment both
continue to reinforce segregation. Studies in metropolitan Chicago

showed that large fractions of black families feared harassment if they moved to white areas. The key to residential stability was white beliefs about the future of the neighborhood.[50]

Housing and the Viability of School Desegregation

Though findings about housing often received little attention in school cases, they were fundamental to the effects of the decisions. In *Milliken I* and the resegregation cases, housing was treated as if it were unrelated to the effectiveness of school desegregation plans. This produced easily predictable failures like the Detroit central city plan.

Viable desegregation plans consider housing in formulating the school plan. Simply ordering school desegregation in the central city while ghettos and white suburbia continue their rapid expansion can be counterproductive. If white families, for example, face a choice between a central city area where all schools have 80 percent black "desegregated" enrollments and dozens of virtually all-white suburban districts, few will chose the city community. A desegregation plan that assumes a static racial boundary is assuming something that no American city possesses. A plan that combines immediately adjacent black and white neighborhoods, for example, when the white neighborhood is already experiencing rapid in-migration of African Americans or Latinos has almost no chance of producing lasting integration. School desegregation transfers in these areas may well further inflame explosive race relations. In such circumstances, choosing the shortest possible busing distances could accelerate resegregation. Some of the most notoriously difficult desegregation situations, such as the bitter confrontation at South Boston High School in the mid-1970s, had short busing times but brought together two groups of disadvantaged students across an explosive racial boundary.

Some of the plans with the least tension have involved long-distance transfers of minority students to suburban schools. A voluntary plan of this sort, METCO, has existed in metropolitan Boston for three decades with few serious problems.[51] Large city-suburban busing plans have been operating for a quarter century with high levels of desegregation and stability in a number of cities with county-wide school systems. Many integrated magnet schools in minority areas have become very popular and receive willing white transferees.

The ghettoization process arising from generations of discrimination is self-perpetuating.[52] Dual markets, mutual fears, unequal market knowledge, mortgage discrimination, and lack of positive models of successful integration made the momentum of past discrimination very powerful. Separate markets in which minority families were less likely to own a home than similar white families and where they usually had to invest in areas that produced smaller gains yield much less accumulated wealth to provide down payments on bigger homes and, therefore, fewer options.[53] Viable school desegregation plans must not be designed in ways that reinforce racial transition and fears; the best plans try to create stably integrated schools that can help support the development of stably integrated neighborhoods.

Fair Housing: The Federal Record

In theory, the federal government committed itself to the principle of fair housing in 1968, but the commitment was limited. In spite of language in the 1968 law that required all federal urban programs to be administered in order to foster fair housing, the 1970s and 1980s brought large additional federal investments in housing *segregation*.[54] The weakness of the 1968 law, which gave HUD no power to impose sanctions even in the face of clear violations, was criticized by HUD secretaries from both Republican and Democratic administrations, most of whom called for stronger enforcement tools. Only the Justice Department could pursue sanctions through lawsuits, and it brought only about twenty fair housing suits a year, though there were an estimated two million violations occurring annually.[55] Not until 1988 was the law strengthened. In early 1995, Roberta Achtenberg, HUD Assistant Secretary for Fair Housing, conceded that "the federal government, including HUD, has a long history of having precipitated and perpetuated housing discrimination." After detailing the ways in which various housing and urban development programs had increased segregation and damaged integrated and minority neighborhoods, she noted that "federal fair housing law has been weak and inadequate."[56]

During more than two-thirds of the time since fair housing became law, the federal government was dominated by conservative administrations deeply skeptical of efforts to remake the segregated housing patterns in the metropolitan areas of the United States.

President Nixon and President Ford attacked strong efforts to integrate suburbia.[57] So did President Carter, during his presidential campaign, when he said that he saw "nothing wrong with ethnic purity being maintained" in urban neighborhoods. Carter said that he thought this was a "natural inclination."[58] Except for HUD Secretary George Romney's brief leadership (before he was fired by President Nixon), there was no serious effort to use federal housing and urban development tools to increase integrated housing in metropolitan areas until the administration of HUD Secretary Henry Cisneros, which began in 1993. Cisneros was hampered by severe cutbacks in the HUD budget and his major legislative initiative to subsidize suburban mobility by the poor was defeated in Congress.[59]

Federal and local housing subsidy programs normally fed money into a segregated housing market. HUD and local housing authorities usually did nothing to address the problems of limited knowledge and fear by tenants and discrimination by landlords.[60] When HUD succeeded in encouraging more subsidized housing in suburbia in response to the 1974 Housing and Community Development Act's requirement for "spatial deconcentration of the poor," there was no serious effort to make sure that minority families obtained access to that housing.[61] Whites rented subsidized suburban housing and minority households remained in the city—increasing school segregation.

There were alternatives. Experiments with housing counseling for subsidized tenants in Chicago and Louisville showed that if minority families were taken to look at housing outside of segregated and racially changing areas, a large fraction of low-income black households were prepared to consider moves even into virtually all-white areas. Moreover, the evidence shows that such moves were highly successful in terms of the children's education.[62] Such a model implemented in Louisville in the mid-1970s was described in research reports and policy debates a generation ago.

After it was directed by the federal district court in St. Louis in 1980 to submit a housing plan to support desegregated education in the St. Louis area, HUD was on official notice to examine the implications of its policies for school segregation. Following that order, HUD commissioned a study of the relationship between subsidized housing and school segregation in three other metropolitan areas. In each, there was a strong relationship between the location and tenancy of subsidized family housing and school segregation. A substantial share of

the segregated minority students in city systems were living in locations determined by subsidized housing policies and practices. In each
area studied, much of the busing required by school desegregation
orders was attributable to the segregation of subsidized housing for
low-income minority families.[63]

By the end of the Carter administration, the impact of the housing policies on school segregation had become clear to HUD officials.
In its final days, the administration sponsored sessions on coordina-
tion of school and housing desegregation policies in various cities,
including Denver. It issued a regulation requiring that housing decisions be taken in light of the implications for school segregation. This
regulation was rescinded in the first days of the Reagan administration and was never put into operation. Regulations implementing the
broad provisions of the 1968 fair housing law were never issued in
the twenty years following its enactment.

Only in the Clinton administration did serious discussion of these
issues resume, but by that time federal housing and urban programs
had become so much smaller that their potential leverage was much
weaker. President Clinton himself proposed massive additional cuts
in HUD following the GOP congressional victory in 1994 and even considered dismantling the department.

When the courts announce that housing discrimination ended
because the fair housing law was passed, they are assuming an
enforcement record wholly at odds with what actually happened. In
the years since fair housing has been enacted, there has been much
larger federal involvement in subsidizing new housing segregation
and resegregation than in ending housing discrimination.

Housing in School Cases: Legal Fictions and Unequal Legal Resources

The federal courts are currently making important decisions on the
basis of fundamentally inaccurate understandings of past and present housing discrimination. The errors can be partially explained
by the fact that housing issues are presented in a skewed way in court
proceedings. The school districts, which try to use housing as a
justification for school segregation, often have the money to create
what appears to be plausible evidence that local segregation is a product of choice by minority and white families, not discrimination. The

plaintiffs usually lack the money to prove the history of housing discrimination. They cannot document the vicious cycles that led to those "choices." They often lack the expertise to attack the validity of flawed survey data assessing the issues of guilt and remedy. Some courts adopt as facts what are speculative interpretations of misleading data used for inappropriate purposes.

School districts typically try to convince the court that mandatory desegregation should end because it makes white flight worse and because it is futile in the face of natural private preferences that constantly expand segregation. A group of hired social science witnesses has testified in many cases that schools are not an important factor in housing decisions that families make, so school policies should not be held accountable for any of the segregation. In the *Pitts* case, for example, the DeKalb County school board hired the leading national experts who worked in judicial battles against desegregation and paid for original surveys in the county. In one year the board spent $441,000 in legal costs.[64]

During the 1980s, the experts testifying for school boards, and the Reagan administration Justice Department also received the only grants from the U.S. Commission on Civil Rights and the U.S. Department of Education for research on the issue of white flight, which the Reagan Justice Department used as a basic argument for dissolving desegregation orders. Professor Christine Rossell, a Boston University political scientist who testified and prepared reports for many school boards, received the only major U.S. Department of Education grant for desegregation research during the twelve years of the Reagan and Bush administrations. Her research was featured in many desegregation cases and in her book, *The Carrot or the Stick for School Desegregation Policy: Magnet Schools or Forced Busing.*[65] David Armor, the most active witness against desegregation, chaired the advisory committee for the U.S. Civil Rights Commission's white-flight study, the only other substantial federally funded work on school desegregation in the 1980s. Armor was active in many of the key cases discussed in this book including Oklahoma City, DeKalb County, Atlanta, Little Rock, Los Angeles, and Norfolk.

Civil rights groups never had sufficient funds to finance a major survey of housing attitudes. The evidence from academic research, however, shows that responses to questions about racial policies depend strongly on how the questions are posed and how the data is analyzed. After a survey was presented in the Kansas City case, for example, and an expert testified that schools were not important for housing choice, a rebuttal witness ran the data and found that if one looked at families with young children, schools were the families most important consideration.[66]

White Flight

In just two years from 1974 through 1976, the facts of white flight changed from an issue the civil rights forces used to try to obtain more far-reaching school desegregation orders to an issue opponents used to defeat desegregation. The decline of white students in city schools as white suburbanization continued had been going on for decades, and it created a central barrier to full desegregation. The policy shift that made white flight an argument against desegregation was the product of both the Supreme Court's *Milliken* decision blocking suburban desegregation and Professor James Coleman's 1975 research on white flight.[67] After *Milliken*, since the courts could not deal with long-term suburbanization trends by including suburban schools in the desegregation plan and the debate turned to the question of whether doing anything within single districts would produce so much white flight that the effort would be futile. In the 1983 Houston case, for example, the court of appeals concluded that school authorities "have no affirmative fourteenth amendment duty to respond to the private actions of those who vote with their feet."[68] Crossdistrict desegregation was rejected in Houston, even though the city had stopped expanding its school district as the city boundaries grew, the year of the *Brown* decision. (The city now has many school districts within its boundaries and a high level of segregation.)

Civil rights advocates had long been concerned with white suburbanization. By 1965, six years before the first busing decision, elementary school statistics showed that there the enrollment of whites in Washington, D.C., was only 9 percent; in Wilmington, Delaware, 31 percent; in St. Louis, 37 percent ; in San Francisco, 43 percent; in Newark, 23 percent; in Philadelphia, 41 percent; in Detroit, 44 percent; and in Richmond, 35 percent.[69] As soon as the Supreme Court ordered urban desegregation, courts began to search for the way to desegregate cities with a heavily minority district. Thurgood Marshall, dissenting in the *Milliken* case, argued that a city-only plan would provide no remedy. On July 25, 1974, when the decision was announced, he said:

> The Detroit school system has in recent years increasingly become an all-Negro school system, with the greatest increase in the proportion of Negro students of any major northern city. Moreover, the result of a Detroit-only decree, the District Court found, would be to increase the flight of whites from the city.... Thus, even if a [racial balance] plan were adopted...such a system would, in short order, devolve into an all-Negro system.[70]

The fears of Justice Marshall were proven correct when Detroit continued to go through rapid racial change. It became a virtually all-black district despite extra money spent to upgrade the schools. Two decades after the Supreme Court's decision, Detroit Superintendent David L. Sneed would report that "the Detroit community has deteriorated dramatically; the concentration of poverty in the city has increased."[71] By 1990, metropolitan Detroit had the most intense residential segregation in the United States and its black students were more segregated than any other metropolitan area except Chicago.[72]

The grim aftermath of desegregation plans focused only on the central city in cities like Detroit, however, was often not interpreted as a confirmation of Justice Marshall's argument that metropolitan desegregation was indispensable. Often it was seen as proving that nothing could or should be done. Almost no attention was paid to the successful city-suburban desegregation plans in many metropolitan areas, most in Southern states with countywide school districts.

In the mid-1970s, housing evidence became a tool for limiting or reversing desegregation orders. Many courts witnessed statistical battles over possible relationships between desegregation and white enrollment loss. The national press gave massive publicity to Coleman's and Armor's claims about white flight and paid much less attention to those who argued that the trends showed the need for more far-reaching remedies.[73] Although there was an intense academic debate on the degree and duration of white flight, researchers agreed that white decline had existed before desegregation and occurred in cities where desegregation was never implemented. In fact, there has been a substantial decline in the percentage of white births in the country.[74] Some court decisions, however, blame all white enrollment decline on busing with no analysis of preexisting trends, birth rates, immigration, or experience of other cities where there has been no busing.

School desegregation was not the sole cause of white enrollment decline, though almost all participants in the debate agree that there are some forms of desegregation plans (particularly mandatory plans busing many white students in heavily minority central cities) that accelerate the decline of white enrollment. On the other hand, the proportion of white students remains much more stable in a number of districts with countywide city-suburban mandatory desegregation. More than half of the nation's largest districts that have been *most* successful in holding their proportion of white students have countywide plans.

Two of the largest of the countywide districts, metropolitan Charlotte and metropolitan Raleigh, North Carolina, actually had a rising proportion of white students in recent years and were growing rapidly in the 1990s. The metropolitan Raleigh (Wake County) schools are as clear a demonstration of the absence of a simple link between mandatory desegregation and white enrollment decline as could be found. The district has large scale mandatory desegregation across city and suburban lines and substantial growth in both the overall district and white enrollment, with minority enrollment up 18 percent and white enrollment soaring 37 percent since 1976.[75]

Raleigh has flourished as a community. *Fortune* rated it top place to do business, especially for knowledge-based industry; *Money* magazine rated it the best place to live in 1995.[76] An early 1995 report found that the Raleigh-area housing market led the nation in increased home value.[77] Its school district is one of the nation's largest, substantially bigger, for example, than those in San Francisco, Boston, Denver, or Atlanta.[78] The success of the metropolitan Raleigh plan does not mean that there is no white flight; it shows that under some circumstances busing of many more students may be linked to greater stability. The greater success of the metropolitan Raleigh district was one reason why adjacent Durham recently voted to merge city and suburban school systems. The Greater Raleigh Chamber of Commerce was convinced that the areawide desegregation was one of the reasons for the economic health of the community and passed a resolution expressing its strong support for the continuation of desegregation in 1995. "On many measures," the resolution said, "our public school system is equal to that of any other urban area in the nation" and noted that only 5 to 7 percent of local students went to private schools, many fewer than in other affluent areas. The resolution hailed the decision to merge city and suburban schools in 1974 and praised the foresight of leaders who "recognized that a strong and prosperous inner-city with a quality school system was a vital element in the future economic growth and prosperity of the entire country." The chamber praised local leaders for decisions "many of which were unpopular in the short term, but which were critically important in the long term." It called on the county to "steadfastly maintain its commitment to racially balanced public schools."[79]

Among the many problems with white flight evidence being used in courts now is that most of it is drawn from experience with the type of desegregation plans that have not been ordered for fifteen years. The claims are also largely based on black-white relationships and the research rarely considers the multiracial schools of many contemporary cities or the fact that the most segregated minority is now Latino. Pure mandatory reassignment plans have rarely been adopted in the past fifteen years. Recent plans tend to provide new educational options and choice as major ingredients.

In a nation where more than a third of the states now have Latino students as their largest minority and Asian enrollments are soaring, using a black-white model is senseless. White flight evidence also usually ignores changing birth rates and immigration, whose effects are sometimes implicitly blamed by courts on desegregation orders.

The Supreme Court returned to the white-flight issue in the 1995 *Missouri v. Jenkins* decision, dealing with it in a variety of ways and reaching decisions that would tend to maximize flight and prohibit some important efforts to offset white decline. The majority opinion expressed the belief that the implementation of an earlier plan limited to the city district was probably the cause of white flight. In response to the requirement to desegregate and to long-term white suburbanization, and the concern about the effect of a mandatory plan under such circumstances, the Kansas City plan attempted to attract white private school and suburban parents into the city schools to offset the continuing residential changes. Justice Rehnquist ruled that this effort to "attract nonminority students not presently enrolled in the KCMSD" was not legal and should be stopped.[80] He said that the requirement was to desegregate the students within the school system, not to attract outsiders. Such a plan would have all schools about two-thirds black at the outset, stripped of some of their special resources, with lowered teacher salaries, and faced with continuing white decline from residential change, even if there were no white flight. The kind of plan suggested by the Court would make all schools largely black in a largely white metropolitan area and would make no effort to compete with private or suburban schools—providing all the ingredients for maximizing white flight.

What Is Known About Housing Segregation

Housing conclusions by courts often contradict established knowledge. The following generalizations would, we believe, be accepted by the great majority of scholars doing empirical work on the development of residential segregation. Though there are major disputes among researchers, generalizations of the sort often found in court decisions and politics are often clearly wrong about areas in which there is little or no scholarly debate. Widely accepted generalizations that simply express demographic facts or are uncontroversial include:

1.   a history of overt housing segregation for black people, who have been more segregated than any other ethnic group since World War I;[81]

2.   segregation in cities was and remains high a quarter century after fair housing laws were enacted;[82]

3.   economic differences explain only a small fraction of the existing segregation. Though incomes differ substantially by race, there is enough overlap of income and variation in housing prices within communities so that there would be no all-black or all-white census tracts in most sections of metropolitan areas if economics determined residence;[83]

    ghettos and barrios are still spreading. Many governmental programs and decisions are related to the origin and spread of minority segregation;

4.   massive discrimination continues in housing and home finance markets. Federally funded tests of housing sales and rental show persisting discrimination against black and Latino homeseekers.[84] The most recent national HUD study found that 53 percent of black renters and 46 percent of Hispanics confronted discrimination during a typical housing search. Among buyers, 59 percent of blacks and 56 percent of Latinos faced discrimination;[85]

5.   subsidized housing has historically been openly segregated in many cities and has produced neighborhood schools extremely segregated by race, income, and a high level of joblessness of parents. Public housing still contributes strongly to school segregation;[86]

6.   minority families prefer integrated communities by large majorities, but their ideal level of integration differs from that of white families;[87]

7. white attitudes toward residential integration have changed substantially in a favorable direction in the last generation even in highly segregated areas, but whites still prefer lower levels of integration than blacks;[88]

8. many long-term effects of prior housing discrimination continue;[89]

9. most suburban middle-class communities exclude subsidized housing, rental housing for families, and affordable housing through official decisions about housing and land use and develop new housing on the edge of suburbia, which is sold to an overwhelmingly white clientele. Schools are important in marketing this housing;[90]

10. major declines in white school enrollment have occurred in central cities and older suburbs with neighborhood schools as well as those with desegregation plans;[91]

11. some of the most rapidly growing school districts in the country have had mandatory city-suburban enrollment for years and have been among the nation's most successful in holding white students;

12. housing subsidies often help resegregate integrated neighborhoods and their schools. That pattern continued long after fair housing became law.[92]

Although many of these assertions are incompatible with conclusions reached by various courts in resegregation cases, they do not deny the presence of significant private prejudice and nongovernmental discrimination. Nor do they show the precise effects of past discrimination. They indicate only broad general patterns of relationships, patterns far more compatible with the Supreme Court's findings of pervasive housing-school interactions in the *Swann* and *Keyes* decisions than with the housing assumptions in the resegregation cases.

Is Segregation Natural and Immutable?

Though there are different ideal levels of integration for whites and blacks, the research on this issue falls far short of supporting the argument that there is an immutable structure of private racial preferences that courts and public officials cannot solve. There is good evidence, in fact, that these attitudes are not purely private, that they are subject to change, and that there is considerable evidence of substantial overlap between black and white preferences. In fact, residential integration has increased significantly in many smaller cities as has acceptance of fair housing in the last generation. The growth of integration occurred even as government policies continued to underwrite segregation. There are stable communities with levels of minority population assumed to be impossible under the preference theory.[93] Research from other areas of civil rights policy, such as school desegregation and attitudes toward election of black political leaders, shows that attitudes change with experience.

Survey research on preferences is often introduced in trials as definitive evidence that segregated housing results from the choices of buyers, not discrimination. This evidence is presented without recognition of two fundamental limitations of surveys: they cannot show the degree to which the attitudes expressed resulted from past discrimination and they cannot show the degree to which attitudes may change in the future. Attitudes, for example, may very well be products of the illegal practices of the past; if they are, they are not natural and private matters but vestiges of that past segregation. Judgments courts must make about legal responsibility are judgments about the continuing influence of past discrimination. Decisions they make about remedies involve estimating not what is practical now but what will happen if the court order alters the status quo in various ways. Survey data has often been used as proof for issues where it is not relevant and may be highly misleading.

In *Dowell v. Board of Education of Oklahoma City*, the Supreme Court made it clear that lower courts must determine whether spreading segregation is a "result of private decisionmaking and economics"[94] The courts normally see only a skewed reflection of knowledge from research because of unequal resources for litigation. Evidence is strong that blacks do not prefer segregation and they would be highly integrated if they lived in the same neighborhoods occupied by whites of similar income.[95]

Courts and local officials often speak of a "tipping point" in racial change, reflecting the belief that there is a certain percentage of black residents in a community that makes total racial transition inevitable and irreversible. Until recent decades, few residentially integrated neighborhoods had ever remained stable because of the block-by-block racial change process adopted by local realtors and property owners to manage increased black housing demand during the decades of overt segregationist policies.[96]

When Thomas Schelling devised the theory of the mathematical incompatibility of the preferences for racial composition of neighborhoods, it seemed to lend scientific status to the tipping point idea.[97] The centerpiece of this theory is that blacks prefer to live in neighborhoods that are 50 percent black and whites prefer to live in neighborhoods that are considerably less integrated and a half-black neighborhood the theory predicts that interracial communities will continue to change until they are all minority, even though almost no one finds that outcome ideal. Surveys conducted in 1978 in the Detroit metropolitan area in which participants were asked about different racial mixes in a block have been widely cited to show that incompatible preferences do exist.[98]

Although differing preferences do present real difficulties for stable integration, there are a number of logical and empirical flaws in the argument presented in court. The first is that integration is increasing and there are substantial numbers of stable integrated communities. According to the preference theory, these things should not have happened. Attitudes are changing; for example, when white households were asked, "if black people came to live in great numbers in your neighborhood, would you move?" the percentage who responded "yes" declined consistently from 78 percent in 1963 to 32 percent in 1990.[99] Although people may prefer a particular racial mix, most say that racial composition is not high among their considerations in housing searches. The best-known surveys of incompatible preferences came from metropolitan Detroit, which had the most severe segregation among large urban communities in 1990. This means that the incompatibilities may be less in other cities. Attitudes changed substantially even among Detroit-area whites between 1976 and 1992.[100] Since white attitudes have been based primarily on experiences with white-black transitions, there may be less fear of change and greater possibility of stability in the emerging multiracial neighborhoods in many cities. The declining birth rate and out-migration of blacks from many metropolitan areas means much less population pressure on integrated areas than in the past. The decline in housing segregation means that black housing demand will not be so concentrated on a few areas. Many communities are also experimenting with ways to break the syndrome of racial change through direct intervention in the housing markets and effective responses to the feared symbols of neighborhood deterioration.

If courts rely heavily on the preference theory to justify returning to segregated schools, they will be limiting the rights of minority students on the basis of the following unsupported assumptions: that the attitudes are inherent, not the product of a history of ghetto creation and expansion under discriminatory policies; that school and housing desegregation would not improve attitudes and increase stable integration; and that the school districts' hired experts are presenting reliable and impartial evidence on attitudes.

In fact, racial preferences are related to a long history of destructive racial change *supported* by public policy and may prove as changeable as many other kinds of racial stereotypes and prejudices have in the last half century.

Toward a Legal Approach Reflecting Urban Reality

If the assumptions about housing in the resegregation decisions are highly questionable and there are serious effects of housing on school desegregation, it is important to consider under what conditions housing violations should lead to additional school desegregation requirements. In the Indianapolis decision ordering city-suburban desegregation, the United States Court of Appeals for the Seventh Circuit formulated standards to judge whether an interdistrict school remedy is an appropriate response to housing discrimination:

1. Discriminatory practices have caused segregative residential housing patterns and population shifts.

2. State action, at whatever level, by either direct or indirect action, initiated, supported, or contributed to these practices and the resulting housing patterns and population shifts.

3. Although the state action need not be the sole cause of these effects, it must have had a significant rather than a de minimis [minimal] effect.

4. Finally, an interdistrict remedy may be appropriate even though the state discriminatory housing practices have ceased if it is shown that prior discriminatory practices have a continuing segregative effect on housing patterns (and, in turn, on school attendance patterns)...[101]

Applying the Indianapolis standards to the housing history of metropolitan America would, no doubt, produce many cases in which the courts would be obliged to consider expanding school desegregation.

The St. Louis case was another example of a potentially crucial development in the law linking housing and school segregation. In its 1980 decision ordering a new desegregation plan, the federal district court ordered the housing agencies to submit a plan to the court to change housing policies in ways that would support school integration. HUD and the local community development agency developed and submitted plans to the court, but because of the replacement of the judge and inaction by the parties, the court never acted on the plans.

Housing as a Path Toward a Solution?

The use of housing issues has evolved radically in school desegregation battles, yet another set of changes is needed if there is to be movement toward integrated neighborhoods with integrated schools rather than a surrender to segregation. Civil rights lawyers in the early years of urban desegregation plans routinely proved how residential segregation was imposed by public agencies as a basic part of winning a school desegregation order outside the South. It was easy to do in most cities because housing discrimination was not hidden until fair housing laws began to appear in the 1960s. In government-operated housing and housing with FHA and VA mortgages, discrimination was particularly blatant. Understanding housing history was a powerful tool for winning desegregation orders by proving intentional official segregation.

The Supreme Court's 5-4 decision in *Milliken I*, however, transformed housing issues from reasons for more desegregation to justifications for less or none. Based on a single district afflicted with spreading segregation (the typical American city profile), opponents argued that resegregation would be accelerated by desegregation and so nothing could be done about it. The white-flight arguments and incompatible preference arguments about the instability of interracial neighborhoods were, essentially, ways of arguing that housing made lasting school integration impossible and, therefore, the effort should be abandoned.

Opponents of school desegregation have been arguing two contradictory things about the relationship between schools and housing. In their white-flight claims, they assume that school desegregation plans have a powerful effect on housing choices, because whites flee the increased contact with minority students. On the other hand, in their theory that people have a natural preference for segregation that is reflected in the private market, they argue that the courts can ignore the interactions between schools and housing issues. Segregation is not a public problem requiring judicial intervention but the result of private natural preferences unconnected to a history of discrimination. Whites simply prefer far lower levels of contact with blacks than blacks do with whites. These contradictory arguments were adopted simultaneously by the Supreme Court majority in the 1995 *Missouri v. Jenkins* decision.

Both of these theories argue that there is a kind of vicious cycle perpetuating and spreading segregation. Both claim that it is results from white resistance to increased presence of blacks in situations where it is possible for whites to leave an interracial institution or community for a segregated white one.

These theories do not explain how it is possible to reconcile the insistence on white opposition to desegregation with the national surveys showing large increases in white acceptance of substantial levels of school and housing integration. One way is to assume that the statements mean nothing. Another, however, is to consider evidence that whites are prepared to accept integration but fear the spread of the ghetto. Much of this resistance may be resistance not to integration but to white fears of resegregation, a fear deeply rooted in many communities by generations of bitter experience.[102]

If the spread of segregated schools and the fear of resegregation compound problems of housing segregation by making whites fearful about moving their children into an area where they will be isolated in minority schools, successful plans for widespread stable integrated neighborhoods with integrated schools may help break this vicious cycle. In fact, there is considerable evidence that strong and extensive school desegregation policies can increase residential integration. A variety of housing policies can help develop better integrated neighborhoods with more integrated schools. Communities should consider the following options.

Housing Counseling

The Kentucky Human Rights Commission was the only civil rights agency in the country to take an early and strong initiative to use housing to help school desegregation. The Kentucky commission put up billboards that said "End Forced Busing"; the next line, however, read "Support Fair Housing." A commission staff member worked to decrease segregation by driving black recipients of rental subsidy certificates around to introduce them to housing options outside the ghetto. About half of these subsidy recipients decided to move to white areas. Under the Louisville school plan, they were immediately exempted from busing, since their moves increased integration. The housing plan allowed recipients of Section 8 housing subsidies to move anywhere in the metropolitan area. Before that time, one half of all black Section 8 families lived inside two school attendance zones in the city. After the plan, four in five were choosing housing outside of those two areas.[103]

Exemption of Integrated Communities From Busing

Many skeptics about school desegregation plans argue that it would be better to deal with the root of school segregation—housing— than to try continually to treat the educational symptoms of residential apartheid. In some cities they point out the irony of busing children out of integrated neighborhoods. Residents who are living in integrated areas bitterly criticize plans that split up their neighborhoods and bus away children who could walk to an integrated school. There are now, however, plans that exempt integrated neighborhoods from busing in a number of cities, some of which show steady reductions of busing as the number of integrated communities increases. Such policies begin to turn vicious cycles into positive cycles of growing integration.

Such policies have been in place for years, for example, in St. Louis and Denver. In Louisville, neighborhoods with enough black residents to meet school desegregation standards regained neighborhood schools. The plan showed the possibility of positive initiatives at low cost. Between 1975 and 1982, the percentage of black students living in predominantly white suburbs nearly tripled.[104] The district was able to exempt thirty-two schools from busing by 1982. As fewer students required busing, the average hour time was cut in half, and the total number of students being bused fell from 18,000 to 11,000 while desegregation was maintained.[105] In Denver, fair housing groups worked with realtors to increase residential integration of Denver neighborhoods so that they could have integrated neighborhoods that would get back their neighborhood schools. This effort was successful in some communities.

Gautreaux: Lessons of a Housing Remedy

The Chicago Housing Authority and HUD were found guilty of generations of intentional housing segregation in metropolitan Chicago in 1969. After the Supreme Court upheld the decision, the courts ordered a set of changes including a larger and more complex approach to the problem of the use of housing subsidy programs to intensify segregation. To help break the pattern of segregation and ghetto expansion in one of the nation's most segregated and resistant housing markets, black families from Chicago housing projects were given counseling about housing opportunities in white areas, escort service, and personal support after their moves. The program was designed to overcome their lack of knowledge about housing in white areas and their fears of violence and intimidation from whites.

Although it began slowly because of intense fear and the lack of experience among eligible households, interest mushroomed after the first groups moved successfully. Once the word got back about the experience of the early participants, thousands applied for the available slots each year. The plan permitted several thousand female-headed poor families to move out of city projects or off the waiting list to suburban private units with rent subsidy certificates.

The program moved children from segregated city schools with low achievement and graduation levels to vastly more competitive outlying suburban schools. The city children had surprisingly successful and positive experiences in the suburbs.[106] The same model has now been expanded under court order to several other cities and is a centerpiece of HUD Secretary Henry Cisneros' "Moving to Opportunity" program.[107] Although the programs have reached only a very small share of segregated minority families, they showed the possibility and potential effects of expanding housing choices for the poor.

Special Mortgage Financing for Pro-Integration Moves

Ohio, the state of Washington, and Wisconsin all have policies providing financial incentives for families whose moves contribute to housing and school integration. Many states have special programs in which they offer a small number of first-time home buyers special low-cost financing to purchase homes. Since mortgage interest is by far the largest cost of owning the home, this is a powerful subsidy.

Civil rights organizations have persuaded these three states to set aside some subsidies for families whose moves increase integration. These subsidies reach relatively few people, but the program illustrates the possibility of using a number of relatively small programs in different ways to produce overall changes.

The legality of the Ohio plan, according to Ohio Attorney General Celebrezze, rested on supporting school desegregation.[108] In 1988, the state housing agency agreed to set aside 5 percent of its low-interest loans for families who move into neighborhoods in which their race is underrepresented in the schools.[109] Approximately 150 people participated in this program each year, half of whom are African American.[110]

The consent agreement settling the metropolitan Milwaukee school desegregation case clearly recognized the housing issue in one of the nation's most segregated areas. It provides state funds for a program to provide families with counseling and information about making moves that promote racial integration, as well as provide low-interest loans to people moving into areas where their racial group comprises less than 15 percent of the population. The state provided 15percent of the state's low-income housing federal tax credits to encourage the development of new affordable integrated housing, and the state housing agency also committed itself to issuing $5 million in mortgage bonds for prointegration sales.[111]

Seattle, Washington, school officials won an agreement with the state housing officials in 1989 to provide up to a $2,000 tax credit to low- and moderate-income home buyers who bought homes in places that would aid school integration. The credits reduced average mortgage payments by 20 percent. The school superintendent noted that even fifty families making such moves would save annual busing costs exceeding the cost of the tax credit in the first year. [112] The policy was designed to reinforce the school district's new 1989 desegregation plan, which was supposed to reward integrated neighborhoods by giving them neighborhood schools.

State and Local Policies for Scattered Site Subsidized Housing

Several highly urbanized states now have considerable experience in developing subsidized housing in normally closed suburban areas as a result of state court decisions or legislation limiting suburban land-use controls. The *Mt. Laurel* plan resulted from the New Jersey Supreme Court's 1983 ruling that exclusionary zoning regulations blocking low- and moderate-cost housing in many communities conflicted with the state constitution. Each New Jersey municipality was required to provide a "fair share" of low- and moderate-income housing based on an assessment of the needs of the state as a whole.[113] The remedy made it easy for developers to sue for and win exemption from zoning regulations in areas that had totally excluded subsidized housing.[114]

The production of many thousands of units of housing under this remedy has shown its potential power. Relatively few of the outlying units, however, have gone to black families because there is an immense unmet need for subsidized housing for white suburbanites, and blacks are unlikely to hear about the units unless integration is a specific goal. This shows clearly the need for more tenant outreach and counseling and integration goals similar to what exists in Louisville and Chicago.

There are similar court orders or state laws in Massachusetts, Pennsylvania, and Connecticut. Local policy has instituted a requirement for affordable units in all major developments in Montgomery County, Maryland, one of the nation's richest suburbs. Clearly there are now ample models to show that such approaches are viable and compatible with both good design and excellent housing markets. If they could be carried out more broadly and tied to housing counseling for potential minority residents, they could have a significant positive effect on school desegregation.

School Construction Choices as Leverage for Integration

Many growing school districts have to make decisions on building schools, particularly in the Sunbelt and in the newer suburbs. Site decisions are crucial to housing markets and to school segregation. A school makes a new housing development much easier to market; school boards usually build wherever developers expand, regardless of the racial consequences. Experience in several communities has demonstrated that developers are willing to negotiate in order to obtain schools. Positive experiences show successes in some cases.[115]

Important experiments in Denver and Palm Beach County have begun to explore the possibilities of using school construction choices to spur residential integration and thus reduce the need for busing. During the 1980s, Denver began several creative efforts to deal with the housing issues underlying school segregation; it developed positive policies to integrate both newly developed and older communities to reduce busing and also moved toward scattered-site public housing. The city council adopted a strong scattered-site policy and built more than 800 units of scattered-site housing; a study by the *Rocky Mountain News* shows that its residents were much more likely than the residents of the old projects to finish high school.

The planned integration in a large new development of private housing on the last large vacant tract in the city is another important example of the use of leverage. A court order prohibiting the construction of new schools that would be segregated stirred fears that the lack of a local school would seriously damage marketing. The problem was solved by an agreement, approved by the board and the court, to design and market the new community for integration; it was implemented successfully according to research by the University of Colorado's urban affairs center.

The same issue arose on a larger scale and from a different source in Palm Beach County, Florida, after the U.S. Education Department found evidence that new schools contributed to "the resegregation of the system as a whole, as well as the disparate treatment of black students." The Palm Beach school district negotiated agreements with various developers to aim for black households at a minimum of 10 percent of the total in developments that would receive neighborhood schools.[116] The experiment showed that many were willing to consider such agreements but it also demonstrated that without clear enforcement authority and sanctions, such agreements would have mixed results. Some developers reached the goal and their new neighborhoods opened with populations producing significantly integrated enrollments at the new schools; in other developments the marketing fell far short. A more targeted and closely monitored process, perhaps building the school only after there was evidence of success with the marketing, might be more effective. In 1995, the metropolitan Raleigh (Wake County) school board entered into its first agreement with a developer.

Ending Urban Apartheid

The school segregation that exists in any given community today shows the enduring effects of practices and expectations rooted in past discrimination in housing. It is, of course, affected by private prejudice and preferences, but those themselves may be products of a long history of discrimination. Contemporary policies also continue to produce segregation and undermine integrated communities and schools. The promise of fair housing has been addressed by only feeble enforcement efforts.

The best way to escape both the destructive trends of spreading segregation and the uncomfortable necessity of outside intervention in local policymaking is to adopt policies replacing the vicious cycles of ghetto expansion with policies fostering integration of neighborhoods and their schools. The Nixon administration examined such a policy and rejected it in an explicit play for white political support. The Carter administration, near the end of its term, was approaching such a policy, but the Reagan and Bush administrations abandoned the effort and worked to dismantle the tools. The Clinton administration reopened the idea of a major attack on housing segregation, but experienced substantial resistance in Congress. There is now ample experience from successful local experiments to provide a basis for mutually supportive school and housing integration policies to overcome the effects of generations of intentional segregation. To make such a policy politically viable, national leaders in and outside of government must systematically examine the results in communities that have provided leadership. Ironically, it may be that the most complex and wide-ranging planning of school and housing remedies would lead to the most natural, stable, and least coercive outcome.

If the courts choose, on the other hand, to use unsupported presumptions and burden shifts about housing issues to justify resegregation of schools, decades of commitment to the goals of *Brown* will give way to seemingly quiet acceptance of segregated schools serving segregated neighborhoods. Housing theories are being presented as key justifications for acceptance of a new *Plessy* in the metropolitan areas of the United States.

A much better path is to accept the unworkability of urban apartheid and to begin to put in place proven and new remedies that could lead toward a more integrated, fair, and workable urban society. In such communities solutions to school segregation issues often could be natural by-products of facing and resolving the deeper issue of racially defined housing, perpetuated through housing markets and housing policies.

CHAPTER TWELVE

Toward an Integrated Future

New Directions for Courts, Educators, Civil Rights Groups, Policymakers, and Scholars

Gary Orfield

The country is betting that segregated schools will work in a multiracial society with a rapidly declining white majority. Courts and local officials rely on false assumptions, committing American society to an inferior education for minority children and the kind of politics, racial beliefs, and social structures that develop in a segregated society. Though we have experienced for generations segregation in the South, we ignore the lessons presented to us from many decades of separate but equal. We are, in essence, sleepwalking back to *Plessy*. This chapter summarizes the unfolding disaster we have observed and outlines how the United States could reverse the growing separation of its children.

This book challenges all of the basic assumptions on which resegregation policy rests. It spells out the meaning of resegregation in the 1990s and analyzes the perverse dynamic that takes shape around resegregated schools. *Brown*'s judgment that segregated schools are inherently unequal remains correct, not because something magic happens to minority students when they sit next to whites but because segregation cuts students off from critical paths to success in American society. Restoring neighborhood schools forces more African American and Latino children into isolated high-poverty schools that almost always have low levels of academic competition, performance, and preparation for college or jobs. Almost no whites end up in such schools under the neighborhood system.

Courts, policymakers, and the press have trusted local school officials to make resegregated schools fair. Usually, no one is required to show that the proposed program for equalizing segregated schools has worked anywhere, with no independent assessment of the results.

When the programs fail, the local school officials lose nothing since the courts seldom require any results and do not punish the administrators. Urban superintendents, who usually last only two or three years anyway, may well be working in another city long before the failure of neighborhood schools becomes apparent. Minority students, however, are punished permanently—they lose their right to desegregation and to judicial mandates for equalizing education. Once a district is pronounced unitary, the historic constitutional debt to minority children is declared paid in full and civil rights groups are told that they must rely on local politicians.

The logic behind resegregation leads not only to meaningless promises but also to pressures that cause professionals to defend the indefensible. Courts and educators must pretend that obviously unequal schools are fair. When discrimination is officially declared to have fully been rectified and the policies for resegregation are accepted by courts and community leaders as educationally sound, the blame for the pervasive inequalities that remain tends to be shifted to minority families and communities, the teachers, and the educational leaders. When discrimination is declared cured, the system can no longer be blamed.

Minority educators find themselves largely confined to jobs in segregated districts and schools and are faced with impossible dilemmas. To get their jobs, educators must claim to be able to do things that no one has actually done on a large scale. Administrators are hired to create an optimistic vision. Those announcing new solutions are celebrated. Urban reform is usually described as a problem of will, leadership, and belief, not as an unworkable structure that needs to be changed. Everyone repeats the popular slogan of the day, such as "all children can learn." They celebrate isolated successes as if such successes were general solutions. They implicitly accept the racial status quo and promise to make it work, as if they know of school policies that can overcome extremely difficult circumstances caused by severe family and community problems in high-poverty neighborhoods. They must not raise issues that alienate the predominantly white and suburban leaders of their state legislature from whom they must seek funds essential to keep the schools open.

In many cities serving mostly poor minority children, conditions and resources are deteriorating fast. Under such circumstances, school politics become even more consumed by cycles of unfulfilled promises and bitter disillusionment. City school systems become numbed by endless rounds of promises, reforms, and failures. The local white establishment feels increasingly justified in taking a critical attitude toward the schools. In some cities, black politicians have now joined in the attack. The predictable failure of inner-city segregated schools then feeds cynicism and generates attacks on the entire system of public education. The failure often reinforces white stereotypes about what critics describe as the inferior culture of minority families, reinforcing growing suburban resistance to providing state resources to heavily minority urban school systems. Increasingly, state governments are moving from aiding urban schools toward seizing control of them and districts that they define as "educationally bankrupt," which usually have large majorities of segregated nonwhite students. When the high-achievement goals of President Bush's America 2000 or President Clinton's Goals 2000 are discussed, the special burdens facing the segregated minority schools are ignored.

Once discrimination is declared "solved" and court protection terminated, the transfer of more resources by whites to the suburbs is legitimized (so long as they do not openly justify such a practice on racial grounds) with whites even going to court to attack vestiges of minority rights *voluntarily* maintained by local school officials. Whites argue, for example, that special searches for black students for an elite magnet school after the court has ruled that the historic debt has been paid discriminates against whites. Lawsuits on this issue were filed in 1995 in several districts, including Boston. School authorities are increasingly frightened to take even politically feasible and necessary steps to deal with obvious inequities.

What Is the Goal?

The political victory of the Right has almost ended intelligent discussion of integration, probably the only viable alternative for successfully organizing the multiracial society emerging in the United States. Integration is not desegregation (though that is a necessary first step), assimilation, or an alternative to ethnic pride. Integration is the goal of sharing major institutions in a way that recognizes and teaches respect for our different cultures as well as our shared goals. It is fully compatible, for example, with efforts to increase understanding and respect for African American or Latino culture and traditions. Institutions moving toward integration must treat students from each background with fairness and respect. These are very difficult goals, but we have learned a great deal about how to reach them in the last two generations. We have all around us in the world the ruins of nations that failed to address such racial and ethnic differences.

No significant policy initiative for urban school integration has been implemented since 1972 and the politics of civil rights have drifted strongly to the right since 1980. The same attack about feasibility was made, however, against the abolitionists, the early civil rights movement, and almost every other successful movement for major social or economic change in American history. Politicians and commentators know what is immediately feasible and what problems the public is not prepared to talk about. Because one of our national parties has succeeded in dominating the white vote for almost thirty years using a strategy of racial polarization, and the other is afraid to discuss race for fear of losing the white vote, little discussion on either the growing inequalities or the successful new civil rights initiatives exists.[1]

Government has gradually been dismantling the commitments made during the civil rights revolution and replacing them with increasingly strident attacks on the poor and the institutions that serve them. The antitax policies that have dominated the country for nearly twenty years mean that no significant new social policies are immediately feasible. Because politicians often believe that they must live within the bubble of what is immediately popular, the job of social researcher should be to describe what is necessary and what is known about the policies that could succeed, and whether such policies are feasible.

During the 1960s, we saw civil rights changes that seemed unimaginable one year become law the next year. Serious thought that had been given to seemingly hopeless reforms turned out to provide the blueprint for the sweeping restructuring of Southern institutions. Clear goals and developed ideas about how to get there existed. Similar work must be done now about the racial future of our metropolitan communities. The policies considered most feasible now concerning school desegregation do not work and may well intensify the underlying problems.

Given our deepening social inequalities, growing racial and class separation within metropolitan areas, and changing population and labor market, any serious move toward equal opportunity must deal with questions of race and educational opportunity. We cannot afford to make irreversible mistakes.

Blocking resegregation is an important but inadequate response. The only real alternative to segregation—which has been the dominant pattern of American racial history—is integration. Desegregation is a first step, but the ultimate goal is to transform segregated institutions into integrated communities. This process has begun but left far from completion by the civil rights movement of the 1960s and the Supreme Court policies of the late 1960s and early 1970s. For a generation, our schools have been left halfway through a revolution that is now threatening to unravel. There has been almost no work on moving from desegregation to genuine integration, moving from the awkward but necessary remedy of busing to the ultimate goal of integrated communities with schools the produce clear gains for minority students. There has been no serious national discussion about how to create schools that succeed in preparing students for a successful multiracial society.

Lessons of Our Research

This study began with court decisions permitting resegregation. Comparing their unexamined assumptions with what actually happened, we found fundamental inconsistencies. Many school leaders go into court claiming that desegregation has failed and promises to protect minority rights in segregated schools. The courts trust local agencies and decide to extinguish the judicially enforced rights for local minority children.

Decades of intense attacks on school desegregation have made proposals for resegregation sound reasonable to many Americans. Readers need to think, however, about what it would be like to apply to their own children the kinds of policies black and Latino families face in resegregation. How would they view a plan to take their kids out of strong schools and send them to schools with huge majorities of disadvantaged children from families facing very severe problems? These would be schools with low parent involvement and very low levels of competition, schools that teachers would try to transfer out of as soon as possible. How would people feel if this were described to them as a benefit, and they were told not to worry about their children having no more rights to court protection because the local school bureaucracy had made an unenforceable promise to upgrade these schools in a way never accomplished before? Such policies affecting black and Latino children, however, continue to be approved by courts and praised by the press and local white leaders. When President Kennedy asked Congress to enact the first major civil rights act in 1963, he asked white Americans to imagine that they were black, and to commit the nation to "treat our fellow Americans as we want to be treated."[2] If one were to spend even a few hours in the classrooms of schools in the ghettos and barrios and the suburbs of any segregated metropolitan area, nothing could be more self-evident that Kennedy's words are not the reality today in resegregated schools.

To learn about the effects of resegregation, we went to communities and found out what happened. Courts and legal experts tend to reason from assumptions, not to study results. The policy debate has been largely about theories, not experience.

In the districts we studied, the compensatory programs that were supposed to guarantee equality were limited, unaccountable, temporary, and without evidence of success. Communities tended to adopt currently popular reforms, thus obtaining favorable press coverage. No permanent commitments were made, and typically no requirement for either results or independent oversight existed.

When the federal courts allowed Norfolk, Virginia, to return to segregated neighborhood schools in 1986, the decision wrote into law conventional conservative criticisms of busing, blaming the plan for white flight and parental disengagement. The new plan was supposed to cure white flight, spur parental involvement in neighborhood schools, and use dollars to improve achievement in the black schools. All of these assumptions turned out to be wrong. After eight years, white enrollment had fallen substantially, parental involvement at all-black neighborhood schools dropped, and racial gaps on test scores were as large or larger than before. The special monitoring committee for the resegregated schools was disbanded.

Policies that provide extra money to segregated schools often are described as better and far less disruptive than desegregation. In its 1977 *Milliken II* decision, the Supreme Court supported this approach in Detroit. Examining the results in four districts, however, no evidence was found that the *Milliken II* plans cured the educational deficiencies. Apathy, inertia, politics, and blind trust in school bureaucracies were common. In Detroit, now the nation's most segregated metropolis, the courts released the state of Michigan from its requirement to pay for educational reforms with no evidence that the programs had improved minority achievement.

In Kansas City, the court relied upon money and choice to achieve desegregation and improve academic achievement. More than $1.4 billion was poured into local efforts. The plan achieved modest success in slowing racial change and producing some educational gains, but the entire approach was successfully challenged in the Supreme Court in 1995.

The treatment of the Kansas City remedy by state officials and the Supreme Court showed the hypocrisy of many critics of mandatory desegregation. Officials said that it would be much better to concentrate on choice and to demand educational improvement. But when coercion was minimized and money was spent to encourage voluntary transfers to transformed schools with remarkable programs, this choice-driven remedy became more controversial than most mandatory orders.

Once they had defeated mandatory desegregation, state and local officials assailed special funding and refused to stick with educational reforms until they produced results for the victims of discrimination. The Supreme Court's 1995 decision in *Missouri v. Jenkins* requires courts to return to state and local control as soon as possible, even if segregation is restored and the local school district lacks funds to continue the educational reforms. The Supreme Court refused to support the lower court's call for actual educational gains and forbade efforts to increase desegregation by offering attractive school choices to attract whites in private and suburban schools.

A handful of school districts achieved national reputations for progress in segregated schools, which they presented as better alternatives to desegregation. The Washington suburb of Prince George's County, Maryland; Atlanta; and Oklahoma City each received extensive national praise for their claims about academic success in segregated schools. Prince George's County test reports were praised by leaders, including President Reagan. For years the school district received intense positive attention from the media. The school district, however, could provide no evidence of its widely accepted claims of sweeping educational gains; recent statewide tests show great problems. Atlanta local leaders dropped a desegregation case in 1973 in exchange for black control, and claimed for years that local students were above national norms.[3] Atlanta was rigging its test data.

Standardized statewide tests eventually showed Atlanta achievement to be among the very worst in the state by high school, in spite of per-student spending about the suburban level.[4] Atlanta had boosted its test scores by using out-of-date testing a low percentage of students, and reclassifying students for testing purposes.[5]

Oklahoma City helped convince the courts to permit resegregation on the strength of its high test scores. Subsequent research showed that the city was testing a very low proportion of its students and flunking many students, something that can increase apparent test scores.[6] No district has produced evidence of equalizing its segregated high-poverty schools.

The Supreme Court now assumes that local officials are purified of the local history of discrimination and will solve racial problems through local politics. Our study of a district with abundant resources, a manageable problem, a highly educated constituency, an African American superintendent, and a liberal tradition, shows few grounds for optimism on this score. Segregation and concentrated poverty rapidly increased in Montgomery County, Maryland, one of the nation's most affluent counties. Left on its own, the district failed to act. It did not even ensure that voluntary choices would be available to low-income families by providing transportation. Magnet plans produced apparent desegregation, but the schools had segregated classes and programs. When challenged by a parent and the press in 1995, the county rapidly backed away from enforcing its weak policies against transfers increasing segregation.

The only community we studied that seemed to have both a viable plan and powerful community support for desegregation was Charlotte, where there had been a quarter century of mandatory city-suburban, county-wide desegregation. The district was gaining in both white students and proportion white enrollment in the 1990s, in spite of long-term mandatory desegregation, and reported substantial academic gains. Even in Charlotte, however, there was a close call when local business leaders became dissatisfied and brought into office a strong superintendent to cut back desegregation. Segregation began to spread as the city increasingly relied on magnet schools. Even in a city with many positive experiences, local control was problematic. In the 1995 elections, however, Charlotte's integrationists captured control of the school board.

Our case studies focused on resegregation. They show that courts and many communities across the United States are quietly turning back to segregation, assuming that it will work this time. Educators are disguising the change, never calling it segregation. Judges hope that discrimination is no longer a problem and that new programs administered by local school bureaucracies will make separate schools equal. The courts assume that they can safely retire from the field. They assume, incorrectly, that the underlying problem of housing discrimination has been solved.

The Politics of Resegregation

One of the ironies of the resegregation battle is that though the reversals are clearly driven by politics, the political context is strangely missing from most policy debates. The judicial and political pressure for resegregation arose from decades of major changes growing out of five presidential election victories by a virtually all-white party opposed to civil rights. Conservative presidential victories from 1968 to 1988 and hundreds of Nixon, Reagan, and Bush federal court appointments created a situation in which conservative claims have been repeated so often that they now are widely accepted as facts. The two Democratic presidents elected since the civil rights era have been moderates who said nothing in favor of urban school desegregation.[7] The language of segregationist Alabama Governor George Wallace ("forced busing") has become the mainstream press description for urban school desegregation. Stephan Lesher's recent study of Wallace concludes that Richard Nixon actually moved the Republican party well to the right of Wallace during the 1968 campaign.[8]

The Nixon administration and twelve Reagan-Bush years followed by the Gingrich Congress produced extreme racial polarization in politics. Among whites, though support for desegregation continued, the issue of racial justice went to the bottom of the list of national priorities. In 1995, 56 percent of whites thought that blacks were as well off or better off than whites in terms of education in spite of massive gaps.[9] Conservative politicians won white votes by telling them that civil rights policies had gone too far and were hurting whites.[10] No powerful defense of civil rights and no leadership helping the public understand the persisting inequality in educational opportunities for minority students existed.

Judicial decisions usually reflected the political change after time. The Supreme Court ended progress against segregation after President Nixon's four appointments. The Rehnquist Court, with its Reagan-Bush majority, worked actively to dismantle desegregation. Presidents Nixon, Ford, Reagan, and Bush claimed that racial problems had largely been resolved, that discrimination was uncommon, that courts should do less, and that local control was best. They appointed all the new Supreme Court justices for a quarter century. Their positions are now being read into the Constitution by most of their appointees. Skillful mobilization of white fears produced political victories that led to restaffing of the courts, which led to decisions interpreting away constitutional requirement.

If, as this book argues, we are in the midst of a historical reversal and that reversal is neither impelled by public demands nor producing benefits, it is logical to wonder why we were not informed. We have a set of national institutions that provide for division of power and for self-criticism. During this period, there has usually been a division between the president and Congress, and we have very extensive and powerful national media as well as the world's most powerful and respected universities. This should be enough to guarantee a well-informed debate on fundamental questions about the future of American education and race relations.

Yet, as the schools move back toward segregation, few efforts have been made to examine its effects. The Supreme Court decisions received little mass-media attention. A century earlier, when the Supreme Court upheld policies mandating racial separation in *Plessy*, similar disinterest existed. In both periods, the Court was following earlier political changes, and the interest of whites had moved to other issues.

Political changes made the resegregation seem unsurprising and sensible. The political and court changes are often viewed as if they were responses to public opinion turning against desegregation or to civil rights policies failing. But the courts were actually leading, not following, public opinions. Neither whites nor minorities have given up on the goal of integration, and opposition to busing was much higher two decades ago.[11] Both white and minority families share a belief that an integrated society with integrated schools would be better.[12] A 1995 national survey of urban school board members found that 85 percent believed that desegregation remained important.[13]

Although the mass media does have a great deal of independence and power, they, like the Democratic party, chose not to use it. One reason is that they tend to define the range of political debate by what the leaders of the two parties say. When both parties have become fundamentally dominated by large contributors, and the arena of decisive electoral battles has become white suburbia and the South, defining issues becomes difficult. Civil rights and minority community organizations tend to get serious media coverage only in times of obvious crisis. As the population is increasingly suburban and has no personal experience of social inequality, newspapers faced with declining readerships tend to seek suburban readers. The problem is compounded by the fact that most newspapers treat education as a low-prestige beat to be covered by a relatively inexperienced journalist who tends to cover mostly school district press releases and events at board meetings. Most do not seriously examine the accuracy of local school district claims about plans for separate by equal schools.

The silence of the universities is more surprising. During the civil rights movement, research on desegregation was abundant. Government and foundations pumped dollars into race relations work. It seemed as if the academic world was a strong resource for the civil rights movement, but it turned out to be only a fair-weather friend. When the government was supporting civil rights, the issue became a central focus of research. Once politics changed and research funding dried up, so did most academic involvement. Part of the logic of resegregation is the cutoff of most of the information about segregation and its consequences. The federal government published no basic statistics on national school segregation levels since the Carter administration. The research community and most research funders tend to follow rather than challenge political cycles.

Only a handful of researchers continued to work on desegregation after policies shifted, a new education agenda launched, and research money shifted toward the issues of the Reagan agenda. Since 1980, much more money was spent by school boards and the Reagan administration to create evidence to justify resegregation than on discovering ways to make desegregation work. Civil rights organizations had no money to sponsor serious research. Nor did federal civil rights agencies fund such studies once the Reagan administration consolidated control of the U.S. Civil Rights Commission, which had been an independent agency very actively concerned with school deseg-regation for the previous six administrations.[14] The federal desegre-gation research program in the National Institute of Education and the federal grant program funding projects an research on successful race relations in schools (the 1972 Emergency School Aid Act) ended with the first Reagan budget.[15]

Research priorities were redirected to the priorities of the "Excellence Movement," which emphasized tests, more science and math courses and other requirements, support for private schools, curriculum content changes, and market-based approaches.[16] After the 1983 *Nation At Risk* report, issues of equity virtually disappeared from the national and state education agendas. The basic focus of research shifted away from larger issues to change within schools and classrooms.

Researchers seldom investigate the continuing validity of the cen-tral claim of the *Brown* decision, that "separate is inherently unequal." There have been few systematic comparisons between white and minority schools in states or metropolitan areas, though such work is possible with new state assessment data. Often states will release data showing the strong relationship between poverty and achievement without ever mentioning that almost all of those poverty-impacted schools are segregated minority institutions.

In social science research and public debate, issues of systematic racial inequalities became uncommon after the early 1970s. The impact of desegregation in providing what minority families sought—better opportunities and success in a multiracial society—was rarely studied. A handful of researchers, including Robert Crain, JoMills Braddock, James McPartland, and Amy Stuart Wells, have documented long-term benefits of desegregation,[17] but their work received only limited attention. Other work showed that blacks attending integrated high schools have much greater college success.[18] Children in the most segregated inner-city schools are so isolated from realistic competition and assessment that they and their parents believe they are headed for success although they are actually achiev-ing a level so low that failure in college is foreordained.[19]

What research has been done is often ignored. The public is seldom informed that there are proven and relatively simple techniques, such as having students work in interracial study groups on academic tasks, which produce both academic gains and increases in positive racial attitudes.[20] Many minority supporters of neighborhood schools do not know that research shows that strong teachers and a demanding pre-collegiate curriculum are seldom found in high-poverty segregated schools,[21] or that minority parents report desegregated schools to be more responsive to minority parents and community groups than all-minority schools, which are often swamped by other problems.[22]

Research results are commonly interpreted through a very different lens than those for other programs. The federal desegregation assistance program, whose evaluations showed clear benefits, was the largest education program eliminated by the Reagan administration.[23] It is vital that academics and journalists insist that we look at the actual results of the new policies.

Desegregation Critics

Desegregation policies are attacked from a number of directions. The segregationist policies of the pre-civil rights South were rooted in theories of white supremacy, caste purity, and tradition. The contemporary legal and political attack argues about states rights, local control, democracy, and the proper role of the courts, combined with a neoconservative attack saying that desegregation is futile anyway. The attack from some African American politicians, educators, and bureaucrats, on the other hand, tends to mix elements of attacks on flawed policies, black power and Afrocentric theories, remembrances of the pre-desegregation era, and reaction to what is seen as a theory that black progress depends upon contact with whites. Oftentimes the coalitions backing resegregation are a strange and temporary alliance of people holding a variety of inconsistent beliefs.

Ending court-ordered desegregation has been supported by black mayors in several major cities, including Denver, Minneapolis, and Cleveland. This has often been incorrectly interpreted by the press as evidence that blacks no longer support school desegregation. Some leaders are reacting, as did Booker T. Washington a century ago, to what they see as a very limited range of options in an increasingly racially polarized society where judicial protection of the suburbs forecloses the best form of desegregation. Clearly, desegregation has little relevance within many of the largest cities. A number of the biggest urban districts are one-sixth or less white.[24] Some districts face senseless orders sending students from all-black, schools to three-fourth black schools which have a few poor whites. Many residents of those areas assume that desegregation is infeasible everywhere; perhaps the deepest damage of the Supreme Court's decisions is the incapacity of many local leaders today in the metropolitan North to even *imagine* integrated education. Few are acquainted with the models of success- ful metropolitan-wide desegregation in the South.

Other black critics believe that racial inequalities can be overcome by racial pride and higher aspirations. The Afrocentric curriculum movement and the creation of black male academies as alternatives to desegregation echo the experiments of the black-power movement in the early 1970s. It was not accidental that the first of these acade- mies was created in a Milwaukee school, left totally segregated because *Milliken I* blocked full desegregation in one of the nation's most residentially segregated metropolitan areas. This approach attempts to resolve inequalities by changing consciousness. Virtually no evidence exists that emphasis on culture can overcome the enor- mous problems facing schools of concentrated poverty or even that minority aspirations are low.[25] Black students, in any case, typically report aspirations as high or higher than whites.[26] Their problem is unequal preparation. The popularity of this experiment is clearly related to a sense of desperation, as is the subsequent turn by some of those leaders to private or corporate-run schools as a solution.

Research shows that desegregation opens richer opportunity net- works for minority children, but without any loss for whites. Part of the benefit for minority students comes from learning how to func- tion in white middle-class settings, since most of the society's best opportunities are in these settings. In contrast to the critics' assump- tions, the theory is not one of white racial superiority but a theory about the opportunity networks that historic discrimination has attached to white middle-class schools and about the advantages that come from breaking into those mobility networks.

Research has been mainly about effects of desegregation on minor- ity students, with a central focus on the way it works or fails to work to open doors into the mainstream of the society and the economy. This might have been a reasonable model when there was a vast white majority in the country, but there are now growing regions where whites need a path to success in a multiracial community with a white minority. Recent surveys show a growing perception that there are benefits from desegregation for whites.[27] Perhaps the mood of minority critics would change if desegregation debates could be framed around the possibility of mutual benefits of the kind recently affirmed in a survey of white and African American college students in Indiana.[28] Developing a multiracial conception of the benefits of desegregation is part of the process of moving toward genuine integration.

Possible Futures

The nation today is experiencing the quiet consolidation of a system of segregation and inequality. Much the same thing happened after *Plessy*. Generations passed as segregation was consolidated and built into the fabric of our developing metropolitan areas. Rigid segregation was followed by dramatic increases in the inequality of resources; there are signs of the same trend now. As we face resegregation and inequality, it is urgent to seek policies that lead back toward the vision of *Brown*.

Steps Toward Integration

There are many ways in which the country could begin to move toward integration. Although court battles are posed as choices between resegregation and preserving the existing desegregation plan, a desegregation plan is merely an imperfect and partial step toward the ultimate goal of integrated schools that serve stably integrated communities. Many of the old plans are seriously out of date, both in terms of not reflecting the current demography of the community and by not incorporating the lessons of research. They can be improved greatly.

Since *Brown*, the responsibility for desegregation has been focused on the courts. Now, with the Rehnquist Court pushing for judicial withdrawal, local leaders face possibly irreversible commitments to segregation. Civil rights lawyers, enforcement officials, and national educational, journalistic, and philanthropic leaders need to examine these choices and insist on serious consideration of the consequences.

Although the discussion is often framed as if desegregation is merely one of various possible educational treatments, it actually has a different logic, different goals, and vastly different roles for schools and educators. Compensatory education is designed to raise test scores of at-risk students through targeted educational programs designed to make up for what the students have missed, adding programs and staff to a weak school. It cannot change conditions outside the school. Desegregation aims to create connections with new opportunities that will change a student's life chances not only through academic achievement but through better access to jobs, higher education, and roles in community leadership.

Desegregation's aims are transformative—to create new institutions with stronger educational programs and positive race relations. These goals include helping whites overcome racial stereotypes and learning to function more effectively in an interracial society. Some of these objectives cannot, in their nature, be attained within segregated schools.

Supporting the goals of integration does not mean supporting all desegregation plans. Some make little sense or are even counterproductive. Much minority criticism of desegregation arises from either senseless "desegregation" or unfair treatment within desegregated schools. Local civil rights lawyers should, for example, end policies that transfer minority children from a ghetto to another poor, heavily minority central city school or that send a handful of white children to each city school. The best policy in such a situation might aim to achieve substantial desegregation in fewer schools and work for interdistrict transfers for other students. Insensitive and unfair policies or practices within some desegregated schools must be targeted and corrected.

Policies to preserve and improve desegregation are not in conflict with compensatory education. As the Supreme Court recognized in *Milliken II*, the history of discrimination has produced educational damage that needs attention whether or not desegregation takes place. Our analysis of *Milliken II* plans does not reject such programs but concludes they must be better designed and monitored much more strongly if there are to be real benefits. The specific recommendations that we offer could begin to turn communities from resegregation toward genuine integration.

Blocking Resegregation

If better desegregation strategies are to be achieved, it is first necessary to block the rush to end court orders. The leverage of the courts has been critical in the history of urban desegregation. A court battle may redirect energy in the short term from the productive improvements into an adversarial attack on the performance of the school district, but this may be essential. Such efforts should be accompanied by an offer to negotiate legitimate problems and a strong emphasis on strengthening real benefits for students. Plaintiffs should suggest specific meanings for educational equality and god faith compliance by the school district and urge expansion of successful elements. They should work to maintain judicial oversight until there is clear evidence that the unequal opportunities growing out of a history of discrimination have actually been corrected.

The standard for court oversight should be the provision of real opportunities long enough to make up for the cumulative effects of generations of discrimination. If minority children in segregated high schools, for example, have been denied a fair chance to be equally prepared for college, there should be clear evidence of major gains on this issue before a court order is terminated. If both educators and community groups realized that there was a strongly focused commitment to getting actual results, the debate would become quite different on all sides. Under the Supreme Court's 1995 *Jenkins* decision, courts will have to link the outcomes they require with explicit findings that the educational inequalities are the direct result of previous segregation. Since this was not previously necessary, additional hearings may be required.

Civil rights lawyers facing unitary status proceedings should fully investigate the districts asking for dismantling, not only showing what elements of the plan were never fulfilled, but also looking for new violations, such as construction of new schools that would obviously be segregated and thus undermine the stability of desegregation elsewhere. Many growing districts have built such schools and permitted erosion of desegregation in a number of ways. Policies on student and teacher transfers and on segregation within schools often produced new violations.

Resegregation cases have been skewed by the lack of resources to represent the interests of minority children. Effective representation would surely slow resegregation by creating a significant possibility that the court might tighten rather than end judicial mandates. This is a crucial time for philanthropies to invest in strong legal representation of minority children and the research needed to meet the requirements of the courts. It is also time for a key role to be played by the U.S. Justice Department's Civil Rights Division and the Education Department's. Too many cities are being resegregated by default.

Effective litigation strategies must include educating the public. What courts order and how administrators respond both are strongly affected by the public climate. Civil rights groups must not only battle in court but also must explain the costs of segregation and the value of desegregation to the public. Believing inaccurate political claims that court-ordered plans have huge costs and produce educational harm is, of course, strongly related to more critical attitudes toward desegregation.[29]

Better information about benefits and the attitudes of students and families actually experiencing busing would doubtless improve attitudes and make courts and administrators more conscious of consequences. The climate within which negotiations took place would change. The deeper changes needed to turn desegregated schools into successfully integrated schools require active support by school personnel, who are much more likely to work for goals they understand to be educationally and socially beneficial. Civil rights groups need to try to change the debate from whether or not to resegregate to how to get the greatest gains for all students, a question on which civil rights advocates and educators have the same long-term interest. Civil rights groups should also challenge local schools of education and education organizations to provide professional leadership for effective multiracial schools.

Monitoring, Assessing, and Improving Plans

Day-to-day operation of desegregation plans produces some legitimate complaints. The only mechanism provided by most court orders for dealing with problems in the plan—convincing a lawyer to file a formal motion and trigger a court hearing—is much too cumbersome, costly, slow, and adversarial to effectively resolve conflicts. It also excludes direct involvement from educators and community leaders. Expert oversight and negotiations among the parties or among experts trusted by the parties and school system professionals offer a better way to diminish conflict and improve plans. Local leaders should not assume that the only choice available is between the status quo and resegregation. An improved desegregation plan is often a far better alternative.

Monitoring offices and citizens committees can identify and help solve problems. The complaints of minority communities about in-school segregation, unfair discipline, unfair magnet selection mechanisms, and other problems should be taken seriously and so should complaints about racial conflict. Many complaints can be solved in ways that improve education and are consistent with the goals of desegregation. Good solutions will also often aid many white children.

The Role of the Courts

Courts are not ideal institutions for restructuring racial opportunity in schools, but they are the best we have. Their performance can be substantially improved. They lack electoral legitimacy, technical expertise, and staff resources necessary to keep track of a large bureaucracy, leading many to conclude that pursuing court-ordered change is futile. Courts became involved, however, only because local officials discriminated for generations and refused to act. Our studies show that many local officials still passively accept or actively favor segregation and do little or nothing to enforce equity when the court withdraws.

After *Milliken II* limited desegregation, courts were given the supposedly simpler and less intrusive job of repairing the educational harms of segregation. If local school administrators both knew how to overcome inequalities in minority schools and would do it, a court would only have to order states to provide money for a time. Courts did just that, turning both money and the responsibility for overseeing its use to the local school bureaucracy, but the assumptions were wrong. School systems have rarely been able to mount broadly effective compensatory programs, even with much larger and longer-term resources than those provided by most *Milliken II* orders. Urban school districts usually lack the stability and the focus to implement any complex change on behalf of politically weak constituencies.

Most courts have been passive in enforcing their orders. The court usually bestirs itself only when a lawyer makes a motion. Since the civil rights lawyers have little or no capability to monitor the orders, they rarely act. Lawyers for parties do not have the necessary expertise in understanding implementation or in analyzing the data that could show benefits and failings of programs. They also lack time and money needed for this task.

Only in the face of flagrant violations do courts do anything to justify the claim that they are "running the system." Our study indicates that courts rarely act to assure benefits and often require no serious accountability.

Courts possess ample authority to institute much more effective procedures without adding substantially to their burdens. They can deal with their most important weaknesses by appointing experts to advise the court. Many issues disputed in the courts can actually be resolved quietly if the court has a representative who understands the data and perspectives of the professionals involved. Although such experts or special masters with professional training in the issues before the court are only advisors, their presence can be an incentive for the parties to avoid easily disprovable claims of the sort commonly made and accepted in courts.

The federal district court in San Francisco, for example, has required the parties to nominate experts they trust to serve on a committee that advises the court on the implementation of the plan. The court selects from among the nominees and appoints one from each party's lists and the experts are then responsible only to the court. The committee is given full access to district data and personnel and makes findings and recommendations. A number of its recommendations for major change have been accepted and implemented. All of its decisions have been unanimous through 1995, showing that there are many issues on which experts selected by all sides agree.

The San Francisco process produced radical educational reforms. The reports to the court resulted in a far-reaching strategy of requiring actual progress for minority students or replacing entire school staffs and creating new kinds of schools. Before this was done, an analysis of data showed little effect from most court-ordered programs. In recent years both the schools threatened with dissolution and those actually dissolved and reconstituted have shown substantial real progress for minority students.[30]

Courts have some special strengths—removal from politics and the ability to stay with a complex issue long enough to implement change. Most urban school systems are crippled by bitter politics and the replacement of superintendents every two years or so. Courts are often not disrupting a stable and effective local educational structure but lending an element of continuity to a turbulent and sometimes chaotic institution in which no one addresses difficult long-term issues.

Good monitoring requires the courts to set specific goals against which to evaluate compliance. Otherwise the court will often have no alternative but to accept the district's version of its own successes. A court after *Jenkins* needs to delineate what it finds to be the harms of segregation and specify what must be accomplished to remedy local violations.

Since making these specific *Jenkins* linkages between historic violations and continuing effects requires a great many complex and subtle judgments, courts must necessarily rely on those who have been the closest observers of these long-term realities. Long-time minority educators, parents, community leaders, local researchers, and school board members within a school system or in local institutions of higher education have experience that deserves particularly close attention in this regard.

Courts should not assume that the "harms of segregation" have been cured when great inequalities remain. To realize the Supreme Court's goal of restoration of minority children to the condition their community would have faced in the absence of generations of educational discrimination, short-term programs with no discernible results are obviously inadequate.

Local Educational Leaders

Most local school leaders have never had to make a serious decision about the future of race relations in their schools. They could shift the blame to the courts. Now that the issue is coming back to local school boards, local educators have a heavy responsibility. They should look at the record before they resegregate. If neighborhood schools had positive effects, cities that have maintained them such as Chicago, Detroit, Atlanta, and Washington, D.C., would have excellent schools rather than many ranking among the nation's worst. School officials should study nearby big cities to see how well the inner-city segregated neighborhood schools actually work before creating more.

Educational leaders should also be careful to avoid a classic fallacy—reasoning from isolated best cases about compensatory programs. Before accepting an alternative, board members, superintendents and community groups should ask for proof that the reform has been successfully implemented district-wide in segregated schools in some city and independently assessed. Almost all of the suggested reforms will fail this test. The proper stance should be great caution in betting the future of the city on an untested plan to equalize segregated schools. They should require independent evaluation.

Whether or not there is a desegregation plan, local educators need plans for developing positive race relations and racial equity in the schools. These are questions fundamental to the future of schools and communities undergoing vast demographic change.

School officials need to think about successful integration as a long-term goal and build it into the administrative structure, hiring and training decisions, and the assessment system. We understand far more about the possibilities and conditions for effective interracial schools than was known in the era of *Brown*. Understanding and using this knowledge is a vital part of contemporary professional leadership.

Typically, school districts provide human relations training to faculty and staff only when desegregation begins. Such training makes a difference in both education and academic achievement and should be built into district processes. Teachers, many of whom may be themselves products of segregated education, should be trained in methods that have the greatest academic benefits for all students and provided with continual support to make the changes needed to implement those procedures. The potential benefits of desegregation for white students as well as students of color are more likely to be realized in a school where there are positive role models from the racial groups represented in the school and where teachers have learned to work effectively across racial lines.

Much was learned during the 1972-1981 period when the federal government financed desegregation aid and research. Realizing the full benefits of desegregation takes commitment within the school district and each school. They need methods of avoiding classroom segregation, unequal counseling, discipline, and other practices that have the effect of separating students within schools.[11] Successful desegregation does not involve taking something from whites to give to blacks but rests on a series of changes that have benefits for all groups. There are demonstrated techniques that focus upon successful classroom integration, and produce both academic gains and positive racial attitudes.[31] The Student Team Learning Techniques developed at Johns Hopkins University, for example, demonstrate substantial gains as do techniques developed by Elizabeth Cohen at Stanford.[32]

Research

It is important to both local and national debates that there be a revival of research work on urban segregation and desegregation in

the universities with support from government and major foundations. For most of a generation, there has been little serious intellectual work on race relations in American schools or on conditions of
successful multiracial education. Little work has been done on segregation and desegregation effects on Latino students who will soon be
the nation's largest minority population. Researchers should meet to
formulate new agendas of basic questions, courses and seminars
should be supported on leading research campuses, and public and
private research agencies should support this work. We do not, for
example, have even basic data on segregation in the multiracial
schools developing in our coastal cities. Basic research and reliable
data are essential for improving policy.

Conservative administrations cut off research funding. The federal government went from active support of desegregation research
under President Carter to support only for research creating evidence
to support the Justice Department's resegregation drive under
President Reagan. As a new education agenda was launched,
research money for desegregation dried up in most private foundations, too. The issue of equity vanished from the national and state
education agendas.[33]

The Role of the Media: Analysis
Not Cheerleading

As key participants in an increasingly interracial society, reporters,
writers, and editors need to consider their role carefully. Effective
public discussion of school resegregation requires full information
about the positive as well as the negative perspectives on civil rights
policies. Politicians at all levels often yield to temptations to exploit
racial fears. As the courts retreat and research is limited, choices are
being made. The local press tends to accept uncritically whatever the
local school bureaucracy says without any of its normal skepticism
about improbable claims.

Resegregation decisions should be covered as major public choices
and with the kind of skepticism that the press might direct at any large
change undertaken with great optimism but no model of success.
Coverage should include looking closely at any evidence that proposed
programs have actually worked on a large scale in segregated school
systems. There should also be coverage of the actual condition of segregated schools in nearby cities that have neighborhood schools. The

press should also investigate and report problems with the existing plan and ideas for resolving them. Surveys probing fundamental goals of families, not asking a few leading questions, can also make valuable contributions. Like other institutions of the local establishment, the tendency is for the press to be swept into the cycle of justifying resegregation. It is one of the only sources, however, of vitally important independent information.

Federal Guidelines

The Justice Department and the Education Department are two federal agencies that have general responsibility for civil rights enforcement that have not played a positive role in school desegregation policy. President Reagan's Justice Department was at the center of the drive for resegregation. Unfortunately, neither the Clinton Justice Department's Civil Rights Division nor the Education Department's Office for Civil Rights (OCR) provided strong leadership on the large issues left unspecified by the courts. The Justice Department tends to await complaints, not actively monitor cases it brings.[34] The Education Department's Civil Rights office has created no standards or serious monitoring of educational results of desegregation plans. Although it is severely limited by congressional language forbidding the OCR to require busing, there is no reason that it could not offer standards for effective desegregation and good faith compliance, giving some specific meaning to the sweeping language of the Supreme Court's decisions. In the past, the federal courts have shown substantial respect for the professional judgment of the Education Department on matters of educational policy related to civil rights.

Cross-District Plans

Civil rights groups and school districts in cities and racially changing suburbs would all benefit from extending desegregation to the suburbs. Though this may seem an odd issue to raise in a time of abandonment of much more limited plans, the real choice about the future is between accepting resegregation and finding a path toward viable and lasting desegregation. The most stable desegregation plans are plans that include cities and suburbs. Many of the problems of older plans relate directly to their limited reach and their inability to deal with the on-going suburban exodus that is now in its fourth decade.

In districts with large minority enrollments, broader plans lessen the incentive of whites and middle-class minorities to flee the city and can provide city children access to suburban resources and to far more competitive schools. Opportunity theories of desegregation work best when plans include the entire urban areas allow placing most students into predominantly middle-class schools. Such plans increase stability by raising the costs of flight and creating better options for those who stay. In such communities, high-status families have to be concerned about the schools serving the poor since their children share the same schools. Business must care because there is nowhere else to go for workers. Such plans create a vested area-wide interest in success and they have the demographic stability needed to permit long-term efforts to upgrade schools as we observed in the Charlotte study.[35]

Since the late 1970s, there have been several federal court cases that have enabled considerable numbers of students to cross district lines. In two cases, large voluntary inter-district transfer policies have been funded by state governments as a result of school desegregation litigation. Language in the Supreme Court's 1995 decision, *Missouri v. Jenkins,* raises higher barriers in federal courts. There are probably still cities where a metropolitan case could be fought successfully in federal court; one possibility is Denver, where the state constitution was amended to prevent expansion of the city school system in the midst of the initial desegregation case.[36]

Although the school choice movement threatens to foster resegregation by both race and class, it also has positive possibilities for cross-district desegregation. Many states now provide rights to transfer to schools of choice in other districts but do not provide the information systems, the transportation, the counseling, and other elements needed to make this opportunity genuinely available to low-income segregated minority families. Nor do they prohibit transfers that intensify segregation. Without strong civil rights policies, choice plans can pay to transfer of white students from integrated city schools to all-white suburbs. Good choice plans can aid desegregation through equity elements such as strong public information and personal outreach, free transportation, enforceable desegregation goals, and prohibition of transfers increasing segregation. Information is especially important for families whose social networks may not automatically bring them information about schools, whose primary language is not English or who are economically disadvantaged.

Civil rights groups and urban school boards share an interest in explor-
ing the possibility of more extensive desegregation remedies under the
state constitutions. Unlike the federal constitution, education is an
explicitly established right in many states. State constitutional rights
could provide the basis for state orders that would permit desegregation and educational reform across district lines. Clearly where a state
has acted to increase segregation or to block desegregation, it is liable
to a judicial remedy. The first full-scale effort to define such state rights
in Connecticut was rejected by the trial court in early 1995 but
remained under appeal at this book's printing.[37] The second major case
was filed in metropolitan Minneapolis-St. Paul in September 1995.[38]

Housing

Policies for housing integration could take a significant part of the
desegregation burden off the schools in a society where young households typically move every three years. Desegregation is a limited
experience when students must make morning and afternoon trips
across the racial boundaries between two separate worlds.

School desegregation is often criticized as a treatment for a symp-
tom of the underlying problem, segregated housing. Analyses including Massey and Denton's *American Apartheid* argue that spatial isolation
by housing is the root system of inequality in metropolitan America
and the central reason for the cumulative and self-reinforcing nature
of social division and inequalities. Working on the housing issues in
combination with school desegregation opens the possibilities of
much more powerful remedies.

The goal of better integrated schools in integrated neighborhoods
with less busing fits much better with the values that huge majorities
of Americans express than turning back to segregation. In surveys,
most Americans strongly support integrated schools but want educational reform, choice, and more direct parent and community
involvement in schools. African American parents want integrated
schools in the communities where they live. Only a tiny minority
want to live in all-black areas or attend all-black schools. School and
housing policies could break patterns of discrimination and move
toward natural integration.

School desegregation can foster housing desegregation and housing policies can reduce the necessity for busing. Uncoordinated housing policies operating in markets with traditions of segregation,

however, will often exacerbate school segregation by destabilizing interracial communities.

School districts should request housing and related agencies for support, formally asking housing and community development agencies to examine each of their programs to develop plans to prevent its use in ways that increases school segregation by increasing segregated housing. The school plan should reward integrated neighborhoods.

In growing school districts, developers of new housing should be required to prepare and implement plans for marketing their housing to an integrated clientele before the school district will construct the new school.[39] In exchange for the increased value that a new school gives the developer whose housing becomes more marketable, it is reasonable to expect that the developer should not increase segregation but will aid neighborhood desegregation. To the extent that this involves including more affordable housing in new communities, this would help address another school problem—almost all new suburban communities are being built without any housing affordable to teachers educating their children. As one of the largest local employers and one that tends to have a diverse workforce, school districts can also help by providing fair housing advice and support for their own staffs.

Effective school desegregation plans should include as much as possible of the local housing market, should be supported by vigorous fair housing enforcement and by strong policies permitting families receiving subsidized housing to move out from ghettos. Local and state civil rights agencies should act against mortgage and insurance discrimination. Counseling should be provided to minority families receiving rent subsidies offering housing choices including outlying largely white communities with the best job opportunities and most competitive schools. At a time when massive changes in HUD-subsidized housing policies will confront many families with new housing decisions, desegregation policies could have a particularly substantial effect. School desegregation plans should reward in stably integrated communities by ending busing there.

State school and housing officials should be especially sensitive to developing problems of suburban segregation. Projections show vast growth of suburban minority school enrollment in the next generation and massive movement of whites to outer suburbs, but most suburbs have no experience and few tools for dealing with segregation and racial transition, which can rapidly transform a community.

Without early and effective planning, many older suburbs will face relatively rapid racial resegregation in schools, accompanied by a dramatic change in their housing markets. Ending busing won't stop this —many such communities have no busing—but strong policies supporting integration may help substantially.

Courts must decide whether housing segregation is the result of discrimination by public agencies. Courts often reach *ad hoc* conclusions reflecting the judge's personal impressions rather than a serious examination of knowledge on the subject.

The white flight to suburbia, for example, that judges believe is caused by busing, may turn out to be almost identical to that experienced in similar cities with no busing. Since findings of fact are rarely reviewed by the higher federal courts and those findings may end desegregation, errors may never be rectified. Courts should not adopt neighborhood schools as a solution to white flight without understanding both that white declines are occurring in most cities that have neighborhood schools and the amazing stability of some systems with city-suburban busing. The courts should consider appointing an expert witness responsible to the court, perhaps someone from a local sociology or urban planning program, to ensure full consideration of the relevant factual issues.

The initial Supreme Court decisions on busing recognized the intimate interaction between school and housing, but that awareness has rarely affected policies. During the last years of the Carter administration, the Justice Department actually sought combined school and housing remedies. One of those cases was successfully litigated before the Reagan Justice Department dropped the idea. There have been proposals to revise federal, state, and local housing policies in ways that would make school busing less necessary over time. Though there are no quick remedies to housing segregation, working on the problem could move us closer to school desegregation without busing. This goal reflects the desires expressed by a majority of Americans in national surveys. Most Americans express strong support for integrated schools but want educational reform, choice, and more parent and community involvement in schools. African American parents say they want integrated schools closer to home. Properly designed education and housing policies could move the nation toward those goals.

School districts should work with housing and community development agencies to support racial integration. School policies should reward integrated neighborhoods by establishing integrated neighborhood schools. Minority families who receive rent subsidies should receive extensive counseling that includes information about housing options in outlying white suburbs where there are usually better job opportunities and more competitive schools.[40] Programs of this sort in Chicago, Hartford, and Cincinnati have found many minority families interested in such opportunities. Research in metropolitan Chicago has shown large school benefits associated with such moves.[41]

Similarly, when the issues are raised before school boards either before or after unitary status proceedings, school boards need much better advice about the nature of housing policy and the options they have for using their leverage to encourage changes in neighborhood segregation and resegregation. With the exception of a handful of communities, there has been little effort to produce the kind of positive interaction between school and housing policy which could lead toward stable integration. School systems are the most powerful local institution with direct interest in stable interracial communities. School authorities should ask both public and private institutions to cooperate in the development of better integrated housing, stabilize neighborhoods threatened by residential resegregation, and break up the concentrations of extreme poverty in housing projects that confront schools with almost impossible tasks.

What We Have Learned

As this book goes to press, the trend toward resegregation is manifest across the country. The Supreme Court approved the first big city desegregation order outside the South in Denver in 1973. The Denver federal district court approved resegregation in September 1995. There are challenges to existing desegregation orders in cities from Minnesota to Florida, from Massachusetts to California. Politicians with no direct role in local cases, such as the mayor of Indianapolis and the governor of Arizona, are jumping into local disputes, trying to take political credit for ending busing. In the course of a few years, the awareness that the Supreme Court has approved resegregation has spread across the country and has carried with it the impression that the era begun by *Brown* is rapidly coming to an end.

We are now far into a cycle of blaming the local school authorities for the dismal educational consequences of policies that confine urban poor minority children to the nation's most isolated schools and housing policies that keep them in communities devastated by joblessness and crime. With little analysis, some of our largest cities are closing down the only major bridge from the ghettos and barrios to middle-class America. Once we accept resegregation as normal and educationally advisable, it will be natural to blame urban school leaders for the poor performance in their schools. Administrators in urban districts inherit weak and often rigid systems, neglected facilities and overburdened staff. They struggle to stem decay.

Two or three years later, leaders are fired or leave and go off to make similar promises in another city. Cities experience a well-paid parade of illusionists. The constant change tends to divert attention from the fact that we have an unworkable structure whose results are dismally predictable without even knowing who is running things or what this year's reform program is called. This does not mean that leaders are not sincere in their beliefs, just that the problems are far beyond their capacity to change in a broad and lasting way. Conservative critics are now using the failure of school reform promises to attack the entire structure of public education, proposing to replace it with a voucher system.

If discrimination and segregation are defined as non-problems and unequal schooling persists, the other logical target for attack is the intellectual capacity of minority students and families. If they are being given a fair chance and failing, the logic of segregation says, they or their families or their culture must be inferior. If they are inferior, there is little that can be done and there is no need to give much priority to the futile task. This tone is apparent in a number of recent court decisions.

The real roots of the problem, however, lie in the social and economic crises of our cities and the systematically unequal educational opportunities offered to poor and minority children. Desegregation, properly understood, is an attack on the underlying system of inequality and a demand that the effective institutions and opportunities be shared with those who have historically been treated most unfairly. If we are to avoid the brutal logic of segregation and to learn from the poisoning of social and educational possibilities in the South for generations after *Plessy*, we must raise the stakes, spell out the logic of *Brown* and the integration movement, and make much more careful judgments about our common future.

We need a serious debate on the ways to achieve a successful multiracial society. For white leaders, who are often sorely tempted by the politics of racial polarization and scapegoating, there needs to be a clear recognition of the fact that when we celebrate the Tricentennial of American Independence, there will be a huge nonwhite majority in our country if well-established demographic trends continue. The leaders of what seem likely to be the last generations of a predominantly European-origin America need to consider not only what the current majority prefers but also what will produce a viable society for their children to live in when their descendants will be worried about minority rights for whites.

What we do now, in either discarding or building upon the possibilities of *Brown* will do much to shape how we proceed through the vast demographic transition that the Census Bureau predicts will make our school age population less than two-fifths white by 2050. It would be much better if we enter that transition with multiracial public schools that offer equal opportunity, strong protection for minority rights, and training to live in a profoundly multiracial society.

Brown opened a path to a viable future for American society. Forty years later, we know much more the reasons why separate schools are usually unequal and about the preconditions necessary for effective interracial schools. The stakes are much higher today, not only because of the increase in the minority population but also the ever increasing necessity of education for economic success. The experience of *Brown* and the results of resegregation have given us lessons that we ignore at great cost.

There is nothing in the experience of the United States since *Plessy v. Ferguson* to suggest that racially separate schools will ever be equal so long as the rest of society is profoundly unequal. Choosing resegregation means choosing greater inequality and risking the future of our multisracial society.

Notes

CHAPTER ONE

1 *Bd. of Educ. of Oklahoma City v. Dowell*, 498 U.S. 237 (1991).

2 *Freeman v. Pitts*, 112 S. Ct. 1430 (1992).

3 *Missouri v. Jenkins*, 115 S. Ct. 2038 (1995).

4 *Bd. of Educ. of Oklahoma City v. Dowell*.

5 *Green v. Sch. Bd. of New Kent County*, 391 U.S. 430 (1968).

6 *Freeman v. Pitts*, 112 S. Ct. 1430.

7 Richard Kluger, *Simple Justice* (New York: Vintage Books, 1975), 253.

8 Herbert Brownell with John P. Burke, *Advising Ike: The Memoirs of Attorney General Herbert Brownell* (Lawrence: University of Kansas Press, 1993); Mark Stern, "Presidential Strategies and Civil Rights: Eisenhower, the Early Years, 1952-54," *Presidential Studies Quarterly* 19, no. 4 (fall 1989): 769-95.

9 G. Edward White, *Earl Warren: A Public Life* (New York: Oxford University Press, 1982) 166-68.

10 J. W. Peltason, *58 Lonely Men: Southern Federal Judges and School Desegregation* (New York: Harcourt, Brace and World, 1961).

11 Ibid.; Reed Sarratt, *The Ordeal of Desegregation* (New York: Harper and Row, 1966).

12 Gary Orfield, *The Reconstruction of Southern Education: The Schools and the 1964 Civil Rights Act* (New York: John Wiley, 1969).

13 *Green v. Bd. of Educ. of New Kent County*, 391 U.S. 430.

14 Harry S. Dent, *The Prodigal South Returns to Power* (New York: John Wiley & Sons, 1978).

15 H. R. Haldeman, *The Haldeman Diaries: Inside the Nixon White House* (New York: G. P. Putman's Sons, 1994), 126.

16 Ibid., 126-30, 142, 183-84, 276; Leon Panetta and Peter Gall, *Bring Us Together: The Nixon Team and the Civil Rights Retreat* (Philadelphia: Lippincott, 1971).

17 Sue Davis, "Justice Rehnquist's Equal Protection Clause: An Interim Analysis," *University of Nebraska Law Review* 63 (1984): 288, 308.

18 Senate Committee on the Judiciary, *Hearings on the Nomination of Justice William Hobbs Rehnquist*, 99th Cong. 2d. Sess., 1986, 161-162.

19 Ibid., 325.

20 Davis, "Equal Protection," 308-309.

21 *Delaware State Bd. of Educ. v. Evans,* 446 U.S. 923 (1975).

22 *Columbus Bd. of Educ. v. Penick,* 443 U.S. 449 (1979).

23 *San Antonio Indep. Sch. Dist. v. Rodriguez,* 541 U.S. 1 (1973).

24 *Milliken v. Bradley,* 94 S. Ct. 3112, 3134-41 (1974).

25 Judge Avram Cohn, letter to author, 4 May 1994; Detroit case is described in detail in chapter 6.

26 The national and regional desegregation trends are described in chapter 3.

27 See chapter 3.

28 Bruce Oudes, ed., *From: The President: President Nixon's Secret Files* (New York: Harper and Row, 1989), 399.

29 Oudes, *From: The President, Nixon to John Ehrlichman,* 19 May 1972, 451.

30 Ibid.

31 Ibid.

32 Gary Orfield, *Congressional Power: Congress and Social Change* (New York: Harcourt Brace Jovanovich, 1975), 182-84; G. Orfield, *Must We Bus? Segregated Schools and National Policy* (Washington, D.C.: Brookings Inst., 1978), 247-54.

33 George H. Gallup, *The Gallup Poll: Public Opinion 1935-1971* (New York: Random House, 1972), 1934, 2009.

34 Orfield, "Desegregation Aid and the Politics of Polarization," *Congressional Power,* chapter 9.

35 *Adams v. Richardson,* 356 F. Supp. 92 (D.D.C. 1973), was the first of many orders.

36 *Columbus Bd. of Educ. v. Penick,* 443 U.S. 449 (1979); *Dayton Bd. of Educ. v. Brinkman,* 443 U.S. 526 (1979).

37 "What Carter Believes: Interview on the Issues," *U.S. News & World Report,* 24 May 1976, 22-23; Bell record is summarized in 95th Cong. 1st sess., *Congressional Record* daily ed., (25 January 1977), S1301-06.

38 The program was combined with a number of small grant programs and a substantially smaller total amount of money was sent to the states to spend on whatever they thought best. No state used it to set up a desegregation aid program. Most states simply distributed the money on a per capita basis to school districts. See John Ellwood, ed., *Reductions in U.S. Domestic Spending* (New Brunswick, N.J.: Transaction Books, 1982), 191-98.

39 Ibid., 35.

40 House Committee on the Judiciary, Subcommittee on Civil and Constitutional Rights, *Hearings on School Desegregation,* 97th Cong. 1st sess., 1981, 614, 619.

41 *Education Week,* 24 November 1982.

42 U.S. National Center for Education Statistics, *The Condition of Education* (Washington, D.C.: GPO, 1993), 100. The trends had shown falling public and rising private enrollment in the 1970-84 period. (Ibid.)

43 Herman Schwartz, *Packing the Courts: The Conservative Campaign to Rewrite the Constitution* (New York: Charles Scribner's Sons, 1988); *New York Times,* 30 November, 1995.

44 Edwin Meese III, *With Regan: The Inside Story* (Washington, D.C.: Regnery Gateway, 1992), 316-17.

45 P. Karatinos, "*Price v. Austin Indep. Sch. Dist.*: Desegregation's Unitary

Tar Baby," 77 W. *Educ. L. Rep.* 15 (1992); see also *Price v. Austin Indep. Sch. Dist.*, 729 F. Supp. The Austin Independent School District, Planning and Development Office, March 1994.

46 Karatinos, "*Price v. Austin.*"

47 *Tasby v. Wright*, 713 F.2d 90 (5th Cir. 1993).

48 *Stell v. Board of Public Education*, 860 F. Supp. 1563 (S.D. Ga. 1994)

49 *Cleveland Plain Dealer*, 25 August 1994, 6-B.

50 Patrice M. Jones, "School District Seeks Release From Edict on Cross-Town Busing," *Cleveland Plain Dealer*, 5 January 1995, 1-B; "Court Oversight of Denver Schools Is Ended," *New York Times*, 13 September 1995, B7; Peter Schmidt, "U.S. Judge Releases Wilmington Districts from Court Oversight," *Education Week*, 6 September 1995, 9.

CHAPTER TWO

1 Portsmouth Public Schools, *Community Schools, Update*, October 1994.

2 Editorial, "Desegregation: Board Must Vote for Student Achievement," *Minneapolis Star Tribune*, 26 June 1995, 8A.

3 Stanley Lieberson, *A Piece of the Pie: Black and White Immigrants Since 1880* (Berkeley: University of California Press, 1980); Douglas S. Massey and Nancy A. Denton, *American Apartheid: Segregation and the Making of the Underclass* (Cambridge: Harvard University Press, 1993).

4 A 1995 national survey showed that less than a fifth of whites knew that African Americans were doing much worse than whites in terms of jobs and income, and that only 30 percent of whites, compared to 84 percent of African Americans, believed that "past and present discrimination" were major causes of racial inequality. (*The Washington Post*, 9 October 1995, A22); another national survey, by the Gallup Poll during the same period, showed that only 6 percent of whites believed that racial discrimination against blacks was a "very serious problem," and only 23 percent more believed it was "somewhat serious." (*USA Today*, 9 October 1995, 5A.)

5 *Plessy v. Ferguson*, 163 U.S. 537 (1896) 559-60.

6 Ibid., 562.

7 Earl Warren, *The Memoirs of Earl Warren* (New York: Doubleday 1977), 2-3.

8 Ibid., 296.

9 *Milliken v. Bradley*, 94 S. Ct. at 3145.

10 John D. Long, *The Republican Party: Its History, Principles, and Policy* (Boston: Lindsay and Co., 1888).

11 V. O. Key, *Southern Politics in State and Nation* (New York: Alfred A. Knopf, 1949).

12 Stanley P. Hirshson, *Farewell to the Bloody Shirt: Northern Republicans and the Southern Negro, 1877-1893* (Chicago: Quadrangle Books, 1968), 26-27.

13 C. Vann Woodward, *Reunion and Reaction: The Compromise of 1877 and the End of Reconstruction* (New York: Doubleday Anchor Books, 1956).

14 C. Vann Woodward, *Origins of the New South, 1887-1913* (Baton Rouge: Louisiana State University Press, 1951), 466.

15 Ibid., 468.

16 Harry S. Dent, *The Prodigal South* (New York: John Wiley & Sons, 1978); Kevin Phillips, *The Emerging Republican Majority* (New York: Doubleday Anchor, 1970).

17 Thomas Byrne Edsall and Mary D. Edsall, *Chain Reaction: The Impact of Race, Rights, and Taxes on American Politics* (New York: W. W. Norton, 1991); Stanley B. Greenberg, "From Crisis to Working Majority," *The American Prospect* 7 (fall 1991):104-17; Gary Orfield, "Racial Transformation and Political Failure: Republican Polarization and Democratic Denial," working paper, seminar on Future Directions of American Politics and Public Policy, Harvard University, Cambridge, Mass., May 1993.

18 Gary Orfield, "Congress and Civil Rights: From Obstacle to Protector," in *African Americans and the Living Constitution*, ed. John Hope Franklin and Genna Rae McNeil (Washington, D.C.: Smithsonian Institution Press, 1995).

19 *Pasadena City Board of Education v. Spangler*, 427 U.S. 424 (1976).

20 Orfield, "Congress and Civil Rights."

21 *Slaughter House Cases*, 893 U.S. 36 (1873).

22 *Cumming v. Board of Education*, 175 U.S. 528 (1899), cited in Mark V. Tushnet, *The NAACP's Legal Strategy Against Segregated Education, 1925-1950* (Chapel Hill, Univ. of North Carolina Press, 1987), 22. James D. Anderson, *The Education of Blacks in the South, 1860-1935* (Chapel Hill, Univ. of North Carolina, 1988), 193, 263.

23 *Civil Rights Cases*, 108 U.S. 3 (1883).

24 *Missouri v. Jenkins*, 115 S. Ct. 2038, 2056 (1995).

25 See chapter 11.

26 John Hope Franklin, "Jim Crow Goes to School," in *The Negro in the South Since 1865*, ed. Charles E. Wynes (New York: Harper Colophon, 1965), 147.

27 Louis R. Harlan, *Separate and Unequal: Public School Campaigns and Racism in the Southern Seaboard States, 1901-1915* (New York: Atheneum, 1969), viii.

28 Ibid., 12-13.

29 Franklin, "Jim Crow," 148.

30 *The Public Papers of Woodrow Wilson*, quoted in Lawrence J. Friedman, *The White Savage: Racial Fantasies in the Postbellum South* (Englewood Cliffs, N.J.: Prentice-Hall, 1970), 155.

31 Frank R. Parker, "*Shaw v. Reno*: A Constitutional Setback for Minority Representation," *PS: Political Science and Politics* (March 1995):50.

32 Friedman, *The White Savage*, 164.

33 *Missouri v. Jenkins*, 115 S. Ct. at 2056.

34 Ibid. at 2065.

35 *Plessy v. Ferguson*, 163 U.S. 53, 551 (1896).

36 Ibid., at 550.

37 Jack Temple Kirby, *Darkness at the Dawning: Race and Reform in the Progressive South* (Philadelphia: J. P. Lippincott, 1972), 24.

38 *Buchanan v. Warley*, 245 U.S. 60 (1917).

39 Loren Miller, *The Petitioners: The Story of the Supreme Court of the United States and the Negro* (Cleveland: Meridian Books, 1967), 246-50.

40 Gunnar Myrdal, *An American Dilemma: The Negro Problem and Modern Democracy*, vol. 2 (New York: Harper and Row, 1944), 624.

41 *Plessy v. Ferguson*, 63 U.S. 537, 551 (1896).

42 *Bd. of Educ. of Oklahoma City v. Dowell*, 111 S. Ct. 630, 635, 639-40 (1991).

43 *Armour v. Nix*, slip opinion (N.D. Ga. 1979).

44 *Freeman v. Pitts*, 112 S. Ct. 1430 (1992).

45 Gallup Poll data; see discussion in chapter 4.

46 *Missouri v. Jenkins*, 115 S. Ct. at 2053-2056.

47 Ibid., at 2060.

48 Glen C. Altschuler, *Race, Ethnicity and Class in American Social Thought, 1865-1919* (Arlington Heights, Ill.: Harlan Davidson, 1982), 7, 83.

49 Allan Chase, *The Legacy of Malthus: The Social Costs of the New Scientific Racism* (Urbana: Univ. of Illinois Press, 1980).

50 Charles Murray and Richard Hernstein, *The Bell Curve* (New York: The Free Press, 1994), 61-62.

51 Stephen Jay Gould, "Curveball," *New Yorker*, 28 November 1994, 139.

52 C. Vann Woodward, "The Case of the Louisiana Traveler," in *Quarrels That Have Shaped the Constitution*, ed. John A. Garraty (New York: Harper and Row, 1966), 157.

53 Robert J. Harris, "The Court as Ally of the South," in *Black Americans and the Supreme Court Since Emancipation*, ed. Arnold M. Paul (New York: Holt, Rinehart and Winston, 1972), 32. The book reprints part of Harris's 1960 book, *The Quest for Equality* (Baton Rouge: LSU Press, 1960).

54 Lois B. Moreland, "Minorities in the Politics of 1980," in *The Presidential Election and Transition 1980-1981* ed. Paul T. David and David H. Everson (Carbondale: Southern Illinois Univ. Press, 1983), 104.

55 Lou Cannon, *Reagan: The Role of a Lifetime* (New York: Simon and Schuster, 1991), 521.

56 The others were Andrew Johnson and Ronald Reagan, Barbara Sinclair, "Governing Unheroically (and Sometimes Unappetizingly): Bush and the 101st Congress," in *The Bush Presidency: First Appraisals*, ed. Colin Campbell and Bert A. Rockman (Chatham, N.J.: Chatham House Publishers, 1991), 170. Bush later signed a weaker version of this bill.

57 Maureen Dowd, "Getting Nasty Early Helps G.O.P. Gain Education on Thomas," *New York Times*, 15 October 1991 A1, A18; Michael K. Frisby, "Race Tactic Deplored but Is Called Effective," *Boston Globe*, 16 October 1991, 1, 8; R. W. Apple Jr., "Senate Confirms Thomas 52-48, Ending Week of Bitter Battle," *New York Times*, 16 October 1991, A1, A19.

58 Altschuler, *Race, Ethnicity and Class*, 6-7.

59 Booker T. Washington, "Atlanta Exposition Address," in *The Voice of Black Rhetoric*, ed. Arthur L. Smith and Stephen Robb (Boston: Allyn and Bacon, 1971), 99.

60 Booker T. Washington, *Up From Slavery: An Autobiography* (Garden City, N.Y.: Doubleday, Page and Co., 1901).

61 David Levering Lewis ed., *W. E. B. DuBois: A Reader* (New York: Henry Holt and Co., 1995), 327.

62 David R. Berman, "Takeovers of Local Governments: An Overview and Evaluation of State Policies," *Publius* 25, no. 3 (summer 1995):55-70; Fern Shen and Charles Babington, "Maryland, Baltimore Plan Overhaul of City Schools," *The Washington Post*, 22 January 1966, D1, D6; Terry M. Moe, ed., *Private Vouchers* (Stanford, California: Hoover Inst. Press, 1995), 1-18.

63 *Newsweek*, 22 February 1993, 54, quoting Michael Casserly, director of the Council of the Great City Schools.

64 John Edgerton, *Speak Now Against the Day: The Generation Before the Civil Rights Movement in the South* (New York: Alfred A. Knopf, 1995).

CHAPTER THREE

1 Much of the data included in this chapter was first released by the Harvard Project on School Desegregation in a report issued by the National School Boards Association. See Gary Orfield with Sara Schley and Sean Reardon, *The Growth of Segregation in American Schools* (Alexandria: National School Boards Association, 1993).

2 Eric M. Cambum, "College Completion among Students from High Schools Located in Large Metropolitan Areas," *American Journal of Education*, 98 no. 4 (August 1990):551-69.

3 U.S. Department of Education Office for Civil Rights Data in, Gary Orfield, *Public School Desegregation in the United States*, 1968-1980, Tables 1 and 10, and 1991 Center for Education, Statistics, Common Core of Data Public Education Agency Universe.

4 1994 Census Bureau projections indicated that Latinos will be the largest minority by 2020, with nearly 16 percent of the population. See "Americans in 2020: Less White, More Southern," *New York Times*, 22 April 1994. The Census Bureau has projected that the U.S. population will be 22 percent Latino and 14 percent African American by 2050 if trends in the early 1990s continue. The Latino share of the U.S. school enrollment should surpass the African American share in the early twenty-first century. See U.S. Bureau of the Census, P25-1104, Tables A, 2, 3, cited in *Population Bulletin*, 49, no. 2 (September 1994):9.

5 Computations from U.S. Department of Education, Common Core of Educational Statistics.

6 Greg J. Duncan, *Years of Poverty, Years of Plenty* (Ann Arbor, Mi: Inst. for Social Research, 1984).

7 Christopher Jaeger, "Minority and Low Income High Schools: Evidence of Educational Inequality, in Metro Los Angeles," working paper no. 8 (Chicago: Metropolitan Opportunity Project, 1987).

8 Peter Scheirer, "Metropolitan Chicago Public Schools: Concerto for Grades, Schools, and Students in F Major," Metropolitan Opportunity Project, University of Chicago, 1989.

9 Gary Orfield, *The Growth of Segregation in American Schools: Changing Patterns of Separation and Poverty Since 1968* (Alexandria: National School Board Association, 1993), Table 5.

10 Ibid., Table 4.

11 Southern Education Reporting Service in Reed Sarratt, *The Ordeal of Desegregation* (Harper & Row, 1966), 362; HEW Press Release, 27 May 1968; OCR data tapes; NCES Common Core of Data Statistics, 1991-92.

12 Orfield, *Growth of Segregation,* Table 7.

13 Ibid., Table 8.

14 Statistics computed from National Center for Education Statistics, Common Core of Education Data for the 1991-92 School Year, by Sara Schley and Sean Reardon, Harvard Graduate School of Education; Orfield and Monfort, 1988.

15 *The Condition of Education 1993:* 100.

16 *The Condition of Education 1994:* 110.

17 U.S. Census Bureau, *School Enrollment, 1992,* Table A1, Table C.

18 Ibid.

19 Gary Orfield, Franklin Monfort, and Melissa Aaron, *Status of School Desegregation, 1968-1986. Segregation, Integration, and Public Policy: National, State, and Metropolitan Trends in Public Schools* (Alexandria: National School Boards Association, 1989), 1.

20 Gary Orfield and Franklin Monfort, *Racial Change and Desegregation in Large School Districts: Trends Through the 1986-1987 School Year* (Alexandria: National School Boards Association, 1988).

21 Orfield and Ashkinaze, 1991, 113.

22 U.S. Bureau of the Census, 1991b:5.

23 Orfield and Ashkinaze, 111, Orfield and Monfort, 1988, 11.

24 Orfield and Monfort, "Racial Change," U.S. Civil Rights Commission, *New Evidence on School Desegregation,* 1987.

25 Peter Scheirer, Poverty Not Bureaucracy," working paper, Metropolitan Opportunity Project, Univ. of Chicago, 1991; the following chapter segment draws heavily on Orfield and Sean Reardon, "Race, Poverty, and Inequality."

26 Ibid.

27 Scheirer, Table 13.

28 Computations from Ohio Department of Education data by Sean Reardon.

29 National Assessment of Education Progress, *The Reading Report Card: Progress Toward Excellence in Our Schools: Trends in Reading Over Four National Assessments, 1971-1984* (Princeton: Educational Testing Service, 1985).

30 P. Kaufman and M. M. McMillen, *Dropout Rates in the United States* (Washington, D.C.: National Center for Education Statistics, 1990), 5.

31 Because dropout rates are calculated a number of different ways, rates may not always be comparable across districts or metropolitan areas. In this paper, we cite two basic kinds of dropout rates— *annual (or event)* rates and *cohort* rates. Annual rates give the percentage of students entering a particular grade (usually ninth or tenth) who have dropped out by the time their cohort graduates four or three years later. There is a great deal of variation even among the way these rates are calculated in different studies and in different cities. Therefore, in this paper we present dropout rates from only one study at a time, and then only to compare districts within a

particular metropolitan area. Our intention is not to provide definitive reports of actual dropout rates, but only to show that they differ sharply by race, SES and location.

32 Philip Burch, *The Dropout Problems in New Jersey's Big Urban Schools: Educational Inequality and Government Inaction* (New Brunswick, N.J.: Rutgers Bureau of Government Research, 1992), ix.

33 Study Commission on the Quality of Education in the Metropolitan Milwaukee Public Schools, 1985; John F. Witte and Daniel J. Walsh, *Metropolitan Milwaukee District Performance Assessment Report*, staff report to the Study Commission on the Quality of Education in the Metropolitan Milwaukee Public Schools, August 1, 1985.

34 Los Angeles County Office of Education, *The Demographic and Education Conditions of Public Schools in Los Angeles County 1987-1988: A Statistical Report*, 1989.

35 Henry Jay Becker, *Opportunities for Learning Curriculum and Instruction in the Middle Grades*, Report No. 37 (Baltimore: Center for Research on Elementary and Middle Schools, Johns Hopkins University, 1990); Doug MacIver and Joyce Epstein, *How Unequal Are Opportunities for Learning in Disadvantaged and Advantaged Middle Grade Schools?*, Report No. 7 (Baltimore: Johns Hopkins University Center for Research on Effective Schooling for Disadvantaged Students, 1990).

36 See Jeannie Oakes, *Multiplying Inequalities: The Effects of Race, Social Class, and Tracking on Opportunities to Learn Mathematics and Science* (Santa Monica: RAND, 1990), figure 2.3.

37 Ibid., figures 3,4 and 3.5.

38 Ibid.

39 Ibid., Figure 4.3.

40 NAEP data reported in Educational Testing Service, *The State of Inequality*, (Princeton: ETS, 1988).

41 Gary Orfield, Howard Mitzel et al., *The Chicago Study of Access and Choice in Higher Education*, University of Chicago, Committee on Public Policy Studies, 1984, p. 117.

42 Oakes, *Multiplying Inequalities*, 66.

CHAPTER FOUR

1 *Freeman v. Pitts*, 503 U.S. 467 (1992).

2 Interview with Marcia Borowski, March 5, 1993.

3 National Center for Education Statistics, *The Condition of Education 1994* (Washington, D.C.: Government Printing Office, 1994), 272-73, 277.

4 Telephone interview with Norma Cantu, then counsel for the Mexican-American Legal Defense and Education Fund, 10 February 1993. Cantu became assistant U.S. secretary of education for civil rights in the Clinton administration.

5 Ann Bradley, "Education for Equality," *Education Week*, 14 September 1994, 29-30.

6 Peter Schmidt, "L.A. Decree Would Reassign Teachers, Redistribute Resources Among Schools," *Education Week*, 11 December 1991, 1, 11.

7 Bradley, "Education," 31-32.

8 *Hobson v. Hansen*, 265 F. Supp. 902 (D.D.C. 1967); Donald L. Horowitz, *The Courts and Social Policy* (Washington: Brookings Institution, 1977), chap. 4, "Equal

Spending Order Brings Inequality," *The Washington Post,* 9 February 1975, A16.

9 See *Sheff v. Weicker,* 609 A.2d (Conn. Sup. Ct. 1992); the trial court rejected this effort in April 1995, *Sheff v. O'Neill,* CVS 9-0360977S, slip op. (Hartford/New Britain Sup. Ct. April 12, 1995). This decision was appealed to the state supreme court.

10 Gary Natriello, Edward L. McDill, and Aaron M. Pallas, *Schooling Disadvantaged Children: Racing Against Catastrophe* (New York: Teacher's College Press, 1990).

11 Ina V.S. Mullis and associates, *Report in Brief: NAEP Trends in Academic Progress, Achievement of U.S. Students in Science, 1969 to 1992, Mathematics, 1973 to 1992, Reading, 1971 to 1992, Writing, 1984 to 1992* (Washington, D.C.: GPO, 1994), 19. Between 1973 and 1993 the percentage of black high school dropouts among young adults fell from 22 percent to 13.6 percent. See National Center for Education Statistics, *Mini-Digest of Education Statistics 1994,* (Washington, D.C.: GPO, 1994), 37.

12 Orfield and Ashkinaze, chap. 5.

13 Gary Orfield with Sarah Schley and Sean Reardon, *The Growth of Segregation in American Schools* (Alexandria: National School Board Association, 1993).

14 Samuel S. Peng and Susan T. Hill, *Understanding Racial-Ethnic Differences in Secondary School Science and Mathematics Achievement,* U.S. Department of Education, February 1955, 19-21.

15 Sabrina Hope King, "The Limited Presence of African-American

Teachers," *Review of Educational Research* 63, no. 2 (summer 1993):124.

16 Ibid., 126.

17 Ibid., 132.

18 Rafael Heller, *What Affirmative Action? Where are the Minority Educators in Metropolitan Chicago?* (Chicago: Chicago Urban League and Latino Inst., 1992).

19 National Center for Education Statistics, *National Digest of Education Statistics 1992* (Washington: GPO, 1992), 79; Richard J. Mumane and associates, *Who Will Teach: Policies That Matter* (Cambridge: Harvard Univ. Press, 1991), 63-65; Orfield, *The Growth of Segregation in American Schools.*

20 National Center for Education Statistics, *The Condition of Education 1994* (Washington, D.C.: GPO), 68-70.

21 Less than a fifth of black women had a child before marriage in the 1940s (approximately the rate of illegitimacy for white babies in the late 1980s), but the percent of black births to unmarried mothers rose to 38 percent by 1970 and shot up to 64 percent by 1989. See U.S. Census Bureau, *The Social and Economic Status of the Black Population in the United States, 1973* (Washington, D.C.: GPO, 1974), 3; U.S. Census Bureau, *The Statistical Abstract of the United States 1992* (Washington, D.C.: GPO), 69.

22 Ibid., 48. SAT score comparisons have many limitations since the test-taking population is not a sample of the overall student population and different states and regions have very different policies about requiring the SAT for college

applications. National Center for Education Statistics, *The Condition of Education, 1995* (Washington, D.C.: GPO, 1995):v.

23 "The Marva Collins Story," (CBS television broadcast, 13 November 1981).

24 *Stand and Deliver* (Warner 1988).

25 Rodney, Ho, "After the Buses," *The Virginian-Pilot and The Ledger Star,* 17 January 1993, A1 and A12.

26 Ibid., A12.

27 *Milliken v. Bradley,* 433 U.S. 267 (1977).

28 Gary Orfield, "Hispanics," in Arthur Levine and associates, *Shaping Education's Future* (San Francisco: Jossey-Bass, 1989), 55-56; Gary Orfield, "Exclusion of the Majority: Shrinking College Access and Public Policy in Metropolitan Los Angeles," *Urban Review* 20, no. 3 (fall 1988):147-163.

29 Robert Lissitz, *Assessment of Student Performance and Attitude: St. Louis Metropolitan Area Court Ordered Desegregation Effort,* (report to Voluntary Interdistrict Coordinating Council, 1992).

30 Gary Orfield et al., *Desegregation and Educational Change in San Francisco: Findings and Recommendations on Consent Decree Implementation,* report to San Francisco Federal District Court, 1992.

31 Ibid.

32 Ibid.

33 William Celis III, "Heads of Big City Schools Need Political Skills to Last," *New York Times,* 17 February 1993, B9.

34 Orfield and Ashkinaze 1991, chap. 5.

35 *Education Week,* 26 April 1995, 19.

36 Michael J. Puma et al., *Prospects: The Congressionally Mandated Study of Educational Growth and Opportunity* (Bethesda, Md.: Abt Associates, 1993), XXXI-XXXIII.

37 Ibid., XXXII.

38 Ibid., xxxiii.

39 *Dowell v. Board of Education of Oklahoma City Public Schools,* 778 F. Supp. 1144 (W.D. Okl. 1991).

40 Bill Zlatos, "Running Up the Score," *Pittsburgh,* 3-9 March 1994.

41 Jennifer Jellison, *Failed Promises of Local Control in Oklahoma City* (Cambridge: The Harvard Project on School Desegregation, 1996, in press).

42 Zlatos, 1994.

43 See Phillip Burch, *The Dropout Problem in New Jersey's Big Urban Schools: Educational Inequality and Government Inaction* (New Brunswick, N.J.: Rutgers Bureau of Government Research, 1992); Gary Orfield and Lawrence Peskin, "Metropolitan High Schools: Income Race, and Inequality," in *Education Politics for the New Century,* eds. Douglas E. Mitchell and Margaret E. Goertz, 1991; Doug MacIver and Joyce Epstein, *How Equal Are Opportunities for Learning in Disadvantaged and Advantaged Middle Grade Schools?* report no. 7, The Johns Hopkins University, Center for Research in Effective Schooling For Disadvantaged Students, 1990.

44 See *Riddick v. Sch. Bd. of Norfolk, Va.,* 627 F. Supp. 814 (1984), aff'd, 784 F.2d 521 (4th Cir.), cert. denied, 479 U.S. 938 (1986).

45 Gary Orfield and Franklin Monfort, *Racial Change and Desegregation in Large School Districts*

(Alexandria: National School Boards Association, 1989).

46 Ibid.

47 Ibid.

48 Orfield and Ashkinaza, ch. 5.

49 Ibid.

50 Gary Orfield and Franklin Monfort, *Racial Change*, 10.

51 Statistics computed from data tapes of Education Department Office for Civil Rights and Common Core of Education Data.

52 Report of Bernard Gifford to Judge Paul Egly, Superior Court of Los Angeles, October 1978.

53 Office for Civil Rights and Center for Education Statistics data tapes, U.S. Department of Education.

54 Wake County Public Schools Enrollment data.

55 *Milliken v. Bradley*, 418 U.S. 717 (1974).

56 *Missouri v. Jenkins*, 115 S. Ct. 2038 (1995).

57 *Cleveland Plain Dealer*, 12 February 1994, March 3, 1995, March 4, 1995.

58 *New York Times*, 18 June 1995, 26.

59 *Report of the Twentieth Century Fund Task Force on School Governance* (New York: Twentieth Century Fund Press, 1992), 4.

60 Resolution of Board of Trustees, Austin Independent School District, 13 April 1987.

61 There are extremely strong relationships between education, income, knowledge about politics, and voting rates. In the 1992 election, for example, 41 percent of high school dropouts voted compared to 81 percent of college graduates. See U.S. Bureau of the Census, *Voting and Registration in the Election of November 1992* (Washington, D.C.: GPO, 1993). The gap widened in the 1994 elections. "Low Income Voters' Turnout Fell in 1994," *New York Times*, 11 June 1995.

62 *Dowell v. Bd. of Educ.*, 778 F.Supp. at 1190.

63 Jellison, "Failed," 1996.

64 Ibid.

65 Peter Schmidt, "Problems with Launch of Choice Plan Place Indianapolis Officials Under Fire," *Education Week*, 29 September 1993.

66 American Institutes for Research, *Magnet Schools and Issues of Desegregation, Quality and Choice*, 1993, 11.

67 Ibid.

68 Since the study also suggested that rates of white flight were not significantly different from those found in districts with mandatory busing, school districts could end up with greater costs and no more stability. Ibid. at 16.

69 Rita E. Mahard and Robert L. Crain, "Research on Minority Achievement in Desegregated Schools," in *The Consequences of School Desegregation*, ed. Christine H. Rossell and Willis D. Hawley (Philadelphia: Temple University Press, 1983), 103-125.

70 Janet Schofield, in *Handbook of Research on Multicultural Education*, James A. Banks and Cherry A. McGee Banks (New York: McMillan Publishing, 1994).

71 Mark Granovetter, "The Micro-Structure of School Desegregation," quoted in Amy Stuart Wells and Robert L. Crain,

"Perpetuation Theory and the Long-Term Effects of School Desegregation," *Review of Educational Research* 64, no. 4 (winter 1994):531.

72 Eric M. Cambum, "College Completion Among Students From High Schools Located in Large Metropolitan Areas," in *American Journal of Education*, 98, no. 4 (August 1990):551-69.

73 Ibid., 531-55.

74 *USA Today*, 12 May 1994, 8A.

75 *USA Today*, 12 May, 1994, 8A.

76 Frahm, 1993:A1.

77 Gallup, vol. III:2323.

78 Gallup Report, February 1981:29.

79 Jaynes and Williams 1989:128-29.

80 *Phi Delta Kappan*, unpaginated insert, September 1994, 43.

81 Louis Harris and Associates, 1978:38.

82 Harris and Associates, *The unfinished Agenda on Race in America*, report to the NAACP Legal Defense and Education Fund, January 1989, appendix B.

83 It is not unusual for the public to hold contradictory views about controversial issues. For example, a large majority of the public want to cut welfare but, at the same time, a substantial majority also say they would like to do more to help poor children. See *US Today*/CNN Poll, in *USA Today*, 8 December 1994, 6A.

84 "Poll Shows Wide Support Across U.S. for Integration," *Boston Globe*, 5 January 1992.

85 Harris Survey, *Boston Globe*, 26 May 1981, 2.

86 "Poll Shows," 15.

87 Possible approaches will be discussed in chapter 11.

88 Scott Wade, "NAACP, Teachers, Union Seek Delay of Busing Vote," *Louisville Courier Journal*, 9 October 1991, A1.

89 Jim Adams, "Division of Blacks Over Busing Is Ironic," *Louisville Courier Journal*, 8 October 1991, B1.

90 Ibid.

91 Stan McDonald and Scott Wade, "Whites Divided Over Plan to End Forced Busing," *Louisville Courier Journal*, 27 October 1991, A1.

92 Ibid.

93 John B. Conahay and Willis D. Hawley, *Reactions to Busing In Louisville: Summary of Adult Opinions in 1976 and 1977*, 1979, 9. Unpublished study on file at the Center for Policy Analysis, Duke University.

94 There are, of course, localities where opinions may diverge and where there may be special problems with the plan or an absence of real desegregation.

CHAPTER FIVE

1 See *Adkins v. School Bd.*, 148 F.Supp. 430, 434-36 (E.D. Va. 1957), aff'd. sub nom *School Bd. v. Adkins*, 246 F.2d 325) 4th Cir. 1957), cert. denied, 355 U.S. 855 (1957).

2 *Beckett v. Sch. Bd. for the City of Norfolk*, 148 F.Supp. 430 (E.D. Va. 1957), aff'd. sub nom *School Bd. v. Adkins*, 246 F.2d 325 (4th Cir. 1957), cert. denied, 355 U.S. 855 (1957).

3 Ibid.

4 Race Rel. L. Rep. 955 (1958).

5 *Brewer v. School Bd.*, 434 F.2d 408 (4th Cir. 1970), cert. denied, 399 U.S. 929 (1970).

6 *Brewer v. School Bd.*, 456 F.2d 943 (4th Cir. 1972), cert. denied sub nom. *School Bd. v. Brewer*, 406 U.S. 933 (1972).

7 *Riddick v. School Board of City of Norfolk*, 784 F.2d 521, 541 n. 18 (4th Cir. 1986), cert. denied, 479 U.S. 938 (1986).

8 Plaintiff's Post-Trial Memorandum at 10-11, *Riddick v. School Bd.*, 627 F.Supp. 814 (E.D. Va. 1984) (No. 83-326-N).

9 John McManus, "Busing: End of An Era?" *Norfolk Compass, Ledger Star*, 27 September 1981.

10 Norfolk City School Board, *Survey of the Norfolk, Virginia Public Schools V.1*, June 1955, 75.

11 Petition for a Writ of Certiorari to the United States Court of Appeals for the Fourth Circuit at 1A, *Riddick v. School Bd.*, 627 F.Supp. 814 (E.D. Va. 1984) (No. 83-326-N).

12 Recorded in Respondent's Supplemental Brief on Petition for a writ of certiorari to the United States Court of Appeals for the Fourth Circuit at 4, *Riddick v. School Bd.*, 784 F.2d 521 (4th cir. 1986) (No. 85-1962).

13 McManus, "Busing: End of an Era?"

14 Marjorie Mayfield, "Chaos Absen in Roll Call of Schools," *The Virginian Pilot and Ledger Star*, 16 August 1987.

15 Thomas Johnson, interview by authors, 18 March 1993.

16 Ibid.

17 A "Top Justice Official Speaks Out on Ruling in Norfolk Busing Case," *The Virginian Pilot and Ledger Star*, 16 August 1987.

18 David J. Armor, Ph.D., *An Evaluation of Norfolk Desegregation Plans* (December 1982), 16.

19 Leslie Carr and Donald Zeigler, "White Flight and White Return in Norfolk: A Test of Predictions," *The Sociology of Education* 63 (1990):272-82.

20 *Riddick v. School Bd.*, 627 F.Supp. at 822, aff'd, 784 F.2d 521 (4th Cir. 1986), cert. denied, 479 U.S. 938 (1986).

21 Armor, *Evaluation of Norfolk*. 274.

22 Ibid.

23 Armor, *Evaluation of Norfolk*.

24 Ibid., 274.

25 David J. Armor, Ph.D., "Response to Carr and Zeigler's "White Flight and White Return in Norfolk," *The Sociology of Education* 64 (1991):134-39.

26 Carr and Zeigler tested Armor's hypotheses that "if busing continued after 1981, the loss of white students would have been 4.4 to 8 percent annually," and "as a corollary, the percentage of white students in the schools would have declined to 32 or 36 percent" overall in the district. Carr and Zeigler, "White Flight," 274.

27 Ibid., 275.

28 Ibid.

29 Ibid., 274.

30 Ibid., 281.

31 Ibid., 137.

32 Leslie G. Carr, "Reply to Armor," *The Sociology of Education* 64 (1992):223-27.

33 Armor, "Response."

34 Carr, "Reply to Armor," 226.

35 *Riddick v. School Bd.*, 627 F.Supp. at 821, aff'd, 784 F.2d 521 (4th Cir. 1986), cert. denied, 479 U.S. 938 (1986).

36 Diggs and Tucker Schools were consolidated to create Campostella School.

37 Lucy Wilson, interview by authors, 18 March 1993.

38 Poverty was measured by the percentage of students whose low family incomes qualified them for free lunch. No other statistics relating to poverty are kept by the district. Peggy H. Lee, Senior Director, Child Nutrition Service, Norfolk, Virginia, letter to author, 25 March 1995.

39 Data for 1986-87 from Norfolk Public Schools (NPS), 7th Day Enrollment, 10 September 1986. Data for 1993-94 from 30 September 1993 Membership NPS. These figures include pre-kindergarten.

40 In 1986-87, sixth graders were reassigned from elementary to middle school. Therefore, the overall population changes that occurred from 1985-86 to the 1986-87 school year do not reflect overall losses in population, but changes in what level of education students were attending. However, since the sixth grade attendance areas are consistent from 1986 to 1993-94, comparisons are possible. Data for 1986 to 1987 from NPS 7th Day Enrollment, 10 September 1986.

41 Data for 1993-94 from NPS, 1st Day Enrollment, 7 September 1993.

42 See *Riddick v. School Bd.*, 784 F.2d 521, 541 n.18 (4th Cir.) cert. denied, 479 U.S. 938 (1986).

43 Calculations derived from data in the following sources: Data for 1982-83 from NPS, 7th Day Enrollment, 8 September 1982. Data for 1983-84 from NPS, 7th Day, 7 September 1983. Data for 1984-85 from NPS, 7th Day, 12 September 1984. Data for 1985-86 from NPS, 7th Day, 11 September 1985.

44 City Planning and Codes Administration, City of Norfolk, *Comparison: 1980 Units by Valuation, Southside Hampton Roads Communities*.

45 Ibid.

46 Ibid.

47 Ibid.

48 Ibid.

49 Ibid.

50 Dr. Paul Schollaert, interview by author, 18 March 1993. See also Amy Goldstein, "Scholar Sees Mistake in Study's Conclusions About Busing, Learning," *The Ledger Star*, 3 January 1983. Schollaert produced the study under contract for *The Ledger Star*.

51 Ibid.

52 Ibid.

53 Gary Orfield and Franklin Monfort, *The Status of School Desegregation: The Next Generation* (Alexandria: National School Boards Association, 1992), 21, 22.

54 Federal Bureau of Investigation, *Crime in the United States 1980, Uniform Crime Reports* 133, 134.

55 Ibid.

56 John McLaulin, interview by author, 20 March 1993.

57 Ibid.

58 Deborah M. Jewell-Jackson, "Ending Mandatory Busing for Desegregation in Norfolk,

Virginia: A Case Study Explaining the Decision Making Process in a Formerly De Jure Southern School District" (analytic paper presented to the faculty of the Graduate School of Education of Harvard University in partial fulfillment of the requirements for the Degree of Doctor of Education, 1995).

59 Carr and Zeigler, "White Flight," 272-82.

60 As quoted in Carr and Zeigler, "White Flight," 279.

61 Carr and Zeigler, "White Flight," 272-82.

62 Ibid., 279.

63 Ibid.

64 Record at 635, *Riddick v. School Bd.*, 627 F.Supp. 814 (E.D. Va. 1984) (No. 83-326-N).

65 Ibid., 607-27.

66 *Community Oversight Committee Report*, 31 August 1990, p. 3.

67 Vivian Ikpa, "The Effects of Changes in School Characteristics Resulting From the Elimination of the Policy of Mandated Busing for Integration Upon the Academic Achievement of African-American Students," *Educational Research Quarterly* 17:1, 19-29.

68 Ibid., 19.

69 Ibid., 23.

70 Ibid., 24.

71 Ibid., 19. The t-test statistical procedure was performed to determine if a statistically significant difference existed between the SRA composite test scores of African American students during the existence of busing and the scores after the elimination of the busing policy. Ikpa concludes that the mean difference was statistically significant. (p.5)

72 Ibid., 28.

73 Department of Research, Testing and Statistics, NPS, *1991 ITBS Test Results for Target and Non-Target Schools* (July 1991), 13. Scores for later years provided by Department of Research and Testing, NPS.

74 All calculations were conduced by using original test score data collected by school and provided by the school system for various years, rather than the scores presented in summary reports presented by the school system.

75 Armor, *Evaluation of Norfolk*, Figure 5.

76 Ibid.

77 Vanee Staunton, "Report Faults Norfolk's Neighborhood Schools," *The Norfolk Pilot and Ledger Star*, 4 May 1994, A1 and A14; Lise Olsen, "Harvard Report Distorts Facts, School Officials Say," *The Norfolk Pilot and Ledger Star*, 4 May 1994.

78 Though these are sixth-grade scores, a middle-school grade, the data were separated to analyze scores based upon a child's fifth-grade school.

79 McLaulin, interview.

80 Gary Orfield, *The Reconstruction of Southern Education* (John Wiley and Sons, 1969).

81 *Riddick v. Sch. Bd.*, 627 F.Supp. 814, 818, aff'd, 784 F.2d 521 (9th Cir.), cert. denied, 479 U.S. 938 (1986).

82 Armor, *Evaluation of Norfolk*, 11.

83 Community Oversight Committee Report, 31 August 1990, 32.

84 Rodney Ho, "After the Buses," *The Virginian Pilot and The Ledger Star*, 17 January 1993, A1 and A12.

85 *Riddick v. Sch. Bd.*, 627 F.Supp. 814, 825, aff'd, 784 F.2d 521 (4th Cir. 1986), cert. denied, 479 U.S. 938 (1986).

86 Ibid.

87 Ibid.

88 Wilson, interview.

89 Dr. John Foster, interview by author, 18 March 1993.

90 NPS, PTA Membership and Volunteer Hours, 1991-93 and 1984-85.

91 Ho, "After."

92 The Center for Research on Effective Schooling for Disadvantaged Students, *Five Practices Encourage Parent Involvement in Urban Schools* (Baltimore, MD: The Johns Hopkins University, October 1991).

93 Ibid.

94 Amy Goldstein, "Living Near School Is Not Important, Educator Believes," *The Virginia Pilot and Ledger Star,* 13 April 1982.

95 Frank Hassell, a private consultant for the Norfolk Redevelopment and Housing Authority, interview by author, 20 March 1993.

96 Michael Bernard, ed., *Volunteers in Public Schools* (Washington, D.C.: National Academy Press, 1990).

97 *Brown v. Bd. of Educ.*, 347 U.S. 483, 74 S. Ct. 686 (1954).

98 Plaintiff Posttrial Memorandum at 84, *Riddick v. Sch. Bd.*, 627 F.Supp. 814 (E.D. Va. 1984) (No. 83-326-N). During the 1950s, the city displaced 29 percent black households; during the 1960s, the city displaced more than 8 percent of black households; and during the 1970s, the city displaced nearly 9 percent of black households, all by some form of clearance or public action. Plaintiff Posttrial Memorandum at 85, *Riddick v. Sch. Bd.*, 627 F. Supp. 814 (No. 83-326-N).

99 See, e.g. Norfolk Redevelopment and Housing Authority Report, May 1957, 6, 7; Frank Sullivan, "Benefits Seen for All of City by Chairman," *Norfolk Virginian Pilot,* 4 October 1949, 1, 22.

100 Trial Testimony of Yale Rabin, record at 1547, 1557, *Riddick v. Sch. Bd.*, 627 F. Supp. 814 (No. 83-326-N); Plaintiff Posttrial Memorandum at 88-89, *Riddick* (No. 83-326-N).

101 Denise K. Schnitzer, Acting Grants Writer at Norfolk Public Schools, provided information based on 30 September 1992 enrollment data indicating that 95.1 percent of the students attending Tidewater, 82.8 percent attending Roberts Park, 75.5 percent attending Young Park, 60 percent attending Bowling Park, and 61.8 percent attending Campostella live in public housing. In contrast, only .2 percent of the students attending Lindenwood, 1.4 percent attending St. Helena, 1.9 percent attending Monroe, 12.5 percent attending Jacox, and 35.1 percent attending Chesterfield live in public housing. Based on 30 September 1992 enrollment data, about 40 percent of the children attending target schools live in public housing.

102 Plaintiff Posttrial Memorandum at 86, *Riddick v. Sch. Bd.*, 627 F. Supp. 814 (No. 83-326-N).

103 *Riddick v. Sch. Bd.*, 627 F. Supp. 814, 826, aff'd, 784 F.2d 521 (4th Cir.), cert. denied, 479 U.S. 938 (1986).

104 Written response from Dr. Forrest R. (Hap) White, budget director

for Norfolk Public Schools to Gary Orfield, December 1994.

105 NPS, 13 September 1993 enrollment and Carr, "Reply to Armor," 226.

106 Letter and regression analysis charts addressed to Dr. Forrest R. White, budget director, Norfolk City Schools from Hunter Kimble, associate policy specialist, Commonwealth of Virginia, Department of Education, 1 December 1993.

107 See, for example, Final Report of the National Assessment of the Chapter 1 Program, *Reinventing Chapter 1: The Current Chapter 1 Program and New Directions* (December 1993). This report found that disadvantaged children in schools with high rates of poverty performed much more poorly in school when compared with disadvantaged children in schools with less poverty. The report concludes that the achievement gap between disadvantaged and other students means that schools with concentrated poverty will have much greater difficulty in meeting the National Education Goals set by the National Education Goals Panel.

CHAPTER SIX

1 *Brown v. Bd. of Educ.*, 347 U.S. 483 (1954).

2 *Bradley v. Milliken*, 433 F.2d 897 (6th Cir. 1970), aff'd, 484 F.2d 215 (6th Cir. 1973), rev'd sub nom. *Milliken v. Bradley ("Milliken I")*, 418 U.S. 717 (1974).

3 *Bradley v. Milliken*, 484 F.2d 215 (6th Cir. 1973), rev'd sub nom. *Milliken v. Bradley ("Milliken I")*, 418 U.S. 717 (1974).

4 *Milliken v. Bradley ("Milliken I")*, 418 U.S. 717 (1974).

5 *Milliken v. Bradley ("Milliken II")*, 433 U.S. 267 (1977).

6 Ibid. at 280.

7 Ibid. at 287-88.

8 Ibid. at 280.

9 *Green v. County Sch. Bd.*, 391 U.S. 430 (1968).

10 The so-called *Green* factors have become the most commonly used guide to determine whether a school district is "unitary" or desegregated. *Green* required that desegregation be achieved in the following areas: the student body, faculty and staff, transportation, extracurricular activities and facilities. These factors were measures of progress toward meeting the goal specified in *Green* to create a "system with out a 'white' school and 'Negro' school, but just schools." Ibid. at 441.

11 *Jenkins v. Missouri*, 1955 U.S. Lexis 4041; 63 U.S.L.W. 4486.

12 For a detailed history of the Detroit case, see Elwood Hain, "Sealing Off the City: School Desegregation in Detroit" in *Limits of Justice*, ed. Howard Kaldoner and James Fishman (Cambridge, Mass.: Ballinger Publishing Co., 1978). See also, Phillip Cooper, chap. 5 in *Hard Judicial Choices: Federal District Court Judges and State and Local Officials* (New York, Oxford: Oxford University Press, 1988).

13 *Bradley v. Milliken*, 402 F. Supp. 1096, 1138-45 (E.D. Mich. 1975), aff'd, 540 F.2d 229 (6th Cir. 1976), aff'd sub nom. *Milliken v. Bradley*, 433 U.S. 267 (1977).

14 Ibid. at 1136-38.

15 The state cofunded the reading, in-service training for teachers, counseling/career guidance, and testing components.

16 *Bradley v. Milliken*, 402 F. Supp. at 1145.

17 Stuart Rankin, interview by author, 3 February 1994.

18 *Bradley v. Milliken*, 476 F. Supp. 257, 258 (E.D. Mich. 1979).

19 DeMascio's departure was prompted by what the court of appeals called "bitter feelings: [as quoted in *Bradley v. Milliken*, 620 F.2d 1143, 1150 (6th Cir. 1980)] that have developed" because of DeMascio's reluctance to respond adequately to the plaintiff NAACP's motion to desegregate three all-black regions in the city. DeMascio, in his original order, had left those school regions all black. Although the court's order only refers to defendants, the Stipulation included all parties in the case, including the plaintiff NAACP. For a detailed discussion of these events see Cooper, *Hard Judicial Choices*, 128.

20 Avem Cohn, transcript of address delivered at the University of Michigan, 1989, 6.

21 U.S. District Court Judge Avem Cohn, interview by author, 30 May 1993.

22 Ibid.

23 Arthur Jefferson, interview by author, 5 May 1993.

24 United States District Court Monitoring Committee, *Overview of the Detroit Desegregation Case* (Detroit: Detroit School District, June 1984), 4.

25 *Bradley v. Milliken*, 585 F. Supp. 348, 349-50 (E.D. Mich. 1984), judgment vacated, 772 F.2d 266 (6th Cir. 1955).

26 For a summary of these appeals, see, *Bradley v. Milliken*, 828 F.2d 1186 (6th Cir. 1987).

27 United States District Court Monitoring Commission, Monitoring Commission Report of the United States District Court Monitoring Commission for the Detroit School District, *Profiles of Detroit's High Schools: 1975-1984* (Detroit, October 1984), Aii. As is common in the evaluation of many remedial programs studied here, monitors often look first to evaluate implementation of programs; that is, monitors measure how the programs were set up. This type of evaluation does not measure the effect of programs on their intended beneficiaries.

28 United States District Court Monitoring Commission, *Overview and Status of the Detroit Desegregation Case* (Detroit: June 1984).

29 Ibid.

30 Ibid.

31 Ibid.

32 Ibid.

33 *Bradley v. Milliken*, Stipulation of the Parties Regarding Funding and Implementation of the Court-Ordered Educational Components, Attorneys Fees and Costs, 29 June 1981.

34 Arthur Jefferson, interview by author, 19 January 1994.

35 Ibid.

36 The state standards correspond to the number of items correct on a given test section and vary

depending upon each subject and grade level.

37 Henry Woods and Beth Deere, "Reflections on the Little Rock School Case," *Arkansas Law Journal* 44, no. 4 (1991).

38 Pulaski County School Desegregation Case Settlement Agreement (March 1989, as revised 28 September 1989), 23.

39 *Little Rock Sch. Dist. v. Pulaski County Special Sch. Dist.*, 716 F. Supp. 1162, 1190 (E.D. Ark. 1989), order rev'd in part and dismissed in part, 921 F.2d 1371 (8th Cir. 1990).

40 Ibid. at 1189.

41 To desegregate the schools, the district also uses a so-called majority to minority transfer program that allows students to transfer across district lines to schools where their race is in the minority, so long as the transfer does not negatively affect racial balance in the sending school. This program is used in conjunction with magnet schools and several "interdistrict schools," some of which are located in the predominantly white Pulaski County school district and in the predominantly black Little Rock district. The interdistrict schools are overseen by both the Little Rock and Pulaski County school districts and offer specialized programs similar to the magnet schools in an effort to attract a diverse student body.

42 The Eighth Circuit, however, described this outcome as "far from certain." *Little Rock Sch. Dist. v. Pulaski Special Sch. Dist.*, 921 F.2d 1371, 1385 (8th Cir. 1990).

43 *Little Rock Public Schools, Little Rock*

School District Desegregation Plan, 29 April 1992.

44 Ruth Steele, Superintendant of Little Rock School District from 1989 to June 1992, interview by author, 18 March 1993.

45 Chris Heller, interview by author, 20 March 1993.

46 *Milliken II*, 433 U.S. at 280.

47 Steele, interview.

48 Horace Smith, interview by author, 20 March 1993.

49 Office of Desegregation Monitoring, U.S. District Court, Little Rock Arkansas, 14 March 1994.

50 *Pulaski County School Desegregation Case Settlement Agreement*, 24-25.

51 Danny Shameer, "Black White Test Score Gap Lingers After Decade," *Arkansas Democrat-Gazette*, 19 August 1993.

52 "Summary, Conclusions and Recommendations," in *1991-92 Incentive Schools Monitoring Report* (1992), 31, referring to Stanford Achievement Test results, districtwide comparative data, 1992 and 1993.

53 Judge Susan Webber Wright, written statement to the Little Rock School District and Counsel, 19 March 1993.

54 Ibid.

55 Ibid.

56 U.S. District Court Judge Susan Webber, letter to author, 24 January 1994.

57 Office of Desegregation Monitoring, United States District Court, Little Rock, Arkansas, *1994-95 School Racial Balance Monitoring Report: Little Rock School*

District, North Little Rock School District, Pulaski County Special School District, 31 January 1995, 5.

58 Ibid., 11.

59 Melissa Guldin, associate monitor, Office of Desegregation Monitoring, interview by author, 17 March 1993.

60 *Memorandum of Understanding,* Order of Chief Judge Frank A. Kaufman, U.S. District Court, 30 June 1985.

61 John Murphy, interview by author, December 1993.

62 Attorney George Mermick, interview by author, 15 February 1994.

63 Prince George's County Schools, *A School System of Choices,* 1987.

64 Edward Feleyg, interview by author, 10 March 1993.

65 Attorney George Mernick, interview by author, 15 February 1994.

66 *Second Interim Report of the Community Advisory Council on Magnet and Compensatory Educational Programs to the Prince George's County Board of Education,* 26 March 19687, 23.

67 Michael K. Grady, *Report of the Academic Effect of Educational Equity Efforts in Prince George's County,* (Maryland: Office of Research and Evaluation, Prince George's County Schools), 2.2.90.

68 See, e.g., *Reinventing Chapter I: The Current Chapter I Program and New Directions,* final Report of the National Assessment of the Chapter I Program, December 1993.

69 *Third Interim Report of the Community Advisory Council on Magnet and Compensatory Educational Programs,* 12 September 1988.

70 For a discussion of this issue, see John J. Cannell, *Nationally Normed Elementary Achievement Testing in American's Public Schools: How All Fifty States Are Above the National Average* (West Virginia: Friends for Education, 1987).

71 *1990-91 Interim Report of the Community Advisory Council,* 20; Response by the Board of Education of Prince George's County to the 1990-91 Interim Report of the Community Advisory Council, 19. Superintendent Edward Felegy, interview by author, 10 March 1993.

72 The term unitary, as it applies to school systems, might be best understood as being the opposite of dual, which implies that a district essentially maintained two school systems, one for white students and one for black students.

73 Dan Robertson, director of planning for the AISD, letter to author, 15 February 1994.

74 Robertson and Jim Raup, attorney for McGinnis, Lochridge and Kilgore, letter to author, 15 February 1994.

75 Ibid.

76 Ibid.

77 Ibid. at 2.

78 Abel Ruiz, interview by author, 21 April 1993.

79 AISD Attorney William Bingham, interview by author, 20 April 1993 and Edward Small, former school board member, interview by author, 20 April 1993.

80 Austin Independent School District, *Resolution of the Board of Trustees,* 13 April 1987, 1.

81 Catherine Christner, et al., *Priority Schools: The Fifth Year* (Austin, Tex.:

Austin Independent School District, 1992), 17.

82 Ibid.

83 Christner, et al., *Priority Schools*, 11.

84 Loretta Edelen, member of Priority Schools Monitoring Committee, interview by author, 21 April 1993.

85 Blanca Garcia, member of Priority Schools Monitoring Committee, interview by author, 21 April 1993.

86 Joseph Higgs, president of Austin Interfaith, a community organization of thirty interdenominational congregations, with black, Mexican American, and white members, interview by author, 21 April 1993.

87 Catherine Christner, Evaluator, Office of Research and Evaluation, AISD, interview by author, 19 April 1993.

88 Austin Independent School District, Department of Planning and Development.

89 Bernice Hart, interview by author, 20 April 1993.

90 Garcia, interview by author, 21 April 1993.

91 Robertson, interview.

92 *Milliken II*, 433 U.S. at 280.

93 *Third Interim Report*, 12.

94 *Milliken I*, 418 U.S. 717, 815 (1974) (Marshall, J., dissenting).

CHAPTER SEVEN

1 Frye Gaillard, *The Dream Long Deferred* (Chapel Hill: University of North Carolina Press, 1988).

2 *Swann v. Charlotte-Mecklenburg Bd. of Educ.*, 402 U.S. 1 (1971).

3 *A Report to the Court in Compliance With Request From District Court*, 1 April 1975.

4 *Charlotte-Mecklenburg Schools: Pupil Assignment Changes, 1974-1987*. Although racial balance figures were not provided annually for every school in the district, they were included for those schools affected by school board actions. It was assumed that any and all schools that had fallen out of compliance in one year were affected by school board actions the following year, and thus were included in the enclosed reports. Chris Folk, former assistant superintendent of the district, confirmed the validity of this assumption (phone interview with author, 11 January 1995). The compliance guidelines used here are those that were specified by the court in 1980: no more than 15 percentage points above the percentage of black students in the entire district for elementary schools; and no more than 50 percent black for secondary schools.

5 Computation of U.S. Census data tapes, 1990.

6 *Charlotte-Mecklenburg Schools Enrollment 1968-69 through 1990*, undated Charlotte-Mecklenburg Schools (CMS) document. *Charlotte-Mecklenburg School Facilities Master Plan Draft*, a joint venture of the CMS Board of Education, Mecklenburg Board of County Commissioners, and Charlotte City Council.

7 Gaillard, *The Dream*, chap. 11.

8 Roslyn Arlin Mickelson and Carol Axtell Ray, "Fears of Falling From Grace: The Middle Class, Downward Mobility, and School Desegregation," *Research in Sociology*

of Education and Socialization 10 (1994): 207-38.

9 CMS and Charlotte-Mecklenburg Planning Commission, *Charlotte-Mecklenburg School Facilities 2002 Master Plan Draft* (October 1993), 3.

10 Ibid.

11 Michael J. Stolee, *A Plan for the Charlotte-Mecklenburg Public Schools,* January 1992.

12 For a fuller discussion of this phenomenon, see Mickelson and Ray, "Fears," 207-38.

13 Ibid.

14 Gaillard.

15 Ibid.

16 Ibid. 166.

17 For math and reading combined, scores of black third graders climbed from the twentieth to the forty-eighth percentile; black sixth-grade scores jumped from the twenty-eighth to the fiftieth percentile; and black ninth-grade scores increased from the twentieth to forty-sixth percentile. White scores also rose significantly, hitting the eightieth percentile by 1985. See Gaillard, 166.

18 Ibid.

19 Ibid.

20 Gaillard and Mickelson and Ray.

21 National Commission on Excellence in Education, *A Nation at Risk: The Imperative for Educational Reform: A Report to the Nation and the Secretary of Education* (Washington, D.C.: GPO, 1983).

22 Mickelson and Ray, 10-13.

23 CMS, *Student Assignment Plan: A New Generation of Excellence* (19 March 1992), 1.

24 Stolee, "Plan," 5-6.

25 Louise Woods, interview by author, 10 August 1994.

26 CMS, *Student Assignment Plan,* 3.

27 *Charlotte Observer,* 26 September 1993.

28 Joe Martin, interview by author, 11 August 1994.

29 John Murphy, interview by author, 12 August 1994. Also described in Denis P. Doyle and Susan Pimentel, *A Study in Change: Transforming the Charlotte-Mecklenburg Schools,* March 1993, 535.

30 Louise Woods, interview.

31 Confirmed by Carol Gerber, assistant to Jim Clark, special assistant to the superintendent and board liaison, 12 January 1995.

32 Joe Martin, interview.

33 Stolee, "Plan," 13.

34 *CMS Magnet Schools Program* (25 February 1993), 8.

35 Denis P. Doyle and Susan Pimentel, "A Study in Change: Transforming the Charlotte-Mecklenburg Schools," *Phi Delta Kappan* 74, no. 7 : 538.

36 CMS, "Action Steps: A Five-Year Plan in Three Phases," *Student Assignment Plan: A New Generation of Excellence,* 19 March 1992.

37 John A. Murphy, *Student Assignment Plan: A New Generation of Excellence,* 19 March 1992, 11.

38 *The Charlotte-Mecklenburg Schools' Magnet School Program: "Creating a New Generation of Excellence,"* submitted to the U.S. Department of Education Magnet Schools Assistance Program, 25 February 1993, 8.

39 Ken Garfield and Kevin O'Brien,

"Black Leaders Work to Delay Charlotte Magnet School Plan," *Charlotte Observer*, 31 March 1992, 1A.

40 Ibid.

41 "Charge to the Committee of 25," endorsed by the board of education, 14 July 1992.

42 Annelle Houk, phone interview by author, 5 August 1994.

43 Susan Burgess, interview by author, 10 August 1994.

44 *James E. Swann et al., v. The Charlotte-Mecklenburg Board of Education*, Civil Action No. 1974, Order, Filed April 17, 1980.

45 E.g., *Charlotte-Mecklenburg School Facilities 2002 Master Plan Technical Notebook, Final Report of the Citizen Advisory Committee on the School Facilities Master Plan*, 6; and Memo from the Education Committee of the League of Women Voters (LWV) of Charlotte-Mecklenburg to the CMS Board of Education, dated 12 December 1994, 9.

46 LWV/CM Question 1: Drift Toward Desegregation, 29 January 1994, 1.

47 The figures cited in the district's response—31 and 29, respectively—contradict those cited in a later, more detailed document, *Demographic Changes in the Charlotte-Mecklenburg Community: A Proposed Agenda for Action*, 13 April 1994. It was assumed that the figures cited in the later document are the correct ones—an assumption confirmed by independent analysis—and therefore the corresponding substitutions were made in the quotation above. Enclosure from Memo, "Subject League of Women Voters' Report," from John A. Murphy to the Board of Education, 8 February 1994.

48 "Charlotte-Mecklenburg Schools Monthly Membership at End of Month 0, 8/22/94—9/2/94," 4 September 1994. Total number of black elementary students in pre-dominantly black schools was 6,264. Total black enrollment at elementary level was 18,283.

49 "Demographic Changes in the Charlotte-Mecklenburg Community: Implications for School Integration: A Proposed Agenda for Action," CMS staff discussion paper, 13 April 1994.

50 E.g., Enclosure from Memo, "Subject: League of Women Voters' Report."

51 Ibid.

52 Ibid., 23.

53 Ibid., 17.

54 "Demographic Changes in the Charlotte-Mecklenburg Community," 16.

55 Memo to the Board of Education of the Charlotte-Mecklenburg Schools, from the Education Committee of the League of Women Voters of Charlotte-Mecklenburg, 12 December 1994.

56 Murphy, *Student Assignment Plan*.

57 *Charlotte-Mecklenburg Schools' Magnet School Program*, 7.

58 Ibid.; Mike Stolee, "A Proposed Pupil Assignment Plan for the Charlotte-Mecklenburg Public Schools," 18 February 1992, 148 (emphasis in original).

59 Susan Leboki, Vice President, LWV, letter to author.

60 *Transportation*, undated CMS document, received 8 October 1994. The undated data included in the district's response were difficult to

interpret. Although several figures were provided for the "estimated number of students eligible for transportation," it was unclear whether these were the number of students who were actually bused. The fact that the cited figures, when combined, represented more than 80 percent of the total school population would seem to cast this interpretation into doubt.

61 The numbers include students bused for all purposes, including but not limited to desegregation. Student percentage is calculated by dividing the total number of students bused by the annual enrollment. Average miles/day were calculated by dividing the total miles per day by annual enrollment. North Carolina Dept. of Public Instruction, *Transportation Annual Report*, provided by Norfleet Gardner, Chief Transportation Consultant, 10 January 1995.

62 Roslyn Mickelson, Ph.D., *Committee of 25 Pupil Assignment Subcommittee Report*, ed. A. Leon Miller, presented to the Board of Education, 19 July 1994.

63 "Information Concerning the "Shadow Zone" consisting of three areas: a walk zone, a one-mile extension and a four-mile extension," enclosure of correspondence from district, 9 October 1994.

64 Mickelson, *Committee of 25*, 7.

65 CMS Staff, *A Review of the Committee of 25's Report on Student Assignment*, July 1994, 4.

66 Ibid., 3.

67 *Committee of 25 Response to the Staff Response to Report*, undated. Murphy, *Student Assignment Plan*, ??

68 *Pupil Assignment Subcommittee Report to the Board of Education*, February 1994, 15.

69 "Integrated Neighborhoods," enclosed in correspondence, 7 October 1992, from CMS to the author.

70 *Committee of 25 Pupil Assignment Subcommittee Report*, 15.

71 "New Studies Say Scattered-Site Public Housing Is Working," *The Leader*, 9 July 1993, 1A.

72 Dr. John Murphy, "The Numbers That Count," *The Washington Post*, 3 May 1994, 8A.

73 "Don't Blame Busing," *Charlotte Observer*, 12 May 1994, 10A.

74 Neal Mara and C. J. Clemmons, "School Board in Hands of Backers of Reforms," *Charlotte Observer*, 8 November 1955, 1A, 18A; Editorial, "Reaffirmation for Schools," *Charlotte Observer*, 22A.

75 "People" column, *Education Week*, 17 January 1996, 5; Personal communication to author from Professor Roslyn Michelson, Univ. of North Carolina at Charlotte, 12 January 1996.

CHAPTER EIGHT

1 Chip Brown, "Montgomery Schools: A New Set of Values," *The Washington Post*, 20 July 1981, B1, B3.

2 History of the policies evolvement differed depending upon which school officials characterized events. However, the only official, documented characterization of events received by researchers came from School Superintendent Paul Vance, whose July 1 letter to

Gary Orfield and Susan Eaton describes the 1983 amendment that laid out this stipulation. On file with the Harvard Project on School Desegregation, Cambridge, Mass.

3 In 1990, Montgomery County was the seventh wealthiest county in the United States as measured by per capita income. The wealth per pupil in Montgomery County was $375,093 in 1993. The per pupil expenditure was $7,377. The wealth and expenditure per pupil in Montgomery County far exceeded the state averages in wealth per pupil at $219,365 and per pupil expenditure at $5,823.

4 Floyd W. Hayes, *Politics and Expertise in an Emerging Post-Industrial Community: Montgomery County, Maryland's Search for Quality Integrated Education* (Office of Program Research, U.S. Equal Employment Opportunity Commission, 1985), 1.

5 Roscoe Nix, interview by author, 8 April 1994.

6 The school system is divided into twenty-one cluster areas.

7 For example, in 1970, 92 percent of Montgomery County students were white, just 5 percent were African American, 2 percent were Latino, and 1 percent were Asian. By 1993-94, 58 percent of students were white, 19 percent were African American, 11 percent were Latino, and 12 percent were Asian.

8 Poverty rates in the schools also have risen. In 1993, 21 percent of elementary schoolchildren had family incomes low enough to participate in the Free and Reduced Meals Program. In the 1992-93 school year, more than 9,000 stu-

dents—about 8 percent of the Montgomery County Public School (MCPS) population—needed English As a Second Language classes. The increase in the number of non-English-proficient speakers has risen dramatically since 1979, when about 2,000 students required such services.

9 According to MCPS Department of Educational Accountability Studies, this decline was driven by a declining white population that was consistent with national patterns of declining birth rates among whites. Stated in John Larson et al., *Microscope on Magnet Schools, Secondary School Magnet Programs,* Department of Educational Accountability, MCPS, October 1990, 1; *Montgomery County Public Schools Enrollment by Race and Ethnic Groups: 1968-1993.*

10 Harriet Tyson, interview by author, 9 March 1993.

11 Blair Ewing, interview by author, 7 March 1994.

12 Brown, "Montgomery Schools," B1, B3.

13 Superintendent Paul Vance, letter to authors, 1 July 1994; Memorandum from John C. Larson to School Superintendent Paul Vance, 27 June 1991, 3; John C. Larson, telephone interview with author, 6 July 1994; Barron Stroud, director of quality and integrated education, interview by author, 7 April 1994.

14 *Student Enrollment by Race and Ethnic Group: 1988-1993: Free and Reduced Meals Summary Report,* 29 November 1993.

15 Maryvale was 57 percent African American/Latino and all the other

schools in Maryvale's cluster area remained predominantly white, suggesting that transfers or boundary changes might have been feasible. All of the elementary schools in the Rockville cluster, where Maryvale is located, had space available as of 1993-94, according to MCPS utilization rates. Utilization rates were as follows for the four other elementary schools in the Rockville cluster: Barnsley, 88 percent; Flower Valley, 89 percent; Meadow Hall, 81 percent; Rock Creek Valley, 68 percent. *Requests FY 95 Capital Budget and the FY 1995 to 2000 Capital Improvements Program,* submitted by School Superintendent Paul Vance to the MCPS Board of Education, 2 November 1993.

16 Montgomery County Board of Education, *Quality Integrated Education Policy.*

17 Larson, interview.

18 Larson, interview; Vance, letter to author.

19 Larson, interview.

20 Montgomery County Public Schools, *Educational Load Variables for Schools in Spring,* 1993.

21 Anne Briggs, director of facilities management, MCPS, interview by author, 8 April 1994.

22 Vance, letter to author. Larson, interview.

23 The analysis of transfer requests conducted in this report is not an analysis of the 1994-95 transfer regulations or of adherence to those regulations that were put in place in 1994. Rather, the analysis is based upon 1991 and 1992 data and measures of segregation that were in place during those years. During

those years, officials used the 20 percent differential rule explained in earlier sections of this chapter.

24 Gary Orfield, *op cit.,* Table 3.

25 For the most recent discussion of this fact, see Douglas Massey and Nancy A. Denton, *American Apartheid: Segregation and the Making of the Underclass* (Cambridge: Harvard University Press, 1993). See also Gary Orfield, *The Growth of Segregation in American Schools: Changing Patterns of Separation and Poverty Since 1968* (The Harvard Project on School Desegregation & National School Boards Association, December 1993).

26 See for example, Paul A. Jargowsky and Mary Jo Bane, "Neighborhood Poverty: Basic Questions" in *Inner City Poverty in America,* eds. Lynn and McGeary (Washington, D.C.: National Academy Press, 1990).

27 According to school district data, about 17 percent of the elementary school population qualified for free and reduced lunch in 1988. Calculations derived from data found in *Free and Reduced Meals Summary Report,* Years 1988-89, 29 November 1993 and *Student Population by Race and Ethnic Group: 1988-1993.* According to a July 1 memo to authors, about 21.5 percent of all elementary students qualified for free and reduced meals in 1993. Therefore, poverty, overall, increased about 4.5 percentage points, but concentrated poverty increased at a much more dramatic rate, especially for black and Latino students.

28 Calculations derived from data found in *Free and Reduced Meals* and *Student Population.*

29 Edmund W. Gordon, *Study of the MCPS Minority Achievement Plan,* 1990 and Minutes of the Board of Education, 28 August 1991, 20.

30 Department of Educational Facilities Planning and Capital Programming, MCPS, 18 February 1994.

31 Wayveline Starnes, coordinator of enriched and innovated instruction, interview by author, 7 April 1994.

32 Larson, et al., *Microscope,* E-4.

33 Ibid.

34 Edmund, *Study,* 235-36.

35 Ibid.

36 Calculations derived from data found in MCPS, *Student Transfer Report,* Department of Management Information and Computer Services, 11 July 1994.

37 Starnes, interview.

38 John Larson and Rita Kirshstein, *A Microscope on Magnet Schools, 1983 to 1985: Implementation and Racial Balance* (The Department of Educational Accountability, July 1986), E-9.

39 Ibid.

40 The elementary schools include East Silver Spring, Rolling Terrace, Forest Knolls, Takoma Park, and Montgomery Knolls.

41 Larson and Kirshstein, *Microscope,* 3-33.

42 Ibid., 3-38.

43 Ibid., E-7.

44 Ibid., E-8.

45 Calculations derived from data found in *Student Transfer Report.* The effect of white transfers in and out of magnets was as follows

for the ten Blair magnet schools: East Silver Spring, -8 white students; Forest Knolls, -2 white students; Highland View, -8 white students; Montgomery Knolls, +9 white students; New Hampshire Estates, +8 white students; Oak View, +37 white students; Pine Crest, -3 white students; Piney Branch, -2 white students; Rolling Terrace, -5 white students; Takoma Park, +10 white students.

46 Jeffrey Henig, *The Exercise of Choice Among Magnet Schools: The Montgomery County Case and Its Implications* (George Washington University, April 1993), 6.

47 Jeffrey Henig, "Choice in Public Schools: An Analysis of Transfer Requests Among Magnet Schools, *Social Science Quarterly* 71, no. 1 (1990): 80.

48 Henig, *Exercise,* 6.

49 Ibid.

50 Superintendent Paul Vance, interview by author, 8 April 1994.

51 Calculations derived from data found in *Student Population by Race and Ethnic Group: 1988-1993,* Montgomery County Public Schools.

52 Larson and Kirshstein, *Microscope,* 3-33.

53 Larson, et al., *Microscope,* 2-3.

54 Larson and Kirshstein, *Microscope,* 3-33.

55 In 1988, 799 white students attended magnet schools in this cluster and five years later, in 1993, 1,060 white students attended these same schools. The number of African American students attending these schools has declined from

356 in 1988 to 317 in 1993, an 11 percent drop. The number of Latino students has increased only slightly from 249 to 267, an increase of 7 percent. Most of the Latino students are concentrated in the Rock Creek Forest School. The number of Asian students in this area is still small but increased 35 percent since 1988, when 57 students attended the schools. In 1993, seventy-seven Asian students attended the Bethesda-Chevy Chase magnets. *Student Population by Race and Ethnic Group, the Blair Cluster,* Montgomery County Public Schools, October 1993.

56 Larson and Kirshstein, *Microscope,* 3-33.

57 San Hankin, "Maryland Rental Discrimination Suit Settled," *The Washington Post,* 14 May 1988, A10.

58 Briggs, interview; Stroud interview; Starnes, interview; Ewing, interview.

59 Stroud, interview; Starnes, interview; Briggs, interview; Ewing, interview; DiFonzo, interview.

60 Starnes, interview.

61 Telephone discussion with Judith Bresler, 21 July 1994.

62 Asian student transfers were counted as having no effect on racial balance, as no schools were disproportionately Asian in 1991.

63 Bresler, interview.

64 Judith Bresler, general counsel for MCPS, confirmed July 21, 1994, that the district does not provide free transportation to students who transfer from their home schools.

65 Lauri Steel and Roger Levine, *Educational Innovation in Multiracial Contexts: The Growth of Magnet Schools in American Education,* prepared for the U.S. Department of Education under contract by American Institutes for Research, Palo Alto, California, July 1994, 101.

66 All racial compositions based upon 1991 enrollment data, *Student Population by Race and Ethnic Group: 1988-1993,* supplied by the Montgomery County Public Schools. However, in the case of the Oak View school, 1992 enrollment data was used to determine racial disproportion because county school officials in 1991 decided to move a heavily white magnet program out of Oak View by the 1992 school year because of overcrowding, knowingly reducing the white enrollment at that school. In 1991, Oak View was 42 percent white; the following year, 1992, it was 6 percent white.

67 The net effect was derived through simple arithmetic. The number of approved requests that worked in favor of desegregation was subtracted from the number of requests that worked against desegregation.

68 Larson, interview; Bresler, interview. That formula targets schools as needing controls if their racial enrollments fall within a range of plus or minus 1.5 standard deviations from a racial group's share of total overall enrollment at the district level. This standard would permit transfers that can increase the segregation of Latino and African American students and hinder desegregation efforts.

69 Paul Vance, letter to author, 1 July 1994. This document was released by the school district to the Washington-area media. On file

with the Harvard Project on School Desegregation.

70 *Success for Every Student Plan: Vision and Goals, Outcomes, Strategies and Assessments,* 6 January 1992, updated 14 April 1994, 3.

71 Ibid., 14.

72 *Memorandum to Members of the Board of Education From Advisory Committee on Minority Student Education,* 25 July 1994, iii and 1.

73 Ibid., 1.

74 *Success for Every Student Plan,* 7.

75 Ibid.

76 *Memorandum to the Board,* 3B, Figure 4.

77 Ibid., 3C, Figure 5.

78 After the initial ninth-grade test, students who fail are permitted to take the Functional Test again in subsequent years in order to earn a diploma.

79 Steve Ferrara, Maryland State Department of Education, interview by author, 11 July 1994.

80 Daniel Koretz, *Trends in Educational Achievement,* Congress of the United States (Congressional Budget Office, April 1986).

81 CTB McGraw Hill, Burlington, New Jersey. CTB McGraw Hill publishes the California Achievement Test. New norms were not established until 1991.

82 School officials were unable to locate the data that would have made it possible to aggregate these scores back to the race/ethnicity level. Larson, interview, 12 July 1994.

83 Because Asian students are not historically included in desegregation plans, comparisons will be made between whites and the other two minority groups, African Americans and Latinos.

84 These data represent the first administration of the CRT test in Montgomery County. Only math tests were delivered.

CHAPTER NINE

1 Greg Canuteson, interview with author, 26 August 1992.

2 *Missouri v. Jenkins,* 495 U.S. 33 (1990). In fact, the Supreme Court affirmed the ruling with the caveat that instead of ordering the property tax increases himself, Judge Clark should have instructed the school district to do so. The reprimand was a matter of procedure rather than substance; the property tax itself was upheld narrowly by a 5-4 vote, and the Supreme Court also affirmed the scope and content of the remedy.

3 In the St. Louis plan, as the result of a settlement agreement, the suburban districts of St. Louis agreed to participate in a two-way transfer plan, whereby white students could transfer into inner-city magnets and minority students who wished to could transfer from city schools into outlying district schools. Meanwhile, a mandatory reassignment plan within the St. Louis district, which had been established earlier, was continued. Thus, participation was "mandatory" for the suburban districts but not for individual students. See *Adams v. United States,* 620 F.2d 1277 (8th Cir.).

4 Arthur Benson (plaintiffs' lawyer), 1.

5 Ibid.

6 Ibid., 3.

7 *Adams v. United States,* 620 F.2d at 1280-81 (8th Cir.); *United States v. Missouri,* 363 F. Supp. 739, 746-47 (E.D. Mo. 1973).

8 *Kansas City Star,* 6 January 1976, A3.

9 In four academic years — 1986-87, 1988-89, 1990-91, and 1991-92 — the percentage of non-minority students slightly increased.

10 *Kansas City Star,* 7 June 1977, A3.

11 Memorandum Opinion, Judge Russell G. Clark (No. 77-0420-CV-W-4), 14 June 1985.

12 *Jenkins v. State of MO,* 672 F. Supp. 400, 403 (W.D. Mo. 1987).

13 *Kansas City Times,* 1 October 1976, A2. Sue Fulson, interview by author, 26 August 1992.

14 *Kansas City Times,* 6 December 1976, A1, A8.

15 *Kansas City Times,* 1 September 1977, B4.

16 *Kansas City Times,* 23 September 1987, A9.

17 *Milliken v. Bradley,* 94 S. Ct. 3112, 3122 (1974). As the result of this ruling, suburbs could only be forced to participate in metropolitan busing plans if the plaintiffs could prove that they had either caused, or were substantially affected by, the segregation of the inner city.

18 David Tatel, phone interview by author, 22 February 1993. See, e.g., *Morritton Sch. Dist. No. 32 v. United States,* 606 F.2d 222, 228 (8th Cir. 1979) (en banc) for a case in which the 8th Circuit Court of Appeals rejected a district court's similarly limited interpretation of *Milliken,* and found that school districts that were not constitutional violators could be included in an interdistrict remedy where the effects of the unconstitutional actions of another party (here, the state) were felt in those school districts.

19 807 F.2d 657, 695 (8th Cir. 1986).

20 Judge Russell G. Clark, interview by author, 2 September 1992.

21 Ibid.

22 Arthur Benson, interview by author, 7 August 1992.

23 Order, 12 November 1986, Russell Clark.

24 Judge Russell G. Clark, interview by author, 2 September 1992.

25 Ibid.

26 Benson, interview.

27 Clark, interview.

28 *Jenkins by Agyei v. State of Mo.,* 855 F.2d at 1312 (8th Cir. 1988). A state judge recently found that the state of Missouri's method of allocating funds to its school districts to be inequitable and violates the state constitution. The KCMSD was specifically cited as one of the districts harmed by this system. See *Committee for Educational Equity v. State of Missouri,* No. CV 190-1371CC; *Lee's Summit School District R-VII v. State of Missouri,* No. CV 190-510CC.

29 Order, 15 September 1987, Clark.

30 Ibid.

31 Annette Morgan, interview by author, 13 July 1992.

32 Order, Clark, 21.

33 Morgan, interview.

34 *Kansas City Star,* 19 August 1988, A1.

35 *Missouri v. Jenkins,* 495 U.S. 33.

36 *Kansas City Star,* 26 July 1990, A1.

37 KCMSD Exhibit 8, received by the District Court on June 2, 1993.

38 Current expenditures do not include capital outlay, debt service, adult and community education. Note (1) of Table 2, "Summary of Financial Data of School Districts by County—1991-92 (Six-Director Elementary and High School Districts)."

39 According to some district officials, using the number of "eligible" pupils to calculate per pupil costs is an overestimate because it only includes students who actually attend classes. In their view, expenditure per *enrolled* pupil is a fairer measure, since "expenditures... do not decrease if a child is absent." (Ibid.) According to the "enrolled pupil" measure, for example, per-pupil costs in the KCMSD were only $8,506 in 1992, compared to the $9,412 figure cited by the DESE. Because the number of enrolled pupils will always be greater than or equal to the number of eligible pupils, all of the figures cited in the DESE figures may be reasonably interpreted as slight overestimates. It is important to note that the differences between enrolled and eligible pupils do not necessarily "even out" across districts. For various socioeconomic and demographic reasons, attrition rates are probably higher in urban areas like Kansas City than in rural or suburban districts. Thus, if only the figures for eligible pupils were used by the DESE, the gap between per-pupil costs in Kansas City and per-pupil costs elsewhere in the state would probably diminish slightly.

40 "Current Expenditures per E.P." and "Total Expenditures per E.P.," computer printout from DESE, supplied by Tim Jones, Desegregation Services.

41 This discrepancy, it should be noted, should not be construed as evidence that the district received ample funding before the remedy. Urban districts typically receive higher per-pupil funding than the state average, because they invariably confront a much more formidable set of socioeconomic obstacles than the rural and suburban districts of which the state average is primarily composed (e.g., higher crime and pregnancy, lower attendance and retention, higher capital maintenance costs, etc.). In fact, for fiscal year 1985, the other major urban district in the state of Missouri—St. Louis —spent 20 percent more than Kansas City in current expenditures per enrolled pupil and 16 percent more than Kansas City in total expenditures per enrolled pupil. (Some of this discrepancy was probably due to the fact that St. Louis settled a desegregation suit of its own in 1982, and the settlement agreement provided for additional expenditures. St. Louis was also receiving large state assistance from a series of desegregation orders beginning in 1980.)

42 Kent John Chabotar, "Measuring the Costs of Magnet Schools," *Economics of Education Review* 8, no. 2 (1989): 169-83, 174.

43 Ibid.

44 It should be noted that this breakdown of cost is deceptive in two ways. First, the court provided for only minimal salary increases until 1990, when much larger increases were granted. Thus, comparing aggregate program, capital, and salary costs ignores

the fact that the latter component has only been fully in effect for three years, while the other two components have been in effect since the inception of the plan. Secondly, comparing "fixed" costs for capital improvements to "variable" costs for programs and salary increases overlooks the fact that capital facilities are designed to last for decades, while salary and program expenditures do not have comparable longevity.

45 Figure obtained from Dan Estel, Interim Director, KCMSD Budget and Fiscal Planning Department, 14 April 1994.

46 State's Payment Under Joint and Several Liability as of March 31, 1993: Salary Account.

47 For construction and major renovations $400 million from "State's Payment Under Joint and Several Liability as of March 31, 1993: Capital Account. Exhibit Ward 2, submitted 18 May 1993. Additional $35 million (for additional maintenance costs attributable to magnet facilities such as extra utilities, security, custodial staff, athletic facilities, square footage, etc.) estimated by Roger Lee, Director of Budget, KCMSD, 13 September 1993. For capital-related costs $435 total derived by combining these two figures.

Tim Jones, who handles Kansas City for the DESE's Department of Desegregation Services, asserted in a phone interview that at least $12 million of the $35 million maintenance amount was paid for through the desegregation budget 14 September 1993. (It is unclear what fraction of the $23 million remainder is part of the desegre-

gation budget and which is part of the regular operating budget.) Thus, the total amount of desegregation expenditures that can be attributed to capital construction and improvements is at least $412 million, 35 percent of the total cost, and may in fact be closer to $435, or 38 percent.

48 Figure obtained from Dan Estel, Interim Director, KCMSD Budget and Fiscal Planning Department, 14 April 1994.

49 Among those persons interviewed who were critical of the allegedly extravagant expenditures for capital improvement: Elister Dewberry, attorney for the teacher's union, interview by author, 13 August 1993; Michael Fields, Assistant Attorney General for the state of Missouri, interview by author, 27 August 1992; Mark Bredemeier, primary spokesperson for Landmark Legal Foundation, a conservative think-tank and public interest law firm, interview by author, 21 July 1992; Richard Nadler, community activist, interview by author, 20 July 1992.

50 Scott Raisher, Jolley, Walsh, & Hager, P.C., legal counsel for American Federation of Teachers Local 691, interview by author, 24 September 1993.

51 Order, filed 25 June 1992, Judge Russell Clark, 7.

52 1992-93 salary schedules for the local suburban districts—Blue Springs, Blue Valley, Center, Grandview, Lee's Summit, North Kansas City, Olathe, Shawnee Mission, and Kansas City, Kansas —collected by the AFT Local 691, and compared with the 1992-93 KCMSD salary schedule. Data

obtained from Scott Raisher, Jolly, Walsh & Hager, P.C., legal counsel for AFT Local 691.

53 Order, 12 November 1986, Judge Russell Clark, 3.

54 In the initial court order, Judge Clark recommended a voluntary interdistrict transfer plan, whereby suburban districts wold agree to accept KCMSD transfers, and thereby help achieve racial balance within the district. Yet, the task of enlisting suburban cooperation was not assigned to any specific party, and no "carrots" or "sticks" were included to enjoin suburban participation. The state, which had worked hard to release the suburban districts from liability at the inception of the case, did almost nothing to encourage suburban districts' participation in a voluntary transfer scheme. By January 1994, only one district had joined the VIDT scheme, accepting a total of ten students (of which nine were still enrolled as of April 1994). Thus, the VIDT component of the plan, lacking enforcement components, so far has had only a negligible desegregative effect.

55 Eugene E. Eubanks, interview by author, 13 April 1994.

56 Ibid.

57 Diane Vaughan, interview by author, 13 January 1993.

58 Ibid.

59 Dr. Charles Allen, former KCMSD Coordinator of Testing, phone interview by author, 25 August 1993.

60 "1992 Reading, Language, and Math Means and Adjusted Means for Four KCMSD Cohorts Based on Analyses of Covariance for ITBS Grade Equivalent Scores," KCMSD Research Office, 27 January 1993. The means were covaried on minority status, 1992 SES, as measured by reduced/free lunch, and test score the first year of the cohort. Significance was determined at the 0.05 level. In reading, the performance gap was statistically significant for all four cohorts and ranged in magnitude from 0.19 years to 0.67 years. In language arts, the achievement gap was significant for only one of the four cohorts (0.32 years). In math, the achievement gaps for three of the four cohorts were statistically significant and ranged in magnitude from 0.28 years to 0.40 years. Because the students enrolled in magnet and nonmagnet schools did not do so as the result of a random sampling process (illustrated by the fact that magnet students consistently *began* at higher achievement levels), the covariance analysis and test of statistical significance is not strictly appropriate. For example, even when the test controls for initial test scores, magnet schools may have selected (either actively, through specialized recruitment, or passively, through self-selection) for particular qualities that also facilitate higher test scores and thus could have confounded the data.

61 Matrese Benkofske, Program Evaluator, Evaluation Office, Desegregation Planning Department, *Process/Product Evaluation (Summative): Foreign Language Magnet Elementary Schools, 1992-1993,* KCMSD, February 1994.

62 Interviews by author, KCMSD Research Office, April 1994.

63 Data on KCMSD scores obtained from "Math, Reading, and Language Achievement, KCMSD 1986 vs 1992," Defendant's Exhibit KCMSD #34, submitted to the Court on 27 January 1993. Data on changes in ITBS/TAP norms obtained from Table 5.31, "Comparisons of 1992 National Norms With 1988 and 1985 Norms," in *Technical Summary I: Riverside 2000* (Riverside Publishing Company: Chicago 1994) 153-56.

64 Among the two most prominent research reports documenting potential biases in measurements of above-average achievement are: Dr. John J. Cannell, *National Normed Elementary Achievement Testing in America's Public Schools: How All Fifty States Are Above Average,* 1987; Robert L. Linn et al., *Comparing State and District Test Results to National Norms: Interpretations of Scoring "Above the National Average* (Center for Research on Evaluation, Standards, and Student Testing), 3-5.

65 Ibid.

66 Data obtained from *District Elementary, Middle, and High School Profiles, 1989-90 through 1992-93,* KCMSD Research Office.

67 Ibid.

68 Ibid. Data are not based on a true cohort.

69 *Jenkins v. Missouri,* 855 F.2d 1295, 1302 (8th Cir. 1987).

70 Ibid.

71 The analysis was completed as follows. First, the number of white suburban/private students enrolled in each year of the plan was subtracted from the total number of white students and the total enrollment. Actual white enrollment was used, not percentages. Second, a new minority percent was calculated. Third, the attrition rates were calculated for the seven years of the plan and for the seven years prior to the plan. The difference between the two was applied to the white enrollment for each year and the total enrollment was adjusted to reflect the number of whites subtracted due to the ANAF. Fourth, a new minority percent was calculated (the district's projected racial percentages).

72 *Non-Minority Retention 1991-92 to 1992-93* and *Non-Minority Retention 1992-93 to 1993-94,* KCMSD Research Office, April 1994.

73 *Racial Breakdown of Student Membership of Area School Districts: Percent Black,* KCMSD Exhibit 7, submitted to the Court, January 1993.

74 *Desegregation Achieved in Various Urban Desegregation Plans,* KCMSD Exhibits 10-12, submitted to the Court, January 1993.

75 1995 *Jenkins v. Missouri,* U.S. LEXIS 4041, *58; 63 U.S.L.W. 4486.

CHAPTER TEN

1 "A School System of Choices," *Prince George's County Public Schools Magnet Catalog, 1988-89,* 2.

2 Michelle P. G. Norris, "Schools Bask in National Spotlight," *The Washington Post,* 21 September 1989, A6.

3 Md. State Dept. of Education Division of Planning, Results, and Information Management, *Maryland Public School Enrollment— by Sex and Race/Ethnicity,* 30 September 1992.

4 U.S. Census Bureau and County Data Book, 1988, 241.

5 Gary Orfield and Franklin Monfort, *Racial Change and Desegregation in Large School Districts*, (Alexandria: National School Boards Association, 1989).

6 *1990-91 Interim Report of the Community Advisory Council on Magnet and Compensatory Education*, 23 May 1991, 23.

7 *Swann v. Charlotte-Mecklenburg Board of Education*, 402 U.S. 1 (1971).

8 *Vaughns v. Bd. of Educ. Prince George's County*, 355 F. Supp. 1051 (D.Md. 1972).

9 *Alexander v. Holmes County Bd. of Educ.*, 396, U.S. (1969).

10 *Prince George's County Public Schools Racial/Ethnic Enrollments*, Pupil Accounting and School Boundaries, 1984.

11 James Garret, A Committee of 100 Member and community activist, interview by author, 9 March 1993.

12 Robert Green, *Final Report on Desegregation of Prince George's County Public Schools*, submitted to Chief Judge Frank A. Kaufman, 11 March 1985.

13 Valerie Kaplan, interview by author, 8 March 1993.

14 *Milliken v. Bradley*, 94 S. Ct. 3112 (1975).

15 "*Milliken* relief" is a desegregation compensatory measure often used at schools with high minority enrollments where demographics make it difficult to desegregate.

16 Plaintiff Attorney George Mernick, interview by author, 15 February 1994.

17 Hardy Jones, interview by author, 11 March 1993.

18 *Memorandum of Understanding*, Order of Chief Judge Frank A. Kaufman, U.S. District Court, 30 June 1985.

19 Board of Education member Marcy Canavan, letter to author, 21 December 1993.

20 The Committee of 100 includes ten members appointed by each of the nine board of education district representatives and ten appointed from the community at large. As prescribed by the original Memorandum of Understanding, a monitoring subcommittee includes eight members selected by plaintiffs. This subcommittee has twenty-four members.

21 George Mernick, attorney for the plaintiffs, interview by author, 15 February 1994.

22 School Superintendent Edward Felegy, letter to author, 31 January 1994.

23 Ibid.

24 James Keary and David Alan Cola, "PG Schools to End Busing After 21 Years: $346 Million Plan Seeks Return to Neighborhood Schools," *The Washington Times*, 22 July 1994, A1, A11.

25 *A School System of Choices*, 2.

26 Dr. John Murphy, interview by author, 5 December 1992.

27 Thomas Hendershot, interview by author, 9 March 1993.

28 John A. Murphy and Susan Pimentel, *Applied Anxiety: Organizing for Educational Results* (distributed at Harvard Graduate School of Education Conference on School Choice, 1993), 2.

29 *Magnet School Enrollment, September 30, 1993,* prepared by the Pupil Accounting and School Boundaries, Prince George's County Public Schools.

30 Dr. Joyce Thomas, interview by author, 9 March 1993.

31 Edward Felegy, interview by author, 10 March 1993.

32 Hardy Jones, interview by author, 11 March 1993.

33 *Interim Report of the Community Advisory Council on Magnet and Compensatory Education,* 23 May 1991, 17.

34 *Prince George's County Public Schools Racial/Ethnic Enrollments,* Pupil Accounting and School Boundaries, and *Semi Annual Report to the Court,* November 1993, U.S. District Court for the District of Maryland, 2.

35 Ibid.

36 Thomas, interview.

37 Felegy, interview.

38 Attorney George Mernick, telephone interview by author, 15 February 1994.

39 *Semi-Annual Report to the Court,* Board of Education, Prince George's County (November 1992), 4.

40 *The Memorandum of Understanding,* U.S. District Court for the District of Maryland, 21 June 1985, 2.

41 *Semi-Annual Report to the Court,* Board of Education of Prince George's County, U.S. District Court for the District of Maryland (November 1993).

42 Mernick, interview.

43 *Semi-Annual Report to the Court,* 5.

44 These schools differ from "dedi-cated" magnet schools in which the entire school is transformed into a magnet.

45 "Magnet School Program Enrollment," Pupil Accounting and School Boundaries, 30 September 1992.

The reported median positive effect is 9.8 percent. "Positive effect" is defined as the percent that the school has become better desegregated because of the magnet program.

46 *The Washington Post,* 14 January 1988.

47 "A School System of Choices," *Prince George's County Public Schools Magnet Catalog, 1988-89.*

48 Murphy and Pimentel, "Applied Anxiety," 4.

49 *1990-91 Interim Report of the Community Advisory Council on Magnet and Compensatory Education,* 23 May 1991, 21.

50 *Magnet and Milliken II Programs, 1987-88: A Summary of the Survey Results of Principals, Teachers and Parents,* Prince George's Department of Evaluation and Research, January 1989, 1.

51 Retha Hill, "In P. G., A Game of Blame: Powers at Odds in School Dispute," *The Washington Post,* 11 April 1994, D1; "Prince George's: Views in Black and White" *Washington Post,* 7 August, 1994, A1

52 Retha Hill, "In Pr. George's, Business vs. Schools: Superintendent Blamed for Chill in Once Warm Relations," *The Washington Post,* 31 January 1994, B1.

53 Retha Hill, "Felegy Feeling the Heat: P.G. Superintendent Support Eroding," *The Washington Post,* 1 June 1994, D1.

54 Lisa Leff and Michael Abramowitz, "PG Report Assails Failing Schools, Questions Safety," *The Washington Post*, 23 September 1993, A1.

55 Dr. Louise Waynant, interview by author, 10 March 1993.

56 Hendershot, interview.

57 Sarah Johnson, interview by author, 9 March 1993.

58 Felegy, interview.

59 Alvin Thornton, phone interview by author, 12 February 1993.

60 Ibid.

61 Ibid.

62 *Third Interim Report of the Community Advisory Council on Magnet and Compensatory Educational Programs*, 12 September 1988.

63 For a discussion of this issue, see e.g., John J. Cannell, *Nationally Normed Elementary Achievement Testing in America's Public Schools: How All Fifty States are Above the National Average* (West Virginia: Friends for Education, 1987).

64 See, e.g., Daniel Koretz, *Trends in Educational Achievement* (Congressional Budget Office: April 1986).

65 *Third Interim Report of the Community Advisory Council on Magnet and Compensatory Educational Programs*, 12 September 1988, 29.

66 Wayant, interview.

67 *Maryland School Performance Report, State and School Systems*, 1992, 10, *Washington Post*, 26 May, 1996, B1.

68 Maryland State Department of Education, telephone discussion, 7 February 1994.

69 Joyce Thomas, letter to author, 18 June 1993.

70 See, e.g., *Second Interim Report of the Community Advisory Council on Magnet and Compensatory Educational Programs*, 26 March 1987, 13.

71 Marcy Canavan, interview by author, 11 March 1993.

72 Michael Grady, Director of Research and Evaluation, *Agenda for Research on the Magnet and Milliken Schools of Prince George's County*, Prince George's Schools, 1990.

73 Waynant, interview.

74 *1990-91 Interim Report*, 21.

75 Hardy Jones, interview by author, 11 March 1993.

76 Alvin Thornton, telephone interview by author, 12 February 1993.

77 Ibid.

78 Alvin Thornton, letter to author, 24 January 1994.

79 Felegy, interview.

80 Johnson, interview.

81 *1990-91 Interim Report*, 21.

82 Thomas, letter.

83 Jones, interview.

84 Hill, "In P.G.," D1.

CHAPTER ELEVEN

1 *Missouri v. Jenkins*, 63 U.S.L.W. 4486 (1955).

2 Computations from 1992-93 Common Core of Educational Statistics, U.S. Department of Education.

3 *Swann v. Charlotte Mecklenburg*, 402 U.S. 1, (1971).

4 *Keyes v. School District No. 1*, 413 U.S. 189, (1973).

5 Paul R. Dimond, *Beyond Busing: Inside the Challenge to Urban*

Segregation (Ann Arbor: Univ. of Michigan Press, 1985), 106-7.

6   Ibid., 111.

7   Ibid., 113.

8   *Plessy v. Ferguson*, 163 U.S. 537, 551 (1896).

9   Gary Orfield, "Ghettoization and Its Alternatives," in *The New Urban Reality*, ed. Paul Peterson (Washington, D.C.: Brookings Inst., 1985); Gary Orfield, "Federal Policy, Local Power, and Metropolitan Segregation," *Political Science Quarterly* 89 (winter, 1975): 777-802; Gary Orfield, "School Segregation and Housing Policy: The Role of Local and Federal Governments in Neighborhood Segregation," *Integrated Education*, 48-53.

10 Gallup Poll in *USA Today*, 16 May 1994.

11 Beth J. Lief and Susan Goering, "The Implementation of the Federal Mandate for Fair Housing," in *Divided Neighborhoods: Changing Patterns of Racial Segregation*, ed. Gary Tobin (Newbury Park: Sage Publications, 1987), 227-67. HUD's failure over twenty years to enforce civil rights requirements for subsidized housing was documented in the *Dallas Morning News* Pulitzer-prize-winning series, "Separate and Unequal: Subsidized Housing in America," 10-18 February 1985; more recent shortcomings were documented in U.S. Commission on Civil Rights, *The Fair Housing Amendments Act of 1988 — The Enforcement Report* (Washington, D.C.: GPO, 1994).

12 "Fair Housing Enforcement Needs Additional Improvement," *Civil Rights Update*, December 1994/January 1995, 3, 8.

13 John Yinger, *Housing Discrimination Study: Incidence of Discrimination and Variation in Discrimination Behavior*, report to U.S. Department of Housing and Urban Development, October 1991.

14 Studies of enforcement reflect complex political and institutional processes with very imperfect compliance. See, e.g., LaNoue and Lee, *Academics in Court: The Consequences of Faculty Discrimination Litigation* (Ann Arbor: Univ. of Mich., 1987); Kenneth J. Meier and Joseph Stewart, Jr., *The Politics of Hispanic Education* (Albany: SUNY Press, 1991); Michael A. Rebell and Arthur R. Block, *Educational Policy Making and the Courts* (Chicago: Univ. of Chicago Press, 1982); John B. Williams III, Desegregating America's Colleges and Universities (New York: Teachers College Press, 1988); Richard Neely, *How Courts Govern America* (New Haven: Yale Univ. Press, 1981); Donald L. Horowitz, *The Courts and Social Policy* (Washington, D.C.: Brookings Inst., 1977); Jeffrey A. Raffel, *The Politics of School Desegregation* (Philadelphia: Temple Univ. Press, 1980).

15 *Missouri v. Jenkins*, 115 S. Ct. 2038 (1995).

16 C. Van Woodward, *The Strange Career of Jim Crow*, 2d ed. (New York: Oxford Univ. Press, 1966).

17 *Keyes*, 413 U.S. 210 (1973).

18 *Missouri v. Jenkins*, 115 S. Ct. 2038.

19 *Armour v. Nix*, No. 16708, slip op. (N.D. Ga. 1979).

20 Ibid.

21 Ibid.

22 Ibid.

23 Ibid. The Court describes tipping as involving "elements of fear, personal prejudice, and other psychological and economic factors [which] may partly explain the evolution of transitional neighborhoods from totally white to almost totally black composition, leaving few integrated neighborhoods existing in the Atlanta area today."

24 Orfield and Ashkinaze, 1991, chap. 5.

25 *Armour v. Nix*, 446 U.S. 930 (1980).

26 *Hills v. Gautreaux*, 425 U.S. 284 (1976).

27 HUD Asst. Secretary Roberta Achtenberg, address at Univ. of Pennsylvania Law School, 24 March 1995.

28 Clement E. Vose, *Caucasians Only: The Supreme Court, the NAACP, and the Restrictive Convenant Cases* (Berkeley: Univ. of California Press, 1967), 3. Oklahoma City was one of the cities that originally set out racial zoning; see *Dowell*, 244 F. Supp. 971, 975 (1965).

29 *Corrigan v. Buckley*, 299 F.2d 899 (D.C. Cir.), appeal dismissed, 271 U.S. 323 (1926). In dismissing the case, Justice Sanford found the challenge "so insubstantial as to be plainly without color of merit and frivolous." Two decades would pass before the issue wold come back to the Supreme Court (Vose, 18).

30 271 U.S. 323.

31 *Shelley v. Kraemer*, 334 U.S. 1 (1948).

32 Gunnar Myrdal, *An American Dilemma*, vol. 2 (1946; reprint, New York: Harper Torchbooks, 1962), 623-24.

33 Charles Abrams, *Forbidden Neighbors* (New York: Harper and Row, 1955), 235.

34 Douglas Massey and Nancy Denton, *American Apartheid: Segregation and the Making of the Underclass*, 54.

35 U.S. National Commission on Urban Problems (Douglass Commission), *Building the American City: Report of the National Commission on Urban Problems to the Congress and to the President of the United States*, House Document 91-34 (Washington, D.C.: GPO, 1968), 163.

36 Orfield, "Ghettoization"; Orfield, "Role," 48-53; Gary Orfield "Federal Policy, Local Power, and Metropolitan Segregation," in *Political Power and the Urban Crisis*, ed. Alan Shank (Boston: Holbrook Press, 1976).

37 U.S. Commission on Civil Rights, *Home Ownership for Lower Income Families: A Report on the Racial and Ethnic Impact of the Section 235 Program* (Washington, D.C.: GPO, 1971).

38 Brian D. Boyer, *Cities Destroyed for Cash: The FHA Scandal at HUD* (Chicago: Follett Publishing, 1973); Leonard Downie, Jr., *Mortgage on America* (New York: Praeger Publishers, 1973), chap. 3.

39 See statistics on Section 8 programs in Robert Gray and Steven Tursky, "Local and Racial/Ethnic Occupancy Patterns for Hud-Subsidized Family Housing in Ten Metropolitan Areas," *Housing Desegregation and Federal Policy*, ed. John Goering (Chapel Hill: Univ. of North Carolina Press, 1986), 235-52.

40 The number of authorized additional subsidized housing units was cut nearly in half in the first year of the Reagan Administration. See John William Ellwood, ed., *Reductions in U.S. Domestic Spending*

(New Brunswick: Transaction Books, 1982), 268.

41 John Goering, Ali Kamely, and Todd Richardson, *The Location and Racial Composition of Public Housing in the United States* (Washington, D.C.: U.S. Department of Housing and Urban Development, Dec. 1994), 2.

42 Ibid.

43 Gary Orfield, "Housing and School Integration in Three Metropolitan Areas: A Policy Analysis of Denver, Columbus and Phoenix," submitted to U.S. Department of Housing and Urban Development, HUD Order No. 5007-80, 17 February 1981.

44 *Gautreaux v. Chicago Housing Authority*, 480 F.2d 210 (7th Cir.), cert. denied, 414 U.S. 1144 (1974).

45 *Gautreaux v. Chicago Housing Authority*, 296 F. Supp. 907, summarized in *Hills v. Gautreaux*, 425 U.S. 284, 288 (1976).

46 It is worth noting that President Reagan actually took steps to further hinder integration when he rescinded a regulation requiring housing authorities to report racial statistics. See U.S. Department of Housing and Urban Development, Notice H81-12 (18 October 1981).

47 *Walker v. U.S. Department of Housing and Urban Development*, 734 F. Supp. 1289 (N.D. Tex 1989).

48 Scott Cummings and Wayne Zatopek, "Federal Housing Policy and Racial Isolation in Public Schools: The Case of Dallas," in *Racial Isolation in the Public Schools: The Impact of Public and Private Housing Policies*, ed. Scott Cummings, report to U.S. Department of Housing and Urban Development by Institute of Urban Studies University of Texas at Arlington, 1980, 194-95.

49 "HUD's Responses to Plaintiffs' Requests for Admissions," *Walker v. U.S. Department of Housing and Urban Development*," 11 May 1994, 1.

50 Taub, Taylor, and Dunham, *Paths of Neighborhood Change,* Chicago Sun-Times poll, 1983.

51 Orfield, "Ghettoization."

52 Ibid.

53 Kain, 1993.

54 U.S. Commission on Civil Rights, 1971.

55 During the Reagan years, the Justice Department began asking for more narrow remedies than had been requested earlier and used some of its scarce litigation resources to sue those trying to manage stable integration with racial quotas in their buildings, an enterprise supported by Jesse Jackson and part of a consent agreement with the NAACP, which the Justice Department intervened in a successful effort to overturn.

56 Address at University of Pennsylvania Law Review Forum, Philadelphia, 24 February 1995.

57 *Nixon: The Third Year of His Presidency* (Washington, D.C.: Congressional Quarterly Inc., 1972), 23.

58 Betty Glad, *Jimmy Carter: In Search of the Great White House* (New York: Norton, 1980).

59 "Outcry Stalls Housing in Baltimore Suburbs," *National Fair Housing Report* 4, no. 6 (November-December 1994), 6.

60 Daniel H. Weinberg, "Mobility and Housing Change: The Housing Allowance Demand Experiment," in *Residential Mobility*

and Public Policy ed. W. A. V. Clark and Eric G. Moore (Beverly Hills: Sage, 1980), 168-93, shows limited mobility; U.S. Department of Housing and Urban Development, *Gautreaux Housing Demonstration* (Washington, D.C.: GPO, 1979) documents fear and lack of knowledge as basic barriers to using Section 8 subsidies in suburbs for city black residents during startup period of *Gautreaux* program.

61 Richard Stuart Fleisher, "Subsidized Housing and Residential Segregation in American Cities: An Evaluation of the Site Selection and Occupancy of Federally Subsidized Housing," (Ph.D. diss., Univ. of Illinois, 1979); Robert Gray and Steven Tursky, "Location and Racial/Ethnic Occupancy Patterns for HUD-Subsidized Family Housing in Ten Metropolitan Areas," in *Housing Desegregation and Federal Policy,* ed. John M. Goering (Chapel Hill: Univ. of North Carolina Press, 1986), 235-52.

62 J.E. Rosenbaum, L.S. Rubinowitz, and M.J. Kulieke, *Low Income Black Children in White Suburban Schools* (Evanston: Northwestern Univ. Center for Urban Affairs and Policy Research, 1986).

63 Gary Orfield and Paul Fischer, *Housing and School Integration in Three Metropolitan Areas: A Policy Analysis of Denver, Columbus, and Phoenix,* report to HUD, 1981.

64 Letter to author from Marcia W. Borowski, 5 January 1995; DeKalb County Public Schools, "Summary of DeKalb School's Legal Expenses Requested by F. Pauley."

65 Christine Rossell, *The Carrot or the Stick for School Desegregation Policy:*

Magnet Schools or Forced Busing (Philadelphia: Temple University Press, 1990).

66 Testimony of D. Garth Taylor, Kansas City school desegregation trial, Federal District Court, Kansas City.

67 Coleman, Moore, and Kelly, 1975.

68 *Foss v. Houston Indep. Sch. Dist.,* 669 F.2d 218, 288, citing Supreme Court decision in *Pasadena City Bd. of Ed. v. Spangler,* 427 U.S. 424 (1976).

69 U.S. Commission on Civil Rights, *Racial Isolation in the Public Schools, Appendices,* 1967, 2-12.

70 Thurgood Marshall, "Nos. 73-434, 73-435, and 73-346, *Milliken v. Bradley,* read in Court by Justice Marshall, typescript in Thurgood Marshall papers, Manuscript Division, Library of Congress.

71 Address of Supt. David Sneed to Council of Urban Boards of Education Conference, New York, 1 October 1994.

72 Reynolds Farley, Carlotte Steeh, Maria Krysan, Tara Jackson, and Keith Reeves, "Stereotypes and Segregation: Neighborhoods in the Detroit Area," *American Journal of Sociology,* 100, no. 3 (November 1994): 751; U.S. Department of Education data tapes: 1992-93.

73 An account of the controversy is given by G. Orfield in "Research, Politics, and the Antibusing Debate," 42 *Law and Contemp. Prob.* (autumn 1978): 141-49.

74 U.S. vital statistics data from the 1960s through the 1980s show that non-whites consistently had larger families than whites and that whites were having children below the replacement level since the early 1970s. See *Statistical Abstract of*

the United States 1992 (Washington, D.C.: GPO, 1992), 67. See also Ben J. Wattenberg, *The Birth Dearth* (New York: Pharos Books, 1989).

75 Enrollment data from districts; for overall projections see Charles D. Liner, "Update: School Enrollment Projections," *School Law Bulletin*, Univ. of North Carolina 26, no. 1 (winter 1955): 16-18.

76 *Boston Globe*, 12 February 1995, 1.

77 National Association of Realtors data for period between the last quarter of 1993 and the final quarter of 1994, in *Investor's Business Daily*, 10 February 1995, A17.

78 National Center for Education Statistics, *Characteristics of the 100 Largest Public Elementary and Secondary School District in the United States: 1991-92* (Washington, D.C.: GPO, 1994), 12.

79 Greater Raleigh Chamber of Commerce, Resolution Concerning the Wake County Public School System, 24 May 1995.

80 *Missouri v. Jenkins*, 115 S. Ct. 2038, 2051.

81 Charles Abrams, *The City Is the Frontier* (New York: Harper Colophon, 1967), chap. 5-8.

82 Robert D. Bullard, J. Eugene Grigsly III and Charles Lee (eds.), *Residential Apartheid: The American Legacy.* Los Angeles: UCLA CAAS, 1994.

83 Massey and Denton; Kain, 1993.

84 Margery A. Turner, "Discrimination in Urban Housing Markets: Lessons From Fair Housing Adults," *Housing Policy Debate* 3 no. 2 (1992):185-215; George Galster, "Racial Discrimination in Housing Markets in the 1980s: A Review of the Audit Evidence," *Journal of Planning Education and Research* 9 (1992): 165-75.

85 Turner, "Discrimination," 197.

86 Orfield 1981, Cummings and Zatopek, 1980.

87 *USA Today* poll, in *USA Today*, 22 September 1989. In a 1989 national poll, only 10 percent of blacks expressed a preference for a "mostly black" neighborhood, but 53 percent lived in one; Farley et al., footnote 72.

88 Farley, Steeh, Krysan, Jackson, and Reeves 1994.

89 Kain 1993; Gary Tobin, ed., "The Costs of Housing Discrimination and Segregation: An Interdisciplinary Social Science Statement," in *Divided Neighborhoods: Changing Patterns of Racial Segregation* (Newbury Park, Calif.: Sage Publications, 1987): 268-80.

90 A 1995 study by the Federal Reserve Bank of Boston found that the forty communities in greater Boston with the highest housing price growth in the 1988 to 1994 period had the highest scores on standardized tests and the communities with the lowest scores had housing prices rising only one seventh as fast. (Steve Bailey, "Top Schools, Pricey Homes Linked," *Boston Globe*, 22 May 1995).

91 Orfield and Monfort, 1988.

92 U.S. Commission on Civil Rights, *Low Income Homeownership;* Richard Stuart Fleisher, "Subsidized Housing and Residential Segregation in American Cities: An Evaluation of the Site Selection and Occupancy of Federally Subsidized Housing" (Ph.D. diss.,

NOTES

Univ. of Illinois, Urbana, 1979);
Robert Gray and Steven Tursky,
"Location and Racial/Ethnic
Occupancy Patterns for HUD-
Subsidized Family Housing in Ten
Metropolitan Areas," in *Housing
Desegregation and Federal Policy*, ed.
John M. Goering (Chapel Hill:
Univ. of North Carolina Press,
1986), 235-52.

93 Taub, Taylor, and Dunham.

94 *Dowell v. Bd. of Educ. of Oklahoma
City*, 111 S. Ct. 630, 638 (1991). This
was done against the strong dissent
of Justice Marshall, who argued
that illegal segregation should not
be excused simply because it may
be self-perpetuating.

95 George C. Gallster, "Residential
Segregation in American Cities: A
Contrary Review," *Population
Research and Policy Review* 93, 95
(1988), cited in Boger, John
Charles, "Toward Ending
Residential Segregation: A Fair
Share Proposal for the Next
Reconstruction," 71 *N.C.L. Rev.*
1573 (June 1993).

96 Karl E. Taeuber and Alma F.
Taeuber, *Negroes in Cities, Residential
Segregation and Neighborhood Change*
(New York: Atheneum, 1969),
chap. 5.

97 Thomas Schelling, *Micromotives and
Macrobehavior* (New York: W.W.
Norton, 1978).

98 Reynolds Farley, Howard
Schuman, Suzanne Bianchi,
Diane Colasanto, and Shirley
Hatchett, "Chocolate City, Vanilla
Suburbs: Will the Trend Toward
Racially Separate Communities
Continue?" *Social Science Research*, 7
(December 1978): 319-44.

99 Anthony Downs, "Policy
Directions Concerning Racial

Discrimination in U.S. Markets,"
Housing Policy Debate, 3 no. 2 (1992):
697; Farley et al. shows that even in
metropolitan Detroit white attitudes have improved significantly
though black attitudes became less
favorable.

100 Reynolds Farley et al., "Stereotypes and Segregation: Neighborhoods in the Detroit Area,"
American Journal of Sociology, 100,
no. 3 (November 1994): 750-80.

101 637 F.2d 1101, 1109 (7th Cir. 1980),
cited in Thomas M. Dee and
Norella V. Huggins, "Models for
Proving Liability of School and
Housing Officials in School
Desegregation Cases," *Urban Law
Annual* 23 (1982): 111.

102 Taylor Taub and Dunham found
that interracial neighborhoods in
Chicago tended to stabilize when
people believed that stability would
remain, not when there were certain proportions or conditions.
Commitment of powerful local
institutions to maintaining integration played an important role.

103 Kentucky Commission on Human
Rights, *School and Housing
Desegregation Are Working Together in
Louisville and Jefferson County*, Staff
Report 83-5, 1983, 5.

104 Ibid.

105 Some of this is attributable to
declining birth rates, but it is
worth noting that white flight has
not been a big problem in
Louisville. In the decade from
1981-82 to 1991-92, black enrollment (as a percentage of the total)
fluctuated less than 2 percent actually dropping in the final seven
years of that span. School system
data printouts supplied by *The
Louisville Courier-Journal*.

405

106 Rosenbaum, 1991.

107 *National Fair Housing Advocate*, 5, no. 1 (January-February 1995): 5.

108 Op. Ohio Att'y Gen. No. 87-095 (1987).

109 Zupanc, "Two Pro-Integrative Groups Get State Funds," *Sun Observer*, 15 February 1989.

110 Suja A. Thomas, "Efforts to Integrate Housing: The Legality of Mortgage-Incentive Programs," *New York University Law Review*, June 1991.

111 Leadership Council for Metropolitan Open Communities, Recent Developments in Housing, October 1989, 3-4.

112 *Seattle Post-Intelligencer*, 1 June 1989, B1.

113 The assessment is made by a state agency, the Council on Affordable Housing (COAH).

114 Ibid. at 452-53.

115 *Palm Beach Sun-Sentinel*, _____ 1994.

116 "Affordable Housing and Racial Balance," Palm Beach County School Board Report, 6 June 1990; *Sun-Sentinel*, 31 May 1990.

CHAPTER TWELVE

1 Tom Wicker, *Tragic Failure: Racial Integration in America* (New York: William Morrow & Co., 1996).

2 John F. Kennedy, *Public Papers of the Presidents of the United States* (Washington: Government Printing Office, 1964), 469.

3 Orfield and Ashkinaze, 118-19.

4 Georgia Department of Education, "1986-87 Student Assessment Test Results: Summary" (Atlanta: June 1987);

Orfield and Ashkinaze, 121-29.

5 Orfield and Ashkinaze, 118-22. Similarly, in Oklahoma City, the first case in which the Supreme Court approved of resegregation, an investigation for the Education Writers of America by journalist Bill Zlatos showed a similar set of tactics to increase apparent achievement levels, including exclusion of an unusually high percent of students from the test-taking population. Bill Zlatos, "A Stellar Test Score Performance —But at What Cost?", *In Pittsburgh*, 10 March 1994.

6 Jennifer Jellison, "Oklahoma City Resegregation: Promises and Regrets," Working Paper (Cambridge: Harvard Project on School Desegregation, 1996).

7 Tom Wicker, *Tragic Failure: Racial Integration in America* (New York: William Morrow and Company, 1996).

8 Stephen Lesher, *George Wallace: American Populist* (Reading, Mass.: Addison Wesley Publishing Co., 1994), 4023-403.

9 *Washington Post* poll, 8 October 1995: A26.

10 Only 30 percent of whites thought that "past and present discrimination is the major reason for the economic and social ills blacks face." Ibid., A22.

11 See poll data in chapter four.

12 Gallup poll in *USA Today*, 12 March 1994: 8A.

13 Council of Urban Boards of Education, *Still Separate, Still Unequal: Desegregation in the '90s* (Alexandria, Va.: National School Boards Association, 1995), 3.

14 The commission was reconstituted under White House control in 1983 after President Reagan asserted the authority to fire commissioners opposed his policies. Following the reconstitution, the head of this once independent agency, Clarence Pendelton Jr, said that he was "proud to be on President Reagan's team." The commission stopped criticizing school desegregation reversals. (Letter from House Subcommittee on Civil and Constitutional Rights Chairman Don Edwards to *New York Times*, 30 October 1985.)

15 The National Institute of Education's research program was announced in the NIE publication, *Grants for Research on Desegregation: Fiscal Year 1981*. Washington, D.C.: Government Printing Office, 1980. The grants "approved for funding" but never funded included basic research on the relationship between housing and school segregation, conditions for effective instruction in interracial classes, the educational consequences of desegregation for Latinos, the effects of desegregation on college and graduate education, and other subjects. (Memorandum from Jeffrey M. Schneider, NIE, to Gary Orfield, "NIE approved by unfunded desegregation research," 6 May 1982). The federal desegregation aid program had financed a series of major studies on the impact of programs to make desegregation work more effectively. (System Development Corporation, *The Third Year of Emergency School Act (ESAA) Implementation*, Report to U.S. Office of Education, March 1977).

16 Forty-seven states adopted the basic approach proposed by the commission. (Gail L. Sunderman, "States and the Educational Excellence Movement: The Politics of School Reform," unpublished Ph.D. dissertation, University of Chicago, 1995.)

17 Wells and Crain, 1995.

18 Eric Camburn, *American Journal of Education*, 1990.

19 Camburn, 1990; Espinosa and Ochoa, 1986; Orfield, "Race: How Equal Is Opportunity in Indiana Schools" in *High Hopes, Long Odds*, report number 7A. Indianapolis: Indiana Youth Institute, 1994.

20 The Student Team Leaning Techniques developed at Johns Hopkins University, for example, show substantial gains as did research at Stanford University. (Robert E. Slavin and N. A. Madden, "Schools Practices That Improve Race Relations, *American Educational Research Journal*, vol. 16, no. 2 (1979), pp. 169-80. Elizabeth G. Cohen and Rachel A. Lataon, "Protecting Equal-Status Interaction in the Heterogeneous Classroom," *American Educational Research Journal*, vol. 32, no. 1 (Spring 1995), 99-120.

21 Jeannie Oakes, Rand report; ETS report.

22 Orfield, 1994, 10-11.

23 Ellwood, 1982, 96-98. The program was consolidated with other much smaller programs into a block grant

which was not directed at desegregation purposes and not used for that purpose by the states; benefits are reported in John E. Coulson and associates, *The Third Year of the Emergency School Aid Act (ESAA) Implementation*, Santa Monica: System Development Corporation, 1977.

24 Computations from U.S. Department of Education Common Core of Education Statistics.

25 The director of Detroit's pioneering Afrocentric educational approach in more than two hundred schools conceded that "there is no research base," said Dahia Shabaka, Director of African-Centered Education at the University of Michigan on 2 June 1995. "If it fails, it will not be any worse than what is already happening to our students."

26 A recent statewide survey of black and white students and parents in Indiana, for example, documented aspirations as high or higher than white aspirations among both students and parents. (Gary Orfield and Faith Paul, "Indiana Dreams," Report No. 1 in *High Hopes, Long Odds* series. (Indianapolis Youth Institute, 1993), 3-5; reviews of the national research literature show the same pattern.

27 By 1994, 42 percent of Americans believed that desegregation had "improved the quality of education for whites." *USA Today*, CNN,

Gallop Poll, in *USA Today*, 12 May 1984, 8A.

28 Computations from Indiana Youth Opportunity Study data tape. Most black and white students said attending integrated schools was an advantage.

29 We have found only one survey that measured the degree of knowledge about the facts of desegregation and the way knowledge was related to beliefs and attitudes. That study found that both whites and blacks were very likely to be misinformed about key issues. A majority of both blacks and whites, for example, thought that busing for desegregation cost more than ten times its actual share of the school district budget and more than a fourth of each group thought that "white student test scores have fallen sharply in desegregated schools, though researchers were virtually unanimous in reporting no such damage. (Opinion Research Corporation, "Public Knowledge and Attitudes Regarding School Busing," report to U.S. Commission on Civil Rights, November 1972.)

30 San Francisco Unified School District, *Longitudinal Study of Attrition, Retention and Test Score Growth for Elementary, Middle and High School Students*, Submitted to Federal District Court, 12 October 1995.

31 Jane R. Mercer, Peter Iadicola, and Helen Moore, "Building Effective Multiethnic Schools:

Evolving Models and Paradigms," in Walter G. Stephan and Joe R. Feagin, eds., *School Desegregation: Past, Present, and Future* (New York: Plenum Press, 1980), 281-308; Elizabeth G. Cohen, "Design and Redesign of the Desegregated School," in Ibid., 251-280; John E. Coulson and associates, *The Third Year of the Emergency School Aid Act (ESAA) Implementation* (Santa Monica: System Development Corporation, 1977); Janet Ward Schofield and H. Andrew Sagar, "Desegregation, School Practices, and Student Race Relations," in Christine H. Rossell and Willis D. Hawley (eds.), *The Consequences of School Desegregation* (Philadelphia: Temple Univ. Press, 1983), 58-102; Jeannie Oakes, *Keeping Track: How Schools Structure Inequality* (New Haven: Yale Univ. Press, 1985); Anne Wheelock, *Crossing the Tracks* (New York: The New Press, 1992).

32 Elizabeth G. Cohen and Rachel A. Lotaon, "Protecting Equal Status Interaction in the Heterogeneous Classroom," *American Educational Research Journal*, 32 no. 1 (spring, 1995):99-120.

33 Gail L. Sunderman, "States and the Educational Excellence Movement: The Politics of School Reform," (Unpublished Ph.D. diss., Univ. of Chicago, 1995).

34 Kim McCullough, "Consent Decree Violated, Faculty Integration Back on the Agenda, *Catalyst*, vol. 6, no. 4, 30; Alan Richard, "Federal Agency Tells District 7 to Hire Minorities," *Spartanburg, S.C. Herald-Journal*, 28 September 1995, D3.

35 Orfield, 1996.

36 *Colorado Constitution*, Article XIV, Section 3, and Article XX, adopted November 1974.

37 *Sheff v. O'Neill*, "Memorandum of Decision," 12 April 1995, CV89-0360977S; George Judson, "Connecticut Wins School Bias Suit," *New York Times*, 13 April 1995, A1, A11; Richard Weizel, "Loosers of Suit Vow to Overcome," *Boston Globe*, 23 April 1995, 42-43.

38 Johanna Richardson, "Suit Seeks Minn. Backing of Desegregation Plan," *Education Week*, 4 October 1995, 12, 16.

39 Policies of this sort have been tried in Denver and Palm Beach County, Florida.

40 Gary Orfield, *Toward a Strategy for Urban Integration* (New York: Ford Foundation, 1981); Orfield, "Federal Agencies and Urban Segregation: Steps Toward Coordinated Action," in Orfield and Taylor, *Racial Segregation: Two Policy Views* (New York: Ford Foundation, 1979).

41 James Rosenbaum, 1991.

Index

in North, 6, 15
outdated policies of, 113
policymaking, 73
Prince George's County magnet
  schools and, 272-274
Reagan administration and,
  16-18, 342
Rehnquist's views of, 9-10
vs. resegregation, 103-106
school segregation inequalities as
  issues in, 70-71
in South, 14-16
standardized tests scores and,
  105, 130
success of, 22
Swann case and policies of, 179
unpopularity of, with whites, 22
"white flight" as criticism of, 314-318
Desegregation Assistance Centers, 16-17
Desegregation law. *See also specific
cases and laws*
judicial philosophy shift and, 4, 6,
  18-19
after *Milliken I* case, 15, 78
Plessy case and, 31-33, 345
resegregation and, 5-6
trends in, 26-27, 29-31
Desegregation Monitoring
  Committee (DMC), 255-256
Detroit (Michigan) school system
compensatory programs in,
  148-156, 174-175
resegregation in, 10-13, 336-337
Disinvestment, housing, 305
Dissimilarity index, 181-182
"Diversity profile," 213
DMC, 255-256
Douglas, William O., 11
Douglass, Tiana, 101
Dowell case
decision of, 1-3
historical context of, 5-6
housing segregation and, 41,
  293, 302
integration policies and, 2
local government and, power of,
  35, 101
resegregation and, 1, 3, 18-19

school segregation and, 320
"separate but equal" policy and, 93
unitary status and, 3, 20-21
Dropout rates, 66-67
D'Souza, Dinesh, 27
Dual system, segregated, 3
DuBois, W. E. B., 47-48

Edelen, Loretta, 171
Edenfield, B. Avant, 21
Edmunds, Ron, 82
Effective School Model, 82
Effective Schools Program, 93
Ehrlichman, John, 12-13
Eisenhower, Dwight D., 6
Eisenhower administration, 6
"Eliminating the Gap: Assuring that
  All Students Learn," 24
Emergency School Aid Act (1972),
  14, 16, 25, 91, 265
The End of Racism (D'Souza), 27
Enrollments in schools, 62-63, 194
Equal education, commitment to, 26
Equity Committee, 101
Escalante, Jamie, 67-68, 86
Esselman, Mary, 260
Eubanks, Eugene, 255
"Excellence Movement," 342

Fair housing law (1968), 299, 310-312
"Fairshare distribution" of homes,
  126-127
Farley, Reynolds, 127
Federal Housing Administration
  (FHA), 40, 303, 305
Felegy, Edward, 164-165, 272-273, 279,
  285-286
FHA, 40, 303, 305
Final Judgement for Unitary Status, 154
Flannery, Nicholas, 296
Ford, Gerald, 311
Foster, John H., 118, 135
Fourteenth Amendment, 6, 34, 56
Franklin, John Hope, 37
"Freedom of choice" busing policy, 180
Freeman v. Pitts. See Pitts case
French Immersion program, 212
Functional tests, 232, 235, 282